DISCRETIONARY JUSTICE

Discretionary Justice

Pardon and Parole in New York from the Revolution to the Depression

Carolyn Strange

NEW YORK UNIVERSITY PRESS
New York

NEW YORK UNIVERSITY PRESS
New York
www.nyupress.org

© 2016 by New York University
All rights reserved

References to Internet websites (URLs) were accurate at the time of writing. Neither the author nor New York University Press is responsible for URLs that may have expired or changed since the manuscript was prepared.

ISBN: 978-1-4798-9992-0

For Library of Congress Cataloging-in-Publication data, please contact the Library of Congress.

New York University Press books are printed on acid-free paper, and their binding materials are chosen for strength and durability. We strive to use environmentally responsible suppliers and materials to the greatest extent possible in publishing our books.

Manufactured in the United States of America

10 9 8 7 6 5 4 3 2 1

Also available as an ebook

For my parents, inspirations in life and learning

CONTENTS

ACKNOWLEDGMENTS

This book could not have been conceived without the assistance of staff at the New York State Archives and Library. The head of research services, Dr. James D. Folts, is renowned among state historians for his expertise and commitment to facilitating users' projects. My debt to Jim is considerably greater, as he was instrumental in opening the archives' collection of over 8,000 clemency case files to researchers in 2009. After I began to explore this extraordinary body of evidence he informed me that records of the state parole board were underutilized and possibly of interest. Through his encouragement I applied for a Larry J. Hackman Research Residency grant, and after I received this award in 2012 I embarked on a much larger project, incorporating the analysis of executive and administrative discretion. Two other staff members made signal contributions along the way: Nancy Horan, an astute librarian who frequently untangled the complexities of statutory history; and Monica Gray, the archivist who processed the clemency case files and produced a database of key factors in each file. It was truly a pleasure to be guided by such dedicated professionals.

A team of research assistants and collaborators on related projects helped to expedite and enhance my study. For their assistance in the collection of archival evidence in Albany I am grateful to Joseph Gibbons and Nicole D'Anna, and to William Meredith, recommended to me by Richard F. Hamm. At the Australian National University Robyn Curtis has been an efficient fact-checker and copy editor, and Daniel McNamara, Ian Wood, and Joshua Wodak have taught me a great deal about data management and mining through our co-authorship of a related publication. I am grateful to the Australian Research Council for the funding (DP110105284) that allowed me to hire these assistants. Another former student, Hilary Howes, deserves special mention. Now an established historian, she did a superb job of culling early governors' papers for references to pardoning, and we have since become friends and colleagues.

It is humbling to consider the number of scholars who have contributed to the book's conceptualization and completion. David Tanenhaus, Richard F. Hamm, and Andrew W. Arpey provided critical advice at the earliest stages of the project. James Phillips and Lawrence Pesky kindly supported my application for a Huntington Library fellowship, which I was fortunate to receive in 2014. Mariana Valverde allowed me to work among my former colleagues at the Centre for Criminology and Socio-Legal Studies at the University of Toronto in 2010. My Australian colleagues have played equally significant roles. My fellow members of the School of History's book writing group helped me to reconceive the introduction, and the former head, Angela Woollacott, unfailingly supported my goals from the moment she welcomed me. I am privileged to work in a school whose graduate students and faculty regard collegiality as a guiding light.

When fearless colleagues become fast friends, debts turn into bonds. Sandra Wilson has pushed me to think more clearly about clemency, and I have greatly enjoyed our discussions, even when she has turned them into writing boot camps. Mark Finnane has been a mentor since we first met in 1992, and I continue to admire and benefit from his innovative approaches to criminal justice history. Robert Cribb proceeded from offering surgical criticism on the original grant proposal to becoming a close collaborator, co-editor, and treasured friend who has steered me from intellectual pitfalls. Tyrell Haberkorn has debated the distinctions between impunity and discretionary justice with me since we met in 2012. I could not have wished for a better interlocutor (or cookie baker).

At NYU Press I wish to thank Clara Platter, who supported this project from my first approach. Constance Grady has been an extremely efficient editorial assistant, whose advice on the technical aspects of the production has been invaluable. The press sought out three anonymous reviewers of my proposal and final manuscript. Although I wish I could thank them personally I can safely say that the manuscript benefited from their criticism.

My final thanks go to a scholar and friend whose role in the completion of this book was unparalleled. When the project looked unlikely to get off the ground, Lorna Weir offered her home, where compassion and lively conversation flourished. There are few ideas in this book that cannot be traced to our kitchen table dialogues.

Introduction

Pardon and Parole in the Empire State

The Great Seal of the State of New York features two goddesses who stand astride a shield that depicts the sun rising over the Hudson River. Justice appears on the right, carrying her scales and clutching a sword; her sister, Liberty, holds a staff topped with her cap as she kicks aside a crown. Designed in 1778 by the governor and chancellor of the state, it replaced the previous seal of the Crown with a new image that encompassed the Revolutionary generation's dual aspiration—to retain the rule of law and the principles of British justice while simultaneously unshackling the Republic from monarchial governance.[1] In the state of New York the power of the people to elect their leaders would replace the sovereign's inherited rule over his subjects. Nevertheless, the state's first constitution, and each one that followed, vested the ancient prerogative to pardon in the office of the governor. Liberty put her foot to the Crown, but she did not dislodge executive discretion. Her incomplete move raises two questions: How did the royal prerogative of mercy transform into gubernatorial clemency? Why did the governor's discretion over criminal sentences persist despite the emergence of parole in the late nineteenth century? The answers to these questions lie in the state's unique blend of colonial legacies and modernizing ambitions.

Historians of modern punishment have rightly named New York the nation's chief engine room of penal innovation. Enlightenment thought and humanitarian ideals found fertile ground in the state, producing a revolt against painful and spectacular forms of punishment and their replacement by imprisonment in the half century following the Revolution.[2] By the 1820s, New York's Auburn State Prison, a massive penitentiary that combined solitary confinement with congregate labor, became a model institution that inspired copies around the world. New York's Prison Association, incorporated in 1846, was founded decades after Philadelphia's equivalent, but it quickly became one of the country's leading voices in penal reform.[3] Within a generation of its founding, the association conducted a comprehensive study of the penitentiary system in North America, spearheaded the National Prison

Association in 1870, and played a leading role in the establishment of the International Prison Association.[4]

In the post–Civil War period New York legislators turned the state into an incubator of cutting-edge penal practice. By authorizing indeterminate sentencing provisions and nurturing the reform principle of punishment, New York experimented early with the notion of progressive penology. A small town in upstate New York made history in 1876, as the New York State Reformatory became the nation's first reformatory for adult males.[5] Built in the town of Elmira, its institutional managers acquired the discretionary authority to determine when an inmate had reformed and when he might be granted release on parole. The Prison Association hailed the Elmira Reformatory as a symbol of penal progress while pointing proudly to the groundwork it laid for parole in the 1840s through its committee to assist and monitor released prisoners. By the turn of the twentieth century New York surged further forward with a state parole system, buttressed by statutes that enabled and later dictated indeterminate sentences for all but the most serious offenders. In the latter decades of the Progressive Era it continued to lead other jurisdictions by adding a state board of probation, prison-based psychological clinics staffed by leading behavioral and social scientists, and institutions for the confinement of "defective" delinquents. By the 1930s New Yorkers could justly boast that the state had one of the most comprehensive and advanced criminal justice systems in the world.[6]

Excelsior (meaning "still higher") was the Great Seal's motto, and it was an apt term to characterize New York's leadership in penal practice. When it came to the field of discretionary justice, however, tradition clung. The constitution granted the chief executive unchecked authority to grant pardons, to commute sentences for non-capital offenses, and to reprieve individuals sentenced to death. No state governor wore a crown or held a scepter, but the chief executive's authority came to be called "the one-man power," and it struck many critics as discordant in a republic. From the third constitutional convention in 1821 straight through to the 1915 convention, delegates vigorously debated executive discretion. Outside these arenas, legal publicists turned the sovereign prerogative into a contentious issue, charging that it violated the principle of proportionality and defeated deterrence. The foremost opponent of the prerogative power to pardon was Francis Lieber, a German immigrant who fled Prussian autocracy for American liberty, eventually calling New York home. A political scientist and law professor at Columbia University, Lieber inspired later analysts of the pardon power who advocated the alternative of an advisory board of experts capable, they asserted, of appraising clemency petitions dispassionately. New York was out of tune with most states, which turned toward administrative means of dispensing discretionary justice in the late nineteenth century.[7] Humming along in harmony with its colonial past, rather than joining the national chorus, the Empire State retained a relic of royalist clemency.

By granting the leading edge of penal change the limelight, historians of modern criminal justice have left lingering practices in the shadows. If we search for the enduring role of executive discretion, a problem pondered from the first rumblings of Revolution, we find few scholarly signposts. Theoretical accounts of long-term penal change are attracted, like penal histories, to the distinct identifiers of modern punishment: the prison, parole, the expert. David Garland observes that Foucauldian, Marxist, Durkheimian and Weberian approaches all fix on "a particular cultural trait or characteristic of modern society . . . and explicate it in terms of a particular theory of social structure or social change."[8] The apparatuses of penal discipline that deprived criminals of liberty became the modern substitutes for torture and public executions. The clinical probings of the "psy" professionals differed from the exhortations of the chaplain. And the parole officer's questionnaire was the cold contrast to the sting of the warden's whip. Yet sovereign justice remained in place. The royal pardon's extensive use declined sharply after the eighteenth century, but not to the extent claimed in standard accounts of penal modernity. We need only consider the Queen of England's posthumous pardon of 306 World War I deserters in 2006, or Illinois governor George Ryan's pardon of four men sentenced to death, and his commutation of a further 167 death sentences in 2003 to be reminded that jurisdictions that introduced parole over the late nineteenth and early twentieth centuries did not dispense with executive discretion.[9]

Skyrocketing imprisonment rates and rising concern over wrongful convictions, particularly in death penalty states, have recently turned scholars toward the study of clemency—the modification of criminal sanctions through constitutional authority, not statute law. Like the monarch's royal prerogative of mercy, modern forms of clemency include the suspension of fines, the commutation of prison sentences, the pardon of convicted criminals, and the reprieve of death sentences. For federal offenders, the president holds this power, and governors have the authority to grant clemency for inmates in state institutions, where the vast majority of prisoners serve time. While studies of the presidential pardon power in historical perspective continue to multiply, histories of gubernatorial clemency remain scarce. Furthermore, studies of parole and related administrative means of modifying criminal sentences rarely integrate an analysis of executive discretion, which transformed, rather than disappeared, as indeterminate sentencing and parole emerged.[10] Pardoning was not simply parole's pre-modern forerunner, and parole's origins lie deeper in the past than penal historians have suggested.

New York provides the ideal setting to explore discretionary justice's complex history. From the Revolution onward, various forms of conditional liberty, military parole, and discharged prisoner programs developed alongside pardoning, sometimes at odds, at others in concert with it, and ultimately intertwined. How did advocates of a historically regal prerogative argue in favor of its retention? Why did state-administered parole merely overshadow executive clemency without overtaking it? What conflicts and accommodations occurred in this mixed marriage of pardoning and parole? And how did prisoners and petitioners negotiate the distinct but related routes to release and relief from punishment? These questions prompt the chapters that follow.

***

Histories of mercy in the ancient world and the pre-modern past help to inform the analysis of clemency's enduring presence. The Romans chose Clementia, a goddess associated with mercy, to stand for a personal ethic and a pre-Christian social ideal, as well as a force that "constructs peace from war and restores harmony where discord has reigned." When the emperor granted clemency to subjects who appeared in "abject submission," he demonstrated his authority virtuously, with no suggestion of weakness.[11] In sixteenth-century France, the tale of a humble pardon petitioner could touch the clement heart of the sovereign. In a strongly hierarchical structure, royal pardons could bring peace and assist the poor at the same time that they augmented the monarch's status.[12] Douglas Hay's germinal analysis of "property, authority and the criminal law" in early modern England has influenced a generation of scholars who have applied his analysis of mercy to numerous jurisdictions and periods.[13] Whether examining modern North America or colonial Africa, historians have shown how the "calculated blend of terror and mercy under the strict rule of law" has upheld hierarchies of class, race, and gender through the clement treatment of individuals.[14] Among American historians, in contrast, the power dynamics of mercy have attracted comparatively little attention. Historian Vivien M. L. Miller rightly observes that "historical treatments of clemency in its wider social and cultural context are conspicuous by their absence."[15]

Scholarly interest in the history of discretionary justice in the United States gravitates to the White House, not to the prerogative powers of governors.[16] The presidential power to pardon became a sticking point in constitutional negotiations in the 1780s, when radicals were averse to any hint of royal prerogative until a New Yorker, Alexander Hamilton, invoked the need for political stability and won over opponents of expansive executive power. Enlightenment exponents could reject the custom of divine kingship and still consider it necessary to preserve "core elements of monarchy."[17] Consequently, the president, like his imperial Roman counterpart and the erstwhile King of England, should hold unchecked power to grant clemency through the Constitution. Scholarship on the different presidents' use of their power and the shifting political contexts in which they granted or denied pardons boomed after Gerald Ford's preemptive pardon of disgraced President Richard Nixon in 1974.[18] President Bill Clinton's spate of last-minute pardons in 2001 and George W. Bush's questionable commutation of a Republican staffer's sentence for obstructing justice placed a chill on presidential pardoning, at the very point when the number of federal prisoners seeking executive clemency began to rise sharply.[19] State governors, led by Ryan, began to take a different course by commuting death sentences and by pardoning prisoners, especially wrongfully convicted inmates. In a climate of penal populism, the ancient prerogative of mercy is as political today as it was when the nation was founded.[20]

Most studies of state governors' prerogative to pardon approach the subject through the history of capital crime and punishment, which emphasizes sovereign authority's endurance in modernity, yet this concentration fosters a distorted image of the power to commute sentences as a matter, always, of life and death.[21] Hollywood hasn't helped. In crime melodramas, such as *I Want to Live* (1958), the camera shifts from the deathwatch cell to the governor's mansion, and it cuts to close-ups of the clock and the telephone. Will it ring? Will she live or die?[22] Real life did conform to silver screen portrayals of gubernatorial mercy in New York, though not until 1930: this was the year when the state's chief executive assumed exclusive authority over death penalty cases, and the Board of Parole became responsible for assessing petitions in all other cases. Prior to that point, New York's governors appraised pleas for mercy by and on behalf of all offenders, from minor miscreants to murderers.[23] This chronology leads to two further questions: How did New York's chief executives regard and exercise the most individual of their powers, and how did prisoners experience changes in clemency procedures after indeterminate sentencing and parole were introduced?

The history of the pardon has developed largely in parallel to the history of the parole, written primarily by criminologists and socio-legal scholars.[24] Although they are not framed as histories, the leading works in this field indicate the need for an integrated approach to the analysis of discretionary justice. Jonathan Simon's *Poor Discipline* applies a Foucauldian lens to interpret the ways in which modern parole "normalized" offenders, and he connects this mode of discipline to deeper historical practices of clemency in which religious and secular authorities demanded sureties for good behavior and relied on families and communities to monitor and regulate deviance.[25] Published in 1993, when a "flight from discretion" was well underway in penal justice, Simon's book reveals how "psy" professionals accrued discretionary authority over the release of prisoners in the early twentieth century. Another foundational study, published by Sheldon Messinger and his colleagues, examines California's legislative debates and parole board records to explain why a rehabilitative justification for parole emerged belatedly: in the first twenty years of its existence (the mid-1890s to the mid-1910s) the California Board of Parole operated chiefly to relieve the governor of his responsibility to review pardon petitions against excessive sentence, and to reduce prison populations.[26] Parole operated for decades in that state in direct association with pardoning, and both forms of discretionary release relied upon informal decision making and personal judgments of great consequence to the prisoners under their authority.

Unlike the power to pardon at the federal level, hybrid models of discretionary decision making developed in most states, which established boards to process pardoning and parole requests and to provide advice to the governor. Consequently, studying parole in combination with executive discretionary justice is more faithful to historical practice than are narratives of penal modernity that emphasize the taming of discretion.[27] New York, one of the first states to introduce parole, was a laggard when it came to assigning clemency petitions to administrative review in 1930. In contrast, Florida established a board of pardons in the 1890s but it did not introduce a parole board until 1941. Nevertheless, pardons in that state resembled parole in Florida because they typically imposed conditions upon released prisoners (to lead a "sober, peaceable, law-abiding life"), and because they carried the threat of a return to prison.[28] In Texas, the formal conjunction of parole and pardon review took place in 1905, although the governor could overrule any board decision. In both of these former slave states, white plantation owners and families employing servants often promised to employ pardoned offenders as a means to maintain their control over African American workers, historian Ethan Blue argues. This discretionary practice was less a modern form of parole than an updated system of peonage.[29]

State-by-state studies of pardoning and parole—alert to the demographics, economies, and politics of each jurisdiction, and attentive to the individuals and groups involved in decision making—must form the necessary foundation for a nationwide analysis of discretionary justice. New York was not just another state: it was the Empire State, almost a nation unto itself by the mid-nineteenth century, when 10 percent of Americans were New Yorkers. By the turn of the century it towered over other states in the size and diversity of its economy and population.[30] There were three and one-half million inhabitants in the boroughs of New York City alone in 1900, and by 1930 this number almost doubled, with more than half of its population foreign born.[31] Not surprisingly, New York developed a parole system run by state agents long before southern and sparsely populated states followed suit. But in the mid-1920s, when a law-and-order agenda eroded earlier support for progressive penology, New York was also the first state to turn its back on parole. Riots at two of New York's state prisons in 1929 created a crisis of confidence in New York's capacity to fight crime and to punish fairly and effectively. Out of this crucible the merger of parole and pardoning under one board was forged almost a century after Francis Lieber had advocated this modern alternative to an imperial model of clemency.

Recent advocacy of large-scale narrative political history sets a new agenda for an understanding of criminal justice, charted through pardoning and parole.[32] In New York, concerns over the constitutionality and exercise of discretionary justice were hot political issues from the first days of the republic to the mid-twentieth century. The intensity and tenor of those debates shifted over that long period, but one matter remained constant: the significance of discretionary justice as a means for convicted offenders to seek relief from punishment. Although criminal justice historians have connected long-term transformations in state punishment to economic and social change, to emergent strategies of law and order, and to new regimes of knowledge, similar attention to discretionary release is lacking. Authoritative surveys, such as Lawrence M. Friedman's 1993 classic, *Crime and Punishment in American History*, and more recently Elizabeth Dale's *Criminal Justice in the United States* (2011), analyze the infliction of punishment in great depth but refer only briefly to pardoning and parole.[33] Compared to our deep knowledge of the factors that consigned offenders to prisons and the gallows we know surprisingly little about discretionary justice, the power to shorten sentences and spare life.

The 1970s was a period when academics and criminal justice practitioners began to question the project to transform preexisting models of criminal justice into an expert-orchestrated science, and David J. Rothman led the way with two major historical studies, *The Discovery of the Asylum* (1971) and *Conscience and Convenience* (1980).[34] Rothman was on a mission to expose the arrogance of penal professionals, including those involved in the screening of prospective parolees. His scathing account of modernizers' self-serving ambitions casts correctional officials and experts in starring roles, but he sets no scenes for executive clemency, and governors make cameo appearances only when their actions are tied to parole's administration. If we highlight professional hubris and institutional stasis we leave out the plot twists of penal modernization. Accordingly, a larger cast of actors appears in this book: the governors who exercised personal discretion; the prisoners, their families, and advocates, who used customary appeals in pardon and commutation petitions; and the public, which weighed the costs and benefits of discretionary justice in legislative and constitutional deliberations, surveys, and the popular press.

The epistemic transition from sovereign justice to discipline is nowhere more powerfully drawn than in Michel Foucault's *Discipline and Punish* (1975). Initially, historians were dubious of the book's concern with discourse, its selective references to institutional practice, and its inattention to individual actors' motivations. Even criminologist Stanley Cohen, who reviewed the book in 1978, found that Foucault concentrated on origins and ruptures, rather than processes and people, because "he is not really an historian."[35] Such criticism is warranted only to the extent that Foucault confines his analysis of sovereign power to its heyday, the period prior to the ascendance of penitential punishment. Judged as a history, *Discipline and Punish* fails to grapple with the persistence of executive discretion in modernity. Nevertheless, Foucault provides historians with analytical tools that can pick out the contrasting characteristics of sovereign and disciplinary power. Perhaps in ways he did not anticipate, these tools can also unpack how and why parole emerged and pardoning persisted. The technology of parole developed in step with regimes of surveillance, inspection, and normalization, all of which colored penal administration in disciplinary society. In New York the state shifted the responsibility for processing clemency petitions to the revamped parole board in 1930, but the state's chief executive—the inheritor of sovereign authority—retained the sovereign power to permit death and to preserve life.

Discretionary decision making expanded rather than contracted in the modern administrative state. Enlightenment thinkers such as Montesquieu and utilitarian philosopher Jeremy Bentham laid out programs for the rationalization of justice in order to combat the arbitrary and capricious nature of pre-modern punishment.[36] The replacement of severe and bloody punishment with fixed terms of imprisonment was a measure of their success. Despite the embrace of certainty, discretion seeped into old and new cracks in the criminal process: victims' decision to report or to disregard an offense; grand jurors' inclination to indict or to find that evidence of criminal culpability was doubtful; prosecutors' willingness to offer a plea or their determination to apply the law strictly; jurors' readiness to render verdicts in strict alignment with the law or to nullify; and judges' use of their power to suspend or set minimal sentences, or to impose the strictest sentences under the law. The introduction of probation and the increasing use of plea bargaining further extended the optional expansion or contraction of penal sanctions.[37] Unlike these other forms of discretionary justice, the pardon and parole differ; they come into play only after courts set penalties—fines, imprisonment, death. In New York, the state constitution and subsequent statutes imposed nothing more than parameters within which chief executives and boards wielded their authority to pardon or grant parole. State governors' exercise of discretionary power could not have been more profound: it spelled the difference between those offenders who did, and those who did not suffer the full impact of criminal penalties.

***

Thanks to New York's rich repository of archival and published primary records, it is possible to plot the arc of persistence and change in discretionary justice.[38] Forty-nine men served as governor from the Revolution to the Depression, and many of the records concerning their pardon practice have survived.[39] Chapter 1 uses the public papers and messages of New York's first and longest-serving governor, George Clinton, to document the military and political context in which the chief executive exercised his authority to modify punishment. Because the first constitution, inspired by the surge of confidence in democratic rule, determined that the legislature must pardon in capital cases, pardons granted through statutes document the bifurcated nature of mercy in the Revolutionary era. George Clinton, who governed New York for the first eighteen years of its statehood, could pardon only in non-capital cases, yet he inherited powers greater than those of his British predecessor, who had rendered his pardoning decisions in consultation with his provincial Council under the authority of the crown.[40]

Historians agree that post-Revolutionary New York, more than any other original state, invested considerable authority in the chief executive, embodied by Clinton.[41] A towering military figure and popular leader, he was elected while serving in the Continental Army. Wearing these two hats in the midst of war, Clinton made tactical use of the pardon as well as the dispensation of military paroles, and his public papers detail how he weighed mercy against severity in his responses to judgments handed down in civil courts and courts-martial. In the decade after hostilities ceased, legislators began to reduce the number of capital statutes and to approve plans for the state's first penitentiary. By the time John Jay, New York's second governor, took office in 1796, the state aligned with the move made in Pennsylvania and Massachusetts toward imprisonment as the new form of punishment for serious offenders.

As the nineteenth century approached, the era of public whippings and hangings, the punishment prescribed for a wide range of felonies, drew to a close. New York's age of the penitentiary opened with the construction of Newgate Prison in lower Manhattan in 1797, and long penal sentences replaced physical punishment and death for felons thereafter. Enlightenment-inspired alternatives to sanguinary justice and Quaker-led faith in penitence triumphed, but only for a short while, as the prison became dangerously crowded and escape attempts and inmate riots were put down with brutal violence. In response to these problems the governor's power to pardon assumed a new role by releasing a steady stream of prisoners. Traditionalists, who hankered for the old days of public floggings and hangings, decried the release of criminals through executive mercy, and they complained that governors of the early nineteenth century pardoned indiscriminately. Fortunately, the journals of executive pardons, commutations, and respites (a ten-volume set that begins in 1799) allow a more complex story to be told. Discretionary justice in the early national period was more selective than hardliners claimed, and historians have assumed.

Chapter 2 analyzes how pardoning became a factor in the management of new and old hierarchies in New York's canal era. Although African Americans made up a small number of penitentiary inmates, they represented a significant quotient of New York's diverse population, greatly outstripping their proportion in the population of other northern colonies and states. After the Revolution slavery remained legal in New York, and the road toward gradual abolition took twenty years to roll out. In 1799 the legislature finally prohibited the traffic in bonded labor, but the pardon of slaves on condition of their "transportation" became a means for masters to weasel their way around this prohibition, allowing them to sell slaves outside the state. Property also superseded democratic rights in the state's relationship with indigenous peoples, as land-hungry speculators set their sites on Indian land. Prior to the Revolution the state acknowledged treaty Indians' right to self-govern, but it quickly encroached on the rights of Native Americans after the war, including the Iroquois nation in New York. Then, in 1821, this pluralist approach came to a symbolic end. In the state's last legislated pardon, clemency's coercive face showed itself in the stark wording of a statute that pardoned Tommy Jemmy, a Seneca man prosecuted for the murder of a Seneca woman in treaty territory. That act simultaneously pardoned one Indian and declared the state's sovereignty over all matters of criminal law, treaty or no treaty.

The completion of the Erie Canal in 1825 carved a path for the state's economic ascendance in the antebellum era and earned New York a nickname that stuck: the Empire State. Many New Yorkers, not just native peoples and slaves but also the tenant farmers of the Hudson Valley, were unimpressed, and they protested that the state government had failed to deliver on the egalitarian promise of the republic. The use of the pardon power became bound up in the search for stronger anchors to democratic principles. On the federal scene disputes over executive pardoning authority drifted into "philosophical obscurity" in the nineteenth century, but in New York this was not the case, as constitutional conventions drew delegates who lined up for and against gubernatorial discretion.[42] Chapter 3 examines the records of the two conventions (1821 and 1846) in which delegates vigorously tackled the question of the one-man power. Beyond this formal scrum, a pioneering generation of social scientists and penal theorists devised a two-pronged attack on gubernatorial discretion, arguing that mercy, granted by the chief executive, was incompatible with democratic justice, and that pardons distracted prisoners from correcting their characters. But the traditional reliance upon one elected authority, open to scrutiny, attracted greater support in New York. When French social surveyors Gustave de Beaumont and Alexis de Tocqueville visited the U.S. in 1831 to study the prison system they found it curious to find royalist pardoning in the republican homeland of penal innovation.

The alternative to executive discretion—granting the power to the legislature or an appointed board—proved politically unpalatable at a point when divisive local and national issues polarized state party politics. New York's constitution consequently expanded the governor's authority to pardon in 1821 and only moderately trimmed it in 1846. New York governors also proved that pardons could resolve crises that politicians had produced. In 1823, Governor Joseph C. Yates stepped in to pardon inmates whom enthusiasts of isolation had experimented on in Auburn State Prison. As philosopher John Locke and common law theorist William Blackstone had urged, pardons were most beneficent and just when they rectified injustice; clemency affirmed the fallibility of men, not the failure of the rule of law. Governor John Young claimed he acted on this basis in 1847 when he pardoned eighteen prisoners who had been sentenced harshly for their role in a tenant revolt against the great landlords of New York. Young later disclosed to a friend: "If I err at all I feel it should be on the side of mercy."[43] No less than in 1777, the governor deployed mercy to quell a political crisis and to subdue disorder.

Chapter 4, which covers the mid-nineteenth century to Reconstruction, utilizes the first batch of an extraordinary run of clemency case files, and these records complement governors' published papers and messages to the legislature. Chief executives recorded surprisingly lengthy and moving accounts of their motivations behind granting or denying clemency; even so, the internal records of clemency review allow the historian to peer more deeply into the inner workings of the pardon power. In the collection's first decades, most files pertain to petitioners who were ultimately successful in their bids for clemency. Because few unsuccessful files have been preserved it is impossible to determine patterns of refusal versus success. Nevertheless, correspondence in the files that remain, including remarks by the governor and his clerk, plus letters from prisoners, their families, and their supporters, provides an intimate sense of the clemency process prior to the large-scale introduction of parole.

The most obvious feature of the clemency files is the preponderance of male cases: only 4.2 percent of the files preserved from the late nineteenth century concern female prisoners. Nevertheless, their political significance outweighed their frequency, thanks to the American woman's rights movement, with its leadership drawn from New York starting in the 1840. Agitation against women's inequality under the law, civil and criminal, cast women's cases in a light that exposed the larger question at the heart of every plea for mercy: Should the law apply equally to all, or should clemency recognize the frailties and vulnerabilities of certain individuals or types? Chapter 5 examines elite debate over this question, which intensified in the mid- to late nineteenth century, and highlights cases that provoked national attention. The capital cases of Maria Hartung and Roxalana Druse proved so contentious that the New York legislature attempted to pass laws that would resolve this vexing question without requiring the governor to render an unpalatable decision. Although "fancy" prisoners—white, wealthy, and well connected— could usually drum up support for clemency, the rarity of such persons among the criminally sentenced meant governors could anticipate that the press and their political enemies would keep a hawk eye on their moves in such cases.[44] The Walworth murder case of 1873, involving the killing of a father from a nationally prominent family by his own son, demonstrated that privilege could be a liability as well as an asset, and that the prospect of a pardon was never axiomatic.

In pleas for clemency the word of respectable citizens and religious, business, and political leaders counted in prisoners' favor; the approval of district attorneys and judges mattered even more. The files of successful petitioners, as well as governors' public papers, confirm that chief executives rarely commuted sentences or pardoned offenders without the endorsement of at least one of these officials. Petitioners had little control over these assessments, although family members and other advocates sometimes called up local lawmen in an attempt to garner their support. More commonly, seekers of mercy tugged on community ties and plugged into organizational networks to solicit support. For the average prisoner—the poor man, the recent immigrant, and members of racial minorities—a personal link to a higher-status individual or membership in an association willing to stand up for one of its members was a precious resource. Above all, prisoners with strong family and neighborhood connections who appealed for mercy with requisite humility and avowals of reformation stood a fair chance of a pardon. Nevertheless, no plea was a sure bet: some governors were generous, others stingy, and many were accused of favoring the wealthy and influential, although no New York governor came close to being impeached for the misuse of his discretionary authority.

In the Gilded Age the first generation of penal reformers made great strides in New York, where the Elmira Reformatory symbolized the state's endorsement of the principle that punishment ought to reform and release ought to be earned. Pioneering penologists decried the aleatory nature of pardoning. Why should a prisoner's early release depend on the sympathetic heart or the tough mind of an elected politician? And why should the hardship a criminal's absence imposed on his dependent family members—the most frequently cited ground for clemency—matter more than the sound appraisal of his reformation? Indeterminate sentencing and the institutional management of parole were reforms conjured to replace pardoning, but they produced problems only the governor could rectify, which recast sovereign authority as a corrective to penal modernization. Superintendent Zebulon Brockway was initially a star on the international stage of progressive penology. Then, in the 1890s, allegations of cruelty and favoritism added to evidence of Elmira managers' abuse of their statutory authority to revoke parole flared into a scandal. The *New York World* led a spirited campaign on behalf of Brockway's "boys," and it inspired Governor Roswell P. Flower to intervene. As Governor Young had done seventy years earlier, he used his superior constitutional power. Flower pardoned Elmira inmates on the basis that reformatory staff had "overpunished" young men. The mixed marriage of pardoning and parole was off to a rocky start by the turn of the century.

The principle of parole as a discretionary means to prepare inmates for freedom and to reduce the risk of recidivism turned out to be more resilient than Zebulon Brockway's reputation, and New York provided further endorsement by establishing a State Board of Parole in 1901. Chapter 6 considers the first two decades of the board's operations and examines how the extension of parole and indeterminate sentencing to cover inmates in the major state prisons recast the role of executive clemency. In addition to a sample of the clemency case files from this period, this chapter draws on the records of the Parole Board's hearings held at the Auburn State Prison from 1905 to 1919. Most studies of parole in Progressive Era New York have capitalized on inmate case files from Elmira or the Bedford Hills Reformatory for Women, where the most advanced psychological appraisals of deviance were implemented in institutionally managed parole operations.[45] However, the records from the largest state prisons, which incarcerated male and female felons, reflect the ways in which the majority of New York's inmates experienced discretionary release—as a largely personal and decidedly unprofessional mode of character assessment and job placement.

The average prisoner released on parole in the early twentieth century was a male inmate from one of the state prisons. New York remained the nation's leading jailhouse in the Progressive Era, and the state's Board of Parole was assigned responsibility to review applications from prisons that held thousands of inmates, with a substantial proportion reflecting the rise of immigrants in New York from Italy and southern and eastern Europe, plus an increasing number of African Americans. Few of the uniformed applicants for parole resembled the suited men who served on the three-person board: white Anglo-American men of standing, appointed for their political loyalty and community stature, not their expertise in behavioral science. Parole board hearing records (frequently verbatim) indicate how little trust its members placed in expertise and how firmly they relied on what they believed to be common sense. In these interview transcripts we hear bold prisoners complaining that their rights to a fair hearing were denied. We also hear how disrespectful backchat provoked jibes from the board in response. Parole was far less professional as its advocates had hoped it might be, and less expert-driven than historians have claimed.

As the paroling of felons from the state prisons became an established form of discretionary release, governors of the early twentieth century began to grant fewer pardons and to commute sentences more frequently. Occasionally governors pardoned inmates who could not meet the new requirements of parole, based on their low intelligence or limited capacity for work on release. The board had jurisdiction over inmates serving indeterminate sentences but the governor could still grant clemency to any offender, including those serving long mandatory sentences. Whenever this occurred, these prisoners became "special clemency cases," and governors referred their files to the Board of Parole for discretionary release. Thus, the historic gubernatorial practice of attaching conditions to pardons without any means to enforce them transformed into a cooperative venture in which the executive relied on parole procedures that included the prospect of reimprisonment if discharged prisoners violated their parole conditions. The rise of parole in the Progressive Era produced a new interwoven pattern of discretionary justice.

The final chapter traces the political machinations and public outrage that led to the formal merger of pardoning and parole, a deal brokered by Governor Franklin D. Roosevelt. In some respects, which his contemporaries failed to note and criminal justice historians have overlooked, the seeds of that merger were planted during the Revolution under George Clinton, since he handled the parole of military captives and the pardon of wartime offenders, while the legislature had jurisdiction over capital offenders.[46] But the 1930 merger of pardoning and parole blended tradition with novelty: the fate of capitally convicted offenders now lay in the governor's hands alone; an administrative body of appointees and civil servants processed all other clemency petitions; and a Division of Parole employed scores of agents to evaluate released prisoners during a different kind of war, this one against Prohibition-era gangsterism.[47]

Brash newspaper headlines seared fear of a crime wave into public consciousness in the postwar years, and governors, particularly Democrat Alfred E. Smith, faced unprecedented pressure to justify every decision. By the mid-1920s, however, scandals over the Parole Board's bungling of discretion generated greater discontent than concerns over gubernatorial clemency. In the press and in the Republican-dominated legislature, troops lined up to fight crime by tougher measures. Under the leadership of State Senator Caleb H. Baumes, New York clawed back earlier indeterminate sentencing provisions, replacing them with a string of statutes that put a stranglehold on parole eligibility. As of 1926 the so-called Baumes Laws imposed mandatory life sentences on four-time felony offenders. Ironically, the governor's pardon power survived this campaign, partly because supporters of the statute recognized the value in preserving gubernatorial discretion: if minor and nonviolent offenders faced unduly harsh sentences, the chief executive could intervene. Ultimately New York's inmates, overcrowded in the antiquated state prisons and deprived of hope of release, spoke louder than politicians. Violent rebellions at Clinton and Auburn State Prisons in 1929 achieved what constitutional convention delegates and high-minded critics of the one-man power had failed to accomplish: the establishment of a new system of discretionary justice in which a board would process clemency requests along with parole applications. Without constitutional amendment and without dislodging the chief executive's prerogative powers, the modern face of discretionary justice took shape.

When ex-governor Roosevelt left Albany for Washington he packed his concerns over the administration of discretionary justice. As president, he authorized a study of release procedures in every state and the federal penal system.[48] Like this book, this massive survey studied pardoning in tandem with parole, but it portrayed the latter mode of administrative release as the modern substitute for an earlier, personal mode of relief from punishment. This succession analogy, which most historical studies of parole reinforce, does a disservice to the long and tangled roots of parole and pardoning, which reach back to the Revolution, with wartime paroles. By the mid-nineteenth century they grew through discharged prisoners' services, intertwined with charitable aid. The federal survey's separate volumes also overlooked the interrelatedness of executive and administrative discretion, which emerged in New York in the late nineteenth century and persists in the twenty-first century, with calls to revive and reinvigorate pardoning to undo the unjust outcomes of draconian sentencing and risk-averse parole.[49] This advocacy will become more robust once it is grounded in histories of discretionary justice, conducted state by state. There is no better place to start than the Empire State.

1

Governing Mercy in the Emerging Republic

The evacuation of English occupying forces from the southern tip of New York was an event worth celebrating. Exhausted but triumphant, a band of Continental troops paraded into Manhattan on November 25, 1783. General George Washington led his men on horseback and George Clinton, his loyal brigadier general, rode at his side. Clinton was also governor of New York, but he had split his duties since 1777 between fighting the enemy and presiding over civilian affairs. As the occasion also signaled the start of the government's long-awaited jurisdiction over the entire state, Clinton, the state's chief executive, hosted a lavish post-parade reception to honor the commander in chief. The wine flowed freely at Fraunces Tavern that chilly evening, and many toasts rang out through the night. By the ninth round it was Washington's turn: "'May justice support what Courage has gained!'"[1] This lusty call heralded the dawn of the unified republic. It also posed a challenge: What would republican justice entail?

The convulsions of revolution generated as much anxiety as hope among elites and commoners, particularly in New York, where many of the former colony's richest merchants and largest landowners, the great landlords of the Hudson Valley, rallied to the republican cause without embracing its egalitarian prospects. The spirit of democracy raised alarm in Whigs and royalists alike, and slave owners clung as long and as hard as they could to keep their human property in bondage and to profit from their sale. Anglo-European settlers' encroachment on native land in the state's interior gained murderous momentum rather than slackening with American independence. The protracted English occupation of New York, longer than in any other state, presaged that much of the past would linger in its future, including in the administration of criminal justice. When the Revolution bestowed independence on New Yorkers it came in the guise of ordered liberty.[2]

From the moment New York cast its lot with the other rebel colonies the implementation of republican justice confronted the question of discretion, previously defined through the royal prerogative of mercy. Colonial governors had exercised this power on behalf of the king, and the revolt could have done away with executive pardoning along with the monarchy. Instead, New Yorkers chose tradition. The state's first constitution assigned sovereign discretionary power to the elected governor, and New York entrusted its chief executive with significant decision-making authority over criminal sanctions, thanks to the reluctant revolutionaries who drafted the plan of government in 1777.[3] The only measure of caution regarding the governor's prerogative was the constitution's determination that legislature would exercise discretion over death sentences for murder and treason. Still, the governor could grant pardons for all other felonies punishable by death, and recommend that murderers and traitors be granted mercy.

As New York consolidated sovereignty over its territory and jostled for economic and political ascendency among the former colonies, the character of discretionary justice drew from the colonial past and English customs as much as it blazed a new republican trail. During the War of Independence, prior practice served both military and civil purposes, and George Clinton's multiple roles—brigadier general of the state militia, brigadier general in the Continental Army, governor and commander in chief of the militia—greatly amplified his capacity to seek order and stability in granting mercy to the enemy, external and internal. The Articles of War authorized Clinton and his field officers to release combatants "on their parole," technically to effect prisoner exchanges but often, in practice, to relieve prisoners' suffering and to reduce the costs of their keep.[4] Disloyalty and disaffection toward the cause of revolution were thorny problems that undermined the war effort, and wartime statecraft included the use of courts-martial to supplement civil courts. After the war, the felonies that preoccupied colonial authorities—horse theft, burglary, robbery, and forgery—were the crimes that led most frequently to questions about the proper role of discretionary justice.

By the close of the eighteenth century the customary penalty of death for property crimes came under scrutiny in New York as Enlightenment aspirations and humanitarian ideals won converts, including the governor. In the final years of his remarkable eighteen-year tenure, George Clinton prodded the legislature to endorse Cesare Beccaria's dictum on the virtue of milder but more certain punishment.[5] A new governor, John Jay, claimed the honor of overseeing New York's adoption of long-term imprisonment with hard labor in place of the death penalty. By the close of the century the state finally made the leap toward revolutionary penal reform, but there was no taste for meddling with the inherited monarchical model of executive pardoning.

Governing, Ruling, and Pardoning in Colonial New York

New York's establishment as an English colony in the late seventeenth century began with a massive land grant from King Charles II to his brother James, the Duke of York. In the king's estimation the power to pardon would play a critical role in the imposition of English rule after the surrender of the Dutch in 1664. Thus, the "Duke's Laws" assigned to James and his appointed agents "full and absolute power and authority to Correct punish Pardon Governe and Rule . . . according such Lawes Orders Ordinances Direccons and Instruments as by our said dearest Brother of his Assignes shall bee established." Pardoning did not entail the suspension of power or weaken royal authority: mercy was a central pillar of "His Majesty's Laws and Justice."[6]

Pardoning's historic association with mercy and mildness and its capacity to compensate for unbending law has never been simply benign, as Douglas Hay and subsequent historians of discretionary justice have underlined.[7] The Duke's Laws made no secret of mercy's capacity to reinforce rule. The king's newly conquered territory, far from European jurisdictions, was modeled on these Old World customs of rule, and in the colony of New York, as in monarchies, governors' pardons, commutations, and reprieves selectively validated appeals that expressed "supplication and consciousness of right."[8] The monarch delegated his royal prerogative to his appointees, and New York's governors exercised that power in all cases other than treason and willful murder. For these latter offenses, governors could reprieve offenders under sentence of death, which suspended case outcomes until "his majesty's pleasure be known."[9]

In the colonial period, the most graphic illustration of mercy's relationship to punishment took place in 1741, in the context of an uprising among free and enslaved blacks in New York City.[10] An earlier slave insurrection in 1712 prompted the Provincial Assembly to enact a law to prevent, suppress, and punish offenses committed by "Negro, Indian or Mulatto" slaves.[11] The statute stipulated that all such persons judged guilty "shall suffer the pains of Death in such manner and with such circumstances as the aggravation or enormity of their Crimes." In 1741, this latest "plot" sent panic through colonial Manhattan, and authorities responded with hasty trials, followed by brutal mutilations, hangings, and burnings at the stake: twenty-six African Americans and four whites were executed (only blacks were burned at the stake).[12] Conditional pardons in the form of transportation far outnumbered executions, however. In March 1741 Lieutenant Governor George Clarke promised "His Majesty's most gracious Pardon" to anyone who came forward with damning evidence; in addition, he dangled the reward of freedom to slaves willing to implicate plotters.[13] In the service of imperial mastery and white hegemony the ploy of coercive persuasion worked.[14]

English governors were not averse to unleashing the full force of the law, but they were as certain as their imperial masters that this force be measured.

New York's tenant farmers posed an ever-present threat to order, not to mention the economic interests of the colony's great land barons. In 1766 Lieutenant Governor Cadwallader Colden ordered out regiments to put down a violent uprising that had simmered to a boil over the previous decade among the tenants of the upper Livingston Manor. By selecting the judges to preside over an extraordinary sitting of the supreme court, Colden could count on the effective prosecution of the alleged ringleaders on the charge of treason. Most rioters confessed to lesser crimes and faced imprisonment, banishment, fines, and whippings for their temerity. William Prendergast was the only traitor to face the terrible penalty for his crime: to be hanged, drawn, and quartered. But the sentence was not carried out. With peace restored on the landlords' terms, the judges and the governor concurred that "the salutary medicine of the public prosecution" had been administered. The imperial masters, satisfied that the conviction had produced "the desired effect upon the local rebels," considered the rebel leader a fit subject for the king's pardon.[15]

Under the framework of colonial governance, royal governors shared their prerogative power with the provincial elite, and they were as intent as the landlords on keeping the "leveling spirit" in check. New York was a notoriously "factious colony," in which effective prosecution and punishments were impeded in lawless districts in the decade leading up to the Revolution.[16] Well before the Revolution occurred, New York's heterogeneous population expressed its selective respect for the rule of English law. Settlers refused to cooperate with investigations and evaded arrest, while jurors, particularly in rural districts, frequently reached verdicts that defied the evidence presented in court. As a result, executions were far less common than they were in England by mid-century. After the horrible welter of executions in New York in 1741, seventy-eight capitally convicted offenders were hanged in the final three decades of imperial rule.[17]

The right to trial by jury was one of the benefits the British had offered the people of New York after the Duke's Laws replaced the Dutch inquisitorial system of prosecution, and any governor who contemplated withdrawing that right knew he could be recalled by his superiors and subject to intense criticism in the colony. By the 1730s, judges of session courts, who were nominated by local assembly representatives, were content to allow jurors to determine the law, not just facts.[18] Colonial officials were perturbed that jurors took advantage of this latitude by shirking their duty to convict on compelling evidence of guilt. As Goebel and Naughton observe: "the diet of the inferior courts had become unbalanced by superabundance of assaults, batteries, routs and riots. It could not be corrected by active prosecution there because juries would not convict."[19]

In formal terms the Province of New York could boast impressive trappings of legality. From 1692 the supreme court justices rode on circuit; the colony was the first to establish a bar association in 1709, and by 1758 its supreme court bench was manned by professional lawyers.[20] Yet these outward signs of legal order cloaked Britain's waning ability to solidify rule and maintain order under the law. Keeping the wealthy and influential locals onside was one means to do so, but it required English governors to exercise caution in appearing too aristocratic. In the early eighteenth century distance helped. In the conquered territory, communications with the home government were so slow and irregular that nominal superiors often cut deals with the representatives of leading landholder and merchant families who dominated the executive council.[21] These powerful "'men of estate and ability'" believed they should have a say in all matters of government, no matter what a governor's royal instructions might state.[22] In the interest of governing without provoking resistance, Henry Clinton, royal governor between 1743 and 1751, acceded to the Provincial Assembly's demands for greater control over finances, and these concessions were never regained. Lieutenant Governor Cadwallader Colden had a poor opinion of New York's great landlords, whom he accused of being "an American feudal aristocracy, and among their tenants an oppressed class of peasants." Still, he knew better than to ignore powerful locals in his use of discretion over tenants' punishment, as the 1766 trials suggest.[23]

The Governing Council's meeting minutes confirm that governors customarily consulted colonial elites on prospective reprieves and pardons. These records also show that the judiciary took a direct role in pardoning beyond simply recommending mercy. Judges in colonial New York suspended sentences and granted stays of execution, allowing pregnant women to deliver prior to serving their sentences, and some judges preempted governors altogether, by pardoning offenders and imposing conditions upon them. By mid-century, these expressions of colonial independence through the modification of punishment became more common. In 1773, Governor Tryon received a letter from supreme court Justice Robert Livingston, who informed the king's representative that he had just granted a pardon to a counterfeiter, one William Hurlbuton, on condition that he implicate greater offenders.[24] The stirrings of rebellion in the colony in the 1750s and '60s only heightened as local political and legal figures took the liberty to determine when, and for what reasons, mercy might be extended.

Sparks of rebellion lit up the colony as Governor William Tryon, the last of the royal governors, sat down to pen a response to the home government's request for a report on the state of affairs in New York. In June 1774, he dutifully wrote that a "Royal Government" had been in place since 1694 and that its "constitution nearly resembles that of Great Britain and the other Royal Governments in America." The colony was administered by a governor who worked with a twelve-member council, appointed by the Privy Council, and representatives whom voters elected to the popular assembly. But Tryon had only to glance at the charred ruins of the governor's mansion, burned down by anti-royalists in 1773, to register that rebelliousness had reached a tipping point.[25] Lest the assembly give further support to uprisings, Tryon prorogued the legislature several times, but this action only confirmed rebels' charges that the king's representative was trampling their cherished liberties. New York's powerful Whig merchants and landowners, chafing at the parliamentary chokehold on commerce and local governance, now joined leveling tenants and plotting "Negros" in their defiance of law and order under imperial authority.

Once full-scale war erupted in 1775, the British retained a small but vital foothold in the southern counties of New York, including the strategic port of New York.[26] At war with the populace he had tried to govern, Tryon made use of British reinforcements, a considerable supply of munitions, and a subtler weapon—his delegated authority to pardon—without having to trouble himself by consulting a council. In October 1778, "His Excellency William Tryon, Esq., governor and commander in chief of the province of New-York," issued a "proclamation in pursuance of an act of Parliament . . . to pardon all, and all manner of treasons and misprisions of treasons, by any person or persons."[27] Tryon attempted to lure his subjects back to the imperial fold in the name of His Majesty, but the king's representative was not the only authority to follow that course. The republicans who took up arms against Tryon shared his appreciation of mercy as a tactic of war.

The Constitution of 1777 and the Composition of Gubernatorial Pardoning Power

Among the New Yorkers who advocated outright rejection of English rule rather than trying to gain greater independence within empire was George Clinton (1739–1812). A distant relative of the royal governor, Henry Clinton, the future state governor could not have been more distinct in his politics. George Clinton was a farmer and representative of Ulster County, and he was one of the assemblymen Tryon had tried to hush, to little effect. Clinton served as a clerk of the Court of Common Pleas from 1759, and he evolved into a passionate opponent of royalist government. His father's deathbed wish was, "Preserve your country's freedom."[28] Although Clinton senior reportedly issued this command to each of his four sons, George, the youngest, went the furthest to fulfill his father's hopes as a soldier and a statesman. In both positions George Clinton ensured that sovereign authority would survive the revolution.

Constitutional histories of pardoning, along with contemporary studies of the president's unfettered executive authority, have framed the history of state constitutions as comparatively cautious and more inclined to constrain gubernatorial discretion.[29] Some states set that course in the first days of the republic. Under instructions from the Continental Congress to organize government in keeping with the principle of the authority of the people, radically inclined state politicians feared assigning the power to pardon to a single individual, even if that officeholder, unlike the monarch, was elected. The memory of royal governors' attempts to abrogate colonists' rights in the last days of imperial rule was fresh and sore, so simply replacing appointed delegates of the king with elected stand-ins was a prospect most states found distasteful. New Hampshire shared with the other New England colonies a long-standing suspicion and resentment of royal power, and its first constitution assigned the pardoning power to the legislature. Georgia took no chances. That state restricted the governor to recommending pardons, subject to the legislature's review. In Massachusetts, Virginia, New Jersey, and Pennsylvania, the first constitutions authorized the governor to pardon only in consultation with their respective executive councils.[30]

New York was an outlier. It was not the sole state to vest its chief executive with the pardon power (Maryland, Delaware, North Carolina, and South Carolina did as well); however, New York alone combined gubernatorial authority with direct popular election and a three-year term of office.[31] New York's governors were not granted the power to veto legislation or to exercise patronage freely, but the first constitution assigned them a place on the Councils of Revision and Appointment, serving with the judges of the supreme court, the chancellor, and members of the state senate. The governor nominated both the chancellor and judges, whose selection was subject to the Appointment Council's review. Daniel J. Hulsebosch rightly identifies New York's governor as "one of the strongest in the states."[32] Indeed, New York's investment in gubernatorial authority set the precedent for the federal Constitution's even greater reliance on executive discretion.[33]

The first state constitutions were drafted in a time of great upheaval and bloody conflict, so it is not difficult to appreciate how colonial political culture provided ballast as politicians navigated their way toward new modes of governance.[34] The New York Assembly remained loyal up to its final session in 1775, whereupon the most radical representatives began to call for the overturning of royal authority. Elsewhere disaffected New Yorkers were divided over the best course forward, and many, especially those who had profited under royal authority, eyed the radical strains of republicanism with trepidation. The violence and radicalism of groups such as the Sons of Liberty unsettled New Yorkers who fought to preserve the cherished rights associated with British justice from the threat of mob rule.[35] Many elite men judged republicanism to be wrongheaded and unnatural, and some early adherents of Whig resistance, such as William Smith Jr., a respected jurist, decided to defend English rule after the war began.[36] The prominent patriots who continued to work toward independence did so halfheartedly in the hope that republican democracy might restore British liberties, not unleash radical leveling.[37] With battles raging around them and the enemy's stronghold in the state's southern counties, English forces were alarmingly proximate; at the same time, the architects of the new government clung to the familiar conventions of English law and common law culture, which settled their hearts and guided their minds as they refashioned a royal province into a state.

On July 9, 1776, the Continental Congress declared New York an independent state, and soon thereafter the provisional governing authority, the Provincial Convention, struck a committee to devise a new form of government.[38] Members of a more radical bent hoped for a Pennsylvanian model that would weaken the executive in favor of the people. But John Jay, the committee's guiding hand, took greater stock in the counsel of his friend, Edward Rutledge of South Carolina, who advised: "when a state abounds in rascals, as is the case with too many at this day, you must suppress a little of that popular spirit, vest the executive powers of government in an individual that they may have vigor, and let them be as ample as is consistent with the great outlines of freedom."[39] Enemy troops were just fifty miles away and advancing as the committee reviewed Jay's draft constitution, which he presented late in March 1777. With their lives, families, and homes in danger, fear must surely have heightened the delegates' preparedness to approve a constitution that granted the governor considerable powers, checked by the principle of popular sovereignty. These anxieties further galvanized the drafters' Rutledge-tinged certainty that a strong executive was the surest safeguard of liberty.[40]

Shortly after the convention adopted the constitution on April 20, 1777, Gouverneur Morris, had who served with Jay on the drafting committee, griped that the new framework of governance failed to bestow New York's chief executive with "vigor." He expressed his disappointment to Alexander Hamilton, who agreed, adding that Americans expressed too much suspicion of prerogative power and placed too much faith in popularly elected legislatures.[41] Neither man may have been pondering the pardon power in this exchange, but they both knew that New York's first constitution restricted the governor from pardoning offenders found guilty of murder or treason. In such cases he could reprieve and recommend mercy, whereas the legislature had the power not only to enact pardons but also to determine that capital sentences be carried out against convicted murderers and traitors, irrespective of a governor's wishes.

Hamilton's and Morris's carping underplayed the fact that New York State's governors assumed a greater role in discretionary justice than their colonial governors had exercised. In the royal province governors could pardon capital offenders only on royal approval, and His Majesty's ministers reviewed recommendations before they advised the king, which imposed a further body of superior authority. The popularly elected governor of New York, in contrast, simply conveyed his recommendations to the legislature, and he could pardon capital offenders, aside from persons found guilty of murder and treason, without seeking approval from any branch of government. The conditions of war and the strategic military roles New York's first governor assumed made the chief executive-cum-commander a vigorous arbiter of justice. Under the first constitution, and as practiced by George Clinton during the War of Independence, executive clemency power expanded.

Pardoning and Parole in Wartime New York

Because chaotic conditions prevented representatives from holding meetings on a regular basis, the Provincial Convention established a Committee of Safety in the summer of 1775 to render decisions, including the selection of militia officers. In December of that year it commissioned George Clinton as a brigadier general of the state militia. Clinton's qualifications for the position were more political than military, however. After clerking under William Smith Jr. (prior to his Loyalist conversion) Clinton established a successful legal practice in the lead-up to his service in the Assembly, from 1768 to 1775.[42] His forthright anti-Tory sentiments led to his election as a member of the Second Continental Congress, but the request from the Committee of Safety brought Clinton back to defend his home state. George Washington judged Clinton's leadership so admirable that he commissioned him as a general in the Continental Army in March 1777. In an instant Clinton, the Ulster County farmer, became a military man.

General Clinton's popularity with soldiers matched his knack of impressing his military superiors, and this capacity to bridge high and low made him the preferred choice for governor when the first state election was held on July 8, 1777. The state constitution required candidates for governor to have the same property qualifications as the men authorized to vote for them—

one hundred pounds clear of debt—so Clinton's income and holdings easily sufficed. Compared to the vast land holdings and commercial investments of the state's landlords, many of whose ancestors had acquired manors under Dutch and British rule, the status and lineage of New York's first governor were decidedly modest. Clinton appealed to the majority of voters, who rejected the landlord elite's favored candidate, Philip Schuyler; they also chose him over Thomas Morris Scott, one of the founders of the Sons of Liberty.[43] After the election the patrician Schuyler sniffed to John Jay that the new governor's "family and connections do not entitle him to so distinguished a predominance."[44] But nothing could be done: the people had spoken and Clinton was their man, one of a cohort of "new men" thrust into power through the Revolution.[45]

Among the rebellious colonies, New York, as the chief theater of the war, was in a uniquely precarious position.[46] The English bore down from their stronghold to the north, the king's Indian allies threatened in the west, and enemy troops menaced from the south. In the early summer of 1777 disaster seemed imminent as General Burgoyne's forces blazed down the Hudson Valley toward Albany. When Clinton attempted to resign his militia post in May of that year the convention refused to accept it, even after he formally accepted the governorship on 30 July.[47] When General Washington received news of Clinton's election he congratulated the convention on the electorate's choice: "That gentleman's character is such, as will make him peculiarly useful at the head of your State, in a situation so alarming and interesting as it is at present circumstances."[48] Yet, those same circumstances kept Clinton in the field, acting as a military leader, first and foremost.

The governor did not convene the legislature until September 1777, and the first meeting of the newly elected senate and assembly was delayed until 5 January the following year.[49] In the interim, Clinton held office by correspondence, leaving the executive function of government in the hands of the Council of Safety, which the convention established at the close of its final meeting in May of 1777. The constitution was ratified, but the Council of Safety assumed the authority to exercise all functions of government until regular sittings of the legislature could be held.[50] The authority to pardon was one of those powers.[51] In an echo of royal governor Tryon's proclamation, the convention issued an ordinance on May 10, 1777 offering a "free pardon to such of the subjects of the said state, as, having committed treasonable acts against the same, shall return to their allegiance."[52]

Military legal tradition, redefined by the Articles of War, set the boundaries of discretionary justice toward the enemy.[53] English custom adopted the French term *parole* to describe the release of prisoners contingent on their word of honor to respect conditions imposed on their liberty. The aim of parole was not to extract enemy prisoners' allegiance but to induce them to promise to relinquish arms if released. The Articles provided this tactic to allow prisoner exchanges, but the Council of Safety and military officers paroled prisoners for a wider range of motives. In September 1777, the Council paroled captured Cadwallader Colden on terms that must have buoyed patriots' hopes for victory: the former lieutenant governor had to swallow his convictions and his pride as he swore:

> I will not by writting [sic] word or Deed Do or be Privy to any acct matter or thing whatsoever to Promote the Interest Jurisdiction Claim or Authority of the King or Parliament of Great Britain in or over all or any Part of North America, And I Pray God to help me as I shall keep this my Solemn Oath & Engagement.[54]

Military officers could parole enemy captives in the field, and historians have documented the release of many prisoners soon after battles, largely because the resources to feed and clothe militiamen were never secure and invariably poor. But George Clinton's public papers record that officers were the chief recipients of paroles. The general authorized the parole of a British ensign (the lowest ranked of commissioned infantry officers) on account of illness. William Adamson beseeched "Your Excellencey's [sic] Humanaty [sic] & Good Character," and he hoped "Your Excellency will be pleasd [sic] to permit me to go to New York on my Parole, so that I may get some ease, for I cannot live ten days in the Condition I am at present for I can not get Medisons [sic] here." But the ensign absconded, and American authorities suspected he had returned to the enemy.[55] Taking the word of enemies, even gentlemen and officers, was a matter of life and death in time of war.

In addition to New York's military foes, the state faced the "intestine enemy" of loyalism, a threat as serious as British assaults but deeper, darker, and more difficult to dislodge. Among the Council of Safety's responsibilities was oversight of the committee for "Detecting and Defeating Conspiracies," a kind of political police force initiated by the convention late in 1776.[56] In addition to uncovering disloyalty this committee (later called a commission) operated until 1781, and it used inquisitorial tactics to interrogate New Yorkers who seemed averse to independence.[57] Individuals considered disloyal or given to "Evil and Corrupt Intentions" could be charged with "Disaffection" to the "American Cause," and local boards could compel suspects to swear the oath of allegiance, pay fines and, for some men, to enlist. The most serious offenders ended up before the supreme court where they faced criminal prosecution. Commissioners also had the power to banish lesser offenders who refused to demonstrate their support of independence, a punishment that brought ignominy and the likelihood of penury. If petitioners of "Repute & Integrity" were prepared to vouch for suspects willing to declare their allegiance, commissioners could be persuaded to exercise their discretion in keeping with the "Cause of Liberty." In the presence of a constitution but the absence of a government capable of governing, the commissioners claimed it "their Duty not only to secure offenders that they may be bro't to Punishment but also to pardon all such who convinced of their Error are willing to return again to their Duty."[58] Thus, the convention, the Council of Safety and the Commission against Conspiracies each played a part in the pardoning of offenders and disloyal subjects, with and without the conduct of criminal trials, in an atmosphere of unnerving insecurity.[59]

In the first years of independence, military courts came closest to supplying prosecutorial and pardoning procedures bound by law and in adherence to traditions of British justice.[60] Charges were laid, suspects and witnesses were called and examined; evidence was weighed and officers rendered verdicts; and judge advocates or presiding officers imposed sentences, with military personnel enlisted to carry out punishment of life and limb. The Continental Congress adopted the British Articles of War of 1749, but Washington modified them to allow him the discretion to determine the penalties imposed upon Continental soldiers who committed offenses against military discipline.[61] Using these powers, Washington ordered Benedict Arnold's co-conspirator, Major John Andre, to be court-martialed and executed for espionage in 1780, after the discovery of his plot to hand over West Point, New York, to the English.[62] In New York State, federal courts-martial operated alongside state militia tribunals, convened by the governor as commander in chief (although officers in the field also convened them to check serious offenses promptly). Penalties ranged from reprimands and fines to public whippings and hangings, carried out before fellow soldiers, but sentences were often commuted and offenders pardoned in the interest of maintaining fighting morale.

General Clinton advised a forgiving approach in February 1777 after a general court-martial imposed two death sentences for treason, as well as penalties for men found guilty of lesser offenses, including disobedience of "Orders, Neglect of Duty," refusing to march, and "remissness of duty." Writing to the convention, whose approval was necessary before any death sentence was carried out, Clinton recommended that the convicted traitors be "pardoned under the Gallows," since he found the evidence against the men doubtful. More broadly, he thought this dramatic display of mercy would "Answer a better Purpose":

The only use in Punishment is to bring People to a proper sence [sic] of their Duty and as I flatter myself from the Effect, even convening this Court only has already had on the Refractory & Disobedient, that the End will be fully answered tho' these Wretches Lives be spared; nor have I the least Doubt but that the Honorable Convention will extend Mercy towards the first if it can be done in their better Judgment consistent with the public Good.[63]

One year later Clinton told a militia colonel who inquired about the prospect of mercy for privates found guilty of dereliction of duty that his general policy dictated that "as little Severity may be used as possible, as the milder the means to induce the Militia to perform their Duty if effectual, the better."[64] Mercy was calculated political theater, both civil and military.

Ill-advised lenience could also undermine the war effort, and Clinton was equally eager to make this known by supporting severity on select occasions. Another general court-martial, held two months later just north of enemy territory at Fort Montgomery, produced nineteen capital convictions. Jacobus Rose (or Rosa), a private in the King's American Regiment, was found to be the leader of a band that roamed the countryside in civilian garb, recruiting soldiers for the English and skirmishing with members of the militia. The court-martial convicted him and thirteen others of levying war, and it found five men guilty of aiding and giving comfort to the enemy. In the court's opinion, each captive was guilty of "adhering to the King of Great Britain whilst owing allegiance to the State of New York."[65] Could mercy safely be shown on any grounds against such a threat?

With the state's survival on a knife-edge in the spring of 1777, Clinton urged the convention to make a "sudden and severe Example" of these "daring and insolent" offenders. The court-martial had recommended mercy for seven on the basis of "their apparent Distress, open Confession and Promise of Future Obedience of the Laws of the State of New York." The brigadier general disagreed, fearing that locals would "soon take the Law into their own Hands" to avenge the treasonous party's wounding of militia officers during their raids. His appraisal was no exaggeration, since the intensity of direct action frequently spilled beyond the formal proceedings of local committees and boards.[66] The convention issued a high-minded response to Clinton's request, claiming it must advance the cause "in some Cases by extending mercy to mitigate the Rigor of Justice." Nevertheless, it limited its generosity of spirit to two of the condemned: the first, in view of his "extream [sic] youth and it appearing that he has been deluded"; the second, because he had provided evidence against the others and was willing to take the oath of allegiance.[67] In practice, the convention and the brigadier general in the field were not so far apart. Harshness was the necessary counterweight to forbearance in a fledgling state "infested" with loyalists. Republicans showed that they were as adept as royalists at manipulating discretionary justice as a tool of war.

The patriots were not simply fighting a war: they were campaigning for the hearts and minds of a people who had been ruled for a century under the common law, the Bill of Rights, and the principle of trial by jury in a civilian system of criminal justice. The convention, and later the Council of Safety, trod upon those rights and principles when it authorized military courts to try civilians suspected of spying and treason.[68] The convention took this risky path in its legislative response to the "want of Courts properly instituted for the Trial of Treasons and other Offences against this State." The law's passage made up for Articles of War, which did not apply to civilians. Until 1777 New Yorkers could spy for the enemy, recruit men in the king's service, and furnish supplies and intelligence, yet "escape with Impunity."[69] Rosa's undercover loyalist recruiters were hauled before the court-martial under the new law, which came into effect on April 1, 1777.[70] Enfolded in the operation of the Commission for Detecting Conspiracies and the Council of Safety, the militarization of prosecutions for disloyalty made it difficult to distinguish the state of New York from the military regime that operated in the occupied territory. New York was not alone in its resort to alternative tribunals and the short-circuiting of procedural safeguards to check resistance, but this practice lent credence to loyalist accusations that American liberty had come at the cost of British justice. The convention's abrogation of rights—the use of spying, the trial of civilians before military courts, with their fate decided by an unaccountable executive body—provided propaganda material for Tories opposed to so-called democratic governance.[71]

The Provincial Convention did, nevertheless, aspire to institute a civil system of justice from the establishment of statehood. In mid-July 1776 it was impossible to establish a civil government, so existing magistrates and judicial officers were asked to continue to serve, providing that they were "well affected to the Liberties of America." In most parts of the state, local branches of the Committee of Safety examined persons suspected of having committed criminal offenses, which supplemented the work of the Conspiracies Commission against the "disaffected."[72] The convention firmly declared that all New Yorkers derived "protection from the Laws of the same," but the mechanisms of civil prosecution against lawbreakers were rudimentary. Relying on military courts would never amount to an effective or sustainable system of criminal justice, and the most committed of patriots believed that British justice and common law were the best guarantors of liberty.[73]

By 1778, as Governor Clinton tightened his grip on the reins of his new executive office, he decided that citizen-led committees and commissions could "no longer maintain Peace & a due Subordination." The unruliness that plagued many parts of the state confirmed the "necessity of having our Civil Magistrates appointed and our Courts of Justice opened."[74] Although the law allowing civilians to be tried by military courts remained in effect for the duration of the war, the regular courts began slowly to provide a civil system of prosecution and punishment according to common law precedent and criminal statutes. After months of delay following the constitution's adoption, the governor and the legislature began to exercise their authority to reprieve and pardon.

Civil Justice: Moderation and Severity in the Early Republic

On October 6, 1778, Governor Clinton issued a proclamation that offered a reward for the capture of a loyalist guerrilla group suspected of the murder of a major in the New York militia and of numerous burglaries committed several months earlier. Although the war raged on, these captives were prosecuted through the regular criminal courts, which quickly pronounced sentences of death for Claudius Smith and two of his partners in crime. On January 22, 1779, a crowd assembled before the town of Goshen's courthouse and watched as the three men were hanged. Since the jury found the men guilty solely of the burglaries, the governor could have exercised mercy without having to defer to the legislature. Instead, Clinton decided he must act against his natural sympathies in order to show that burglary could not be committed with impunity: "Was I at Liberty to pursue my own Feelings on these Occasions they would incline me to Pardon these Unhappy Culprits but as a Servant to the public they ought not to influence my Conduct."[75]

Amy Augur was more fortunate. When her case came under Clinton's eye, he made no mention of his feelings toward the woman, convicted of the murder of her illegitimate infant, but he reprieved her death sentence and recommended that the legislature grant her mercy.[76] On February 17 the legislature complied with the governor's advice when it passed an act that pardoned Amy Augur. Because she was a "proper object of mercy," the statute stated, the legislature granted her an absolute discharge "of and from the felony aforesaid and the conviction aforesaid and all execution and forfeitures thereon." The news undoubtedly brought relief to the woman, who had since married, but it was newsworthy for another reason: "An Act to Pardon Amy Augur" was the first statutory pardon in the state of New York, issued in accordance with the constitution's assignment of the power to pardon, split between the governor and the legislature.[77]

The initial step toward the regularization of civil criminal justice began in 1777, with the appointment of John Jay as the state's first chief justice. Jay provided a steady hand at the helm of the State Supreme Court of Judicature, which began to travel on circuit during trial terms. General Sessions courts were also established in localities for the trial of non-capital offenses.[78] At the first session of the supreme court, sitting at Kingston on September 9, 1777, Jay used the occasion to exhort the grand jury to perform its tasks without "fear, favour or resentment." They must have a "determined resolution to do [their] duty," in a state of "calm deliberate reason, candour, [and] moderation."[79] Six months later, in the spring term of 1778, Jay and his brother judges faithfully reported to the governor the sentences they had handed down. During the supreme court's sitting in the town of Poughkeepsie, seven men had been convicted on the capital charges of burglary and horse stealing. The judges recommended four to mercy, but for the remaining three they found "no Reasons sufficient to induce us to think it our Duty to recommend them to your Excellency for Pardon." The governor concurred. On April 24, 1778, two of the condemned were hanged: William Smith, whom the judges considered a "notorious villain," along with a tenant of Courtlandt's manor, put to death for two counts of burglary.[80]

Desperate pleas for mercy on behalf of the third man, Myndert Harris, were hastily dispatched to "His Excellency the Honourable George Clinton Esqr. Gov'r and Commander in Chief of the State of New York." The petitioners conceded the condemned man's "Wickedness and Villany," and they allowed that Harris had been justly convicted for burglary; nevertheless, they earnestly prayed that it "may please His Excellency to have Compassion on the most Distressed Father & Mother & Relation of Said Harris, and have Mercy on the Criminal." A second plea for a reprieve came from the grand jury members, a third stressed that Harris had previously served the state as a soldier, and a fourth petition anticipated that "a pardon in his Case, will be more agreeable to the good Subjects in General, than an Execution."[81] This polyphonic pleading paid off. Handed his first opportunity to send a clear indication of his administration's commitment to law enforcement, the governor judged he could limit severity so long as properly conducted trials, convictions, and sentencing had taken place. The execution of two burglars, the first criminals to be executed through the regular criminal courts since the colonial era, was deemed sufficient to pacify the good subjects of New York.

In the early republic, most convicted felons were men and women charged with burglary, robbery, horse theft, forgery, and counterfeiting, not murderers or traitors. Although offenders convicted of these felonies also faced the mandatory death sentence, the governor could pardon such criminals (along with lesser criminals) on his own authority.[82] Governors did not keep a full record of their pardons prior to 1799, so their messages and public papers provide only a partial account of cases in which they granted mercy or recommended that the legislature pass a pardon statute. The record of executions carried out after the multiple hangings of June 1778 and the Smith gang members' executions in January 1779 shows that Governor Clinton used his pardon power sparingly in the lead-up to the reduction of capital crimes in 1796.[83] Of the seventy-eight people executed over this period, more than half were convicted of property offenses (horse stealing, burglary, robbery, forgery, and counterfeiting) and only ten of murder.[84] Compared to the high volume of executions in England over the same period, these numbers are low; however, the state was far less urbanized and its population considerably smaller.[85] In the late eighteenth century, felons convicted in New York knew the threat of execution was real.

The seventeen-year-old horse thief Benjamin Rogers would likely have ended up a hanging statistic had "Benevolent members of Society" not taken up his cause. Horse thieving was one of the capital crimes jurors took most seriously, but Rogers's backers believed it would be unconscionable to execute a youth who had not yet reached the age of majority. From his "loathsome" prison cell in Albany, Rogers wrote the governor directly in the spring of 1778. Seeking the governor's "Pity and Compassion," he admitted his crime but prayed that his "tender years and inexperience" might have "due weight with your Excellencies [sic] humane Breast."[86] The repentant thief's invocation of Clinton's humanity produced the desired result, and the grounds of Rogers's appeal hints at the growing shift to an association of youth with innocence. Additionally, it affirms that the "sentimental capacity of the affections" was a manly virtue respected by elite men of the Revolutionary generation.[87]

In the early national period a man of refined sentiment did not shrink from his duty, nor did he take pleasure in the infliction of stern justice. Nevertheless, New York's legislators were concerned that the governor might be too mild toward criminals. The state's senators responded to Clinton's third message of August 1779 by concurring with Clinton's refusal to reprieve the Smith gang; however, they disapproved of the general's continued use of mercy as a tactic to induce loyalty. "Having vainly tried every lenient Measure," stressed the senators, "we sincerely lament the Necessity which will compel us, by harsher Means, to enforce Obedience to the Laws, and to extend the Protection of Government to all the faithful Subjects of this State."[88] Clinton shied from sternness while the legislature leaned toward tackling lawlessness without exception. It was a recipe for a showdown.

Governor George Clinton. State of New York, Hall of Governors, retrieved from http://www.hallofgovernors.ny.gov.

While the governor's attention was focused on the federal Constitution's ratification in 1787, state legislators introduced a set of statutes to enlarge the number of offenses subject to the death penalty. The "Act for Preventing and Punishing Rapes, and the Forcible Taking of Women," passed February 14, 1787, made any person who should "carnally know and abuse a woman child, under the age of ten years," guilty of rape and subject to the death penalty. In the Province of New York buggery had been a capital offense, but the passage of the "Act for the Punishment of the Vice of Buggery," passed the same day as the rape statute, underscored that the offense would be "from henceforth adjudged felony."[89] The resort to death as deterrence extended beyond sexual and moral offenses. As of 1787, poisoning that resulted in death and stabbings in which victims succumbed at any point up to six months after an assault were to be tried as willful murder, punishable by death.[90] A mere decade since the war against England had ended the people's representatives appeared to be marching backward to bloody justice.

Clinton's fight against federalist ascendency in Washington failed with the adoption of the Constitution, but his struggle against Albany's legislators who favored sanguine punishments continued. The Quakers of Philadelphia were not the only Americans who considered the continuing reliance upon corporal and capital punishment out of kilter with the ideals of the new republic. Most Republicans (including Clinton's nephew and future governor DeWitt Clinton) were in favor of state-led reforms to support charitable and benevolent means to advance civilization, such as publicly funded schools.[91] Campaigners opposed to harsh penalties believed that relying on mercy to ameliorate the criminal law was ineffective and inappropriate. Along with fellow penal modernizers, notably Thomas Jefferson and Benjamin Rush, George Clinton became an acolyte of Beccaria.[92] In his 1794 address to the legislature, Clinton declared: "It is certainly a matter of serious concern, that capital convictions are so frequent, and that so little attention has been hitherto paid to a due proportion between crimes and punishments." The large volume of capital cases placed undue pressure on the governor to use his discretion to pardon and reprieve. Following Beccaria's theory, Clinton stated that the certainty of sanctions, rather than their "sanguinary character," combined with the prospect of pardons, presented a superior means to fight crime. If he could convince the elected representatives to share his sentiments, he trusted that their "wisdom and humanity" might lead them to pass necessary reforms.[93]

In Pennsylvania, where prominent Quakers had greater sway over penal politics, similar sentiments moved the state legislature to restrict the death penalty to murder in 1794 and to substitute imprisonment for felonies previously punished by hanging.[94] As New York's legislators stalled, Clinton's patience frayed. In his January 1795 address he tried to shame his fellow New Yorkers: "It is indeed a subject of melancholy consideration, that our criminal law should be so repugnant to the mild genius of our constitution, and so similar in its punishments to the cruelty of despotic governments." By invoking anti-Tory sentiment, Clinton pronounced New York's criminal justice system "defective" because it derived from "a nation differing from us in manners, government and principles of policy." The best way to honor the ideals for which patriots had fought and died was to make imprisonment the punishment for all felonies (with murder and treason the exceptions) and to reduce the scope and frequency of executive discretion.[95]

Thanks to Thomas Eddy, a Quaker philanthropist and businessman, New York caught up to Pennsylvania in 1796. Like his Philadelphia counterparts, Eddy believed that a penitentiary could end New York's reliance upon "cruel" punishments, but he needed to find a powerful political figure to realize his vision. Philip Schuyler stepped into the role of backer. Never governor, Schuyler remained a Federalist opponent of Clinton's Democratic Republicans, and he became a powerful senator in the state. Schuyler agreed to support Eddy's plan for a prison similar to Philadelphia's Walnut Street Jail after he paid it a visit in 1795. There, he saw for himself how the Quaker-backed prison subjected felons, who were previously whipped or put to death, to cellular isolation under strict discipline. Once George Clinton's governorship finally came to an end Schuyler found it congenial to promote Eddy's plan. The new governor, Federalist John Jay, became the figurehead for New York's move to penitential punishment.

In January 1796 New York legislators introduced a new code of criminal law, under the blandly titled "An Act making Alterations in the Criminal Law of this State and for Erecting State Prisons."[96] Its impact was anything but banal, however, not least as felony offenders were concerned. Henceforth murder and treason remained punishable by death, but imprisonment became the punishment for all other felony offenses previously subject to the death penalty. Clinton paved the way, but his successor took credit for their state's adoption of a penal system distinct from its colonial past. Since Jay's public life had rolled out in a procession of positions, from politician to judge to governor, he had experienced discretionary justice from many angles before he became New York's chief executive. "Our present mild or (as some call it) relaxed system of punishments" deserved a fair trial, Governor Jay proclaimed after two years into office. It was prudent, accordingly, that he give no cause for concern by way of "the frequency of pardons, in cases where the propriety of them is justly liable to doubt and question."[97] At the dawn of a new era in criminal justice executive firmness must compensate for penal mildness.

Conclusion

After the Revolution it took two decades for a new system of justice, patterned on Enlightenment penal principles, to gel, incorporating the ideals courageous patriots had risked their lives to realize. The royal governor's departure in 1775 created a hiatus in executive power, filled first by the Provincial Convention and later by the Council of Safety, which acted in place of the executive in the review of criminal penalties, including the penalty of death. A civil court system closely resembling its colonial counterpart fell into place after the war began, and it managed to produce verdicts and criminal sentences for executive review by 1778. The constitutionally prescribed process of discretionary sentence review, in tandem with the operation of military justice, prevailed throughout the war. As a field commander and chief executive of the state, George Clinton authorized paroles and exercised discretion over all forms of punishment imposed by courts-martial on civilians and military personnel. The prerogative of mercy, with its monarchical origins, was a plank that propped up the conservative wing of the Revolution.

Historians have interpreted New York's reform of its criminal law in 1796, and similar statutes passed elsewhere in the late eighteenth century, as a watershed in the history of punishment, differing only in their explanations of the transition.[98] The most persuasive interpretations tie broader philosophical and political transitions associated with the Enlightenment, democratic revolution, and the rise of humanitarian sensibilities to local issues, personalities, and contingencies. Colonial legacies and Revolutionary innovation blended in New York's first constitution, which granted the governor more power than his colonial counterpart had held, and it assigned him greater discretionary authority than other governors exercised in states where more radical incarnations of democracy flowered. Yet, the leveling spirit was strong enough to inspire the drafters of the constitution to assign murder and treason cases to the legislature's discretion, not the governor's. After 1796 these crimes were the only ones (aside from the early modern throwback, "stealing from a church") to remain capital offenses.[99] Ironically, the chief executive, not the legislature, provided the greater impetus to set the state on its path from pain and death. In New York the inheritor of sovereign authority led the move toward disciplinary penal governance.

George Clinton left office too soon to lend his name to the state's new criminal statute, which included the abolition of whipping and all other forms of public bodily punishment. Nonetheless, his advocacy of penal mildness can be seen as a delayed response to Washington's toast at Fraunces Tavern in 1783. As a military commander as well as a civil leader, Clinton made mercy central to his governing approach, counterbalanced by his conviction that severity must remain a weapon in the arsenal of order. The new governor, John Jay, assumed the mantle of "supreme executive power and authority," which he had written into the constitution two decades earlier. In New York the character of punishment altered without weakening the chief executive's customary vigor to pardon "at his discretion."

2

Mercy and Diversity

The Pardon Power in the Early National Period

New York's answer to Philadelphia's Walnut Street Jail was Newgate Prison, the name Thomas Eddy chose for the state's first penitentiary.[1] Erected in lower Manhattan, Newgate received its first felons on November 28, 1797. The counterfeiters, forgers, and horse thieves who had faced execution prior to that epochal year, and a host of lesser offenders for whom public whipping was a prescribed punishment, confronted a new mode of punishment behind the prison's walls. Newgate answered the search to put the principle of certain carceral punishment proportional to the gravity of offenses into practice but it left a familiar question unanswered: how might penal managers under this new regime take individual characteristics and the circumstance of each case into account? The state's reliance on imprisonment as the principal means of punishing serious crimes led to another more acute problem: overcrowding and prisoner revolts. Executive discretion provided solutions to these fresh dilemmas; at the same time, governors' use of their power to pardon encouraged enemies of the penitentiary ideal to protest that the "mild" system was less effective than the sanguinary system it had replaced.[2]

Examining the finer grain of discretionary justice corrects the portrayal of gubernatorial clemency in the early penitentiary era as the clumsy patchwork on a faulty apparatus of punishment. This version of penal history began in the Progressive Era. One authority, keen to promote parole and indeterminate sentencing, claimed in 1922 that the pardon was a "sop to the discouraged convicts" and that its abuse in the early 1800s had delivered "a body-blow at the efficacy of the penal law."[3] Subsequent histories, including critical accounts of penal reform, have reinforced this reading of executive discretion as a simple counterweight.[4] New York's governors certainly attempted to keep the state's burgeoning prison population manageable, but they granted pardons aware of the need to shield themselves from accusations of sentimentality and charges of corruption. Their struggles and defenses appear in their messages and published papers and in the journals of executive pardons, which begin in 1799.[5] These volumes, comprising the names of the pardoned, the crimes they committed, and their sentences, also include the conditions governors imposed when they granted clemency. Read together, these records show that chief executives of the penitentiary era began to consider new factors in their pardon deliberations: time served, the faithful performance of labor, and inmates' compliance with the new regime of penal discipline based on pre-determined periods of time. The Railroad Age imposed time discipline on American social and economic life by the mid-nineteenth century, but the penitentiary introduced it much earlier. As Foucauldian scholars stress, time measurement became a prime index of the change from sovereign justice to disciplinary governance.[6] Nevertheless, the sovereign retained the power to keep punishment strictly to time or to shorten it.

Supporters and opponents of penal discipline both framed executive discretion as a political issue, but there was little public criticism of gubernatorial clemency's replication and reinforcement of racial, ethnic, and class hierarchies. The distinctions New Yorkers made between free white citizens and the state's African Americans and Native Americans are stark in governors' selective use of mercy in the early national period. After the wave of draconian statutes directed against slaves and free blacks in the mid-eighteenth century, state legislators began to chip away at the edifice of slavery. But these modest moves met resistance in many forms, including slave owners' support for the pardon of slaves serving criminal sentences. This practice allowed masters to evade New York's prohibition against slave trading: by pledging to "transport" their pardoned slaves, owners could sell African Americans to purchasers outside the state. Profit seeking also trumped rights in the state's relationship with indigenous peoples, as land-hungry speculators abused Native Americans' treaty rights over their ancestral lands.[7] Prior to the 1820s, New York's courts largely ignored crimes committed by Indians if they occurred on federally established reservations. However, the attempted prosecution and irregular pardon of Tommy Jemmy, a Seneca man, announced the state's determination to change the policy. The "Act Declaring the Jurisdiction of the Courts of this State," the title of the 1822 statute that pardoned Jemmy, struck a political blow against assertions of Indian self-government, disguised by an act of mercy.[8]

Freedom and democratic rights, empty words to New York's slaves and Indians, were the ideals that gave the deprivation of liberty its meaning and potency in the early penitentiary period: felons must appreciate what they had squandered and what, if truly repentant, they might regain. Efforts were afoot by the early nineteenth century to improve the welfare of the state's most marginalized populations through philanthropic agencies, such as the New York Manumission Society and the Society for the Alleviation of Poverty.[9] But when the state's new penal machinery drew the least powerful into its grips, their only hope of release short of death or escape came in the form of gubernatorial clemency. At an individual level pardoning was a means to reward reform, relieve suffering, and rectify injustice; in broader terms discretionary justice became enmeshed by the early nineteenth century in the problems of prison overcrowding, the endurance of slavery, and the erosion of Native American sovereignty.

The Penitentiary and the Pardon Power

Penal reformers of the Enlightenment era likened long-term imprisonment to slavery to promote its capacity to deter. Beccaria advocated "perpetual slavery" as a substitute for capital punishment because it subjected seasoned offenders to a mode of punishment he thought that free men feared more than pain or death. Inmates who failed to work, or who spoiled or sabotaged the products of prison labor and behaved with insolence toward keepers, suffered even greater pains, much like recalcitrant slaves. Behind the prison's walls, rule breakers were held in dungeons and given a diet of bread and water. The American apostles of penitential punishment carried this message into the design and management of the first state prisons, and legislators in the Northeast were among the first to endorse penal servitude as a means to fight crime more effectively than the inconsistent infliction of corporal punishment and death. Instead of a system of individual ownership and labor extraction by masters, imprisonment would become the means for "society" in a democratic polity to overmaster criminals incapable of mastering themselves. Imprisonment was "the most proper punishment," Beccaria argued: "that kind of slavery, which alone can be called just."[10] Distinguished by the stigma of uniforms and inmate numbers, felons were legally obliged to work in captivity. And for life-sentenced felons, their unending servitude and incapacitation communicated the most potent deterrent message: those who broke the social contract forfeited liberty.[11] The introduction of protracted incarceration imposed a new regime of forced labor and privation, as Beccaria foresaw, but with it an unprecedented role for executive discretion.

New Yorkers struck a hard bargain as they gave up punishment of the body for felonies other than treason or murder, but inmates at Newgate refused to play their part. Prisoners' escape attempts and their violence toward guards led the legislature to authorize the use of the whip in 1819.[12] Consequently, the slave master's disciplinary weapon, and a form of punishment Eddy had hoped to outlaw (and that the legislature had abolished as a punishment for crime in 1796), returned as a tool of prison discipline.[13] With faith in the penitentiary's capacity to master criminals shaken, pardoning compensated for the costs of the state's attempt to punish more effectively.

In a perfectly rational system of proportionate punishment, mercy would become obsolete, Beccaria predicted in the mid-eighteenth century.[14] Thomas Eddy, in contrast, took his inspiration from Quaker convictions as well as Enlightenment philosophy, and he believed in mercy as a reward to recognize improved character and behavior. In his 1801 *Account of the State Prison or Penitentiary House*, written four years after Newgate opened, he wrote at length on pardoning's rightful place in penitential discipline. The Beccarian notion of punishment portioned correctly and delivered inflexibly was a noble but impractical ideal, Eddy could see, but under the present law it was proper for executives to recognize "greater or lesser depravity" through the mitigation of punishment, so long as convicts served time sufficient for penance. Because Newgate's system of strict discipline, religious instruction, and hard labor was designed to awaken inmates' appreciation of freedom, Eddy believed that prisoners whose behavior improved earned the right to be treated mercifully. Whenever executive discretion was prompted by "unequivocal evidence of reformation," convicts could be justly pardoned prior to the expiration of the sentences.[15]

Eddy's rationale of reward connected the traditional consideration of previous good character in grants of pardons to the evaluation of prison-induced virtuous comportment. The worthy recipient of a pardon was the man (the male offender was his default prisoner) who had "conducted himself with uniform decency, industry, and sobriety; and has never attempted to violate any of [the prison's] regulations."[16] Statements of this nature, found in the annual reports and promotional literature of penitentiaries that popped up across Europe and North America, signaled a new disciplinary discourse, according to Foucault. Through the penitentiary's "means of correct training" and the judgments and "normalizing gaze" of keepers, each convict became an object of knowledge.[17] In Eddy's words, keepers monitored prisoners' behavior, but they considered an inmate's "temper, character and deportment" to be most telling. A move toward micro penality was clearly underway in New York's turn to penitential punishment, yet it operated in association with executive discretion. Sovereign mercy served disciplinary ambitions, so long as it was granted with "sound discretion."[18]

In Newgate's first years the number of pardons governors granted indicates that a temperate approach prevailed as New York's penal experiment began. Three inmates were pardoned out of 121 received in 1797, the first year of Newgate's operation. The pace of pardoning rose only slightly as the number of inmates tripled. Between 1797 and 1801, governors pardoned 86 prisoners, among whom 19 had been sentenced to life. Black men and women, who made up one-fifth of Newgate's prisoners, were pardoned at a rate proportional to their numbers: by the end of 1801, 17 were discharged with a pardon.[19] Governor John Jay made it standard practice, as of February 1798, to consult with Newgate's board of inspectors before issuing pardons. This restrained rate of pardoning persisted during the governorships of Morgan Lewis and George Clinton (who returned from the political wilderness to serve as governor again between 1801 and 1804). However, it climbed significantly once evidence mounted that the experiment in penitentiary punishment was faring badly.

After 1807 "virtually indiscriminate pardoning" became a necessity. The prison population ballooned beyond its intended maximum of 400 inmates and expanded to more than 700 inmates by the late 1810s. Governors took to holding "semiannual pardon seasons" in which large groups of prisoners were released en masse.[20] On one day in 1814, for instance, Governor Daniel D. Tompkins pardoned 75 prisoners.[21] The numbers pardoned do not tell the full story, though. In June of 1812 the governor explained to a petitioner that he made it his practice as governor to meet twice a year with a "Board of Judges &c." for the "express purpose of recommending suitable candidates for pardon."[22] Although a number of the "suitable" prisoners possibly bribed keepers or hired persuasive counsel, Tompkins evidently worked with an informal pardon review board, which indicates a degree of discretion at work in executive decision making, not the profligate release of prisoners.

At the close of the second war with Britain in 1815, a post-conflict crime wave triggered the "wholesale use of the prerogative" as a desperate measure. The number of Newgate prisoners released by pardon was ten times greater by the mid-1810s than the number discharged through expiration of sentence, a shocking statistic and a damning blow to those who had backed the repeal of bloody punishment.[23] In a review of the prison's operations, the state senate determined that 77 prisoners were released upon sentence expiration from 1812 to 1816, compared with 740 who received pardons.[24] In his final address to the legislature in February 1816, Governor Tompkins admitted that the mitigation of prison sentences had become unmoored from the principles Eddy had articulated: "the crowded state of the present prison has of late made it indispensably necessary to extend the list of recommendations for pardons to a greater number than would otherwise be deemed proper."[25]

Improper pardoning dissociated mercy from the object of reform, and in New York it also abetted attempts to reinstate older forms of punishment. Evildoers who anticipated a pardon viewed the prison gate as a revolving door, and they had little fear of serving more than a small portion of their sentences, according to the penitentiary's detractors, including members of the legislature. Bills were passed in the mid-1810s to reintroduce the death penalty for crimes other than murder. Contrary to David J. Rothman's claim that no one other than "a few conservatives" wished to see a return to the gallows, a majority of New York legislators supported that retrogressive move; governors, in contrast, resisted.[26] Governor Morgan Lewis, like Jay and Tompkins, fresh from serving on New York's supreme court, disapproved of an assembly bill that would have punished escaped prisoners with death and the further indignity of dissection, even if they had caused no injury through their flight from prison. In Lewis's mind, the impulse to escape sprang from "the love of liberty, which furnishes no evidence of moral turpitude or incorrigible depravity." The legislature passed this bill in 1805, but the Council of Revision vetoed the attempt to reintroduce "the most terrific sanction found in the criminal code of this state." Similarly, Lewis rejected another bill that would have reintroduced whipping for petit larceny, on the ground that the penalty would merely render offenders "obdurate and incorrigible, to the great hazard of public peace and good order."[27] Notwithstanding these defeats, the legislature prevailed in its effort to introduce a regressive Crimes Act in 1808 that reinstated the death penalty for arson in an inhabited dwelling and restored whipping as an optional penalty to a fine or imprisonment for petit larceny.[28] Tompkins, Lewis's successor, expressed his dismay at the revival of the old regime: "it is incompatible with the genius of free government, and the state of civilization and refinement of which we boast."[29]

The legislature could impose harsh laws to express the people's will, but it was powerless to impede executive clemency without a revision to the state constitution. Consequently, Governor Tompkins could argue two opposing positions on discretionary justice. On the one hand, he admonished the legislature for turning its back on the principle that the certainty of mild punishments provided greater deterrence than the unlikely possibility of a whipping or execution; on the other hand, he undermined the certainty of prescribed prison sentences through his liberal use of pardoning. Between Tompkins's first gubernatorial pardon in 1807 and his last on February 21, 1817, he pardoned 1,701 felons, far exceeding the rate of pardoning under previous governors.[30]

If Tompkins felt compelled to use his discretionary powers to keep Newgate's numbers manageable, no one, least of all the governor, anticipated that the practice was sustainable. Executive discretion could not credibly moderate the state's growing number of criminals. Rather than enlarge the scope of pardoning, Daniel Tompkins urged the legislature in 1816 to requisition funds to support a new penitentiary in the northwestern part of the state. By enhancing its capacity to house inmates in separate cells and to put them to productive work, New York's establishment of a new penitentiary responded to two problems that had led the public to lose faith in the penitentiary promise: inmates' ill-disciplined behavior, worsened through overcrowding; and the use of pardoning for purposes unconnected to convict reformation.

Investing in the Auburn Experiment

The establishment of Auburn State Prison opened a new episode in the penal history of the Western world. There is scarcely a history of punishment that does not identify New York's second major penitentiary as the prototype that inspired numerous imitations in other states and around the world over the following decades. In the United States, Auburn's model of silent congregate labor during the day combined with cellular confinement at night was adopted more widely than the more costly Pennsylvania system of solitary labor. Yet, the opening of Auburn made no immediate impact on pardoning practice. For DeWitt Clinton, nephew of the first governor, who assumed office after Daniel Tompkins became vice president in 1817, it was business as usual in the exercise of executive discretion. Proceeding from where the previous governor left off, Clinton pardoned many more offenders than he deemed appropriate. Additional cells for inmates failed to reduce the penal system's reliance on gubernatorial clemency.[31]

Newgate still staggered along after Auburn opened, and it coped badly with almost double the number of offenders behind its twenty-three-foot walls than its designers had originally intended. Clinton was disturbed that its inmates, crammed into "apartments," included the "young and old—the healthy and the unhealthy—the novice and the adept in crime." In short, Newgate had devolved into a "school of turpitude." In his 1819 message to the legislature the governor reported that the frequency of pardoning was regrettable, but he proclaimed: "the executive is reduced to this dilemma, either to exercise the pardoning power to a pernicious extent, or to witness the destruction of the whole penitentiary system."[32] Clinton's point was rhetorical. New York's commitment to penitentiary punishment, both financial and ideological, was far too great by the 1820s to abandon the program of incapacitation, moral instruction, and forced labor. Overcrowding and idleness, not the penitentiary principle or the constitutionality of gubernatorial pardoning, were the problems that led to the state's further investment in penal infrastructure.

After Thomas Eddy, the "father" of the penitentiary in New York, gave up his position as Newgate's chief agent in 1803, other concerns—the provision of education for the poor, the treatment of the insane—commanded his attention. As he surveyed the breakdown of the penal ideals he had attempted to put into practice, he managed to pick out cases that illustrated penitentiary punishment's capacity to reform. Noah Gardiner, convicted on three counts of forgery in January 1796, fit the bill perfectly. Because his trial occurred prior to the reduction of the state's capital statutes, Gardiner was sentenced to death. Governor John Jay recommended that the legislature pass a pardon statute, and it did so, on the condition that Gardiner serve a life sentence at hard labor. As one of Newgate's first inmates, the former forger turned into a model prisoner, and he was placed in charge of the shoe factory, which became one of Newgate's most profitable enterprises. In May 1801, Governor Jay pardoned the man who, five years earlier, had faced death.[33] In recognition of the inmate's "skill, zeal and assiduity" as a laborer, the governor thought it proper "to encourage such laudable and beneficial exertions by freeing the said [prisoner] from imprisonment and hard labor in the said prison." However, it would be improper to restore his full rights of citizenship, Jay decided. The "disabilities resulting from [Gardiner's] conviction" would remain until the former forger proved himself worthy.[34]

The anticipation that Gardiner's citizenship might be restored hinged on his color. Imprisonment stripped white felons of liberty and the rights they otherwise enjoyed as "the wages of whiteness."[35] The advent of sentencing to life imprisonment produced a new cohort of New Yorkers after 1796, but their subjection to forced labor under threat of legally sanctioned punishment took its inspiration from the status of slaves. Like manumission, a pardon could alter that status; the difference was that free blacks in New York, as in other states, coped with civil disabilities that no pardoned white prisoner, no matter how serious his or her offense, could expect to bear.

From Slavery to Freedom? Executive Discretion and Black New York

Revolutionary rhetoric used the metaphor of slavery to add emotional heft to anti-imperial discourse; after the Revolution the seeking of liberty and the meanings of its denial in New York diversified, implicating executive discretion in direct and indirect ways. For African Americans, bondage was a bitter experience, not a metaphor, and many of the state's leading politicians, notably governors John Jay, Daniel D. Tompkins, and DeWitt Clinton, described slavery as a moral evil and an undemocratic anachronism. Despite the outlawing of slave importation in 1785 and New York's prohibition in 1788 of slave imports with intent to export, a further decade passed before legislators made their first step toward ending slavery. The Act for the Gradual Abolition of Slavery, passed in 1799, granted freedom to the children of slaves, but only once they reached adulthood.[36] After 1817, any person brought into the state as a slave became an apprentice after nine months' residence.[37] According to

Mathew Mason this law provided a further push toward gradual abolition (slavery was finally abolished in 1827), but it "emphatically declared New York a free state and proclaimed its legislature's determination to defend it against encroachment from the slave states."[38]

The exercise of pardoning in the early nineteenth century provides further evidence that New York's road to abolition was circuitous in design and duplicitous in execution. Although the abolition act of 1799 allowed slavery to persist, it stirred up white anxiety over the prospect of freed slaves straining charitable relief and turning to crime. It also inspired slaveholders to violate the law's spirit, if not its letter. In this miasma of political and moral compromise, they sought, found, and exploited means to subvert restrictions on the slave trade.[39] The state's foremost antislavery voice, the Manumission Society, protested that criminal courts regularly sentenced convicted slaves and free blacks to transportation, a ploy used en masse to quell the suspected conspiracy of 1741. This use of judicial discretion, the society charged, permitted owners to sell African Americans beyond the state's border, despite the exportation ban in place as of 1788. Although the courts' role in abetting the slave trade has been noted by historians of slavery, New York's governors contributed as well, through their racially regressive applications of mercy.[40]

Like the pardoning of felons in England on condition of transportation to its distant colonies, the banishment and transportation of convicts modified punishment while leading to an uncertain and fearful future.[41] When the legislature formally acknowledged in 1794 the governor's prerogative to attach conditions to pardons, it registered a practice long in effect.[42] Throughout the colonial era royal governors had imposed banishment as a condition of pardons. During the War of Independence, thousands of suspected loyalists were transported out of the state at the behest of executive authorities as well as courts. White, black, and Native American convicts were frequently pardoned on condition that they "depart from this state and never thereafter return." By the late eighteenth century, however, the use and implications of transportation acquired a racial cast. Of 276 pardons granted between 1799 and 1806, 78 were conditional on the prisoner's quitting the state. Notably, slaves made up almost half of those pardoned on condition of transportation, and for these pardoned convicts freedom from prison came at a great price.[43] When governors granted clemency on condition that a slave "leave this state" this rider responded to slaveholders' objections to the state's prohibition of inter-state slave trading. An act of 1790 made this plain in amending the restrictions imposed two years earlier: "Whereas many inconveniences have arisen from the prohibiting the exporting of slaves from this state," the preamble stated. After 1790, courts could recommend transportation as an alternative punishment for any slave, providing "the crime whereof such slave shall be convicted, is of such a nature, that transportation would be a proper punishment."[44] As in other cases in which courts recommended mercy, governors frequently endorsed this advice.

Because slaveholders bore the costs associated with the transportation of assigned slaves, conditional pardons absolved the state of financial and penal responsibility and worked to decrease New York's black population. In October 1797, Governor John Jay issued a pardon for Hester Combs, convicted of petit larceny and sentenced to six months' hard labor. Combs, a slave of one John Elliot, was pardoned "on condition that the said John Elliot . . . send her out of this State and that she do never return to the same again."[45] The master was also obliged to provide the mayor of New York with substantial sureties—two hundred dollars—to assure authorities that he intended to meet his obligation. A woman convicted of arson, a far more serious offense, was pardoned under similar conditions. Sarah, "a slave of William Alexander," was convicted in New York City in 1801 for committing an offense that used a much-feared weapon and a crime almost impossible to prevent. Perhaps her confession led to the short sentence of one year's imprisonment. It may also have induced the convicting judge of the Court of General Sessions to recommend to the governor that the woman be transported rather than imprisoned. The confessed criminal's incarceration in Newgate State Prison would impose a financial burden on its keepers; in contrast, the cost of her transportation would be born by her master. The aging George Clinton pardoned Sarah on the condition that William Alexander "do transport her out of the State and that she never thereafter return to the same."[46] Despite the financial burden of transportation, this pardon condition essentially imposed a small tax on the profits slaveholders could expect to make by selling slaves to buyers in southern states or the West Indies.[47] Hester's and Sarah's sentences consigned them to months of scrubbing floors, washing clothes, and emptying slop buckets in a gloomy and often violent prison; in contrast, their pardons on condition of transportation all but guaranteed they would end their days as slaves in a slave state, under conditions at the very least unfamiliar, and at the worst more brutal and bleak than any slave or prisoner faced in New York.

Offenders such as Sarah could be pardoned as governors pleased, but the legislature was responsible for the pardon of murderers, and then only if the chief executive first recommended a reprieve. In this realm of discretionary justice, blacks and whites, free and slave were technically equal. This did not mean that judges and chief executives weighed mitigating factors equally, though, as the aftermath of James Johnson's conviction for murder indicates. Daniel Tompkins's reasoning in regard to the pardon of the former

slave turned New York City dancer illuminates the racist cast of capital justice. In 1810 Johnson was convicted of killing a fellow African American in
an alcohol-fueled brawl involving his wife and a man who had insulted her.
When the case came before Governor Tompkins, a man whose "repugnance
to the punishment of death" was well known, the convict's chances looked
better than they had at trial, when ill-prepared counsel had defended Johnson
before an all-white jury. Historian Shane White argues that the governor gave
the man no hope of a pardon, but Johnson's lawyers did, at least, persuade
Tompkins to reprieve their client, and the chief executive did consider their
argument that Johnson had been provoked by the victim.[48]

Governor Tompkins's reply to Johnson's counsel was a study in the larger
balancing act between racist reasoning and the rule of law. More than a
brusque dismissal, his refusal to pardon Johnson showed a legally trained
mind at work, weighing his belief in the lower culpability of blacks as a class
of people against his reading of the facts in this case. Tompkins was elected
to office in 1807, and the Republican retained the governorship for a decade,
prior to becoming James Monroe's vice president in 1817. Like fellow governors John Jay and DeWitt Clinton, he was a member of the New York Manumission Society, and supported its African Free School. But opposition to
slavery and patronizing racism were commonly coupled in elite white thinking, as Tompkins's response to the lawyers indicates. "Persons in low life and
indigent circumstances and more particularly negroes . . . are frequently un-
acquainted with the principles of morality and the precepts of religion," he
opened. The governor considered blacks poorly educated and untutored by
"moral and well formed society," which made it difficult for them to appreciate the "legal and moral turpitude, and consequences of particular actions."
Had Johnson been intoxicated, he might have been considered less than fully
culpable. But the facts of this case did not warrant "benignity," Tompkins
decided, speaking both as governor and as a former justice of the supreme
court. The death sentence would stand.[49]

Was transportation benign? This question was argued as free blacks slowly
acquired legal rights over the early nineteenth century. Owners of bonds-
women and bondsmen continued to profit from sentences of transportation,
issued at the discretion of judges, but this was not the reason behind Governor Tompkins's criticism of this practice. In his January 1812 address to the
legislature, he followed his call for the legislature to "devise the means for the
gradual and ultimate extermination" of slavery, "that reproach of a free people," with an attack on the transportation of slaves, which corrupted justice.
Tompkins even claimed that the prospect of a slave's "lucrative disposition"
led masters to "tempt or to entrap the slave into an error; to operate upon his

ignorance or his fears, to confess a charge, or to withhold from him the means of employing counsel for defense."[50] However, the record of Tompkins's pardoning practice contradicts these claims and shows the limit of his stance against racial injustice.

The second volume of executive pardons, covering the period 1806 to 1811, is the first that documents the distinctions governors made between the pardon appeals of African American and white convicts. The name index, with the letter "B" marked against 66 names, reveals that race was at the forefront of the minds of Tompkins and his predecessor, Federalist Morgan Lewis (who served from 1806 to 1807). There is no question that these men pardoned African Americans while being fully aware that such decisions exposed convicts to the possibility of enslavement beyond New York. Of 557 pardons granted over this five-year period, the 66 black recipients of pardons, 34 of whom were slaves, made up just over 11 percent of the total. In many instances transportation was an implied rather than specific condition. "Jacob," a New York City slave convicted of petit larceny in May 1806 and sentenced to two years' hard labor, was pardoned several weeks later by Governor Lewis, "on condition that he leave the state within 60 days."[51] Tompkins adopted the practice when he took office, and he maintained it throughout his governorship.

The proportion of blacks pardoned declined over the 1810s, down to 5.5 percent, but the practice of pardoning in the interest of slave owners persisted. As late as 1816, four years after Governor Tompkins denounced court-ordered transportation and a year before he proclaimed his support for a total abolition bill, he pardoned an enslaved woman, "Rosannah." Convicted of grand larceny in New York City some time in July 1814 and sentenced to four years at hard labor, she left Newgate on January 29, 1816, when Tompkins pardoned her on condition that she be "transported from the state of New York . . . immediately on being liberated."[52] A new sentence of undetermined destination but certain duration awaited the pardoned woman.

In 1712, the year of New York's first major slave insurrection, the Provincial Assembly openly acknowledged that the execution of slaves undercut the profits of masters, and politicians had offered them financial compensation. Prior to the Revolution, royal governors were prepared to grant pardons to slaves on the understanding that owners sell or transport their chattel out of the colony.[53] A century later, after New York prohibited the exportation and sale of slaves, pardons provided a more devious way to compensate slave owners. It would be wrong to claim that this aim was the only motivation for mercy toward African Americans, since the majority of pardons after the turn of the century were granted without imposing conditions. Furthermore, the banishment of pardoned white New Yorkers indicates that the expulsion of convicted criminals was not a racially exclusive form of clemency. Nevertheless, these qualifications do not erase evidence that the state's chief executives, as well its criminal court judges, knowingly favored the economic interests of those who stood to profit financially from clemency. Legislators were not the only decision makers who dragged the state from its potential to lead a "polished and enlightened nation"; chief executives' exercise of discretion was equally implicated in New York's ambivalent passage toward racial equality.[54]

Discretionary Justice and the Struggle for Sovereignty

In his 1812 address to the legislature, Governor Tompkins followed his objection to the transportation of slaves with a call to "ameliorate the condition and cultivate the affections of the natives, who dwell within our territory."[55] Most historians of indigenous-settler relations regard the governor's words as the paternalistic patina on the state's ruthless drive to facilitate private land ownership and capitalistic economic development at the expense of tribal holdings.[56] This process began during the War of Independence, as the state sliced off territory held by "disloyal" tribes and offered it up as military bounty land. Internal colonization took off after the Erie Canal Commission was established in 1810, when the dream of a canal to connect the Great Lakes to the port of New York looked likely to become a state-backed reality. In the colonial era, native-newcomer relations were not so lopsided in the Great Lakes region.[57] The Iroquois Confederacy, which jockeyed for position between French and English imperial interests, commanded respect through diplomacy, trade, and war.[58] Even after the Revolution, the federal government acknowledged that it negotiated with Indian *nations* to determine their territorial boundaries and to delineate their special status as *imperia in imperio*. The criminal justice system played a significant role as well, particularly in New York, where the anti-federalist Clinton and his successors openly defied federal precedence over indigenous-state relations to assert states' rights and to act out a local version of manifest destiny. The imposition of statute law and the modification of criminal penalties through executive clemency became twin strategies in New York's ambition to rule diversity unilaterally.

In the Euro-American mind, the racial characteristics of indigenous people were distinct from those of blacks brought over to the United States from Africa.[59] Centuries of settler-native encounters framed the ways in which new post-Revolutionary relationships were negotiated between federal and state authorities and native peoples. Unlike slaves and free blacks, Indians in conflict with state law could reference the history of European recognition of their right, as natives, to self-governance. The assertion of native sovereignty was especially strong in New York, the principal homeland of the Iroquois Confederacy of Six Nations, the most feared indigenous military force prior to the nineteenth century.[60] Iroquois allies were critical to British ascendency in North America during the French and Indian Wars, and both George Clinton and his brother, James, acquired their first taste of military service fighting in that conflict.

Once the War of Independence divided the British between Whig and Tory, it also fractured the Iroquois Confederacy. The Oneida and many Tuscarora sided with the Americans, and the other four nations adhered to the British, making effective use of raids to cut off vital food supplies and transportation routes in the state's northwest.[61] The Continental Army struck back in the bruising Sullivan campaign, in which James Clinton was joint leader. General Washington instructed troops to carry out a scorched earth policy against the Iroquois allies of the British, involving "the total destruction and devastation of their settlements and the capture of as many prisoners of every age and sex as possible." With clear intent to "terrify and disconcert" the enemy, Washington aimed ultimately to pacify the Indians of New York: "After you have very thoroughly completed the destruction of their settlements," he instructed Sullivan, "if the Indians should show a disposition for peace, I would have you to encourage it."[62] Peace came at a high price to native peoples in the form of a treaty signed at Fort Stanwix in 1784. The national government took land from the disloyal nations and defined new boundaries around their reduced territory.[63]

This post-Revolutionary pact set a new framework for the consideration of terror and mercy in the New York's dealings with Indian offenders against state criminal laws. A subsequent federal treaty, signed at Fort Harmar in 1789, set out the terms of compensation for the sale of Indian land; in addition it introduced a separate article concerning the equal application of the law to Indians and non-Indians:

> Should a robbery or murder be committed by an Indian or Indians of the Six Nations, upon the citizens or subjects of the United States, or by the citizens or subjects of the United States, or any of them, upon any of the Indians of the said nations, the parties accused of the same shall be tried, and if found guilty, be punished according to the laws of the state, or of the territory of the United States, as the case may be, where the same was committed.[64]

Furthermore, Indians and U.S. citizens were both obligated under this treaty to deliver culprits to state authorities, so that prosecutions could occur according to applicable laws. Previously, Indian customs such as "grave covering" and the burying of tomahawks were recognized and used by the British as culturally sensitive ways to compensate for violence and to express the desire for peace and reconciliation.[65] These pluralistic means of recognizing wrongs and offering restitution would henceforth be replaced by strict adherence to Anglo-American rules respecting trial and punishment, with mercy the closest cognate to the restoration of offenders to their communities.

Treaties are one thing: working out intercultural relations on the ground is another. Legal pluralism, as Lisa Ford argues, had something to offer the colonizers as well as those who resisted and adapted to colonization.[66] To define indigenous offenses against Americans as crimes was to place offenses committed against Indians by whites under the same rubric. As late as 1790, news of the murder of two New York Seneca chiefs at the hands of white men prompted President Washington to send his Indian commissioner to express the "Great Chief's" abhorrence over the "injury to our brothers of the Indian nations."[67] The commissioner, Timothy Pickering, was instructed to negotiate peace according to Seneca diplomatic law. Similarly, the state authorities brushed aside calls from Protestant missionaries to prosecute crimes between Indians in their own nations, on the basis that such a policy would stir up resentment and win few converts. Indians agreed for different reasons. Defending traditional means of dealing with offenders was integral to their survival and autonomy.

In 1802 the Iroquois proposed another federally sanctioned grave-covering ceremony after a Seneca man known as Stiff-Armed George stabbed and killed a white millwright. This time, though, the provisions of the Fort Harmer treaty were followed. Much had changed since the 1780s, particularly the ascendance of the state over the federal government in regulating Indian-settler relations. After the stabbing, the chiefs and sachems of the Seneca, Onondaga, and Cayuga tribes, together with white citizens of the town of Canandaigua, met in a council struck to restore equable relations, not to assign guilt or inflict penalties. Red Jacket, a chief representing the Seneca, was in no mood to deal with the state government:

> Did we ever make a treaty with state of New York, and agree to conform to its laws? No. We are independent of the state of New York. It was the will of the Great Spirit to create us different in color: We have different laws, habits and customs from the white people. We will never consent that the government of this state shall try our brother.[68]

When state authorities took the suspect into custody after the council was held, in defiance of Red Jacket's claim, the federal government sat on its hands.[69] By the early nineteenth century, New York's defiance of federal ascendency over Indian relations and land transactions went unchallenged.[70] Red Jacket marched his case to Albany, where he demanded two meetings with the old governor, George Clinton. Discussions between the two leaders failed to resolve the matter to the Seneca's satisfaction: Stiff-Armed George was indicted, prosecuted, convicted, and sentenced to death in February 1803.[71] The pluralistic legal culture that had prevailed in the colonial era was crumbling.

Simultaneously the mechanisms of executive discretion, designed for indigenous people whose land was coveted by state and speculator alike, were just gearing up. On September 3, 1802, the U.S. Secretary of War, Henry Dearborn, wrote to President Jefferson that the Iroquois had presented a compelling argument in the Stiff-Armed George case, and editors across the country published Red Jacket's powerful statement. Mathew Dennis states that the national government favored a pardon after the killer's conviction.[72] However, internal communications confirm that plans for a pardon were underway well in advance of George's trial. Immediately after his meetings with the Indian party, Governor Clinton reported to Dearborn that he had reassured Red Jacket of the state's intention to treat his compatriot respectfully: if the accused man were to be convicted, Clinton said he would reprieve the sentence to allow the legislature time to consider a pardon. President Jefferson supported this course of action. In February of 1803, one week prior to the opening of the trial, Secretary Dearborn conveyed the president's request that the governor consider "the propriety of taking such measures as your own judgement may dictate for procuring a pardon, in case of conviction, of the Seneca Indian."[73]

Although the pardon of Stiff-Armed George demonstrated Red Jacket's skill in playing off hostile powers against each other—in this instance, the state versus the federal government—the statute was lawful: a twelve-member jury had convicted an indicted suspect; the jury and the judge had recommended mercy; the governor had respited the sentence of death; and the legislature had granted a pardon. The state government asserted its might through the suspension of punishment as well as its threat, while the Iroquois received the federal intervention they had demanded. Historians have read the outcome as proof of the Seneca's "residual power . . . a power that was extralegal if not technically legal."[74] In one respect this interpretation is compelling: a recognized leader of a nation, not a mere defense attorney, asserted Seneca sovereignty.[75] Yet there was nothing irregular or extralegal about the pressure Red Jacket used to urge the exercise of execution discretion. Clinton, more than any governor who would follow him, knew this well, having

RED JACKET,
Seneca War Chief.

Philadelphia Published by Key & Biddle

Red Jacket, Seneca chief. New York Public Library, image 809195, retrieved from http://digitalcollections.nypl.org.

considered the utility of mercy under conditions of war. Daniel Tompkins, governor during the War of 1812, shared that experience. Furthermore, the 1787 Bill of Rights proclaimed the legality of petitions directed to the governor or legislature.[76]

The key difference between the case of Stiff-Armed George and other high-profile capital cases was the nature of Red Jacket's argument, not the granting of a pardon in response to political pressure. The legislature stated that it was "expedient to pardon the said George," and it dictated that the "chiefs and sachems of the Seneca nation" were to provide assurances that "the said George shall immediately be set out of this state."[77] The state was content to make the pardoned murderer the Senecas' problem, but unlike slave owners, George's community had no financial or strategic interest in fulfilling the banishment condition. The outcome of this case, an ungainly dance between unequivocal prosecution, explicit recognition of nationhood, and the admission of political expediency, failed to convince either the Seneca or Euro-American New Yorkers that the state law applied either legitimately or equally to treaty Indians.

Red Jacket was a persuasive speaker but a selective historian. The 1803 trial of Stiff-Armed George was not the first time that an Indian had faced the death penalty in New York. Native Americans not indigenous to the state and not signatories to treaties were more vulnerable than members of the Iroquois Confederacy to prosecution and punishment under state law. George Peters, a Brothertown Indian, was tried for the murder of his wife, Eunice, the mother of their three children, in August 1801, and the state executed him on March 26, 1802.[78] The Brothertown did not hold historic title to the land on which they lived. In 1774, the Oneida allowed this Christianized coalition (comprising communities who had migrated from the New York-Connecticut-Rhode Island region) to farm on their traditional lands. When the Oneida withdrew their offer in 1788, the state preempted the land and appointed a superintendent to encourage the Brothertown to adopt private farming, learn trades, and school their children through Christian education. In 1796, the state assumed stewardship of the Brothertown in what it described as "compensation" for their loss of land. Given this context, a homicide involving a husband and wife in this community reflected badly on the missionizing and civilizing agendas of religious bodies and the state. Governor George Clinton stated that a reprieve was appropriate, "considering the ignorance of that unfortunate people, and the nature of our political relation with them."[79] In this instance, the legislature disagreed and refused to grant a pardon. The Brothertown, unlike Red Jacket's nation, were in no position to launch a political or military challenge.

The law of the colonizer fell on two other Native American men who shared Peters's fate prior to the trial of Tommy Jemmy in 1822. Neither case inspired a sophisticated defense of native sovereignty, since one was a Brothertown and the other a Stockbridge. Formerly members of the Mohican nation in Massachusetts, the Stockbridge community had also received a land grant from the Oneida, among whom they resettled after the Revolution in Madison County in upstate New York. Like the Brothertown, they were targeted by missionaries intent on converting Indians to Christianity and to teaching them the skills valued in a market economy, and they were largely converts from the 1740s onward.[80] When the "black robes" looked for success stories to place in their reports to donors, Marie Antone and her family were the type of Indians who suggested their conversion efforts were unwelcome. After a jealous spat with another young Stockbridge woman grew heated, twenty-one-year-old Antone stabbed her rival and left her dead, and an all-white jury found her guilty of murder. Justice Jonas J. Platt duly sentenced her to death on June 28, 1814, but not without a challenge from Antone's father.

Abram Antone protested that the matter was for the Stockbridge to settle, not the laws of New York State, and his family threatened to derail the legal process. According to a local chronicler, "The [Stockbridge] Indians disputed the right of the white-man authorities to interfere with their customs, or to exercise jurisdiction over them in criminal or other cases where the parties were of their race." Without a treaty or Red Jacket's debating acumen to back their claims, the condemned woman's father and brothers chose a more combative strategy, turning up at the scaffold site "painted and equipped in warrior style."[81] The confrontation threatened to turn the ceremony into a violent melee until a local militia captain convinced the family that deadly force would meet any provocation. Shouts of revenge pierced the air as Mary Antone mounted the scaffold, but the family made no move as they watched the grim spectacle of equal justice unfold on September 30, 1814.[82]

A Pardon to Declare the Sovereignty of the State

The pardon of Tommy Jemmy has attracted considerably more attention than the conditional pardons of slaves and the selective use of pardons in the state's dealings with lesser-known indigenous capital offenders.[83] Severity and clemency were both signposts of Indian sovereignty's increasing fragility following the Revolution. In contrast to the earlier tolerance of native spiritual beliefs, the Jemmy case was a turning point in the decline of legal pluralism, argues Lisa Ford. By framing it in terms of discretionary justice as practiced in the early national period, its wider dimensions become apparent, as a decisive moment in state authorities' attempts to govern New York's diverse population. Like the letter "B" inserted beside the names of African Americans in post-1799 executive pardon registers, the word "Indian" flagged white authorities' understanding of pardon recipients so labelled as members of a distinct racial group. Some, like the already-uprooted Brothertown and Stockbridge, were the first to be ruled according New York's criminal laws, notably in cases involving members of their own people. The Seneca were the last. Led by Red Jacket, they were also the most determined to assert their right of self-governance, as they made clear in the way they responded to an alleged murder that occurred shortly before the stop-and-start trial of Tommy Jemmy.

The immediate trigger for the state's determination to pardon Seneca chief Soo-non-gize, also known as Tommy Jemmy, was the "trial" of Joseph Bigbag. Conducted according to Iroquois custom, the ceremony occurred on the same day that Jemmy was arraigned for the murder of a woman the Seneca believed to be a witch. A council of eight Tonawanda chiefs and thirty-nine others from neighboring reservations acted as prosecutors, jurors, and judges in Bigbag's case.[84] After a three-day council, they decided the accused wife killer was innocent. The finding was not so much the issue as was the fact that New York legal authorities failed to prosecute this case, which sachems settled as an internal affair. Thus, when the Seneca handed over Tommy Jemmy to the state for prosecution, the gesture was a challenge, not a concession.[85] "The justices had to have been very aware of the Indian resistance to state criminal jurisdiction and also conscious of the alternative process that the Indians utilized in cases involving members of their own tribes," Deborah A. Rosen observes.[86] They must also have appreciated that the Seneca intended to transform New York's attempt to prosecute Jemmy into a show trial that would clarify, beyond the shadow of a doubt, their standing as a self-governing nation.

First-rate legal talent for the accused, including the redoubtable Red Jacket, gathered in Buffalo, and they fixed on the question of jurisdiction. Jemmy's defenders challenged the basis on which the state claimed the right to put a treaty Indian on trial for an intra-tribal act of violence.[87] The Seneca gambled that the trial would expose New York's abuse of its powers as defined by federal treaties. Thomas J. Oakley, a highly skilled lawyer who had recently served as state attorney general, was Jemmy's defense attorney, but the real star, who captured national press coverage for his eloquent and trenchant assertion of the Seneca's right to autonomous government, was Red Jacket. The case against the state was so compelling that the prosecution requested that the circuit court suspend judgment and refer the case to the next sitting of the state supreme court at Albany. The *Niles Weekly Register* described the un- usual proceedings as a "Singular Law Case," which turned more farcical when the defense appeared before New York's supreme court using the same strat- egy, demolishing the state's misrepresentation of the Seneca as a conquered people who had ceded sovereignty.[88] Faced with incontrovertible evidence to the contrary, drawn from federal treaties, the court dismissed the state's case. The only way left for the authorities to save face was executive discretion.

"Crimes committed by Indians against Indians on Indian reservations" could not go unpunished, New York supreme court justice Ambrose Spencer fumed in his report to Governor DeWitt Clinton.[89] A decade earlier, Gover- nor Tompkins had used patronizing language in support of efforts to inure indigenous peoples to the law and to secure their fealty to the state. Indians, it was thought, could be treated differently from Anglo-Americans because they were ignorant and felt "horror at becoming the objects of punishment by laws which they cannot interpret or comprehend."[90] The mood in Albany had darkened considerably by 1822. According to Spencer the "legal obliteration of indigenous customary law" was the "litmus test of settler sovereignty," and the attempted prosecution of Jemmy had turned into a debacle because the Seneca had clearly proven their right of self-governance. The time had come for the state to grant courts of law "exclusive jurisdiction in such cases."[91] If the state could not overturn federal treaties, the legislature had another op- tion: to pass a law that would pardon Jemmy as an act of state sovereignty over the Seneca. Governor Clinton advised the legislature to pardon Tommy Jemmy, a man who had never been tried, let alone convicted. The pardon was unconstitutional, since the legislature could not pardon offenders prior to conviction. So much for the rule of law. The Act Declaring the Jurisdiction of the Courts of this State formally terminated tribal justice with a bald procla- mation of settler sovereignty, yet it was self-contradictory, since it depended on the sachems and chiefs of the Seneca nation to take charge of "the said Soo-non-gize and transport him out of New York."[92]

Conclusion

The trouble the state took to assert sovereignty through discretionary justice expressed a growing sentiment, which most white politicians and land specu- lators shared, that the indigenous peoples of New York had relinquished their right to dwell in the lands of their ancestors. Their ever-shrinking reserva- tions would mean they must either adapt to and abide by the laws of the state, or move elsewhere in the country, out of the way of American-style prog- ress. White authorities cosseted this hard message in paternalistic discourse.

One year before he pardoned Tommy Jemmy, DeWitt Clinton stated that the Seneca would benefit from the "care and protection" the state currently provided the Stockbridge, Oneida, and Brothertown.[93] The conditional pardon of Jemmy can also be linked to the pardoning of enslaved blacks released from prison into the custody of their owners. Transportation from New York taxed the owners of these pardoned offenders but still allowed them to profit through the slave trade. As the gradual abolition of slavery and growing rates of manumission led to a rise in the number of free blacks in the state's penitentiary, Newgate's inspectors proposed that all black convicts, free and slave, be pardoned and transported to states in the southwest, but the plan was never implemented.[94] The inspectors tried again in 1816, when they recommended the establishment of a penal colony in a remote part of the state. Two years later a special committee of the legislature suggested that all pardoned inmates and those who had completed their sentenced be banished. Even Thomas Eddy, who attributed Newgate's failure to reform prisoners to its incapacity to isolate them, hoped that the new state prison far from the city of New York might provide a more effective form of temporary banishment than Newgate could provide.[95] Until that time discretionary justice was the means through which New York would define and manage its problem populations.

In the lead-up to the convention that revised the first constitution, the question of the pardoning power climbed up the agenda as a possible object of reform. Governors resorted to pardoning in an effort to keep Newgate State Prison from succumbing to the pressures of violence and pestilence, but their use of their authority came at the expense of the penitentiary ideal, fueling the reintroduction of whipping and the expansion of the death penalty's scope. A mood for significant political change pervaded state politics by the late 1810s, but the direction of change was unclear, as inter-party and personal rivalries cross-cut divisions over penal policy.[96] Two generations had passed since John Jay and his fellow drafters had written the first state constitution on the fly. By 1821 it was reasonable to assume that calmer heads might prevail to establish a new framework of government better suited to a state that was vying with its nearest rivals for economic ascendency, now that grandiose plans for the Erie Canal were surging forward. The original drafters decided to split the power to pardon between the executive and the legislature, but there was nothing sacred about this discretionary formula. Many delegates found fault with the use of clemency since the Revolution, but none of them pointed out mercy's reinforcement of racial inequality in the deservedly named Empire State.

3

Debating the Pardon in Antebellum New York

The 363-mile canal that connected the port of New York to the Midwest was a waterway that brought unprecedented prosperity to wealthy individuals and to the state, which vaulted to national prominence in the antebellum era.[1] Although this symbol of modernization profited early investors, including Thomas Eddy, the penitentiary promoter, its impact was uneven.[2] The direction and flow of economic progress left many New Yorkers, notably African Americans, on the margins, explicitly barred from full citizenship and voting rights, and white tenant farmers, many of whom considered their landlords slave masters. Tenant discontent politicized and turned violent over the 1830s and '40s, and governors responded by calling out the militia and making mass arrests. Fifty years after New York's first governor had used terror and mercy in waging war, an internal rebellion thrust chief executives into a similar scenario. But the context had changed. The pardoning of anti-rent rebels occurred in a more democratic period, in which multiple political parties jockeyed for power and all white men, including tenants, could vote.

The extension of the franchise to adult white men and the state's tiny number of free property-owning black men was the 1821 constitutional convention's greatest advance toward the ideal of popular representation. Delegates were prepared to shed the governing skin New York had grown in the context of the Revolution. At the same time, this advancement of revolutionary ideals effectively consolidated a "white man's democracy."[3] The convention's modification of the pardon power carried an equally conservative message. Gubernatorial patronage and the executive council's power of revision were challenged, but when delegates turned to the exercise of discretionary justice they decided to augment the governor's power. Out of step with other states, and out of favor with emerging penological theory, New York stripped the legislature of its power to pardon and handed the exclusive prerogative to the governor.[4] At the following convention, in 1846, opponents of the "one-man power" made greater headway, supported by increasing statistical evidence of its arbitrariness and abuse; however, social scientific arguments concerning its inconsistency with democratic governance proved insufficient to shake New Yorkers from their reliance on executive discretion.[5]

The Empire State gained the pole position in the race to lead the nation in commerce and population growth by the middle of the nineteenth century, but its adherence to historic pardoning models left it in the rear guard of criminal justice reform.⁶ In most other respects a world leader in penal modernization, New York's retention of gubernatorial pardoning, despite constitutional deliberations and sophisticated philosophical challenges, calls for the closer analysis of sovereign power at a time of democratization for white America. Constitutional debates, governors' messages to the legislature, commissioned reports, and the first body of official statistical accounts confirms that executive discretion's viability and merits were strongly challenged in the antebellum era. Concerted attempts to introduce alternatives to executive discretion made little headway against the one-man pardon in New York. And actions spoke louder than the words of constitutional delegates on two dramatic occasions. The solitary-confinement scandal at Auburn State Prison in 1823 and the anti-rent crisis of the mid-1840s demonstrated how governors could use their discretionary authority to rectify problems New York's elected politicians created and its courts failed to resolve. The machinations of state politics and the persuasive claims of pardoning's defenders, both humble and powerful, also account for New York's ongoing and increasing reliance on a regal model of prerogative power.

The Pardon under Constitutional Consideration

Should the verdicts handed down in court be final, subject only to legal appeal? Should the "voice of the people" determine the ultimate fate of criminals? Or should the final outcome of criminal sentences be determined by the stroke of the governor's pen? John Jay and his committee of constitution drafters considered these questions in 1777 with the English forces bearing down on them. When Pennsylvanians did the same they determined that elected representatives could be trusted with oversight of discretionary justice, but New York's patrician framers favored executive power. The circumstances that led to the first governor's use of mercy and severity in time of war to achieve strategic objectives subsided by the late 1780s, as Governors Clinton and Jay sponsored less sanguinary forms of punishment under civil administration. By the early nineteenth century two categories of offenders became the focus of the pardon power: murderers facing the death penalty (a matter for the legislature to determine) and felons filling up Newgate State Prison (released through governors' pardons). The state's new penitentiary at Auburn opened in 1816 with an updated plan for prison discipline, and religious and secular idealists who still believed the penitentiary punished more effectively than the lash and the noose staked their reputations on this innovative institution.[7] The backdrop to the third constitutional convention of 1821 looked nothing like the context that gave rise to the first constitution, so there was no reason to assume that the model of executive power in place since 1777 would hold.[8]

Convention delegates met at Albany in the autumn of 1821 prepared to re-consider the first state constitution, but few of the 126 white men sought rad-ical change.[9] New York's law of 1817, which decreed that all slaves in the state were to be free by 1827, marked the limit of white New Yorkers' prepared-ness to extend the reach of rights among "a great and free people."[10] Many believed that the 1777 settlement should hold and that suffrage ought to be exclusive to white men of property. As a stalwart of conservative republi-canism, the state's chancellor, James Kent, argued against extending suffrage to men who were not their own masters, particularly tenants and laborers under the control of landlords and men of affairs. The majority of delegates countered Kent's distaste for "the extremes of democratic doctrines" by argu-ing that the constitution should not entrench a class system.[11] As Daniel J. Hulsebosch argues, Bucktails (a faction of the Democratic-Republican Party critical of Erie Canal promoter Governor DeWitt Clinton) led the campaign against the Council of Revision's interference in the legislative process and the partisan control of the Council of Appointment. Under Martin Van Bu-ren's leadership, their criticism "fueled the constitutionalization of politics."[12] Rivalry between Van Buren and Clinton, the first governor's nephew, grew over the 1810s and intra-party schisms multiplied. From Federalists versus anti-Federalists in the early republic, New York's political system fractured into a shifting kaleidoscope of factions defined as much by personal enmities and ambitions as ideological distinctions. In such a fiercely partisan legisla-ture many doubted that the pardon power could rest safely in the hands of the people's representatives.[13]

Before the convention did away with legislative pardoning, delegates artic-ulated competing understandings of executive power in a democratic repub-lic. Most of the key speakers—sitting and future supreme court judges, former and future governors, senators, and great landlords—had direct experience of discretionary justice, and these encounters informed their support for the governor's sole authority to pardon. State Senator Peter R. Livingston, a mem-ber of the family of great landlords and legal luminaries, thought that the original framers had erred in granting the legislature a role in pardoning. He reflected that anti-monarchical "prejudices and passions" prevailed in 1777, when "father was at variance with son, and the bands of society were torn asunder." Since that time of trial those hot feelings had cooled, and the defects of popular involvement in pardoning had become apparent. To mix the power to enact law with the power to modify it was a violation of "fundamental principles of government," Livingston advised. By introducing the principle of majority rule over death penalty cases, the original state constitution failed to anticipate the unseemliness produced by close votes in the legislature: "what will be the effect in the minds of the community? All their tender feelings will be exerted, and they will be doubting, whether he ought to be punished or not."[14] Delegates familiar with the assembly's penchant for passionate rhetoric expressed concern that pardoning ought to be more sober and discrete. Nathan Williams was a conservative Episcopalian who considered it offensive that legislatures made impulsive decisions based on group emotion. "Such a body is not the proper sanctuary of justice," he tutted. Fellow Federalist and New York Supreme Court Judge Jonas Platt agreed. The legislature was not a "fit tribunal" to exercise discretion; in contrast, governors were more likely to act with firmness and "steady impartiality."[15]

Not a single delegate supported the freer use of pardoning. The matter on which they differed concerned the question of whether representatives in the legislature were more or less likely than chief executives to be influenced by public opinion. Williams and Platt believed that governors were more reserved than legislators; others argued the opposite. Erastus Root, a leading jurist and distinguished brigadier general during the War of 1812, considered himself a good judge of men's characters. Delegates who thought governors were impervious to pleas for mercy were naive. "Virtuous indeed must that chief magistrate be, who would not bend to such importunities." Without expressly raising the potential of corruption, Root added that "wealthy and influential" petitioners must surely have ways to sway governors.[16] Jurist Ogden Edwards charged that governors were not so much corruptible as overly sensitive to the suffering of criminals and their loved ones. Men "too much influenced by feelings of humanity" frequently succumbed to sentimentality:

> The exercise of the power of pardoning is pleasant—it is humane—it is agreeable to the best feelings of the human heart. But sad experience has taught, that the interests of the community require that the civil arm should be brought to bear with power upon malefactors.

A Bucktail opponent of the Clintonians, Edwards likely aimed his call for manly fortitude at DeWitt Clinton, the sitting governor. Yet he made a wider point: in order for executive discretion to be just, "the governor must nerve himself" against imprecations for mercy.[17] On that score the conservative

Platt could find common ground with Edwards. It was unmanly for governors to reprieve death sentences and recommend mercy because it allowed governors to delegate responsibility and disperse it among legislators. Assigning sole responsibility for the life or death of convicted capital offenders to one man would force him to be decisive. In the interest of justice the chief executive's "strong and resolute hand" must overpower his soft heart.[18]

When Judge Edwards considered whether pardoning accountability could be increased without some sort of oversight, he thought not: he was prepared to transfer pardoning to the governor's sole discretion, but he believed the chief executive's pardons must come with justifications. Ironically, there was greater accountability in the British system, Edwards claimed, since "a pardon never passes the great seal, without containing a recital of the causes for which it is extended." In republican New York, in contrast, "they are granted without a single reason for it." Other delegates agreed with Edwards that governors would be more "watchful" if they were compelled to report the rational grounds for their pardons. In Livingston's opinion, no self-respecting governor would dare risk shame by admitting that "sickly sympathy" had moved him to grant mercy: "Do you think he would dare say, 'I pardoned on account of my tender feelings; or for mere speculation; or in hopes of reformation'?"[19]

The most persuasive support for discrete pardoning came from the state's legal leaders. Chief Justice Ambrose Spencer, the man who later advised Governor Clinton to send a strong message of state sovereignty to the state's native population, based his support for gubernatorial pardoning on his familiarity with Newgate and Auburn State Prisons. Spencer's regular inspections of these institutions convinced him that pardoning was an appropriate response to the swelling prison population. Because it was necessary to release so many prisoners any requirement to provide individual pardon reports would be impractical. Chancellor Kent spoke in more positive tones, drawing on a Hamiltonian understanding of unfettered sovereign mercy.[20] "The ground of humanity" and the "hope of reformation" were legitimate justifications for clemency in Kent's opinion. Besides, the venerable Federalist advised, publicizing the reasons for law's modification was frequently "inexpedient" and "impolitic." After four days of debate the proponents of reporting went down to defeat, although this measure would receive support at the fourth constitutional convention in 1846.[21] In 1821, the vast majority of delegates reached agreement because they regarded the legislature as a body that had grown unsuitable to dispense discretionary justice for ordinary criminal offenses. The chief executive was empowered to pardon as he pleased on the assumption that men elected to that office would act decisively and discretely.

Experimenting with Solitary Confinement

The perception of pardoning in wider spheres of political discussion was considerably more critical than it was on the floor of the convention. At the close of the debate, eighty-nine delegates voted in favor of exclusive gubernatorial discretion and only twenty-nine objected: the pardon power was preserved and personified. In the years leading up to the convention, however, legislators had reintroduced whipping and lobbied for new capital statutes in the late 1810s, in part because they associated pardoning with deleterious mildness. Supporters of penitentiary punishment were equally critical of gubernatorial pardoning and they proposed a variety of solutions. In 1817, a senate committee reported on the problems besetting Newgate and attributed its high rates of recidivism to injudicious pardoning.[22] By 1821 little had changed, despite Auburn's opening. Shortly before the constitutional convention, the legislature appointed a prominent trio of commissioners to review the management of punishment and labor in the state's two penitentiaries.[23] Their 1822 report to the senate presented the first exhaustive review of penitentiary punishment since 1799, and they described the intervening period as a "history of mortifying failures and disappointed hopes." Imprisonment "hitherto conducted" had "wholly failed" to reform; instead, it had spread "the love of vice, and a knowledge of the arts and practices of criminality."[24] A lack of internal discipline and imperfect classification of prisoners was one reason for the penitentiary's failure; another, which they equally decried, was the use of the pardon power as a managerial strategy.[25] Defenders of executive clemency, such as Spencer, might point to its utility in preventing overcrowding, but the commissioners read usefulness as misuse. For the first time, criticism of discretionary justice was backed by statistical evidence, an early index of the turn toward social scientific approaches to penal reform.[26]

To achieve a "more perfect understanding" of the penitentiary's viability, the New York commissioners undertook an "authentic history" in 1822 of the state prisons, based on annual reports, legislative committee proceedings, and the statements of prison inspectors. Their most stunning revelation concerned the frequency of pardoning: of the 5,069 convicts committed from 1799 to 1821, over half—2,819—had been pardoned.[27] The first of Newgate's reports to admit that pardons were issued to deal with an excess of prisoners appeared in 1808. With apparent disregard for evidence that prisoners had repented, the number of pardons mounted. In 1821 two-thirds of repeat offenders committed to Newgate and Auburn State Prisons had previously been pardoned.[28] This information convinced the commissioners that criminals could anticipate "light punishment," which stripped the penitentiary of its "dread and terror." The legislature had tried to compensate by approving the use of whipping as an instrument of prison discipline in 1819, but hundreds of "desperados" were "let loose upon society" by pardon each year, whether or not their punishment was sufficient. Even the success stories looked suspicious. If any of Newgate's or Auburn's inmates became law-abiding citizens, the commissioners attributed their renunciation of crime to accident, not design. By the 1820s critics of the penal system took a dim view of the idealism that had led New York to demand so much of penitentiaries. "That a whole community of intelligent men should have expected such a result, exhibits one of those instances of public infatuation . . . which do not the less excite our wonder when the illusion is past."[29] The *New York Evening Post* agreed. The state had invested too heavily in the penitentiary to abandon it; consequently the time had come to replace sentimental hope and sloppy pardoning with a coldhearted redesign of the experiment, based on facts and "forcible reasoning."[30]

More than a decade before Gustave de Beaumont and Alexis de Tocqueville published their national penitentiary survey to international acclaim, the Society for the Prevention of Pauperism in the City of New York published a humbler study. Its pamphlet, "Penitentiary System of the United States," incorporated the 1822 report of the state senate commission. Although it rejected the idea of returning to sanguinary punishment the society endorsed the commission's conclusion that "the too frequent intervention of pardoning" was a serious defect of the current system, especially in New York, the state in which profligate pardoning was "the most striking and melancholy." Pardons were granted through a "mistaken policy of displaying principles of humanity." Jurors delivered verdicts and nullified their decisions by recommending mercy, and leading citizens lent their names to pardon petitions without considering that their unthinking tenderness "defeat[s] the purpose of the laws." To rescue the experiment, and to resist pressure to extend brutal means of penal discipline, the society's report recommended that "the pardon power be never exercised excepting in extreme cases."[31] This refrain in favor of certain punishment came with a new call, not for more flogging but for stricter isolation.

Solitary punishment was a long-considered penal concept by the 1820s. English reformer John Howard had called for its adoption in the mid-eighteenth century, and subsequent Quaker campaigners had promoted enforced solitude as the best means to induce penitence through contemplation and spiritual guidance. Unlike Philadelphia's Walnut Street Jail, Newgate was built without solitary confinement cells, and Eddy considered this compromise with economy the source of misrule and high recidivism rates.[32] Auburn would be different. The senate's prison report of 1817 supported New York's adoption of the Pennsylvania model of solitary punishment as a means to prevent the riots, fires, and mutinies that occurred repeatedly at Newgate.[33] A block of 285 single cells was installed at Auburn, and the first group of inmates to put the touted benefits of solitary confinement to the test arrived on Christmas Day, 1821. When the Society for the Prevention of Pauperism and the Senate's commissioners extolled this form of punishment in 1822, the experiment was just underway.[34]

Solitary at Auburn was meant to break obduracy and rebelliousness. Wherever this technique had been used, the society's report enthused, "the spirit of the offender was subdued, and a temper of meekness, and evidence of contrition, displayed." The object of isolation was to render the criminal's confinement "odious and mentally oppressive."[35] Again, the society agreed with the senate commission on this point. The reform of prisoners remained a goal, but the protection of society from crime was the cardinal purpose of punishment. "After having for twenty-five years employed our sympathies and resources for the criminal part of our society," its report urged, "it is now our duty to look to the innocent." Industrious, law-abiding citizens whose taxes paid for expensive prisons expected and deserved to be protected from criminals "by any such means as may be most efficient."[36] DeWitt Clinton's successor, Governor Joseph Yates, thought that isolating offenders was the best means to mold them into pliant subjects. In January 1823 Yates used his first address to the legislature to declare he was "perfectly persuaded" that "solitary confinement without labor . . . presents the best means of reclaiming the offender; and according to the benign intentions of our penitentiary system, of fitting him for future usefulness."[37] The legislature supported these words with legislation that enlarged the application of solitary confinement for all repeat offenders to a maximum term of two years. By 1823, Auburn's experiment of solitude was gelling into general policy.

Advocates of solitary punishment could utter a word such as "benign" in combination with "odious" because they considered isolation a progressive alternative to New York's return in the 1810s to the use of bodily punishments. Solitary confinement was compatible with the "mild" criminal code introduced in 1799 because it left the convict's life and limb untouched. And unlike barbaric public punishments, which habituated observers to "spectacles of horror," it did not dull the public mind to suffering.[38] The Pauperism Prevention Society had rashly gambled that if solitary confinement failed it would prove that "the System is intrinsically defective, and out of the compass of perfection."[39] Before long it became apparent that "moral suffering" was as cruel as physical pain, if not more barbaric. When Governor Yates, a former chief justice of the state supreme court, conducted his regular visit to the state's prisons in the summer of 1823 he saw with his own eyes the impact of the punishment he had endorsed.

The profound mental and physical suffering among prisoners held in solitary confinement eroded Yates's and the state legislature's confidence in its continued use at Auburn.[40] Simultaneously, the governor's decision to use the pardon power vindicated the convention delegates who had urged that executive discretion be preserved and enlarged. The warden of Auburn, Gershom Powers, first reported evidence of solitary confinement's cruelty in August 1822, when Clinton was still in office, but it took Yates's 1823 visit before the policy was overhauled. The governor learned that isolated prisoners had suffered higher than average rates of illness and death. These men "languished" in their cells, and the visiting physician reported that their sedentary existence increased their susceptibility to pulmonary diseases and dropsy. Other inmates turned to shocking acts of self-harm and attempted suicide in desperate attempts to end their "mental oppression." Yates's personal interviews of some of the prisoners in question prompted him to issue pardons on the spot for twenty-six men, many of whom he considered in imminent danger of dying; the remainder he pardoned gradually, on the advice of the prison inspectors.[41]

By the end of 1823, the solitary cells at Auburn, which had once held proponents' dreams of mild but odious punishment, were emptied of the "hardened" offenders they had hoped to crack.[42] In Yates's second address to the legislature, in January 1824, he admitted that New York's experiment had failed, and he justified his spate of pardons on this basis: "I have thought [it] proper to pardon a number of the convicts . . . to prevent an undue increase of their punishment, in consequence of a classification, . . . and in pursuance of which, a number of prisoners had been confined in the solitary cells."[43] The conservative delegates to the 1821 constitutional convention may not have agreed with this latest liberal dose of pardons, but the released inmates benefited from the constitution's consolidation of executive discretion.[44]

Penal historians concur that the solitary confinement crisis of the early 1820s generated a compromise in New York's approach to penitentiary punishment. Auburn adopted a plan of congregate labor during the day, solitary confinement at night, and protracted solitary imprisonment only as a means of institutional discipline. Within a decade, the Auburn model inspired similar prisons to be built around the country.[45] Yet, as far as pardoning was concerned, nothing changed, despite continued claims that it interfered with institutional mechanisms that encouraged reform. When the solitary confinement experiment began in 1821, the board of inspectors at Auburn had intended that isolated prisoners would "brood over the horrors of their solitude, and the enormity of their crimes, without the hope of executive pardon."[46] In contrast to the state's disastrous trial of unrelieved solitary punishment, pardoning remained an integral but contentious element in New York's growing penal system, as a growing circle of critics debated the merits of discretionary justice.

Sentiment and Reason: The Social Scientific Analysis of the Pardon in Antebellum America

Since the Revolution, confidence in gubernatorial pardoning mingled with the belief that pardoning ought to withstand the test of reasonableness. John Jay declared in 1798 that the pardon power required "prudence and discretion, and not the wishes or feelings of the governor."[47] Sensible to this expectation, New York governors frequently set out their reasons for reprieving death-sentenced offenders. George Clinton did so when he recommended that the legislature pardon Stiff-Armed George in 1803, and governors frequently cited judges' opinions to stiffen the credibility of clemency. Statutory pardons typically stated the grounds of legislative pardons, and the title of Tommy Jemmy's extraordinary pardon in 1822 declared its political justification. Thus, when Joseph Yates took office in January 1823 (the year the new constitution came into effect) he became the first governor vested with exclusive power to pardon. Assuming this role, he considered it appropriate to declare what motivated him to use his authority, despite the fact that the constitution did not oblige him to do so.

It is unlikely that Airy Thompson set out to make history, but the timing of her trial midway through 1822 made her the first convicted murderer in the state of New York to be pardoned by the governor. A free black woman aged twenty-eight, Thompson gave birth to a girl in the early spring of 1822 in upstate Ontario County. Suspicion of foul play arose when the newborn was found dead with a severe wound to her head. Because Thompson confessed she had struck the fatal blow, her court-appointed attorneys argued a defense of insanity. The case was tried before Justice Platt, the same man who had recently supported the retention of gubernatorial pardoning. After the jury had convicted Thompson, adding a "strong recommendation of mercy," Platt reported the outcome to then-governor DeWitt Clinton and confirmed his support for a gubernatorial reprieve.[48] Since the new constitution was not yet in effect and the legislature was not in session when Clinton received Platt's recommendation, the capitally convicted woman's case landed on Yates's desk in January 1823.

In Joseph Yates's pardon of Airy Thompson he declared the "black woman" a "fit object of our mercy." Proceeding with the royal "we," the proclamation to "the People of the State of New York" stated that "we have pardoned remised and released and by these presents do pardon remise and release the said Airy Thompson of and from the said felony and murder." The governor's explanation quoted at length from the jury's statement, which they had attached to their verdict. According to the law's definition of insanity she was sane, but they believed she had suffered from "temporary visitations of insanity," and imagined that "the pains of childbirth must have been excruciating." Having stated that they had conformed to the "well established and salutary principles of the law," the jury considered it just that Thompson not suffer the sentence of death.[49]

Similar thoughts and feelings had likely stirred Governor George Clinton to reprieve Amy Augur for killing her "bastard" in 1779, but by the 1820s and '30s, men with greater faith in science than in sentiment began to question emotionally tinged motives for mercy, not just in the formal arenas of constitutional debate but in opinionated pamphlets and investigative reports, such as the studies produced by the state senate commission and Pauperism Prevention Society.[50] Now that New York's governors had sole discretion over the fate of murderers, they became easier targets of critics who declared that sympathy had no place in pardoning.[51] Airy Thompson's pardon would hold, but opponents of executive discretion began to question the tender prompts of gubernatorial pardoning and the fading culture of gentility on which it was based.[52]

Pardoning practice studied through social scientific methods began in the 1830s, with the analysis of trends over time and across jurisdictions. Discretionary justice in New York and in other states that had experimented with penitentiary punishment became objects of social scientific inquiry thanks largely to three Europeans.[53] Owing to their groundbreaking survey of North American prisons, *On the Penitentiary System* (1833), Frenchmen Gustave de Beaumont and Alexis de Tocqueville have become familiar figures in penal historiography. Francis Lieber is less well known, but he became a far more significant figure in arguments over the pardon power after he translated the two noblemen's study into English and wrote a lengthy preface. Lieber's reputation as a lecturer with Boston's Society for Useful Knowledge and his membership in the Philadelphia Prison Society secured the deal, but his interest in penology (a word he coined) arose from personal experience.[54] In his Prussian homeland his anti-authoritarian beliefs had led to police harassment and a period of imprisonment. Against police orders, Lieber fled to the United States in 1827, where he linked up with leading prison reform groups, including Philadelphia's Society for Alleviating the Miseries of Public Prisons, founded in 1787. Under its authority Lieber began what became a lifelong study of pardoning practice in his adopted country, and a determination to put an end to executive discretionary justice.[55]

The three investigators came from countries where monarchs and emperors had withheld and granted pardons in times of revolution and war, and this made the men especially sensitive to hints of regal fiat in republican America. In the modern penitentiary stakes, Beaumont and Tocqueville judged that "the State of New York is without contradiction one of the most advanced in the path of reform." [56] Accordingly, they found it surprising that the pardon had been "much abused" in America. More shocking was evidence that New York governors appeared to be the worst offenders. They did not conduct original research to reach this conclusion, which they lifted from a damning report, recently written and published by Irish Catholic pamphleteer Mathew Carey. Beaumont and Tocqueville repeated Carey's claim that governors had released one-third of inmates from Auburn Penitentiary over the 1820s "on the presumption of reformation," and this practice failed to confine pardoning to the correction of doubtful convictions.[57] Lieber, the adopted American, was closer to the ground, and he corrected the visitors' misperception in his translator's notes. New York's governors had not been uniformly liberal in their use of the pardon, and the recently elected governor, William Marcy, had pledged to be less clement. Whether Lieber had cases such as Airy Thompson's in mind, or possibly his own case, he agreed with Chancellor Kent that "no human wisdom" could ensure that the strict application of law would render, in every case, just outcomes.[58]

After Beaumont and Tocqueville sailed back to France as Lieber stayed stateside, adding a lengthy preface to On the Penitentiary System, in which he proposed a formula to recalibrate discretionary justice to conform to the principles of democracy and to shield pardoning practice from emotion. In ancient times, the sovereign's pardon operated when the branches of government "were but illy defined." In Britain and Europe "this power gradually rose into a distinct privilege, cherished by as many rulers, probably, for its great political importance, as for its merciful characters, so grateful to a paternal monarch." Now that democracy had rejected its earlier "religious-political character," Lieber urged, Americans must update the administration of pardoning, since every executive office holder, from the President down to state governors, was subjected to "vehement solicitation and personal prayers." The people, including women and others without full rights of citizenship, were not shy about appealing to the governor, and they turned up frequently to his residence expecting to be seen. No monarch faced such pressure, Lieber observed, since his subjects cold not "accost" the sovereign. In contrast the popularly elected chief executive could expect to hear from "a mother of many children, suffering great poverty, because the arm of stern justice took their protector away from them to be punished in a prison." In Lieber's view, these appeals to one man's sympathy produced unjust decisions, whereas a "committee or chamber of pardoning" would base its decisions on argument and reason.[59]

Lieber's model of discretionary decision making, laid out in his preface, was less innovative than he claimed. Prior to the adoption of the second constitution, deliberations over pardons had been shared between formally separate branches of New York's government. Governor Tompkins reported that he collaborated with the justices of the state supreme court, who made semi-annual visits to Newgate and later Auburn prison, to determine which prisoners might merit pardons. In capital cases, governors publicly and privately conveyed to the legislature their opinions on the appropriateness of persons facing execution as prospective recipients of pardons. When trials concerned the security of the state, during the Revolution and in the War of 1812, the governor as commander in chief corresponded with field commanders on the conduct of courts-martial. And in the state's shambolic prosecution of Tommy Jemmy, DeWitt Clinton worked closely with the legislature as well as the judiciary to come up with a patchwork pardon in 1822. The novelty of Lieber's proposal lay in the challenge it posed to justify a mode of discretionary justice increasingly out of step with New York's international reputation for penal innovation.

The Politics of Pardoning Arithmetic

Prior to the early nineteenth century, the impulse to collect and analyze data concerning the natural and material world was largely a private enterprise.[60] Learned and benevolent societies such as New York's Society for the Prevention of Pauperism used their own resources to interrogate problems and propose fact-based solutions. By the 1830s, "a kind of naïve infatuation with numbers blossomed in the culture."[61] In 1839, for instance, New York adopted a law "Respecting Convictions in Criminal Courts, and to Procure Statistical Information Concerning Convicts."[62] Our rearview vision of the wobbly statistics compiled in the antebellum era need not distort the seriousness with which their authors tried to use numbers for political purposes. If critics of penal justice could embarrass governments with unflattering statistics, then government administrators and executive office holders decided they must fight back with numbers of their own.

At a time of enthusiasm toward moral and social reform, individual social investigators and associations pioneered the interrogation of state institutions, and the administration of discretionary justice was no exception. Matthew Carey (1760–1839) did not confine his reformist impulse to penal matters— urban public health, poor relief and temperance were of equal concern—but he was determined that the Auburn penitentiary ideal not be blighted by current practice. In his *Thoughts on Penitentiaries and Prison Discipline* (1831) Carey criticized the practice of pardoning in New York, having studied its abuse in the 1820s and his pamphlet colored Beaumont and Tocqueville's conclusions. In contrast to Lieber's lengthy preface and the French authors' even lengthier study of the prison system, Carey's report was short, free, and pitched for a broad readership. Basing his study on the senate report of 1822, he cherry-picked the most extreme figures (the pardoning of 803 prisoners out of 975 committed to Newgate in 1816) to imply that nothing had changed since the postwar crime wave. He pinned this figure to his broad conclusion that the "pernicious exercise of the power of pardoning" was "sinister." Carey also alleged that an "iniquitous traffic" in pardons operated at the state prisons, but he did not substantiate his claim.[63] Weak evidence did not reduce the report's impact, however. Despite its spotty and selective statistics, Carey's pamphlet dramatized Lieber's point that "no governor of a state can dispense with the obligation of being judged," a fact that distinguished democracies from monarchies.[64]

By the 1830s governors began to use the resources of their office to commission their own studies of the pardoning power. Governors Enos T. Throop and William H. Seward led the way. Throop, born in 1784, was a circuit court judge and Democratic-Republican allied with Martin Van Buren, whom he succeeded as governor after Van Buren left New York to become secretary of state in 1829.[65] Seward was nearly a generation younger, born in 1801, and he became New York's first Whig governor in 1839, an office he held until 1842. In his earlier role in the state senate in the early 1830s, Seward threw himself into penal reform, in particular the effort to abolish the death penalty. In 1834 he became a founding member of the Whig Party and became associated with its liberal progressive wing. The pair differed in politics, age, and bearing (Seward a fashionable firebrand, Throop a stolid farmer at heart), but both men faced criticism of injudicious and corrupt pardoning practice and they reached the same conclusion: discretionary decision making must become a subject of empirical analysis.

After winning the post of governor in his own right, Throop used his first address to the legislature in January 1830 to reassure members that his first months in office as Van Buren's replacement had seen him pardon solely in regard to "the objects of punishment." This commitment had required that he "resist the most earnest and affecting appeals to my sympathy." As proof he offered evidence that he had pardoned a modest twenty-eight prisoners, and he had refused to commute the death sentences of each of the four men convicted of murder in the previous year. In every case involving clemency he had acted for one of three reasons: doubts concerning guilt; satisfaction of merit after consultation with keepers and judges and interviews with prisoners; and the need to compensate for insufficient "latitude of discretion in the courts." The governor's advocacy of milder laws and a reduction in the number of offenses subject to mandatory life sentences was widely shared, but Throop hoped he could soon support his aims with data from Auburn's "prison books." In 1831 he recommended that "interesting tables be formed" to test the effects of the "mode and degree of punishments" on the incidence of crime. "We should be able also to compare year with year and have some data for regulating our criminal code, and producing a uniformity of sentences."[66] Ironically, Governor Throop's wholehearted support for closer analysis of pardoning practice ultimately lent credibility to Carey's claims. By his third term in office, his rate of pardoning felons had tripled from the rate he set in his first year in office.[67] Throop became an easy target for rival Democrat William L. Marcy, who became governor in 1833 with a promise to turn the books around.[68] Over his six years in office Marcy did not provide tables but simply asserted he had brought pardoning under control, a claim his successor, a Whig, would challenge.[69]

The election of William H. Seward as governor occurred after the electorate decided it was prepared to experiment with a newly minted party that had toppled the Democratic party, which Martin Van Buren had turned into a machine that held onto power over the 1820s and '30s.[70] Determined to bring down their Whig nemesis, Democrats (who retained a majority in the state senate) attacked Seward on a vulnerable flank: the high-minded liberal's use of the pardon power. After his first year in office, the *Albany Argus*, the Democrats' trumpet, slammed the governor for favoring Whig petitioners and denying pardons to their own supporters.[71] Seward counterattacked with statistics of the sort Throop had discussed several years earlier, and the evidence he gathered went further than any previous study in tracking the practice of pardoning over the previous twenty years.[72]

The Whigs had a trumpet of their own in the *Albany Evening Journal*, owned by party powerbroker Thurlow Weed, who devoted six columns of his paper to demolishing the Democrats' accusations of favoritism. The report combined extensive accounts of the cases in which Seward had granted pardons as well as retrospective statistics that set his use of discretion in the context of earlier governors' practice.[73] In January 1841, reelected governor, Seward entered these statistics on the public record. Seward used numbers to prove he was a more circumspect pardoner than any of the four governors who had preceded him—Clinton, Yates, Throop, and Marcy. "I have deemed it my duty to restrict the exercise of the pardoning power, within narrower limits than have been heretofore observed," he boasted.[74] Previous governors had confined their reports to their pardons of felons, but Seward totted up all acts of executive clemency, including their pardons for misdemeanors. Throop had, indeed, begun his governorship as a lean pardoner, granting only 88 acts of clemency in 1829. But Governor Marcy turned out to have been more generous a pardoner than he claimed. The number of pardons he issued in his first year in office, 1833, was double the number in Throop's first year. Seward also revealed that Marcy's use of his executive powers did not diminish over his governorship. According to the governor's numbers, Marcy pardoned a total of 158 convicts in 1838. Once Seward took office, his "narrower" limitations clamped this free flow of pardons into a trickle: 64 in 1839 and 85 in 1840. If anyone doubted his commitment to the faithful discharge of his executive duty to uphold the laws of the state, Seward, an opponent of the death penalty, reminded critics that nine of sixteen murderers sentenced to death in his first term had been executed, and that he had granted clemency to just three condemned men.[75]

Case-by-Case Discretion and the Death Penalty

When antebellum governors turned to numbers and taxonomies of pardon criteria in their public defense of executive discretion, they reached for a reasoned and principled impression of executive discretion that had not been necessary in George Clinton's and John Jay's day. In the late eighteenth and early nineteenth centuries, governors could face accusations of partisanship or favoritism but they faced no questions over their capacity, as white gentlemen, to combine sympathy and sound policy. The constitutional consideration of gubernatorial pardoning, the social scientific tests of discretionary justice, and the state's combative party politics in the 1830s created a climate in which executive power holders learned that expressions of sentiment could be politically costly, particularly when offenders faced the death penalty.

The assignment of the power to pardon in murder cases after the 1821 constitutional convention meant they generated the greatest desire on the part of governors to appear fair but firm. Whether he decided on the fate of a murderer or a minor offender, Governor Throop claimed he simply applied his decision-making formula; other factors clearly entered into his decisions, however. Throop's reports to the legislature regarding convicted murderers indicate he favored offenders who appeared to have turned a course toward moral rectitude. In one of his regular visits to Sing Sing State Prison in 1832, he was pleased to encounter the demure Eliza Comstock, whom he had reprieved from execution in 1830 for the murder of her husband.[76] At her trial in rural Steuben County, she claimed she had dosed the intemperate Mr. Comstock with arsenic to discourage him from drinking. The jury did not believe her, but Throop did, considering her "of good character but ignorant." Happily, Throop reported that after two years imprisonment at Auburn she had "submitted with patience and gratitude to what she considered punishment administered with justice and great mercy."[77]

Seward also acknowledged his sentiments, but he took care to link his feelings with his political and religious values. In his 1841 message in defense of his pardoning practice, Seward laid out a list of categories similar to Throop's and added several more, including cases in which inmates suffered from life-threatening illness, "and a small number in which the appeal for mercy was commended by the sex, the tender youth or extreme age of the prisoner." The miserly pardoner further admitted he granted clemency to individuals who had committed crimes under "mitigating circumstances" and criminals who had demonstrated evidence of "penitence and reformation."[78] Backed against a wall of recrimination over his alleged tenderheartedness, Seward asserted the validity of sympathy in pardoning by filtering it through reasoned categories of deservedness.

In the bear pit of legislative politics, the political arithmetic of pardon deliberations in capital cases attracted the most attention. After 1825, the year when nine men were hanged, the number of offenders put to death began to decline.[79] Legislators abolished public executions in 1836, and this move made many Democrats, as well as Whigs, hopeful that the state might abandon the death penalty outright.[80] Governors Throop and Seward, both public opponents of the death penalty, turned readily to execution statistics to reassure the public and their political opponents that they were prepared to discharge their duty to ensure that the laws of the state be enforced.[81] As they urged legislators to abolish capital punishment or at least restrict it to treason and premeditated murder, they allowed the hangman to continue his grim work.

Efforts to abolish the death penalty and criticism of gubernatorial pardoning converged in the early 1840s through the work of a select committee of the state legislature, which very nearly ended New York's use of capital punishment. In 1832 an earlier committee, encouraged by Governor Throop, advised that the death penalty be abolished, but its recommendation fizzled without leading to a vote.[82] Further defeats occurred in 1838 and 1839, when a subsequent committee recommended against abolition. A Whig majority in the assembly and senate at the start of Seward's second term in 1841, plus support from progressive Democrats such as John Louis O'Sullivan, who headed the committee, put the radical reform in sight. O'Sullivan, a lawyer and publisher of the *United States Democratic Review*, published and distributed the committee's exhaustive *Report in Favor of the Abolition of the Punishment of Death* in April 1841. Once again, it appeared that New York might become a world leader in penal reform.

On top of the study's numerous arguments against the death penalty, including jurors' reluctance to convict, the danger of false confessions, and the difficulty of assessing insanity, O'Sullivan's study underlined that "an essential part of the proposed reform" was the removal "from the hands of the Executive Chief Magistrate of the State of the power of pardon."[83] The abolition bill the committee later introduced lost by only six votes.[84] Out of this defeat the crusade continued on two new fronts, one statistical and the other constitutional: the establishment of the American Society for the Collection and Diffusion of Information in Relation to the Punishment of Death, formed in New York City in 1844, and the growing momentum for a revised constitution that would resolve the tension between manly mercy and evidence-based, council-administered pardoning.

Pardoning Compromised: The 1846 Constitutional Convention

Stirring judicial and legislative ingredients into executive discretion was just one of several new political recipes for pardoning reform offered up during the 1840s, thanks to the holding of the constitutional convention in 1846. The fourth constitutional convention called on delegates to consider the merits of the pardoning regime that had prevailed since 1822 and the possible benefits of its modification. Only one generation had passed since the last convention, but New Yorkers were eager to redraft the state's political blueprint.[85] Major changes to the judiciary were introduced, and further reforms gave the people greater say over those who governed them. An amendment to the procedures governing gubernatorial pardon was introduced as well, but it was largely cosmetic. The constitution New Yorkers adopted in 1846 left the governor's hand, if not also his heart, in discretionary justice.

Momentum in favor of a new constitution derived mainly from opposition to legislative taxing and spending powers and the determination to trust the selection of state and judicial officers to the people, twin elements in what Peter J. Galie refers to as New York's "democratic revolution."[86] The most radically inclined delegates in 1846 hoped to extend the vote to women and affiliates of the Liberty Party, and abolitionists in both major parties pressed for African American men's right to vote, on par with white men.[87] Growing tension between New York's landlords and tenants also prompted the holding of the convention.[88] After decades of protest, the balance of power began to tilt in favor of those who tilled the land, and the new constitution ultimately abolished "all feudal tenures of every description."[89]

Delegates who challenged the scope of power in the executive office were equally ambitious. In keeping with other state constitutional conventions of this period, several members of the committee assigned to consider the "power and duties of the Governor" attempted to divide executive power between departments and office holders. Starting in the mid-19th century, as James A. Henretta notes, the revision of constitutions in most states eroded governors' "focused and coherent executive power."[90] At the New York constitutional convention of 1846, delegates who promoted shared models of pardoning tried to do the same thing but failed; despite the efforts of critics such as Francis Lieber and John O'Sullivan, New York did not fall into line with the emerging trend of divesting the chief executive's prerogative to pardon. Far from "point[ing] toward emerging principles in American constitutional thought," New York's constitutional delegates merely tempered executive discretionary powers.[91] The emerging administrative principle of delegated power became a lost cause for close to a century.

Divisions between and within the states' political parties over parochial and national issues largely account for New York's preservation of a strong executive in charge of pardoning. Although women and African Americans were ineligible to participate in the convention,[92] delegates represented a cross-section of white male New Yorkers, from the mechanics of New York City and the middling farmers of the rural regions in the north and west to wealthy merchants and leading legal figures. No tenants participated, but thirteen delegates who defected from the Whig Party represented the new Anti-Rent Party, formed in 1845 and a political force in its own right by the 1846 election.[93] Democrats dominated the floor, but they were split between Hunkers and Barnburners, with Tammany Hall the backer of most of the New York City delegates. The Whigs were no more united, with conservatives and radicals in their camp siding with Democrats over single issues, including the authority of the governor's constitutional authority to pardon.[94] These slippery alliances and the convention's focus on unchecked legislative power conspired against the attempt to hobble the chief executive's power.

To read the reformers' defeat as inevitable would underplay the passion of their cause and the strength of their convictions. Commanding figures presented compelling arguments in support of decentralized pardoning procedure once the committee assigned to review the "powers and duties of the Executive" set to work.[95] The chairman was a radical Democrat and future state attorney general, Levi Star Chatfield, who had publicly declared his sympathy for the cause of the anti-renters as well as his support for equal black suffrage.[96] Allied with fellow Barnburner Michael Hoffman, Chatfield pressed for an amendment to grant the legislature power to set laws to regulate pardoning.[97] Another influential player was George A. Simmons, a progressive Whig, who later chaired the House Committee on the Judiciary as a congressman. He was the voice of Lieber at the convention, and he offered an alternative that would preserve the existing division of executive power but distribute it among decision makers. Simmons agreed it was time to "prescribe general restrictions and limitations on the pardoning power" so that juries would be less tempted to render verdicts in anticipation of a lax or harsh governor's action; however, he strongly preferred that an executive council, not the legislature, replace independent gubernatorial authority. The New England states used this model, and Simmons thought New York could adopt an advisory board to operate like a court of equity: "Let it consist of the heads of departments . . . and let the Governor consult with them in all cases of pardon." For both men the prevailing model of executive discretionary justice had to go, a prospect that inspired four days of debate.[98]

None of the thirty men who participated in the pardon deliberations envisioned eliminating discretionary justice. The most conservative, such as James Tallmadge Jr., age sixty-eight, one of the oldest delegates, and the only one to have participated in the 1821 convention, predictably held that pardoning authority ought to remain exactly where he had helped to lodge it: in the office of governor. True, some officeholders had handled their power "indiscreetly" (he offered no names), but it was better to "put up with occasional indiscretions than to place embarrassing or prohibitory restraints upon its exercise or to interfere with the proper jurisdiction of the Executive."[99] Another assembly veteran, Whig Robert C. Nicholas, shared the elder statesman's views. If power had been abused, he believed "it was simply from a mistaken feeling of kindness" on the part of governors. Were a board or council to replace the governor, it would "divide this responsibility between individuals." Nicholas warned that distributing the pardon power to many men, rather than one, would lead responsibility to be "frittered away." A prominent Buffalo attorney and judge, Horatio J. Stow, came up with a similar equation: "divide the responsibility, and it would be nowhere."[100]

Defenders of the one-man power included younger men, and they came in multiple political stripes. Lorenzo B. Shepard was a rising star among New York City Democrats, and one of the most avid orators on the pardon power.

At twenty-six years of age, he was young enough to be Tallmadge's grandson, and his youth may have emboldened him to propose the opening amendment to the 1821 constitution. Rather than fragment the governor's power, he believed the new constitution should enhance it by granting the chief executive the authority to pardon "in such manner, on such terms, and under such restrictions as he may think proper." Like his elders, he regarded pardoning as an intrinsically personal attribute: the "ear of the Executive should always be open to petitions and applications for pardon," and the power to grant them was best "deposited in his hands."[101]

In the debates of 1846 concerning the pardon power, unlike those aired in 1821, there were no clear winners. The push for greater regulation and oversight of discretionary justice was met by arguments that pulled in favor of pardoning's personal qualities. In the end, the executive committee landed on a compromise. The majority of delegates agreed that greater transparency in the decision-making process would reduce the impression, if not also the prospect, of unjust pardoning, but they took some time to reach that conclusion. John Louis Stephens, a Tammany man with many allies among the Whigs (including William H. Seward), proposed that "no reprieve, pardon or commutation shall be granted except notice of the application therefore, with the grounds or reasons thereof, and the names of the applicants be given for two weeks prior to such application, in such manner as the Legislature shall determine." Not unlike the publication of wedding banns, the announcement of a prospective pardon was meant to bring the matter before "the bar of public opinion," and to flush out possible objections. Publicizing the names of petitioners would also prevent "men of respectability" from signing petitions. In Stephens's opinion, "the secrecy in which the whole is done invites and encourages recklessness"; conversely, the open operation of discretion would leave every pardon vulnerable to challenge.[102]

Most delegates balked at Stephens's proposal: some thought the proposed reporting requirement would drive petitioning underground and increase the possibility of corruption; others anticipated it would drastically reduce access to compensatory justice. One of the most liberal-minded delegates, Ansel Bascom, worried that subjecting pardon applications to review and publicity would become a "rule to show cause why the pardoning power should not be exercised." And Michael Hoffman grumbled that reporting reasons would provide no means to make the practice of pardoning more democratic. "After [the governor] had exercised the power [to pardon] of what use would it be to call on him, except to get up a newspaper discussion about it?"[103]

Resistance to the greater openness of pardoning led to a blend of Shepard's and Stephens's proposals, which left pardoning in the governor's hands to be exercised as he thought "proper," but subject "to such regulation as may be provided by law relative to the manner of applying for pardons."[104] The committee ended up deciding that governors must annually report the name of each convict pardoned, reprieved, or granted a commuted sentence. The adopted amendment stopped short of compelling the chief executive to declare why he had pardoned, and it rejected Simmons's proposed pardon council. The legacy of the third constitution was long (each subsequent constitution has retained this clause), but its political import was immediate and potent. The retention of the one-man power, vested with added legislative circumspection, set up a test no delegate in 1846 could have overlooked: the prospect that imprisoned anti-rent protestors might be pardoned by the incoming governor.

The Anti-Rent Crisis and the One-Man Pardon

When manorial tenants of the late eighteenth century refused to pay their rent and disguised themselves as they set landlords' property alight, they were difficult to distinguish from the Sons of Liberty, the rebellious colonists who fitted themselves out as "savages" when they dumped tea into Boston Harbor to protest against unfair taxation. In playing at being Indians, they exploited a form of licensed misrule that lent a flavor of authenticity to anti-authoritarian protest.[105] By the 1830s a distant imperial government was no longer the tyrannous authority against which rights-seeking protestors struggled. From the Revolution onward the governor and the legislature had supported the state's landlords and suppressed insubordinate tenants, but sympathetic juries repeatedly stymied efforts to prosecute rebels. By the antebellum era anti-renters' grievances found powerful and more respectable supporters ready to promote their cause.[106] Agitation against "feudal vassalage" funneled its way into legal challenges, constitutional lobbying, and the formation of a political party, and its violent strain became explosive.[107]

In 1839, Governor Seward, hardly the picture of a military leader and a man openly sympathetic to anti-renters' grievances, resorted to General Clinton's tactics by ordering the militia to subdue tenants' protests, which had overwhelmed civil authorities. Seward worked with apprehended leaders, trying to convince them to renounce violence and cooperate with a commission he established to reach a peaceful solution. Five years on, with little to show for their patience, radical malcontents decided that violent action conveyed a clearer political message than legislative petitions. In December 1844, hundreds of men, many disguised as Indians, intimidated and attacked a sheriff, and at two rallies later that month anger and hotheadedness led to three

ANTI-RENTERS STOPPING A SHERIFF.

Anti-renters lying in wait. Source: New York Public Library, image 809195, retrieved from http://digitalcollections.nypl.org.

deaths. The scale of the insurrection, which threatened to engulf the state, produced a consensus, even among anti-rent sympathizers, that "the reign of violence and homicide in the manor counties must be put down," and that those involved in its "'Indian' operations" must be punished. At this moment of violent lawlessness, mercy appeared out of the question.[108]

With Democrat Governor Silas Wright at the executive helm, the state began its first round of successful prosecutions of violent anti-renters in 1845. Hundreds of protestors were rounded up, and the shooting death of a sheriff serving a tenant with orders to pay overdue rent in the summer led to a further crackdown and the arrest of a man called Big Thunder, the faux Indian nom de guerre chosen by anti-rent leader Smith Boughton. A jury convicted him of highway robbery for his interference with the serving of official papers, and two more "Indians" were found guilty of the sheriff's murder. Wright allowed Boughton's life sentence to stand, but he considered it wise to reprieve the condemned murderers and commute their sentences to life imprisonment (militants' threats to burn down villages may have concentrated his mind). From this point forward, Wright refused to concede further ground for the relief of these inmates, or the scores of others who faced harsh sentences after hasty trials.

Before long, this picture of rushed and rough justice began to transform widespread contempt for the rioters into sympathy for the imprisoned felons, many of whom appeared to have been convicted simply for associating with protestors. The governor's intransigence in light of this apparent injustice led anti-rent senators to introduce a proposal in May 1846 that would have replaced executive pardoning with legislative pardoning. William H. Vanschoonhoven, a state senator and one of the proposal's sponsors, who later became a delegate, continued to urge this change during the convention, without success.[109] Neither the new constitution nor the legislature had managed to come up with a means to undo the harshness of the crackdown, but the state election set up a different prospect for relief. The people voted Democrat Silas Wright out of office and Whig John Young was voted in.

Governor Young made no secret of his sympathy for the anti-renters' cause, and some historians contend that he secured the governorship by promising anti-renters he would pardon the prisoners in exchange for electoral support.[110] Contemporaries had good reason to question Young's denial of this charge, since one of his first acts in office was to pardon eighteen protestors convicted on felony charges. "No occasion has before occurred when the Executive authority was solicited by so many citizens to extend all at once the forgiveness of the State so fully to so many of such offenders," Young began his loquacious proclamation. A pardon petition signed by eleven thousand

New Yorkers convinced him that "only a vindictive administration would deny a pardon now." Pardoning violent insurrectionists who had defied the law and killed innocent people risked making a mockery of justice, Young conceded. These men had wrongly "bid defiance to the law," and their prosecution and convictions had vindicated and affirmed law's "majesty." But it was time now for a grand act of sovereign mercy to defuse sympathy for the rebels by releasing the movement's martyrs, and to restore public tranquility. With a nod to Alexander Hamilton's writings on the utility of executive discretion, the proclamation of 6,553 words declared: "it should never be forgotten that it is not severity alone in the administration of justice that secures the fidelity of the People to the Government. But that mercy, when it can properly be exercised, is even more effectual."[111]

The climax of the anti-rent wars in the mid-1840s was the largest and longest-standing agrarian protest movement of the day, and the pardon of the imprisoned combatants flashed across the country's wire services. Young's enemies, mainly carping Democrats, turned the high number of pardoned men, some of them murderers, into a different kind of political arithmetic when they claimed it proved the Whig governor danced to the tune of riotous villains.[112] Within Young's party, critics of the blanket pardon were no kinder, and the governor failed to attract Whig endorsement at the next election.[113] Historians of New York's anti-rent movement have focused on its relevance to contests over property, the shifting definitions of legitimate protest, and the significance of white male producerism in antebellum notions of citizenship. However, Big Thunder and his lesser-known cohort of prisoners likely read Young's pardons differently once they were free to return to their homes and families.[114]

Conclusion

The pardon of the imprisoned anti-renters, like Governor Yates's pardon of inmates locked in Auburn's solitary cells in 1823, dramatized what many delegates to the constitutional conventions asserted, namely that one man, acting through the authority of executive office, could undo injustice wrought by many men, and he would face responsibility for his decision. In addition to the pardon power, the chief executive retained his authority to order the militia to act, and to appoint special prosecutors. His sovereign power of life and death linked the pardon at the mid-nineteenth century to its ancient antecedents, notwithstanding the opportunities presented at the 1821 and 1846 constitutional conventions to consign it to the past. The third constitution removed the executive's patronage privilege by making most appointive offices elective, but it left the governor's authority to grant mercy intact.[115]

What must the real Indians of New York have made of the anti-renters' outlandish dress and their unapologetic claim to ownership of the land they tilled? The state's true native people felt the sharpest edge of state sovereignty through rulings that refused to recognize the various tribes as independent nations, casting them instead as citizens "owing allegiance to the state government; subject to its laws and entitled to its protection as such citizens."[116] Similarly, the seventy-one convicted murderers hanged between 1822 and 1846, mere statistics in governors' messages to the legislature, paid the ultimate price to confirm that chief executives, including abolitionists, were not too tenderhearted to govern.[117] No prisoner thought him- or herself a statistic when crafting a plea for mercy. Convicted offenders and their supporters sought the beneficent face of sovereignty, and a few, like the redeemed murderer Eliza Comstock, appeared to touch the governor's heart. But social scientific probes and political sniping made governors appreciate the risks of pardoning on sentimental impulse. By the mid-nineteenth century, executive discretion became a minefield of political arithmetic, even as it remained a deeply personal practice.

Constitutional reform of the pardon power ended with the Third Constitution, but this did not spell the end to the prominence of discretionary justice on New York's political agenda. Over the following decades, debate over discretionary justice took new routes and different forms, with the Prison Association of New York adding its voice by the mid-1840s. Efforts continued to proffer alternatives to the one-man pardon, but individuals such as Francis Lieber began to work with the association to gather more persuasive proof that gubernatorial discretion must give way to the tide of democratic republicanism. New York was unwilling to part with its reliance upon executive authority at the following constitutional convention in 1867, but it was prepared to lead the nation in the discretionary release of prisoners through reformatory management. The uprooting of the pardon was unnecessary for the seeds of parole to be sown in mid-nineteenth-century New York.

4

The Pardon and the Progenesis of Parole in the Mid-Nineteenth Century

From the early days of the republic, New York's highest-ranking judges inspected prisons periodically on top of their court duties. In 1844 the judge who sentenced anti-rent leader Big Thunder to life imprisonment visited Sing Sing State Prison for the official purpose of informing the state government on its management.[1] John W. Edmonds left the prison shaken, feeling not unlike Governor Yates after he witnessed the condition of prisoners held in solitary at Auburn in 1823. The use of the lash at Sing Sing to punish inmates was rife by the 1840s, and Edmonds considered the warden's regime admittedly cruel.[2] Unlike governors, the judge could not pardon inmates, but his authority did give him the right to recommend that the warden be sacked and his iron rule replaced by a system "mild, humane and just."[3] Edmonds was equally troubled over the fate of prisoners after their release. If prison management were improved inmates could develop habits of industry and learn to tame their criminal propensities, but such gains would wither in a world of hostility and temptation. Edmonds swung into action. Within weeks of his Sing Sing visit he gathered like-minded gentleman who pledged to help him establish an organization "to aid discharged prisoners in their efforts at leading honest lives." The Prison Association of New York (PANY), incorporated in 1846, earned the state's blessing to provide "support and encouragement" to male and female ex-convicts who appeared to be "sincerely penitent."[4]

The members of the Prison Association never doubted the impact they made on the development of parole and indeterminate sentencing in New York and the nation. Despite its significant role in promoting these modern administrative modes of discretionary justice, PANY occupies a hazy place in penal historiography.[5] From the mid-1840s PANY assisted discharged prisoners and participated in their post-incarceration supervision three decades before the Elmira Reformatory opened in 1876, with its internally managed system of graduated release and post-release monitoring.[6] Early experiments with parole in Australia and Ireland were critical to New York's investment in the reformatory, as most histories of penology stress, but the association's early work with released prisoners laid the groundwork for extramural supervision and support to complement institutional reform. The yearning for

manly independence and full citizenship, the ideals that lent anti-rent rhetoric credibility, was the same spirit that PANY hoped to instill in discharged
prisoners.[7] Making men of convicts was the principal goal, but the association
also attempted to aid female ex-prisoners by forming a "female department."[8]
These efforts undergirded the separate-prisons-for-women movement and
the masculine citizen-building rationale of male reformatories, which gained
support over the 1870s. Edmonds's Association opened up a new field of discretionary justice, forming a bridge between earlier benevolent agencies' aid
to indigent and friendless ex-prisoners and "fallen" women and the state-
administered parole system it helped to foster.

PANY's discharged prisoner work, advertised through heart-tugging
stories of lives turned around, opened donors' wallets, and its research on
discretionary release added fresh grist to the anti-pardon mill, still grinding
away twenty years after the 1846 Convention, which introduced only modest checks on the governor's free and expansive power to pardon. In 1849
the Whig-dominated legislature made a further attempt to render pardoning
more accountable, but its effort came to naught, despite Governor Hamilton
Fish's commitment to make it work. Francis Lieber became a gadfly in deliberations over discretionary justice in New York after he joined PANY as a
corresponding member in 1845. Endorsed by the association and backed by
its resources, Lieber designed a survey in 1865 and polled ex-governors on
their use of their pardoning powers. The evidence he gathered of gubernatorial ambivalence over their duties, combined with statistics showing wide
disparities in pardon practice, made PANY confident it could demolish the
one-man power at the 1867 constitutional convention. But it misread the
moment. The committee responsible for evaluating the pardon power concluded that constitutional change would impede rather than enhance justice.
As late as the 1860s, supporters of existing practice, liberals as well as conservatives, still referred to the uniquely personal qualities of the governor's
ear. Even Francis Lieber, who drafted President Lincoln's code of war in 1862,
grudgingly acknowledged that the personal touch must occasionally correct
injustice.

The governor's pardon, administrative discretionary release, and ex-
prisoner supervision became entangled in the mid-nineteenth-century as the
rudiments of parole first took form in New York. Heroic histories of parole
written in the Progressive Era and more recent critical histories of disciplinary
"net widening" provide insufficient room for historical figures' ambivalent,
uneasy navigation between traditional and emergent modes of discretionary release.[9] Discipline after discharge did not supplant sovereign power, as
many histories of parole claim, and secular notions of citizenship did not

shunt aside religious support and moral surveillance. Recent scholarship on the "theological residue" in the modern state underlines that secular agencies, such as PANY, believed firmly in sin, forgiveness, and redemption. Those beliefs, which informed expectations of ex-convicts' behavior and defined their nonconformity in the 1840s, lingered into the reformatory era.[10] To trace the path to modern regimes of citizenship building based on inspection, surveillance, and normalization we must start with PANY's discharged prisoner program. And to understand the organization's support for state-authorized parole and indeterminate sentencing we must consider PANY's frustration, which intensified over the 1850s and '60s, over its limited authority to enforce conditions of release. The cracks and faults in epistemic shifts in governance and the overlap between gubernatorial and administrative modes of discretion become visible once we zoom in on the progenesis of parole in New York over the early to mid-nineteenth century.[11]

Penitential Discharge: Precedents for PANY's Ex-Prisoner Program

The original promoters of imprisonment over pain and death gave surprisingly little thought to the fate of discharged prisoners. When the Boston Prison Discipline Society began its operations in 1825, it expended most of its energy debating the Philadelphia Society for the Alleviation of Public Misery (founded in 1787) over the advantages of the congregate Auburn plan versus the Pennsylvania system of separate imprisonment.[12] The societies sparred over the rival systems' recidivism rates and the proportion of prisoners pardoned versus those released at the expiration of their sentences, but they considered post-incarceration welfare a matter for charity work and poor relief, as well as for the religious organizations involved in chaplaincy and prison-gate missions. By the 1840s, it appeared that such assistance was no longer adequate. In Manhattan alone the number of people released from prison overwhelmed the capacity of churches and benevolent organizations to assist. As Judge Edmonds walked the city streets he observed that "convicted felons, without money, without character, without employment, and without friends, except among the vicious" were "pouring out upon the city." Unless they acquired upright and encouraging friends, he feared their numbers would increase and they would be "left to prey upon the community." Another gentleman who attended the Prison Association's inaugural meeting used a similar metaphor to identify "the skill which can set from the rubbish of evil habit and association, the buried, but not lifeless, energies of goodness." Pollution and purification imagery replicated contemporary moves to treat waste and to sanitize disease-bearing effluent from noxious industries in a time of rapid industrialization and high immigration. Society had a responsibility to assist former prisoners just as it had a vital interest in treating waste wisely.[13]

The gentlemen who began to treat the problem of discharged prisoners in the 1840s saw themselves as innovators who carried a torch lit by earlier visionaries, such as England's John Howard, and tended by subsequent philanthropists. The association's officers thought it wise to keep up with developments in Europe (generally recognized as the leading locus of innovation in the mid-19th century); at the same time they sought inspiration from American precursors. In 1803, while serving as mayor of New York City, Edward Livingston had attempted to reduce crime by providing assistance to people "capable of supporting themselves." Among those who found it difficult to secure employment Livingston included "'discharged or pardoned convicts from the State Prison.'" As mayor, he considered Newgate an improvement over the "bloody code with all its horrors," but its establishment ought not allow society to "'repel'" released prisoners "'from its bosom.'"[14] Livingston referred this advice to the Humane Society of New York, which formed in 1803, and over the following four decades similar charitable and reform organizations engaged in intra- and extramural work with offenders, beginning with youth in the state's biggest city.

Philanthropic efforts to assist and control urban juveniles provided another precedent for PANY's mandate. Two decades earlier the Society for the Prevention of Pauperism set off on a mission to rescue and reform minors, and it formed the New York Society for the Reformation of Juvenile Delinquents in 1822 to lobby for a refuge to accomplish its work. Opened in 1825, New York's House of Refuge for children with criminal convictions or those considered wayward, provided bed and board, rudimentary education, and gender-based work training. It also sought employers for released inmates— mistresses in need of domestic servants and tradesmen in need of laborers and apprentices. In the early national period the "shadow of patriarchal authority" characterized the aid elites imposed on their charges, and it lingered in PANY's proposal to regulate freed prisoners.[15] An expanded system for adults, administered through an incorporated organization, would be original; however, "preserving order and enforcing obedience" was "nothing new," as Edmonds reassured donors. PANY would take charge of those who had failed to govern themselves, whether children or adults, women or men, and impose upon them "the principles upon which our families and our country are governed."[16]

The precedents for PANY's discharged prisoner initiative ranged beyond the sources they identified, particularly race-specific attempts to mold Indians and ex-slaves into citizens. Removal was a policy that offshored the challenge of incorporating individuals who were free but not wholly citizens on account of their race. New York was one of the first states to relocate native people living within the state's borders, and many of its leading citizens supported the African colonization movement, which took off in the late 1810s.[17] Other attempts to manage the multiracial state more directly informed PANY's programs with prisoners discharged from the state's prisons. These programs tried to assimilate indigenous peoples and to prepare free blacks for the demands of citizenship, even though they were barred from the rights and responsibilities of white males. New York's Manumission Society previewed the techniques later used to train children in the House of Refuge when it established an African Free School in the City of New York in 1787. To counter prevailing prejudices against the growing ranks of freed blacks, thought to be inclined toward vice and crime, the school provided basic education and strict moral instruction to instill habits of industry and the capacity for self-support.[18]

Protestant missions in Indian territory followed a similar path to citizenship building, which would become PANY's chief goal in dealing with discharged prisoners. Although religious conversion was a prime objective for most missionaries (with many converts gained during the so-called Great Awakening of the late eighteenth century), they also provided instruction in farming, trades, and domestic craft, all skills necessary to thrive in an alien culture based on private property and a gender division of public and private life. Progressive missionaries stood up for the rights of native peoples against land developers' aggressive attempts to appropriate their lands by law or deception, but nonbelievers, such as Red Jacket, refused to adopt Christian beliefs or customs even when they came with material aid. Similarly, black graduates of the African Free School objected to the curriculum and management style of white educators by the late 1820s, and they pushed for modifications on their own terms.[19] But these stories of resistance and rejection were not the ones featured in associational annual reports. Philanthropists, ever dependent on benefactors' support, preferred to craft tales of aid well used by charges who demonstrated their capacity to end their dependence on charity and their readiness to obey the laws of society.

Compared to missionaries' assimilationist efforts, PANY's program entailed a more secular approach to the preparation of former prisoners for freedom after incarceration. Nevertheless, the committee it formed to oversee discharged prisoners adhered to a biblical script of correction that bid criminals to "go and sin no more." From the first days of the penitentiary, clerics had ministered to offenders to gird them against the temptations and evil associations that lay beyond the prison's walls. Formal religious services and Sabbath schools were supplemented in New York's largest institutions with chaplaincy programs, and students of prison discipline agreed that clerics of impeccable character were essential to guide sinners toward the straight path of conformity to the laws of God and man. When Governor Seward learned that Sing Sing's governance was sliding into a regime of terror, he turned to its Methodist minister, the Reverend John Luckey, to restore the prison to "the principles of Christianity," namely imprisonment as an opportunity for repentance and correction.[20] Luckey saw no distinction between his sense of calling and his professional and personal interest in prisoner welfare. Writing in 1860, he recounted the story of a young convict whose sentence of ten years was about to expire in 1840. Because the "reformed orphan" confessed his sins to Luckey with "tears of contrition," he brought the offender to his own home after he served his full sentence in order "to renew his strength." With Luckey's letter of reference in hand, the repentant criminal sent back letters that described the trials he had faced and overcome.

Had a governor pardoned the prisoner "on the ground of his extreme youth and good conduct," this happy ending would never have occurred, according Luckey. He claimed that the prisoner had told him he was happy the governor had refused to grant him mercy: "'Had I been pardoned, I should, no doubt, have returned to my former course of crime and probably expired on the gallows, and sunk my soul in torment.'"[21] The Prison Association founders shared Luckey's belief that pardons obstructed efforts to build up prisoners' moral resilience, but they doubted that chaplains' ministrations and their efforts to inspire religious awakening could provide anadequate means treat penitential discharge on an industrial scale. Inspired by these precursors and mindful of these concerns, PANY forged ahead in 1844 by establishing a Committee on Discharged Prisoners, headed by a Quaker.

The Gender Agenda of Discharge Management

Isaac Hopper, PANY's first agent in charge of discharged prisoners, had worked in the earlier streams of moral reform and citizenship, which made him a suitable candidate for the new position. Born in 1771 into a Quaker family, he spent his formative years in Philadelphia, where he assisted runaway slaves, both informally and through the lobbying power of the city's Abolition Society. After he helped establish free schooling for blacks in Philadelphia, Hopper moved into the field of criminal justice, first by providing poor relief and then by inspecting public prisons. Working through the Society of Friends, his charitable inclinations extended to native Indian welfare. But a schism with more orthodox Quakers led him to New York in 1829, where he continued to provide shelter to escaped slaves, including some guilty of crimes, and this work contributed to his disownment by the Friends in 1842. Judge Edmonds's 1844 circular to persons interested in forming a prison discipline society came at an opportune point for Hopper, who had just been burned a second time in religious squabbles. Despite his advanced age, he rose to the challenge PANY set him: to take charge of ex-prisoners, both males and females, and mainly individuals who had resettled in and around Manhattan. Who better than a sixty-four-year-old Quaker who had fathered sixteen children in two marriages to pledge that "fatherly reproof, and friendly advice, and encouragement" would transform "delinquents" into "useful and honored members of society"?[22]

With Hopper as its "agent," PANY's Committee on Discharged Prisoners instituted New York's first statewide and state-endorsed release management program for adult females and males, decades before standard accounts of parole date its founding.[23] Although male prisoners greatly outnumbered females, who made up only a small fraction of New York's several thousand prisoners by the 1840s, gender distinctions were paramount in mid-nineteenth-century understandings of criminality, correction, and, as it followed, the programs devised to monitor their release and reintegration.[24] In prison, men were called keepers, officers, and agents, and they were employed to maintain order, to enforce discipline, and to oversee work assignments, which included a wide range of industrial operations in the largest state prisons. The women who supervised female inmates in the "female departments" of Auburn and Sing Sing were called matrons. This title indicated seniority, but it also carried associations with domestic training and medical care, which PANY deemed necessary to train former female prisoners how to cook, wash, clean, spin, and sew. These distinctions were reinforced when it named its New York City headquarters an "office" for the placement of male ex-prisoners. For females, PANY set up a "home."[25]

In a state that denied women the right to vote, despite the attempt to extend the franchise through constitutional change in the 1846 convention, PANY managed the release of female lawbreakers without anticipating their transformation into self-governing citizens. The Committee on Discharged Prisoners repeated its mission like an incantation in its early annual reports: to secure liberated prisoners from "the temptations of want" and to "afford them the means of earning an honest livelihood." This goal did not distinguish between men and women, but it went without saying that the sexes faced distinct forms of hostility as well as temptation. Consequently, the Association's executive set up two separate departments for ex-prisoners, in which Hopper had charge of the men and a committee of ladies (including his daughter, Abby) assumed responsibility for the women.[26]

Decisions concerning PANY's effort to help convicted criminals find work and housing were driven primarily by masculinist precepts. Beginning in the 1830s, organized mechanics protested the development of state prison industries at Auburn and Sing Sing and the exploitive contract labor system, which provided huge profits for private manufacturers at the expense of free labor. The training of criminals in trades that improved their prospects of employment on release was equally galling in the eyes of organized workers. In 1842, the *New York State Mechanic* weighed in on the dispute over the merits of the Philadelphia system versus the Auburn system and blasted New York's use of congregate labor. The *Mechanic* had men like Luckey in mind when it decried the "short-sighted philanthropists who would convert our prisons into seminaries of prisoners." Punishment was meant to strike terror into wrongdoers, not to boost them above honest and industrious laborers in a competitive labor market.[27] The Committee on Discharged Prisoners countered that the male ex-prisoner was society's prodigal son, bearing the "brand of *criminal* . . . still upon his brow."[28] To leave such a man on his own, tempted through poverty to commit crime, was shortsighted, whereas helping him earn his wage through work, enough to support himself and his dependents, made a man of a former prisoner, just as wage labor was meant to make "men" of Indians and former slaves.

Isaac Hopper's office concentrated on equipping male ex-convicts for self-reliance, while the female department operated its "home." Notably, the work of PANY's home for discharged women faced no equivalent organized antagonism to its ministrations. Instead, the female department identified a different public relations hurdle: the broad moral consensus that all female criminals were "fallen." "When a woman is discharged, penniless, or with a few shillings in her pocket, her almost inevitable fate is a return to vice, unless some asylum be at hand for her rescue."[29] To a significant degree, the matrons agreed with the public, since they viewed female ex-prisoners through the lens of sexual immorality and pollution—reclaimable, but more easily and indelibly stained than males. This challenge could be overcome only though strict maternal governance in a homelike setting modeled on "that best of all moral schools, the humane and religious private family."[30] In this respect, female former felons, along with minor offenders released from New York's City Prison and Blackwell's Island Penitentiary, were subjected to the same level of scrutiny applied to their juvenile counterparts in the House of Refuge. However, women discharged from the state's prisons were not compelled to remain; indeed, they faced expulsion if they violated house rules. Until or unless they were assigned to mistresses and masters, residents of the home had to work for their upkeep, and matrons allowed them to remain unless they were disobedient or quarrelsome. "The Home is quite an undesirable a place to bad subjects," the 1850 report declared with some pride.[31] The executive members of the female department were far happier to report that it found "situations" for the majority of its women, by which they meant service positions in respectable homes.

Hopper's accounts of his work with male ex-prisoners followed a different narrative, with manly independence the desired outcome. Using anecdotal evidence to color his summary statistics, he stressed the practical assistance he provided discharged prisoners to become self-supporting. Hopper warmly described the reformation of criminals such as "S____," a young man who had committed grand larceny after falling in with "persons of dissolute character." Prison officers referred him to PANY's office, where he received shoemaking tools after his release. The man later told Hopper that he "supports comfortably by his industry, an aged mother and two sisters." Hopper's office provided men clothes "of a kind that will not attract attention, and point them out as convicts," and it also paid their board if they had no home to go to until they could earn their own keep. One man received a horse and cart; some were given tools for carpentry and smithing; another received a loan to establish a coopering business, and this man's "close attention to business" eventually allowed him to employ several hands. Stonecutting tools from Hopper's office led to another man's smooth transition from prison to wage labor after he had served twenty years in Sing Sing prison for a second offense. "'If I had found such friends when I was first discharged from prison,'" the stonecutter reportedly told Hopper, "'I should not have been there a second time.'"[32]

In the seventh year of its operations, PANY decided it was time to review the work conducted by the office and the home since 1845, and its summary report confirmed that two different missions had emerged. The men's and women's departments both struggled to cope with the discharge from New York's burgeoning prison population, especially in New York City, but they approached this challenge according to different scripts of criminality and correction.[33] Over PANY's first seven years, it "disposed" of 1,854 cases: 977 men and 877 women. Of the men, Hopper reported that 795 were "doing well" or "hopeful." The female department provided more detailed statistics of work placements and moral lapses. The staff found situations for 312 women and reported that a further 35 secured places on their own; less favorably, 24 women were dismissed for "improper conduct" and 114 had returned to "evil courses."[34] Fortunately, no woman had committed a major crime (compared to the nineteen men who ended up back in prison), and a mere handful had committed minor offenses. The home's referrals of women to hospitals, mental asylums, and the Magdalen Home in New York City expressed the matrons' intensive care, training, and moral screening of women, in contrast to the practical aid and support the men's office provided.

As the female department's confidence in its maternalistic model of governance grew, the women in charge of its work came to see that they were subservient to PANY's all-male executive. Ironically, the work of transforming fallen women into morally upright domestics inspired the female department's executive members to rebel against their "parent" organization.[35] In 1853, the year after Isaac Hopper died, Abby Hopper Gibbons led her fellow female department members away from the association her father had helped to found. Once independent they formed the autonomous Women's Prison Association, a bold move that touched off the movement for the separation of female prisoners in purpose-built reformatories.[36] Simultaneously, the women's departure turned PANY into a more expressly masculinist association. Echoing the antislavery slogan, "Am I not a man and a brother?," PANY redoubled its effort over the 1850s and '60s to convince the public that "the convict was a man still."[37]

PANY's Uneasy Relationship with the Pardon

Neither PANY's parables of penitence and industry nor the Committee on Discharged Prisoners' glowing accounts of success should be taken as gospel. Could an octogenarian agent realistically have aided 977 men, let alone kept track of them? The association's bylaws required Hopper to correspond as its agent with prison superintendents "relative to the character and trades of prisoners, and to ascertain previous to the discharge of each prisoner, his feelings, views and capabilities, with a view to making the best arrangements for his future employment." In addition, PANY expected its agent to correspond with employers, keep a record of work assignments, and maintain contact with discharged prisoners. Little wonder, then, that its 1852 review of discharged prisoners acknowledged that the fate of 348 former convicts was "unknown." PANY never contemplated folding its tent, however. On the contrary, it was proud of its cost-effective and humane means of reducing recidivism. Although it continued to struggle against prison superintendents, who resisted the association's attempts to expose evidence of cruelty and mismanagement in the state's penal institutions, PANY had a relatively free hand to run its discharged prisoner program so long as its donors approved of and supported its work.

Under the authority the state granted PANY through its incorporation in 1846, the executive provided advice to the government concerning criminal justice policy, including the care of prisoners after their release. The Committee on Prison Discipline's pardon branch was the companion to the Committee on Discharged Prisoners: the former compiled evidence to attack a long-standing means of prisoner release, and the latter gathered records to prove the superiority of pre-release screening and post-release supervision. The legislature listened. In 1849 and in 1858, new regulations were introduced to govern the granting of pardons by making governors more circumspect in the use of their clemency powers. If PANY could revamp benevolent aid into an "organized systematic method of reaching the convict with elevating remedial influences," then surely executive discretion could be conducted according to the same principles.

From its inception, the Prison Association took a nation-leading role in condemning the executive pardoning privilege, and it was keen to welcome Francis Lieber's assistance. With a year of PANY's founding (and no doubt hoping to enhance its bid for incorporation) it listed a stellar cast of penal theorists and reformers as its "corresponding members," both national authorities and men from England, Prussia, Switzerland, France, and Russia.[38] Lieber was most likely the man who drafted PANY's first public statement against gubernatorial pardoning, since it followed, word-for-word, one of the extended editorial notes in his 1833 translation of Beaumont and Tocqueville's prison study. By 1846, Lieber began to supplement his earlier philosophical pronouncements with nationwide statistics, compiled through PANY's research on prison sentences versus time actually served, and the proportion of pardons to convicts. This supplementary evidence revealed that New York's governors had pardoned inmates in New York's Sing Sing and Auburn State Prisons at about the national average (of 22.03 percent). But since New York's prisons held the largest number of prisoners, the state's governors had to deal with the largest pool of pardon applicants serving time for offences as minor as small fines all the way up to murder.

More troubling to Lieber was evidence that the "greater the crime, the more certain the chance of a pardon." When criminals faced execution or decades in prison, they attracted inordinate sympathy, whereas the petty offender languished, forced to serve out his sentence. To deliver more equitable and impartial justice, the association proposed that New York establish an office of pardon review. Its brief would entail interviewing all prisoners once or twice annually, "to examine the record of their trials, learn the name of witnesses, and examine them, as well as any new testimony which the prisoner may consider important; and when satisfied of his innocence, to

Francis Lieber. Source: New York Public Library, image 430883, retrieved from http://
digitalcollections.nypl.org.

recommend him to executive clemency." Appointed officers from such an inspectorate could sift through frivolous or unmerited pardon requests and prevent governors from having to rely on "interested parties." The current system, which depended on governors' capacity to resist emotional appeals and political influence, could be replaced by one based on "facts not now subjects of record."[39]

Delegates to the 1846 constitutional convention introduced similar proposals, each of which failed, but PANY tried a different tactic. The association became an advocate of tighter restrictions on gubernatorial pardoning and a lobbyist in favor of regulating and rationalizing clemency. In the course of providing its annual report to the legislature in 1849, it provided a long-term review of Sing Sing prisoners, some 7,030 men sentenced from 1817 to 1847. This report determined that 1,617 had been discharged over that thirty-year period as a result of pardons. Prisoners sentenced to seven years or less made up the bulk, but the rate of pardoning for more serious offenders confirmed Lieber's criticism: half of the 120 men serving fourteen-year sentences were pardoned, and nearly two-thirds of life-sentenced prisoners had received pardons.[40] Without adopting PANY's proposal in favor of a pardon board the legislature did act upon its call to shackle executive discretion. The 1849 Act in Relation to Pardons stipulated that for each prospective pardon, an application must first be made to the district attorney of the county in which the prisoner was convicted. Governors, in turn, were to ask the relevant DA for a "concise statement of the case," including "any other facts or circumstances which might have a bearing on the question of granting or refusing a pardon." Finally, the statute required applicants for pardons to publish pardon notices in specified major newspapers.[41] For PANY this was a partial victory. The act referred to "facts" and fact-checking, and it addressed concerns over governors' closed-door consultations with petitioners.

Although the pardon act of 1849 appeared hostile to governors' wide latitude granted under the constitution, its sponsor was the newly elected governor, Hamilton Fish, a Whig and life member of the Prison Association of New York.[42] Within a few months of taking office in January 1849, he became familiar with the problem of unceasing requests for pardons, ranging from lawyers' formal letters and lengthy petitions to brief notes in unsteady hands, and the impromptu appearance of supplicants at his chambers. Fish guessed that the volume of petitions was "almost equal in number to the convictions." In response, he requested that the legislature support "the importance of restricting the exercise of this power." With "proper and judicious regulations," Fish anticipated that pleas for mercy would become less frequent; more significantly, he predicted the pardon power could be "exercised with greater discrimination and safety."[43] Many governors before Fish had sought clearer directives on executive discretion, including Enos Throop, who devised his own formula, and Seward, who had called for an open book on pardoning, but none had overseen the introduction of legislation to accomplish these ends. Thus, elite penal theorists and critics of New York's penal system were not the only ones uneasy with the personal nature and opaque practices of pardoning: by the mid-nineteenth century the quest for reform also came from the seat of executive power.

Governor Fish's letter books, which he maintained over his governorship (1849–50), confirm he did his best to follow the new regulations. After he received a pardon application on behalf of a convict by the name of Ingersol, Fish advised the petitioner he must first publish his notice of application daily for four weeks according to "the law of pardon." The governor appointed the *New York Sun* as the paper to publish notices for New York City cases and the *Albany Argus* for cases connected to all other parts of the state, but notices turned up in numerous papers, likely ones that charged lower fees.[44] On May 28, 1849, the *Brooklyn Daily Eagle* published a notice that "Application will be made to the Governor of the State of New York . . . for a full and unconditional pardon for MICHAEL BRADY." At that point Brady was serving a two-year sentence for grand larceny in Sing Sing; however no petitioner was named, in violation of the rules. Later that summer, Margaret Myers, "in behalf of herself and 3 small children," followed the rules religiously, publishing repeated notices that she intended to apply for the pardon of her husband, convicted of petit larceny.[45] The governor's clerk wrote "Proof of publication," and "proof of notice" on applications such as Myers's, which suggest that his office distinguished between petitioners who had, and those who had not, followed the law.

Once pardon requests reached the governor, Fish, a lawyer who had dealt chiefly with wills and estates, reviewed pardon applications as if he were a one-man court of appeals. When a petitioner requested clemency because he claimed a prisoner was innocent, Fish rebuked him: "there should be as much evidence submitted as would induce a court to order a trial." After applications were lodged, the governor's private secretary sent form letters to prison superintendents as well as judges and DAs for each case he processed: "The Governor desires to be informed of the general character and conduct of the prisoner since his imprisonment and of any other facts within your knowledge bearing on the propriety or impropriety of granting a pardon."[46] Based on this evidence of notices and the governor's terse rejection, the law appears to have worked as intended. Yet, these interchanges were exceptions in the general practice of petition reviews.

The ever increasing volume of pardon applications governors handled, in step with New York's nation-leading prison population, meant that the 1849 pardon law turned out to be unworkable. Delegates wary of altering the state constitution had warned of this likely outcome at the convention held three years earlier. Although the precise number of people who petitioned Governor Fish is unclear, his letterbooks indicate that he responded to over six hundred pardon requests during his tenure.[47] The emphasis on publicity may have opened the process to greater scrutiny, but the Brady notice suggests the rule was flouted, and an unnamed party likely wrote and paid for the notices filed by the indigent Mrs. Myers. There is no evidence in the newspapers of record in New York and other dailies that the number of notices published reached anything close to the total of pardon applications. Yet, when Fish and his successors issued pardons to applicants who presented ex parte applications, they were not violating the law. The final clause of the 1849 pardon act indicated that legislators were as reluctant as the convention delegates had been to restrict executive discretion: the law must be followed, it stated, "unless in the opinion of the governor justice requires that it shall be dispensed with." By the early 1850s, the processing of pardons returned to the status quo ante.

The Committee on Discharged Prisoners also hesitated to hamper gubernatorial clemency, particularly during the tenure of its first agent. Isaac Hopper was happy to use his powers of persuasion to stand up for men with no other advocates, and he was not above requesting pardons for them, despite PANY's formal endorsement of Lieber's criticisms.[48] The association operated at cross-purposes. On the one hand, it presented evidence of inconsistent pardoning practice and traced it to the "one-man" power and the danger of its "prostitution for political purposes"; on the other hand, it solicited pardons for prisoners whom it considered deserving of mercy.[49] Hopper was especially motivated to serve friendless inmates who lacked the capacity to present themselves as fit subjects for mercy, especially African American men. PANY exposed the fact that white prisoners "receive[d] executive clemency much more frequently than the blacks" and reported in 1846 that just one "colored person" had been pardoned from Sing Sing in the previous year.[50] Fellow abolitionist Lydia Maria Child, who wrote a hagiographic biography of Hopper shortly after his death, recalled that he "often applied to the Governor to exert his pardoning power, where he thought there were mitigating circumstances attending the commission of a crime; or when the mind and health of a prisoner seemed breaking down; or where a long course of good conduct seemed deserving of reward."[51]

In practice, Hopper's principles closely resembled the ones numerous governors had publicly declared to justify clemency. While serving as PANY's agent he developed a personal relationship with Governor John Young, who addressed him as "Friend Hopper" in reply to a letter requesting clemency: "'I will pardon any convict, whom you say you conscientiously believe I ought to pardon," Young assured Hopper. Both men preferred "to err on the side of mercy," rather than risk subjecting an innocent or reformed man to misery. The agent in charge of discharged convicts and the executive were mutually reliant. Young admitted as much when he stated he could not properly appraise the number of pardon applications he received. Consequently, the governor found it "'a great relief to find a man in whose judgment and integrity I have such perfect confidence, as I have in yours."[52]

Over the first decades of its operations, PANY's ambition to reintegrate discharged prisoners as productive, law-abiding citizens continued to straddle arguments for and against executive discretion. One reason for this was jailers' and prison superintendents' resistance to the association's legal right to inspect the management of New York's prisons, which undermined the discharged prisoners committee's effort to work with prisoners deemed truly reformed. Drafting pardon petitions, in contrast, allowed PANY to work directly with the executive on behalf of inmates who might not otherwise be considered for institutional discharge. Abraham Beal, the man appointed to replace Isaac Hopper as agent, was thirty years younger than the first agent but he, too, was prepared to petition for pardons. With his background in charity and temperance work Beal was equally given to using the prodigal parable. In 1857, he presented the pictures he had taken of fifty men whom he had helped make the turn to freedom and responsibility, three of whom had been pardoned. "I left the prison, to return (I pray) no more for ever," one pardoned inmate had reportedly stated. Beal believed that "this young man appears to appreciate the blessings of liberty."[53] Since criminals could be likened to patients, suffering from the diseases of criminality and sinfulness, it mattered little how or by whom he was cured. If a pardon quickened and enhanced a man's recovery, why should the Prison Association object?[54] The second reason for PANY's ambivalence toward gubernatorial discretion was its awareness of governors' receptivity to arguments on the basis of human frailty. The capacity of governors to feel pity was the last hope of the condemned, and most officeholders were known to favor particular categories of offenders: the very young, people of previous good character, prisoners suffering from serious illnesses, and individuals whose crimes were committed under duress.

Prisoners whom white authorities considered biologically defective or in a morally compromised mental state were also likely to fare better before the governor than a board.[55] William Freeman, a man of African American and

Native American descent who butchered four members of a white family in 1846, was the first person defended on the basis of M'Naghten Rule, which required juries to consider whether, at the time of an offense, the perpetrator understood the nature of the act and possessed the mental capacity to discern right from wrong. The case riveted the nation's attention to emergent notions of compromised culpability, which percolated at midcentury.[56] Ex-governor Seward's role as defense counsel added a further twist. Freeman's conviction set Seward in two directions: to appeal his client's conviction and, as insurance, to petition the sitting governor, Silas Wright, for a pardon on the grounds that his client's mental state ought to make him a candidate for mercy. Seward's appeal was successful, but Freeman died before he could be retried, and Wright, a Democrat, turned down Seward's plea.[57] "'It would have been pleasant to my feelings to find it in my power, consistently with my sense of duty, to save this man from awful fate impending over him,'" Wright responded to Seward.[58] In time, another governor might have taken pity on the evidently deranged man. PANY's officers who worked with discharged prisoners knew that men of Freeman's station, poor and friendless, could not afford counsel to present petitions. Their sole hope was the prospect of stirring a governor's feelings when he made his prison inspections. Yet, as Wright's response indicated, chief executives of the mid-nineteenth century, including Seward, began to sense more clearly than those in office in the early republic that they must appear not too ready to open their hearts to criminals.

Remodeling the Management of Men

Over the 1850s and early 1860s the national narrative turned into a story of division and conflict: North versus South; free labor versus slavery; manifest destiny versus native sovereignty; temperance versus the liquor interests; men versus women. New Yorkers were also split on these issues, and the state became a hot spot for debate. With the biggest publishing hub in the country and the greatest concentration of organizational headquarters, the city of New York provided a hive for national opinion leaders such as Horace Greeley and William Cullen Bryant, both donors to PANY. Within a decade of its incorporation, the Prison Association attained a national profile through its published reports, which analyzed the administration of justice in every state where officials were willing to answer its questionnaires. Ironically, when it inquired into discretionary release procedures, discharged prisoner services, and pardon practice, it received fuller responses from authorities in Alabama and Georgia than it did from New York's prison keepers.

As PANY's national and international profile grew, lending it an authoritative voice in penal reform, it pressed for a new system of prisoner management locally. The association's principal aim was to solicit state support to complement its approach to the reintegration of discharged prisoners. In keeping with that effort PANY chipped away at executive discretion, not with a view to eliminating the pardon but to refining its features to make it more judicious, less personal and capricious. One expression of the effort to modernize mercy was the passage of an act in 1858 that imposed a file management system on pardon applications and responses. The second, prepared in anticipation of the 1867 state constitutional convention, was an exhaustively researched study, drafted by the redoubtable Francis Lieber, that called for an end to the "one-man" pardon.

Under agents Hopper and Beal, the support of the Discharged Prisoners Committee for pardoning was based on the same sentiments that Thomas Eddy had expressed half a century earlier. They were grounded in Christian notions of redemption and mercy and a commonly shared idea of human nature as fallible and redeemable. The possibility of a pardon kept "hope and good behavior alive in inmates," Hopper stated in 1850. To "deaden this cherished expectation" by denying a convict hope led him to believe that "nothing is to be gained by good conduct and industrious and faithful application to his work."[59] As a leading member of PANY, Hopper was familiar with efforts afoot in Australia's penal colonies and Ireland to turn Christian belief in salvation into systematic experiments of reform through stages. If inmates were made to earn their release by fulfilling a checklist of expectations, their progress to citizenship and freedom could occur in a staged manner, not abruptly at the expiration of a sentence or a pardon.

In 1854, PANY informed the legislature of new schemes operating in British colonies to improve "the management of men" on the path toward release. Captain Alexander Maconochie's penal experiment at Norfolk Island, begun in 1839, was the best known of them, and PANY found his "mark system" worthy of introduction into New York's prisons.[60] The captain's plan revolved around the concept of doing away with sentences of preset periods of time, replacing them with terms prisoners could shorten through the completion of tasks. Maconochie's model assigned credits for good behavior and productivity and imposed fines for poor conduct, charged to each man's "account." He used the term "probation" to describe the second stage of punishment, which involved work outside the prison in gangs. Men who established good records on probationary gangs were granted certificates of good conduct, and at that point they could apply for a probationary pass, the final stage before full liberty.[61]

PANY's Prison Discipline Committee was impressed with Maconochie's defense of his work, but it also published the dispatches that exposed the regime's shortcomings, including insufficient provision of work for proba-tioner inmates, inadequate supervision, and undifferentiated release schemes for women and men. Since the Norfolk Island experiment, other jurisdictions had implemented versions of Maconochie's plan. According to one enthu-siast, the results in Tasmania were "'pleasant and satisfactory in the high-est degree.'" The committee anticipated that Clinton State Prison, opened in 1845 and the newest of the state's three penitentiaries, could provide a suitable testing ground for the system of graduated release. At Clinton, "the labor of the men could be readily adjusted to a system of rewards and punishments, appealing constantly to their moral natures."[62] The ideals of penitence and moral reckoning were fading, outshone by a penal account book.

New York penal reformers were even more impressed by stories of success in the "Irish System" designed by the chairman of the Irish Board of Directors of Convict Prisons and introduced in 1854. Walter Crofton retained Macon-ochie's emphasis on rewards and punishments (with physical force, dietary restrictions, and isolation to be used only as last resorts), and time remained the principal measure of punishment. Prisoners could shorten their sentences not just by working and following the rules but also by passing through stages of discipline and self-improvement. Crofton placed greater emphasis than Maconochie on the value of education, and he insisted that every prisoner, male and female, receive book learning, for which inmates received marks in addition to their prison labor. Crofton aimed to instill in each inmate the capacity to govern his or her own behavior, and the terms he used to iden-tify benchmarks of progress toward liberty were music to PANY's ears: "self-discipline," "self-respect," "self-command," "self-reliance," "self-improvement," and "self-supporting."[63] In keeping with these objectives, Crofton established a series of "intermediate prisons" for men and houses of refuge for women, in which inmates were subjected to less stringent degrees of control and con-finement. Prisoners who could prove their fitness for freedom were eligible for tickets of leave, even if they had not yet served their full terms. In contrast to Maconochie's probationary passes, tickets placed freed convicts under the supervision of the Irish Constabulary, charged with the authority to return released prisoners if they failed to report or committed further offenses. In Ireland and England, this latter provision allayed fears that criminals would simply be let loose without having to complete their sentences. The enlist-ment of the police was unpalatable in New York, the Prison Association felt, so it promoted a modified version of Crofton's system.[64]

More than a decade before the Irish system was put in place, the Com-mittee on Discharged Prisoners had worked with released inmates through agents, and it remained convinced that its workers knew best how to manage men. Nevertheless, PANY continued to gather ideas on discretionary release practice and to solicit ideas from scholars based elsewhere in the United States and abroad. One of its international members was Carl Joseph Anton Mittermaier, professor of law and jurisprudence at Heidelberg, an international authority on criminal law and prison discipline, and a personal associate of Francis Lieber. Having worked for decades at the University of South Carolina, Lieber moved to New York's Columbia College in 1857, where he became a professor of history and political science before leading Columbia's new law school in 1860.[65] Theodore W. Dwight was one of Lieber's Columbia colleagues and later a professor of constitutional law at Cornell University, and he, too, became a major member of PANY's research team. Despite the secular slant scholars of this stature gave the association, Protestant faith in uplift remained a source of energy and inspiration. In 1862, the appointment of Reverend Enoch Wines (1806–79) as PANY's new secretary, the most significant office in the organization, bound its spiritual roots to its growing secular convictions. Wines was a teacher turned Congregational minister and professor of classical languages, and he became a passionate advocate for the revival of the penitentiary as an effective means of punishment and reform. The new secretary's academic training fit him well for PANY's orientation toward social scientific methods and evidence-based reform advocacy.[66] As an officeholder in the association, Wines also played a critical role in bringing the work of prison superintendent Zebulon Brockway, an innovator achieving positive results reforming young offenders in Michigan, to PANY's attention.

This combination of men, ambition, research, and timing turned the dream of testing a modified version of Maconochie's mark system into a reality. Starting in the late 1860s the Prison Association determined that such a bold experiment demanded an entirely new institution—a reformatory for young adult males and first offenders. If New York legislators could be convinced to establish such an institution, the state would lead the world. As the prospect became more certain PANY hardened its stance against the pardon, and it set out to compile the most convincing evidence yet to prove that gubernatorial pardoning had outlived its usefulness.

Surveying Gubernatorial Clemency

When Francis Lieber moved to New York from South Carolina, he left a slave state for a free state just as a war between the North and South began to look inevitable. African American men were free in New York, but race-specific property-owning requirements meant few could vote under the state's latest constitution, and the bloody anti-draft riots in New York City in 1863 sent a chilling reminder that racist violence was not just a southern scourge. Racial injustice was a problem many delegates tried to rectify at the 1867 constitutional convention. Another problem inherited from the state's past was the governor's prerogative to pardon. At this convention, unlike the earlier ones, PANY's survey findings, based largely on Lieber's and Theodore Dwight's research, were scrutinized in detail, although Lieber himself did not attend the convention.

In 1862, Lieber was called to Washington, where he served under the secretary of war and President Lincoln's general in chief to draft a new code of war for the Union. One of the problems Lincoln wished to see resolved was the question of pardons and paroles. The immediate problem was the Confederates' paroling of thousands of captured Union soldiers on condition either that they not serve or that they be exchanged for Confederate captives. Meanwhile, Union commanders were trying their own soldiers and Confederates in the field, in addition to civilians and spies, with inadequate legal instructions. During the Revolution and the War of 1812, the Articles of War had provided guidance, but as John Fabian Witt shows, Lincoln was eager to make his mark by developing the most comprehensive and modern set of guidelines yet written.[67] Lieber obliged the president with a new text to regulate the Union Army's conduct of the war, and the national government adopted it in April 1863.[68] Although Lieber set out numerous provisions to govern military parole (articles 119 to 134), his code imposed no regulations on the president's prerogative to pardon, a tool Lincoln deployed liberally in wartime and that Andrew Johnson, his successor, used even more freely to broker peace with the South in the war's aftermath.[69]

While national tensions preoccupied state political leaders, PANY's executive stuck to its reform agenda in an effort to codify when, how, and by whom discretionary justice could be dispensed. In 1864 the association's Committee on Prison Discipline endorsed a proposal in favor of "a commission or board of pardon, designed to aid the executive by a thorough investigation of the cases brought before them in applications for pardon made by convicts or their friends." The committee dismissed the traditional claim that the hope of pardon encouraged good behavior; on the contrary, it declared that the expectation of clemency "engenders and keeps alive in the convict's breast a feverish and unhealthy excitement, which must obstruct, if not prevent, a permanent reform."[70] Echoing Crofton, the committee stressed that true reform occurs only when the prisoner "calmly make[s] up his mind to submit to the punishment which the law has awarded to him." But they could pin these familiar claims to new evidence by the time they published their report. PANY's research over the early 1860s found that several states—New Jersey,

Connecticut, Minnesota, Nevada, Rhode Island, Massachusetts—had constitutions that restricted or replaced governors' responsibility for pardoning.[71] With New York's population of prisoners the largest in the country, PANY was determined that the state must lead, not follow other states.

A new weapon in PANY's offensive against executive discretion was a survey it commissioned to determine former governors' opinions on executive discretion. Designed in 1865 by Theodore Dwight and Francis Lieber, fellow law professors and PANY vice presidents, it asked former governors to answer seven questions concerning their use and experience of the pardoning power and it requested their advice on its possible reform. Until that point, chief executives' opinions were scattered in state papers and their personal communications, so the surveyors hoped to make governors' misgivings public. In the same year that they distributed their survey, the American Association for the Promotion of Social Science was established, and both of the survey authors were founding officers. However, their affiliation did not make them objective researchers.[72] Lieber and Dwight clearly flagged their desire to gather evidence against executive discretion, as survey "question two" (actually three questions squeezed into one) illustrates:

> Is it, in your opinion, possible that, easily accessible as our chief magistrates necessarily are, the privilege of pardoning can be guarded against frequent abuse and serious mistakes? Does, or does not, the privilege of pardoning, as it now exists, lead, in many cases, to results wholly unconnected with the degree of guilt or the comparative innocence of the convicts, and does not the obtaining of a pardon very frequently depend upon the influence which can be brought to bear on the petition for the pardon, rather than on the merits of the case itself?[73]

No respondent could have failed to discern what the surveyors wished to hear. Nevertheless, the fifteen former governors (plus Supreme Court Chief Justice Salmon P. Chase, formerly governor of Ohio) who sent replies expressed a range of opinions, from solid support for the redistribution of the pardon power to the passionate defense of personal clemency as an attribute of executive office. On balance, the ex-governors favored some modification to the exclusivity of executive pardoning, but the lack of evidence of pardoning abuse and the number of governors who believed in the merits of gubernatorial clemency help to explain why PANY's exhaustively prepared bid to revise the New York State Constitution in 1867 flopped.

PANY published the executive pardon survey responses in the appendix of its mammoth report to the New York legislature on New Year's Day 1867.

From time to time, the association published large national and international studies in its reports, lengthening them to several hundred pages. This one was the largest yet, totaling 547 pages. It also appeared separately as the *Report on the Prisons and Reformatories of the United States and Canada*, with Wines and Dwight as its listed authors. Penal historians have rightly focused on this landmark study for its insight into mid-century shifts in thinking concerning prison discipline the administration of criminal justice.[74] However, historians have shown little interest in the *Report*'s assessment of discretionary release models. The study reviewed Maconochie's and Crofton's systems, as well as the troubling question of the pardon. In addition to its twelve-page analysis of the problem, based on data collected over the previous decades in various states, the *Report* published ten thousand words of governors' commentary on clemency, most of which came from the pens of three former New York governors.

PANY's survey of governors was biased in its design and execution, but its published *Report* of 1867 judiciously included statements in favor of gubernatorial pardoning as well as critical remarks. Among the "matured opinions of gentlemen of large experience and high ability on matters of grave importance connected with the general subject of pardon" were the comments of John King, Whig governor of New York in 1857–58 and seventy-seven years of age when he replied to Dwight's and Lieber's survey.[75] The power to pardon was "an inherent, absolute and essential attribute of the executive," and King claimed he could recall no incident in which it had been abused. Besides, governors customarily consulted the convicting judge in each case, and this meant that "calm and deliberate judgment of an experienced and cultivated mind" guided the chief executive's hand. The constitution must not change, and "the merciful feelings of the heart should never be wholly stifled." The even more elderly Enos T. Throop, having retired to a life of farming, referred back more than thirty years to the messages he had delivered to the legislature, and he reiterated that firm criteria had guided his pardon deliberations. In agreement with King, Throop believed that a governor with "clear views of his duty . . . will discharge it without remorse," and morally unfit candidates for high office were the exception. He rejected the prospect of pardon boards because they split responsibility; moreover, with many men involved in decision making, Throop anticipated they would be "much more accessible to corruption; every member is an avenue through which the wily advocate may approach his object." The ex-governor could see the merit of encumbering the exercise of the pardoning power with "prudential rules," but he believed the "meanest" of prisoners must always have access to mercy, to moderate the severity of the law and to correct its "unequal operation." New York's elderly governors were not the only men who held such convictions. Pennsylvania's former governors William F. Packer and William F. Johnston (a Democrat and a Whig, respectively) agreed, and so did Chief Justice Salmon P. Chase, who saw no benefit in stripping governors or the president of the pardon prerogative: "I am not prepared to say that its exercise would be more wise or more beneficial in other hands, than in those of the state and national executives."[76]

Of all the pardon committee survey respondents, former New York governor Washington Hunt came closest to singing from Lieber's song sheet. In 1860 Hunt sent Lieber a warm letter to congratulate him on the publication of his 1859 book, *On Civil Liberty*, in which his pardon abuse critique appeared in chapter form.[77] In his response to the survey, Hunt agreed it was time to shed "the attribute of the crown," clothed "with an unlimited power," and to replace it with a pardon board. Still, the ex-governor considered clemency a matter that must be treated with delicacy. Whereas Lieber argued that neither infirmity nor family hardship nor previous good character were legitimate grounds for mercy, Hunt admitted he had considered young offenders worthy of a pardon in most cases. In this respect Hunt, a Whig-turned-Democrat, sided with the ex-governors of various parties who contended that the pardon power had not been "abused to the extent as it is sometimes assumed." The issue was not the men in office, who "deem it a point of honor and conscience to discharge the duty independently, unmoved by personal or political influences." Rather, Hunt considered the problem to be men's temptation to "yield to feelings of kindness and compassion." Since "daily appeals and importunities" inevitably challenged a governor's manly resolve, Hunt thought that retired judges, used to recommending mercy on compassionate grounds, would be the best men to exercise the "delicate prerogative."[78]

The Failed Attempt to Reconstitute the One-Man Pardon

Constitutional historian Peter J. Galie refers to the 1867 constitutional convention as the "first failure" in New York's post-Revolutionary reviews of its governing apparatus.[79] The convention took place at the high-water mark of Reconstruction, and the widely shared hope of expanding civil rights and reinvigorating democracy brought energy and purpose to the convention floor. Delegates agreed to make common schooling free, to implement provisions against bribery and corruption amongst officials, and to increase the efficiency of the New York Court of Appeals. But when it came to the greatest symbol of progress—equal voting rights for all men—the Democrats erected a wall of resistance. Another failure of the convention was PANY's proposal to replace exclusive executive discretion with a pardon board, which the convention's Committee on the Pardon Power blocked. Proud of its survey research, national statistics, and international panel of experts, PANY assumed that its status as the nation's leading authority on the pardon power was unassailable.

Francis Lieber did not attend the convention, but Theodore Dwight made an appearance on his behalf, graciously acknowledging that his absent colleague had authored PANY's proposed amendment to the governor's constitutional powers.[80] The sitting governor, Reuben Fenton, supported PANY's stance, and he endorsed it in his 1867 Message to the Legislature.[81] The convention struck a separate Committee on the Pardoning Power on June 20, 1867, chaired by a Republican criminal lawyer, William J. Townsend, and the committee's discussions initially favored the introduction of a board to make pardoning more efficient.[82] Although PANY claimed that most of the ex-governors it surveyed had supported this change, the committee undertook its own survey of several former New York governors whom PANY had not polled, including Horatio Seymour, who supported the existing state constitution. The committee also pored over recent pardoning statistics, which revealed that pardon requests and pardon rates in New York had not risen as high as PANY alleged. Unconvinced that change was warranted, the constitutional committee reached a unanimous decision that the pardon power should remain a matter of executive privilege.[83] True, some states had opted for boards and councils, but twenty-nine had not, and New York would remain one of them.

The Prison Association made a last-ditch attempt to defeat the pardoning power committee's recommendation by appealing to the delegates at large. Theodore Dwight dipped into Lieber's works and sprinkled references to the writings of Beccaria and Tocqueville, but he made no headway. PANY's decision to quote selectively from the 1865 survey of governors backfired. The committee accused Dwight of falsely claiming that every ex-governor had supported PANY's parole board proposal. One delegate commented sarcastically on Dwight's presentation, calling it a "new theory with plausible adroitness." Alembert Pond, a Republican member, acknowledged that PANY's "schemes were perhaps theoretically more perfect than those contained in the present Constitution," but he doubted that introducing a new quasi-judicial review agency would improve access to justice. Former district attorney Elizur H. Prindle believed that pardoning required a human touch. Gaining the "ear" of the chief justice was the right of the "poor man" and his wife, "with tears in her eyes," not just wealthy prisoners who could hire lawyers to prepare "applications in proper form," according to "rules prescribed by the board."[84]

Resistance to the proposal to dislodge executive discretion came, as it had in earlier conventions, from delegates who feared its loss would close off access to justice. Lieber's model of a board acting like a court of equity raised concerns that it would favor elites. This was a plan concocted by and for theorists, not for the benefit of ordinary criminals, in Pond's opinion. He was so perturbed at the prospect of a board that he "scalped" PANY's "elaborate reports":

> Yes, scalped; They have been scalped, and beheaded, and their legs cut off, and bodies burned . . . this Constitution under which we now live has operated beneficially and . . . it should be altered only in the respects called for by the people, or by some popular necessity.

The Prison Association misread the people's mood, and without the juice of popular support the idea of a pardon review board dried into a penological construct. Pond, the fiercest critic of change at the 1867 convention, thought that the 1846 constitution had introduced sufficient safeguards to ensure that pardoning could be conducted properly. Any further refinement could be achieved through statutes. As far as the pardon power was concerned, the delegates to the 1867 convention were in no mood for root and branch change. The Committee on the Pardoning Power, having gathered statistics on New York governors' use of pardoning over the previous twenty years, determined that "the power has been very carefully, judiciously and conscientiously used." The release of "undeserving criminals," they judged, was "so rare as to give no occasion to fear that the public interests will suffer by leaving the pardon power in the hands of the same functionary where it has rested for the last forty-five years."[85]

Conclusion

In 1867 public concern about injudicious pardoning centered on Washington, not Albany. President Andrew Johnson's second Amnesty Proclamation, issued two weeks after the convention resolved to retain executive pardoning, turned "a retaliatory or vindictive policy" toward former rebels on its head by granting a full pardon to all but the chief Confederate officeholders.[86] Federal pardoning protocol was the responsibility of the State Department, which also drafted individual pardons. President Johnson's secretary of state was William H. Seward, who had staked his reputation as governor of New York on his strict regard for pardon reviews.[87] Twenty-five years later, having survived an assassination attempt and supportive of Johnson's efforts at reconciliation, the aging statesman was receptive to southern pardon seekers who "thronged the White House day and night."[88] The Republican-dominated Congress impeached the president but it could not, without amending the Constitution, "deprive the Executive of the power to proclaim the right to maintain the nation's forgiveness and forgetfulness."[89]

The passage of time and the tumult of events beyond his control also changed Francis Lieber's attitude toward executive pardoning. Unlike Seward, however, he managed to keep his personal experiences a private matter. After his escape from Prussia, Lieber knew he faced imprisonment if ever he returned to his fatherland. Under King Friedrich Wilhelm III he had spent several months in prison in the early 1820s, and he remained under suspicion for his republican sympathies after his release in 1825. In 1840 the king's son, Friedrich Wilhelm IV, marked his accession to the throne with a royal decree that offered pardons to former political prisoners, but only those in Prussia, and this chain of events convinced Lieber to draft a pardon petition for the king's consideration. Lieber approached the sovereign with a humble request: "the object of my most subservient supplication requires that I explain my case completely, and I crave therefore a sympathetic ear, that Your Majesty may most mercifully listen to me." Like many other supplicants he believed the monarch could regard Lieber's youth at the time of his offenses a mitigating factor. Since then, he claimed, he had undergone a personal transformation:

> Royal Majesty! I know it, I am no worse than hundreds of those who have been pardoned. I have erred, but I have suffered enough to atone for it. Even if the old belief that the human body renews itself in seven years is unfounded, in three times seven years the inner person certainly changes.[90]

Lieber never referred to his own pardon in his voluminous writings against executive discretionary justice.[91] Yet his experience of arrest, imprisonment, and a pardon granted through the grace of a merciful king must surely have crossed his mind each time he wrote that all states must provide some means to rectify law's capacity to inflict injustice.

The momentum against the governor's pardon prerogative crested at the 1867 constitutional convention and quickly receded. A much larger wave gathered force over the following decade, sufficient to persuade legislators to establish the nation's first reformatory. Although the National Prison Association, which Reverend Wines formed in 1870, took credit for launching the Elmira Reformatory in 1876, it capitalized on thirty years of work conducted by the Prison Association of New York. As a new generation of penal modernizers attempted to push punishment away from profit making, their discomfort with pardoning drifted toward its interference with character correction. When Dwight tried to convince the 1867 constitutional delegates that executive discretion had a "deleterious and disastrous influence upon penal discipline," he attached his critique to "reformatory influences which are, according to modern improved theories, the great influences to be brought to bear upon prisoners."[92] These confident pronouncements generated new questions about the nature of discretionary justice at the dawn of Progressive penology.

5

Reformulating Discretion in the Mid- to Late Nineteenth Century

A single pardon could be "hostile to the ends of justice." Francis Lieber made this point in the 1859 version of his essay on the abuse of the one-man pardon power. Although he was well aware that most prisoners who received pardons were men of low status, Lieber contended that "incalculable mischief may be done by arbitrarily or wickedly pardoning a few prominent and deeply stained criminals."[1] When governors granted mercy toward the poorest of inmates and those sick in mind and body they gave the false impression that gubernatorial clemency operated like a lofty court of equity, blind—like Justice herself—to the divisions of society.[2] In contrast, pardons of high-status prisoners and serious offenders, although small in number, underlined that executive discretion violated the principle of equal justice. Neither penological theories nor constitutional debates persuaded New Yorkers to remove the governor's sole prerogative to pardon, but its place in the politics of punishment did shift in the second half of the nineteenth century for other reasons. The exponential growth in the state's diversifying population, the rise of woman's-rights lobbying, the emergence of new definitions of mental capacity, and the establishment of the first adult reformatory recast discretionary justice's capacity to rectify and to inflict injustice; for governors and pardon petitioners, however, clemency remained as personal and as politically precarious as it was when George Clinton assumed office.

Governors who revealed the inner workings of the pardon process were rare, but most reported on the factors that shaped their decisions, including statements made by judges, DA's and petitioners. John T. Hoffman, who served as an officer in the Prison Association of New York prior to his election in 1869, provided mini-narratives of cases in his public papers. In 1892, after he left office, Governor David B. Hill published a long essay on pardoning, in which he reflected on his experience in having overseen the first execution of a woman in New York since 1852 and the world's first electrocution. Evidence of executive clemency's modernization appeared in fields beyond voltage and technologies of death, particularly in governors' growing inclination to consult medical authorities for definite answers on the question of criminal responsibility. The published records of pardoning and investigative reports on gubernatorial pardon practice include names and decisions, but they also reveal the intimacy of gubernatorial discretion, performed in public office.

New York's unpublished records allow for closer scrutiny of executive discretion at the level of individual cases. In 1858, the New York legislature passed a law that required records related to pardon applications to be kept on file, and thanks to this statute the inner workings of executive clemency can be exposed.[3] In addition to the internal correspondence between officials (pardon clerks, district attorneys, judges, wardens), a wealth of further material, including letters from prisoners and their supporters, interested members of the public, petitions, and newspaper clippings, appears in clemency case files, and not just in high-profile cases.[4] From 1859, when the filing law came into effect, to 1900 a total of 2,644 pardon applications have survived, and basic information from each file has been entered in a database, produced by the State Archives.[5] By supplementing this database, my random sample of 252 case files from this forty-one-year period makes it possible to sketch the broad profile of pardoning practice and to analyze the impact of unique case characteristics on the conduct of clemency.[6] These records reveal that petitions for mercy in the second half of the nineteenth century followed the tone and substance of earlier pardon tales.[7] Despite the introduction of psychiatric expertise into case deliberations, particularly in regard to offenders sentenced to death, applicants still appealed for mercy on well-established grounds of mitigation, and governors continued to respond, commuting sentences on account of youth, infirmity, hardship, previous good character, and the special frailties of old age and femininity.[8] However, the establishment of the Elmira Reformatory in 1876 added a new criterion for clemency: the abuse of administrative discretion produced as the state took its first steps toward Progressive penology.[9]

There is little evidence of the high-level discourse of penal theorists and constitutional delegates in the quotidian business of pardoning. Pardoning's patterns and the peculiarities of individual outcomes become clearest by combining a quantitative and qualitative approach to clemency case files. Petitioners certainly hoped that their submissions would be closely read. They essayed various strategies to solicit mercy, from the modest, carefully worded statement that an offender had suffered enough, to the shrill accusation of injustice and the desperate plea for human kindness. Formal applications were usually drafted by lawyers, and a surprising number of letters came from prominent politicians and business leaders, even in cases involving prisoners from poor families. Nevertheless, the typical file features the words of a family member or advocate writing on a prisoner's behalf, seeking mercy from the state's sovereign authority. The textual trace of their anxious appeals places in the researcher's hands the documents that ended with the chief executive's approval or denial of clemency. When governors considered those pleas they did not simply tick boxes on cover sheets: they opened files full of stories.

Pre–Civil War Pardon Practice under Scrutiny

New York State's first major review of pardoning appeared in time to be tabled at the convention of 1846, but its value to historians exceeds the short time delegates granted it.[10] Concerns over Governor John A. King's apparent laxity with the pardon power prompted the legislature to conduct a further study in 1859. Both inquiries calculated the volume of pardons over time and between governors' administrations, and they also tabulated the period each pardoned offender served compared to his or her original sentence. These historical statistics of clemency are significant in their own right; in addition, they include data their sponsors ignored or overlooked, particularly in regard to the gender, race, and ethnic factors inherent in governors' use of clemency in the mid-nineteenth century.

In 1846 New York's assembly ordered the secretary of state to supply the names, offenses, and sentences of pardoned convicts, plus the date of their pardons, from 1840 to the present. The resulting report showed that 503 pardons and two commutations from death to sentences of life in prison were granted over the terms of four governors. The report's inclusion of prisoners' first names makes it possible to affirm the masculine cast of persons pardoned from the state prison system (at that point Auburn and Sing Sing). Ninety-four percent of the pardoned were males, roughly in proportion to the preponderance of men in these institutions in this period.[11] In 1841, for instance, not a single woman was pardoned from the state prisons. The second-most significant characteristic is the small proportion of violent offenders among the pardoned. Of the ninety-three persons Seward pardoned in 1842, only eight had committed violent offenses or arson, with none convicted of murder. Similarly, Governor Silas Wright, who maintained a hard line against anti-renters during his term, pardoned no murderers in 1845, and only sixteen violent offenders. Prisoners serving long sentences also made up a small proportion of the pardoned in the early 1840s: five were life-sentenced prisoners, and only 14 percent were serving sentences of ten years or greater. Thus, when critics of executive clemency and governors' political enemies complained that dangerous pardoned criminals preyed on the law-abiding citizenry, the new statistical record proved them wrong. The convicts governors pardoned were overwhelming white, Anglo-American male property offenders.[12]

The second major review of pardoning occurred after a sharp rise in immigration over the 1850s, a spike in the prison population, and public outcry over Governor John A. King's pardoning practice. The legislature responded to these issues in 1858 when it called for the formalization of record keeping in pardon applications. Unlike the attempt of the legislature in 1849 that required the publication of petitions in newspapers, the 1858 statute required that all applications to the governor be filed "with a record of the same, and a list of the official signatures and recommendations in favor of such application, and all the original papers on which such application is founded."[13] In the following year New York's senate ordered the secretary of state to produce an overview of the pardons granted over Governor King's time in office (1857–58) and requested that the information appear "in tabular form."[14]

The resulting publication, the 1859 report of the state senate, presented the same data that appeared in the study conducted thirteen years earlier, but it went further by covering all prisoners granted pardons (not just felons at the state prisons), in addition to the conditions governors placed on released offenders. The gender disparity remained the same as it was in the early 1840s, as was the range of offenses. The volume of pardons granted to prisoners had, indeed, climbed over the late 1850s, but so had New York's prison population. Governor King had granted clemency to 237 felons in the two years surveyed—426 when minor offenders were added to the count—but he worked within a prison system whose population had exploded from 1,268 in 1850 to 6,682 by the decade's end. Furthermore, the report indicated that inmates serving short sentences and sentences in lieu of paying fines made up the vast majority of pardoned inmates during King's governorship, consistent with historic trends. Mary Nolan, imprisoned for vagrancy, was pardoned after serving two weeks of a one-month sentence at New York's Blackwell's Penitentiary. King commuted Michael Boyle's ninety-three-day sentence at the Rochester Work House for assault and battery and intoxication to thirty days. Dennis Beahan of Queens was ordered to pay a fine of fifty dollars and to stand committed until he paid, but King pardoned him immediately after his conviction.[15] Pardons of such offenders—many of them Irish and likely recent immigrants serving sentences for minor intra-community offenses—did not incite allegations of unfairness. The reduction of long sentences and the pardoning of violent offenders was a different matter.

Governor King, New York's first Republican governor, got off to a bad start by deciding he need not report his pardoning decisions to the legislature, purportedly under the assumption that the secretary of state's report would suffice.[16] His decision left a vacuum the press was ready to fill with accusations of his excessive mercy. State and national papers and magazines concurred that the man was either too soft or too gullible to allow dangerous criminals to serve minimal sentences. The popular magazine *Harper's Weekly* launched an attack on ill-judged pardoning late in 1857, joining other New York publications in the assault.[17] A cartoon published in January 1858 depicted a burglar counseling his son to thieve. The father assures the boy that the governor will pardon him if he is caught, since notables can always be duped into signing petitions.[18] In an article on "The Pardoning Business," the *Weekly* claimed that "a man sentenced to ten years State's Prison [sic] for heinous crime serves three and is pardoned out." The lesser offender "scarcely remains long enough in prison to make the acquaintance of the turnkeys." Because the "prerogative of pardon" was the only significant power the chief executive retained under the most recent constitution, the paper believed that governors had used it "pretty freely."[19]

The record of executive clemency during King's tenure showed he was less loose with his pardons than his critics, who lined up in greater numbers after a swing toward the Democrats in the elections of 1857, contended. Despite the serious disturbances that rocked the state prison system in the late 1850s due to severe overcrowding and mounting anger over declining work conditions, the great majority of prisoners King pardoned were property offenders and minor offenders.[20] He also trimmed sentences selectively, favoring inmates whose sentences he considered disproportionate to their offenses.[21] Early in 1858 the governor chopped a twenty-year sentence for forgery down to four in the case of George W. Kellogg. The severity of the penalty was a reminder of the time when forgery was punished by death.[22] Kellogg's release after his conviction for bank fraud (on top of an indictment for bigamy) did not inspire cynical editorials about favoritism toward "fancy" white prisoners, but the governor's pardons of inmates convicted of violent crimes attracted greater scrutiny. King was particularly lenient toward men convicted of rape, such as Patrick Anderson, who served only twenty-three months and two weeks by the time King commuted his fourteen-year sentence in 1858. The longest period any convicted rapist spent in prison before King intervened was eleven years, served by James Broome, who had been sentenced to life in 1846. The other six men served an average of just two and one-half years after receiving sentences of terms ranging from ten to fifteen years.[23]

Like Seward, the first Whig governor, King deliberated over harsh sentences fully aware that his political enemies would capitalize on his decisions. Anxiety over rising crime rates and a murderous wave of prison disorder made the atmosphere particularly hostile to clemency in the 1850s.[24] Not just King's Democratic opponents but newspaper editors with Republican sympathies leapt on any digression from severity. In May 1858, as convicted murderer Marion Stout's fate lay in the governor's hands, *Harper's Weekly* threatened King that his party would withdraw its support if he granted a pardon. "Other Governors have exercised the power of pardoning indiscreetly; Governor King has prostituted it."[25] This story appeared on the same day that King commuted an Irish lad's death sentence, imposed for his part in the gang rape and murder of a German woman in New York City's Lower West Side.[26] But Stout was not so fortunate. Despite King's receipt of many prominent individuals' pleas for mercy, including ones from Susan B. Anthony and Frederick Douglass, he declined to intervene, and the man was hanged on October 22, 1858.[27] Periodic executions may not have silenced the governor's critics, but they proved to condemned prisoners and their supporters that mercy was always measured, even in the hands of a man who appeared to pardon freely.

King's detractors overlooked his selective severity, as well as the broader trend evident from the 1840s onward, toward governors' imposition of conditions on released prisoners. The 1846 and 1859 reports showed that among the pardons documented in the two periods, 8.3 percent were conditional. During his governorship King released twenty-four prisoners from state prisons, of whom six were released on condition that they leave their local county, city, state, or the United States. Governors also ordered pardoned prisoners with a view to improving their behavior, in parallel with the rules PANY's discharged prisoner agents imposed on discharged prisoners. When James Hitchcock and Patrick Brennan, sent to prison for four months and three months respectively for "intoxication," were pardoned in 1857 they left prison "on condition that they abstain from the use of liquor."[28] In the 1840s, as the temperance movement gained support in state and national civic life, governors pardoned on the condition that released prisoners conform to the disciplinary expectations used to define responsible citizenship, and this requirement became more frequent by the 1850s.[29]

Although orders to return to a master or father echoed the patriarchal concerns of colonial times, other inmates were pardoned on conditions that foreshadowed the behavioral demands of parole authorities, as Jesse Sims learned. Governor King pardoned Sims after he served one year of a three-year sentence for receiving stolen goods, on condition that he live "a correct moral life, without violating the laws of this State, otherwise he is to be remanded to prison, and serve out the full term of his sentence."[30] But in 1857 no official was authorized to keep track of prisoners such as Sims after their release. Not even PANY's discharged prisoners agent or the managers of its women's refuge home had the authority to compel the reincarceration of wayward ex-prisoners. This problem of inadequate governance of pardoned prisoners after their release was one of the issues reformatory lobbyists seized on as they attempted to extend the disciplinary reach of prisons.[31]

Typical Pardon Practice and the Atypical Capital Offender

Edmund D. Morgan, King's successor as governor and another Republican, was the first to review pardon applications under the 1858 record keeping statute. Within his first months in office he demonstrated how quickly accountability could restore the credibility of discretionary justice.[32] Identifying himself with broader attempts to regularize the procedures governing pardoning, Morgan proudly reported that he took "more than usual pains to ascertain the merits of each application." For every pardon he granted in 1859 (84 from state prisons, compared to 442 refused) he declared he had first consulted the district attorney from the county in which the offense was tried, in order to obtain "full knowledge of the evidence given on trial as well as his views of the case." Executive clemency was no desk job for this governor. In his first summer in office in 1859 Morgan spent several days at each of the state prisons where he met with prisoners, not just their keepers. He started with the backlog of convicts who had previously applied for pardon:

> To each [prisoner] about fifteen minutes were devoted, which was found sufficient to enable the prisoner to tell his own story and to answer any questions I thought proper to put to him. . . . I examined at the prisons in the same way two hundred and three convicts, who from want of friends or the proper opportunity had not previously sought clemency, paying particular attention to those whose length of sentences and good conduct in prison commended them to notice.[33]

Morgan continued to visit the state's prisons each year he served as governor (1859–62). Not even his Civil War duties, which involved drumming up volunteers for the Union, stopped him from undertaking a "personal examination" of pardon applicants.[34] The *Albany Statesman* commented favorably on the governor's policy of firsthand judgment: "one day of contact with these supplicants for mercy gives him a better knowledge of the character and claims of the convicts than a month incessantly applied to the examination of written applications."[35]

Whereas John King reported to Francis Lieber that he had always pardoned with "the calm and deliberate judgment of an experienced and cultivated mind," Governor Morgan was prepared to admit he had made some mistakes.[36] However, in capital case reviews he claimed he invariably reached the correct decision. In his first year as governor one man was executed (iron-worker Michael O'Brien, who had brutally beaten his wife to death), and he commuted the death sentence in two cases, "solely on the ground of insanity." These cases persuaded Morgan that the legislature ought to appoint "some disinterested person, skilled in detecting various forms of [mental] disease" to diagnose such criminals.[37] Examining hundreds of paper applications and personally interviewing hundreds more was already "one of the most onerous and embarrassing duties of the executive," Morgan felt, without having also to appraise the mental state of offenders facing execution. The establishment of a state lunacy commission, manned by medico-legal experts, would take a further fourteen years to occur but Morgan planted this seed at a point of fertile speculation over the nature of the criminal mind and criminal responsibility.[38]

In Mary Hartung's case, a dogged lawyer, not a psychiatric reading of her mind, relieved Morgan of the most embarrassing duty a governor faced in mid-nineteenth-century New York—the prospect of authorizing a woman's execution. Hartung was a German immigrant, married to a saloonkeeper whom she claimed was an abusive drunkard. At her trial she admitted she had been involved in an adulterous affair with one of the household's board-ers, but she testified that her paramour, not she, had dosed her husband with arsenic. After deliberating for two days the jury concluded Hartung was guilty and the judge found the evidence against the accused compelling.[39] Yet this legal finding did not seal her fate. Not since 1852 had a woman been executed in New York, when Ann Hoag was hanged for poisoning her husband, so "that she might have free indulgence with a paramour," the *Brooklyn Eagle* snarled.[40] The alleged means and motives in the two cases were identical, but Hartung was fortunate to have an astute lawyer, William J. Hadley, to defend her.[41] In capital cases more often than minor ones, ambitious and skillful ad-vocates were drawn to the challenge of turning hopeless cases involving poor or minority offenders into atypical cases that could be won on points of law. The African American multiple murderer, William Freeman, was fortunate that William Seward, former governor and defender of the underdog, decided to make a test case of a poor prospect for acquittal.[42] In capital cases with long odds of success a brilliant defense or legal appeal could burnish an attorney's professional reputation, save a client from death, and relieve a governor from the weighty responsibility capital cases entailed.

After the verdict, it appeared that Hartung would share Hoag's fate. Her lawyer followed the usual course in capital convictions: he requested that the governor reprieve his client and commute the sentence of death to one of imprisonment. Clemency appeals in newspapers and letters and petitions sent to the governor made much of her frailty and weak will. More significantly, pleas for mercy turned on the notion that putting a female to death was "repugnant." Despite the outpouring of sympathy toward the adulteress, Governor Morgan told Hadley a pardon was unwarranted. Indeed, the judge's report stated that Hartung was guilty of "a cool premeditated murder of the most revolting character."[43] The governor informed Hadley that his client, a spousal poisoner, deserved no mercy:

> While every application for commutation of pardon shall be decided on its own peculiar facts, I cannot conceive that I should feel authorized in interfering in any case of poisoning where guilt is clearly proved; least of all can I interfere where a husband poisons a wife, or a wife a husband.[44]

Morgan's rebuff led Hadley to pursue other options. Having failed to convince the jury to acquit he struck up a petition campaign, filed a successful writ of error to delay the execution, argued her case before the state supreme court and the state court of appeals, and drafted a bill designed to spare her from death—all without receiving a cent from his client.[45]

As the appeal against conviction dragged on, state legislators responded to Hadley's pressure by passing a bill that divided murder into two degrees, without specifying the means of inflicting death upon persons already convicted of first-degree murder. For decades, critics of jury nullification had mooted the idea that murder be divided into degrees of responsibility. Hadley managed to tip the legislature in the direction of transforming law by tightening up "what had previously been loosely arranged."[46] It soon became apparent that the draft legislation of 1860 was no tighter. Called, ironically, an act "in relation to capital punishment and to provide for the more certain punishment of the crime of murder," the statute rendered the prospective punishment of Hartung and all others facing the death penalty after its passage exceedingly uncertain. The New York Court of Appeals held that the act had inadvertently repealed all previous statutes regarding the penalty for murder, while it also applied (unconstitutionally) to crimes committed prior to its passage. The resulting legal limbo lasted until 1863, when the same court finally held that Hartung could not be tried under the amended murder statute, passed in 1861, in an effort to sort out the mess caused by the earlier one.[47] This end to the legal saga allowed the "man poisoner" to be released from prison after serving three years, and this outcome saved the governor from having to reappraise a petition for her pardon.[48] The Hartung case was a victory for Hadley; it was also a stroke of luck for Morgan, whose reputation as a stickler for form and evenhanded justice remained untarnished.[49] And for Hartung, the result was lifesaving.

The case of Maria Hartung was exceptional on all counts. Most offenders were males from the economic and social margins of the state's diversifying population, facing months or several years of imprisonment for a property or minor violent offense. Representation by a lawyer prepared to take on all three branches of government was a fantasy for the typical person accused of a crime, let alone prisoners convicted of serious felonies. This was one of the key reasons why Radical Republicans at the 1867 constitutional convention stood up for the one-man pardon power. The poor and the poorly represented must never be prevented from seeking mercy. The documents preserved in clemency case files, tied up in pink ribbons, offer reminders that no pardon application was typical to the individuals who faced continued imprisonment or death.

Pardoning's Patterns and Peculiarities

The most important feature of the surviving clemency files is the high rate of successful outcomes, which gives the erroneous impression that governors granted clemency to virtually every applicant.[50] The overall success rate in the 252 cases sampled from the late nineteenth century was 98.4 percent, although governors withheld their grants of mercy on first petition attempts in 17 percent of these cases.[51] Evidently, the secretary of state understood that the 1858 record-keeping statute applied only to those cases in which governors ultimately decided in favor of mercy, likely because inquiries into executive discretion, such as the 1846 and 1859 reviews, were concerned about grants of clemency, not denials. The governor's annual pardon reports, which frequently flesh out the larger corpus of petitions, make it clear that the retained clemency files of the late nineteenth century refer mainly to successful petitions. Prisoners and their supporters who appealed for mercy in person, inmates who served out their sentences before a decision could be made, and those who died before the chief executive made his decision are, unfortunately, underrepresented in the preserved files.

In their messages and annual reports, governors followed the secretary of state's approach, but many chose to report the number of applications they rejected to convey a sense of discernment. Governor John T. Hoffman, a Tammany Democrat in a legislature dominated by Republicans, justified his grants of mercy with detailed reports during his governorship (1869–72). "Although under no obligation to do so," he considered it "proper" to give "the reasons which induced me, in each case, to relieve the convict from the penalties of the law."[52] As an executive member of the Prison Association of New York (PANY) and a former lower-court judge in New York City, Hoffman managed to avoid the tarnish of favoritism and corruption that discolored other Tammany Democrats.[53] Perhaps the impending prosecution of William M. "Boss" Tweed for his abuse of public trust made Hoffman especially forthcoming about his use of executive discretion. In 1870, for instance, he told the legislature he considered more than 1,000 applications made either by "convicts in person" or by "written petition," but granted only 85 pardons, 34 commutations, and 1 reprieve. By comparing Hoffman's record, which includes the first and last names of pardoned prisoners, to the cases entered in the Archives' database, it is clear that many positive as well as negative outcome cases were not preserved. Thus, the records that survive from the last decades of the nineteenth century represent a tranche of petitions, most of which ended in the governor's decision to exercise his discretion in prisoners' favor.

According to PANY and other critics of the one-man pardon, great wealth or high status were necessary to secure a pardon in the late nineteenth century. In its 1867 *Report* on North American prisons the association alleged that "the grant of pardon does not so much depend on the degree of guilt, as on the pecuniary means of the convict to hire [pardon brokers]."[54] But where was the evidence? It bears underlining that the pool of potential petitioners in New York could not afford to pay off corrupt pardon brokers or hire costly legal talent. They resembled the majority of prisoners elsewhere in the industrializing Northeast—poor whites, struggling farmers, and recent immigrants crammed in poorly serviced cities—who fared worst in the prosecutorial and judicial process. They were the individuals against whom complainants decided to press charges and whom police officers decided to arrest. They were the suspects prosecutors decided to try, rather than choosing to drop charges. They were the poorly defended whom judges sentenced severely, or for whom juries refused to recommend to mercy. Even in the nation's largest prison system few convicts came from elite backgrounds or lived in ease. As one delegate to the 1870 National Prison Congress estimated, only "some five percent" of prisoners came from the "well-to-do, educated classes."[55] On rare occasions when white men and women of high status were prosecuted for serious crimes (such as Daniel McFarland, acquitted in 1870 of the murder of his wife's paramour, despite evidence of premeditation), they could usually count on the best defenders—three attorneys, in McFarland's case—to save them from having to petition for mercy.[56] From the 1840s, when alienists and physicians began to testify for the defense in criminal trials, they appeared most often on behalf of the privileged, only rarely for defendants such as William Freeman.[57] The exceptional offenders of high status who were convicted on criminal charges were unlucky compared to their confreres, but compared to the average offender they were in an advantageous position when they plead for mercy. Nevertheless, it would be wrong to conclude that social privilege guaranteed a pardon, or that the typical prisoner did not stand a chance.

What mattered most in laying the groundwork for a successful plea was not the prisoner's status so much as the rank and respectability of a prisoner's supporters. Connections were critical. They made the difference between an embattled wife and children who suffered and sank into destitution while their provider remained in prison and a family reunited. Almost one-third of the case files sampled concern prisoners convicted of property crimes, ranging from petit larceny to major crimes involving fraud and forgery. In terms of his offence and demographic characteristics, Henry Alexander represents the typical applicant for clemency in the late nineteenth century: white, Anglo-American, convicted of a property offence, and sentenced to imprisonment in the state prison system. Ninety-six percent of applicants were male, and a slightly higher percentage of those in the sample were either clearly identified as white or presumed to be, owing to the absence of references to race or "color" in their files.[58] Between 1859 and 1900 only twenty-nine of the applicants were identified as German, Irish, or Italian. A paltry 3.2 percent of files pertain to the cases of prisoners identified as black or colored, which suggests these offenders were left to depend on the slim prospect of impressing a governor on one of his prison visits. However, prison staff were gatekeepers at numerous levels. No matter what a prisoner's status or background, they needed respectable petitioners to turn a hopeless case into a grant of clemency.

According to the documents in Alexander's clemency file, he was convicted of receiving stolen goods and sentenced to five years at Sing Sing State Prison in 1872.[59] The prisoner was a small trader in the clothing business in Albany, which placed him a significant cut above the poorest of prisoners; nevertheless his imprisonment had thrown his family into dire straits. Two years after Alexander entered prison Governor John Adams Dix decided to pardon the man after receiving assurances that his previous character was "very good." More importantly, the prisoner was also a husband and father of a large family with young children. Warden Hubbell of Sing Sing stated that "very many good citizens of the neighborhood where he has lived" were concerned about the family's welfare. After he turned down the first request for clemency, Dix decided to pardon Alexander, since he considered that "the ends of justice" had been served.[60]

Although Alexander's clemency file sustains the governor's public account of his decision, it provides a clear image of what it took to construct a persuasive case for mercy. The prisoner was able to cash in on his reputation with business associates, four more of whom wrote to Dix after the first merchant, and they described the convicted thief as an "honest and upright man." They also dwelt on his "attentiveness to his family" who depended upon him. A further petition stressed the hardship on his dependents, "now in actual poverty and destitution," and "living off charity." The impact of the economic crash of 1873 had begun to bite, making the release of a breadwinner an effective way to reduce the costs of imprisonment and to keep dependents off public relief rolls. This economic rationale may have induced Dix to act in Alexander's favor, but he must also have been struck by the letters that came from the victim. John Claflin owned the store (with offices in New York, Paris, Zurich, and Lyon) from which Alexander had illegally obtained goods worth one thousand dollars. Despite his company's loss, Claflin wrote four letters to the governor over 1873, animated by concern for the prisoner's "suffering family":

> His wife is completely prostrated by grief and his children, six in number, are, with the exception of one girl, too young to do anything for the support of the household. Their family physician informs us that Mrs. Alexander is suffering from heart disease which is greatly aggravated by her present trouble, and we have seen for ourselves that the whole family is extremely destitute and needy.

The victim-turned-petitioner closed by urging Dix that a pardon would be "an act of justifiable mercy," and the governor agreed.[61]

When prisoners of low status in social and economic terms had ties to superiors willing to support bids for clemency, even the most marginal could benefit from gubernatorial clemency. How else might a South American Indian have been pardoned after thieving from her mistress? Victoria Moniqurial's sentence of six months for petty larceny was not particularly harsh, especially in light of evidence that she had stolen family linen and valuable books. The DA in her case wrote in support of her release, and the mistress herself appealed for mercy for this "poor Indian girl," who appeared to suffer in New York's climate. Prison Association officeholders also took up the foreign born convict's cause. PANY's corresponding secretary and Judge Edmonds, the association's founder, both signed a letter claiming that a "designing criminal" had tricked the "half breed or Creole" into committing the theft. The physician of the white mistress, a personal acquaintance of Dix, informed the governor that the lady was so distraught over her servant's suffering that he feared for her nerves, she being a woman of "such exalted character." From an "Indian girl" imprisoned at New York's Blackwell's Island Penitentiary in July 1873, Moniqurial became a pardoned thief before winter set in.[62] The cast of characters in her case is unusual, but the credibility of her supporters was not. In six further sampled cases, victims, mainly of thefts, joined other individuals to petition for mercy, in each instance supporters of considerably higher station than the applicant himself or herself.

The small number of unsuccessful clemency applicants shows that persuasive petitioners and the most sympathetic of characters could not provide a foolproof passport to a pardon. In 1875, an impressive array of advocates appealed to Governor Samuel Tilden to pardon Margaret Caveran, an Irishwoman. No one, including Caveran, denied she had fenced stolen goods (a silk dress a servant had stolen from her mistress). Caveran's petitioners, who called themselves "residents and businessmen of New York," believed what she had told the court: she was a "very respectable" mother who had committed the crime to support her family. The DA and convicting judge found her confession credible, as did an executive officer of the Prison Association, who believed that the fifty-year-old woman, who suffered from heart disease, had been "amply punished for her crime." Since 16 of the 145 sampled files that included indications of offenders' color or ethnicity were Irish, Caveran's background was not an outright barrier to clemency. Nevertheless, Tilden refused to pardon her.[63] Advanced age, ill health, previous good character, feminine domesticity, and the support of superiors—factors that historians have consistently noted as common grounds for mercy—did not spare every offender whose applications cited those factors, even among the prisoners who presented formal written applications, let alone those who appealed to governors from behind prison bars.[64]

A substantial minority—17.2 percent—of the files sampled involved prisoners who were under twenty-one, the age of majority, at the time they were convicted. In the colonial era, notions of innate depravity had supported the use of severe penalties against young offenders; in the nineteenth century broader moves toward the education and cultivation of children into citizenship lifted petitioners' hopes when they cited youth as a ground for clemency.[65] However, under some circumstances an offender's young age could work against him. In the years immediately following the end of the Civil War, public fears of urban disorder rose, as battle-hardened veterans returning from combat appeared to embolden young males to use lethal violence to solve disputes. Nineteen-year-old Anthony Mahn, convicted of murder in the second degree in 1867, was the sort of offender people had in mind when they pondered "the boy problem."[66] At the end of Mahn's trial the judge admonished him for stabbing a fellow youth over a verbal slight, and he identified him as part of a cohort of dangerous ruffians: "you belong to a class of young men in this City who have no respect for the law, and who are ready, upon sudden impulse, to do any deed of violence and crime."[67] The first petition mounted on Mahn's behalf in 1870 was unsuccessful. As one of nine youthful applicants in the sampled files whom governors initially refused to pardon, Mahn was unlucky that Justice Theodore Miller, who presided over his trial, did not tone down his rhetoric when he reported to the governor his opinion of the clemency bid: "In pronouncing sentence I considered that the offense demanded a serious punishment, not only as a just penalty for a wanton and unprovoked crime, but as an example to others who might be prompted to take the law in their own hands without justification or excuse." In his letter to Governor Hoffman, Miller made no reference to Mahn's ethnicity (the name suggests Irish or German origins), but he did draw attention to his class by reference to the densely settled quarter of Lower Manhattan where the crime had occurred. Subsequent applications on Mahn's behalf—six in all— constructed a more forgiving impression of the altercation, more consistent with the definition of manslaughter.[68] If the crime could be seen in that light, the young man's life sentence for murder in the second degree was excessive.[69] Four governors' terms expired before Mahn found a chief executive willing to pardon him, leaving the youth a man of thirty-six by the time Governor Grover Cleveland acted. In granting Mahn's release fourteen years after petitions first rolled in, the governor could now commute his sentence on the grounds that he had served a long sentence and maintained a good record.[70] Cleveland made no formal mention of Mahn's family, but he may also have born in mind his "old and beaten down parents," "broken with grief and toil and in need of their son's aid."[71]

Pardon applicants who could count on family assistance and those whose families enjoyed a respectable reputation were better positioned than those without this clemency capital. Such petitions gained in value when petitioners of high standing endorsed them. When congressmen, senators, and foreign dignitaries wrote to urge mercy, governors felt obliged at the very least to respond, if not also to accede to their requests. In sixteen of the sampled applications men who used the title "the honorable" wrote in support; a further twelve files include letters from senators (state and federal), assemblymen, congressmen, and military officers. If the seventeen business owners, such as Claflin, are added, the number of applications in which men of influence and wealth urged governors to pardon is notable: 35 of the 252 files in the 1859– 1900 sample. Employers of men such as John J. Moran, convicted in 1883 of assault and battery against a woman, were as willing as mistresses of domestic servants to speak up for a good worker. The man who had employed Moran as a plumber and gas fitter stressed that he had always "found him to be honest and reliable." Governor Cleveland also heard from fellow Democrat John J. Cullen, whose endorsement of the man appeared on finely textured paper emblazoned with "State of New York Senate Chamber." New York feminists, such as Elizabeth Cady Stanton, had nothing good to say about husbands who used their fists and boots to assert their spousal rights, but men of substance were prepared to stand behind violent offenders who conformed in other respects to the role of male provider.[72]

Unsurprisingly, prisoners "of some wealth" and influence themselves could call most readily upon elite support in their attempts to solicit pardons. Clothing merchant Owen Tully fit this description. The New York metropolitan press estimated his worth at $30,000, but his preference for public transportation got him into trouble. In a dispute concerning his streetcar fare, Tully, heavily intoxicated, attacked and bit a Brooklyn conductor and a passenger, who sued him successfully for personal damages. Tully hired an attorney to represent him in the civil case, which he lost. After paying $6,400 in damages, he faced a criminal trial on a charge of mayhem. After his conviction he paid his attorney to prepare a bill of exceptions after his conviction, all to no avail. Tully landed in Kings County Penitentiary, facing a seven-year sentence, but at this stage his status and political connections to the "Brooklyn ring" of the Democratic Party worked in his favor.[73] The editor of the *Brooklyn Eagle*, a Civil War colonel, and a state senator all lined up to vouch for Tully as a respectable businessman, husband, and father. Governor Lucius Robinson pardoned Tully in 1876 after he served just one year of his sentence.[74]

Grants of mercy toward well-off Anglo-Americans may appear in hindsight to look inevitable. When governors delivered their annual clemency reports they regularly revealed their minds were swayed by "leading citizens" and persons of "high character," in effect admitting that class and respectability played a significant role in prompting pardons. These code words appeared in letters filed in 61 of the 252 sampled cases. Nevertheless, a close reading of case files confirms that the prominent, not just the poor, required persistence. In Tully's case, for instance, Governor Tilden refused the application for clemency, requiring his supporters to lobby Governor Robinson. Furthermore, the clemency appeals of notorious or prominent prisoners attracted press attention to executive discretion, usually unflattering. Public interest in such cases made governors wary of pardoning members of families whose names appeared on the metropolitan press's "Society" pages.[75]

The Problem of Privilege and the Pardon

Class, gender, age, and ethnicity were more than social categories: they were characteristics that the press composed into narratives for and against clemency. New York City was the nation's nucleus of daily newspapers and periodical magazines, including *Harper's* and *Frank Leslie's Illustrated News*, which catered to an increasingly diverse and expanding readership. Through wire services, stories of New York's criminal convicts and New York governors' use of the pardon power became national news. And when governors aspired to federal office, as Grover Cleveland, Samuel Tilden, David B. Hill, and Theodore Roosevelt did, they were conscious that any controversial grant or denial of mercy could aid or impede their prospects. Lobbyists seeking to advance their interests—medico-legal experts, women's rights groups, ethnic organizations, and reformatory advocates—intervened in the pardon application process whenever a case suited their objectives. Journalists turned these tussles into columns and headlines, but no newspaper had access to the clemency case files that document the micropolitics of overtly political pardons.

When Justice Theodore Miller stated that young men in New York City thought they could take the law into their own hands with impunity, it is unlikely that he had a murderer such as Frank Walworth in mind. Anthony Mahn and Walworth were the same age when they faced trial for murder, but the victim in Walworth's case was his father, Mansfield. In the summer of 1873 a melodrama unfolded in a Manhattan courtroom as the family's history of violent conflict and madness was revealed.[76] Had Francis Lieber been alive when the case came to trial he would have predicted, along with most of the New York press, that a youth with such a pedigree would never be convicted, let alone face a stiff sentence, placing him at the mercy of the chief executive. Many called for a guilty finding, but Walworth's conviction stunned the nation.

The Walworths had been tied to the highest ranks of American law and politics for generations before the family name appeared in crime columns. Frank Walworth's maternal grandfather was a Whig associate of Lincoln's and a hero of the Battle of Buena Vista during the Mexican-American War; his paternal grandfather was Reuben Hyde Walworth, former Democratic senator, judge of the state supreme court, and the last serving chancellor of New York State. Among the family members who testified at Frank Walworth's trial were his maternal uncle, a wounded Union general, and his mother, a respectable and well-educated woman prepared to reveal a history of marital cruelty to save her son. The defendant confessed to the crime, but he claimed he had shot his father to save himself and his mother from a violent abuser. This version of motive sat uncomfortably with the planned nature of the shooting and Walworth's cool manner during the trial, and it divided opinion between sympathy toward a gallant youth and horror over the unnatural crime of parricide. The *New York Tribune*, the *New York Times*, and the *Brooklyn Eagle* formed a chorus of condemnation against sentimentalists who made a hero out of a killer, and they anticipated that Walworth would evade punishment, as the cuckolded Daniel McFarland had through the much-despised "insanity dodge." But the jury surprised everyone, most of all the Walworth family. Walworth was convicted of murder in the second degree and sentenced to life in prison with no recommendation to mercy from the judge or the jury.[77] Nor did the defense counsel lodge a legal appeal. Walworth's fate became a problem for executive justice.

Cynical editors anticipated the "fancy prisoner" would spend about as much time as Owen Tully did behind bars, possibly less. But when the predicted pardon failed to materialize the press moved on, disinterested in the family's struggle to release the young man. The Walworths found that their prominence in the Democratic Party, state and federal, and their prominence in legal circles made them a liability to governors John A. Dix and Samuel J. Tilden, also Democrats. Neither man wished to give the impression of pandering to an influential family, particularly Tilden, who built his national profile as an anticorruption zealot. He banked on that reputation during his governorship of 1874–1876 as he tried to work his way toward the White House.[78] Instead Tilden turned to the state's new Lunacy Commission, introduced in 1874, which Governor Morgan had advocated at the time of the Hartung poisoning case. New York's first lunacy commissioner, Columbia University professor Dr. John Ordrinaux, signed a "lunacy certificate" that reassigned Walworth to the Asylum for the Criminally Insane at Auburn "for appropriate treatment," on the grounds that he suffered from epilepsy. Leading neurologists and psychiatrists in this period were convinced that epilepsy inclined sufferers to violence, and his family hoped his condition would improve if he were treated in a proper asylum. Better yet, he would stand the best chance at improving if he were released into his mother's care. Ellen Hardin Walworth did all she could to press for a pardon.

In many respects Frank Walworth's mother was a typical petitioner: the mother of a son whose physical and mental condition broke down in prison; a widow who had fallen on hard times, forced to support her family through her own wits; and a woman who could call on "intelligent and trustworthy citizens" to support her pleas. Yet Walworth refused to adopt the tone of supplication common in women's clemency requests. Even Lieber was forced to swallow his pride to beg the Prussian king for mercy, but Mrs. Walworth scolded three governors to do their duty. In 1876 she admonished Tilden: "I fear that my son's case has appeared to you as one that would simply appeal to your sympathy, and that you have not thought it worthwhile to examine the proofs [sic] of [my son's] innocence, or of his mental condition since his imprisonment." Tilden, like Governor Dix before him, received Ellen Walworth in personal interviews, and she pestered governors' pardon clerks for further meetings. Tilden offered Mrs. Walworth further medical reviews of her son's condition, but she insisted she had provided him with more than sufficient evidence, as she advised Tilden's clerk:

> Do remind him of the strange fatality by which my son's unfortunate condition of mind was entirely ignored in the verdict against him—and that the verdict was therefore a cruel injustice and a mistake in the administration of the law—a mistake which the pardoning power enables him to correct [sic].

Ellen Walworth grew more insistent after the election of the next governor. Soon after Lucius Robinson took office in 1877, she paid him a visit and followed it up with a didactic letter. "The law has had its way—such a hard and terrible way," so it was up to him, as governor, to "soften Justice with Mercy." "It is your privilege—your right. I know you will not forget this."[79]

When Governor Robinson finally relented by pardoning Frank Walworth on August 1, 1877, he thought it necessary to shield himself from an expected press onslaught.[80] Although his lengthy statement rivaled Governor John Young's declaration regarding his pardon of the anti-rent rebels, Robinson moved from the public sphere of democratic protest to the domestic politics at the heart of this case.[81] The victim, Mansfield Walworth, was cruel: a father who failed to uphold the ideals of paternal authority and a husband who abused his wife, physically and mentally. The son was rash, but he had acted bravely as his mother's champion. Despite claims that Ellen Walworth was a "very artful woman," who had "overinfluenced" Robinson and "blinded" his judgment, the governor made no mention of the woman's acumen.[82] This was a tale of chivalric sacrifice and its tragic costs. Men of "high scientific attainment" had informed the governor that the killer presented no risk to others and that his mental state had become precarious in prison. Thus, it was now "technically proper" to pardon a young man "morally entitled" to release.[83]

Sex Matters and Capital Justice in the Gilded Age

When governors and newspaper editors referred to the question of sex in discretionary justice they did not regard masculinity as a factor that might influence pardoning: they thought solely of women—"the sex."[84] In the late nineteenth century, the proportion of women sentenced for criminal offenses in New York's general prison population remained as low as it was at mid-century. By 1890, the number of prisoners in the state far outstripped that of other states at 11,468. Out of this number, only 1,534 were women, two-thirds of whom were minor offenders.[85] Because serious offenders serving long sentences in New York's state prisons made up the majority of clemency applicants, the female offender was more than a statistical anomaly: she was an exception whom interested parties, for and against women's rights, framed in increasingly political terms over the Gilded Age.[86]

Most governors of the nineteenth century, like Edwin Morgan, pledged their allegiance to equal consideration of men's and women's pardon applications, but the press and petitioners knew perfectly well that sex was central in women's cases, especially those involving spousal relations, and the men who held executive office in the Gilded Age had feminists to remind them of the special status of the female offender in a legal and political system designed and ruled by men. Picking up from the women who had taken over governance of the female house of refuge, advocates of separate prisons for women and lobbyists for laws designed to protect women from marital violence and sexual exploitation gained support across a wide spectrum of the nation by the 1870s.[87] Conservative women such as Ellen Walworth rejected equal suffrage as a goal, but she agreed with most politically engaged women that their home-based moral guardianship earned women a rightful place in public life, including debates over criminal responsibility and capital justice. Feminists strongly opposed male jurors' and judges' construction of the "unwritten law," which protected men from prosecution if they killed out of jealousy or fear of cuckoldry.[88] In contrast, the law unfairly punished women who fought back against their spousal oppressors, men such as the brutish Mansfield Walworth.

When Roxalana Druse was tried for the murder of her allegedly abusive husband, her case posed a political problem for feminists as well as for the governor, Democrat David B. Hill. Druse was a middle-aged mother and wife from upstate New York who shot her husband, William, dismembered his body, and burned his remains with the help of her children. The grisly crime absorbed the entire nation, and her conviction in 1885 and the long period during which the courts considered possible grounds for an appeal created the opportunity for women's rights campaigners to nail Druse's case to their larger political plank—wives' economic dependence on men and, therefore, their vulnerability to spousal abuse.[89] However, the question of marital abuse as grounds for clemency was a matter for the governor to decide.

What would it cost Hill—a Democrat facing a Republican-controlled legislature, president of the state bar association, and a rival of Cleveland's, eyeing the Democratic presidential nomination—to allow the law to take its course? More than a generation had passed since Ann Hoag was executed for poisoning her husband in 1852, and many opponents of the death penalty, in addition to those concerned with the fate of women in a male-dominated justice system, presumed that the practice could be consigned to the past.[90] After her legal appeals failed, Hill issued a reprieve of her execution, during which time he ordered a copy of the transcript from the Hoag trial of 1852. The governor's pardon clerk also looked up Governor Cleveland's report on his commutation of the 1884 death sentence of Agnetta Haight, another husband killer.[91] In this earlier act of clemency, Cleveland had cited Haight's advanced age and illness, and he explicitly denied that any "natural feeling of repugnance" had influenced his decision to commute her sentence.[92] But Druse was healthy, at least in body. Hill cannily exploited the feminist politicization of a wife driven to violence through abuse by resetting the date of her execution just long enough to let the legislative branch debate the possible exemption of women from the death penalty. Just before Christmas 1886 the governor reprieved "the murderess" to permit the consideration of a sex-specific capital punishment bill.[93]

The governor's reprieve statement, published in full in many major newspapers, demonstrated the executive's one-man power; at the same time, his search for a legislative solution carried the risk of appearing unmanly.[94] The *New York Herald* was scathing:

> Why does the Governor not commute her sentence on his own responsibility instead of waiting to hear the view of a republican Legislature in the matter? He has plainly intimated that he does not think it morally right to hang a woman, but he has not the nerve enough to stand by his own convictions.[95]

Hill, a bachelor, defended himself by stating that petitioners for Druse, who based their pleas on a bid for "greater political rights for women," should not "besiege" the executive. He also projected their defeat, since a sex-exempt capital statute would violate the rule of law. Should the legislature pass such an act it would also need to include minors, since, "like women, they have had no share in the making of the law." Hill stood up for sex-neutral punishment by drawing analogies to race and nationality: "The Indians of the State are bound by our laws and required to submit to the punishment provided for their violation, although they have no part in their enactment or any political rights. The same argument applies to aliens." The people's representatives were free to debate the wider issue of "capital punishment so far as it affects women," but it was improper, he concluded, for the executive to pardon "on account of sex."[96]

The letters in Druse's clemency file confirm Hill's awareness that plenty of New Yorkers and correspondents across the nation favored the strict application of the law to uphold masculine domestic authority. "A New York Politician" wrote the governor to say he "approved" of Hill's refusal to commute the sentence of death: "If you pardoned that woman you would never stand a chance of being elected to the Presidency. Unfortunately there is too much leniency shown to females in this country, and they are led to believe they can do whatever they like with impunity." A Mr. J. A. Johner of Brooklyn warned the governor to ignore "those nuisances to society, the 'Woman's rights females'":

> These females have done and are doing more harm to this country than fifty business panics or wars combined. They are fast destroying all the family ties, and have already succeed[ed] in destroying the obedience that wives and children owe to the husband and head of the family; do not listen to these female destroyers.

These petitioners reminded Hill that the pardon of Druse would place patriarchy, the rule of law, and God's commandments under threat.[97]

While the state assembly debated the sex-specific capital punishment bill, Governor Hill appointed three medical commissioners on February 12, 1887, to examine Druse. Each man reported that the murderess was sane now and had been sane at the time of the murder.[98] Then, on February 18, the bill to protect women from capital justice failed by a vote of 72 to 23.[99] Even had it passed the bill would have provided the governor nothing more than a reference point for commuting Druse's sentence, since he could not have applied it retroactively. With no "scientific" rationale for clemency, as Governor Robinson had claimed to justify his pardon of Walworth, Hill allowed the law to take its course: the rope broke Druse's neck and the governor proved he had backbone.[100]

David B. Hill was the governor who oversaw the introduction of electrocution as New York's new technology of death in 1888, and in this capacity he made a study of the state's authority to kill. But he also gave considerable thought to clemency. After his seven-year tenure as governor he wrote a lengthy essay on "The Pardoning Power," published in the highbrow *North American Review*. In Hill's account of executive discretion the Druse

Druse execution. Source: Undated editorial image c. 1887, uncredited source, in Executive Clemency and Pardon Case Files, box 35, folder 28.

case is notably absent; in contrast, he wrote at length about the one-man power, based on his own experience in wielding it and a mini-survey he conducted with ex-governors—Seymour, Tilden, Robinson, Fenton, Cornell, and Cleveland. Their responses supported his belief that the power to reprieve, commute, and pardon belonged exclusively to the executive, operating with "courage, integrity and good judgment." "Mere sympathy" was not a proper ground for mercy in his view, neither the governor's nor the public's; instead, decisions should be made according to "general and consistent rules." Despite this endorsement of rule-bound decision making Hill closed with a note of caution: "It is seldom that there are any two cases exactly alike; and this fact opens up a large field of discretion to be wisely exercised." Perhaps he had the Druse case in mind when he described the pardon power as a "thankless duty to discharge." Ultimately Hill agreed with Shakespeare's Portia, that mercy "becomes the throned monarch better than his crown."[101]

The Elmira Boys and Executive Discretion

Governor Hill's measured endorsement of executive discretion did not diminish his enthusiasm for the new administrative means of determining prisoners' release that were popping up in various northern states. In 1869, Massachusetts led the nation in endorsing the indeterminate sentence, and the National (later American) Prison Association promoted this tool as a vital strategy in penal reform. New York legislators followed suit in 1870 with the state's first indeterminate sentencing law.[102] Because the state's marquee penal institution, the Elmira Reformatory, placed the combination of indeterminate sentencing, discretionary release, and post-release supervision before an international audience, the impact of indeterminate sentencing was greater in New York than elsewhere. With prison agent Zebulon R. Brockway as its head, Elmira's reports of astounding inmate reform inspired the state to introduce a Board of Commissioners for Paroled Prisoners for each prison under a statute passed in 1889. This law also authorized judges to sentence any felony offender to an indeterminate term of imprisonment.[103] This is the framework in which penal historians have set Elmira's history, as the bellwether institution that presaged Progressive penology, for better and for worse. However, the Elmira Reformatory's early history is equally relevant to the history of executive clemency, as its failures in the 1880s and 1890s prompted the use of gubernatorial clemency to remedy the damage unleashed by penal "science."[104]

The Elmira Reformatory formalized the standards against which claims of good character could be made and measured. The word of respectable citizens and the emotional appeals of family members, which continued to have effect in clemency applications, were not relevant to the reformatory's internal discretionary mechanisms. New actors and a new apparatus of discipline and inspection evaluated Elmira's inmates' eligibility for discretionary release. The reformatory was an all-male institution of industry, schooling, military drills, and recreational training, all designed, Alexander Pisciotta states, to "tame and train" the "criminal classes."[105] Since 1862 inmates in New York's state prisons had been allowed to shave time off their sentences, according to a fixed remission schedule, through obedience and diligent work. An Elmira prisoner could reduce his sentence more substantially, but only if could make his way through a labyrinthine set of rules and expectations. Classified into three grades, inmates were ineligible for discretionary release consideration until they could maintain a spotless record in the top grade. The reformatory's Board of Managers and its chief agent, Brockway, sat as the parole board to review each applicant's history, institutional record, and likelihood of reoffending, granting parole only if he had a viable prospect of employment.

Under the Elmira system, more than 80 percent of inmates released at the discretion of the Board of Managers became productive, law-abiding citizens, at least according to the institution's illustrated annual reports, which Brockway marketed to boost his status and to promote the reformatory as a grand success.[106] This gloss of miraculous reform began to dull by the late 1880s, as prisoner allegations of cruelty and unfairness surfaced in clemency appeals and eventually in press accounts. The regime aimed to instill Protestant virtues and drill inmates to become obedient workers, yet it appeared from these exposés that the reformatory's chief agent ruled more like a tyrant than an enlightened penologist. By 1893 the state's chief executive, Governor Flower, became one of Brockway's chief opponents, and he used the same weapon Governor Yates had deployed in 1823 to address Auburn's solitary confinement scandal: executive discretion.

From Elmira's opening years, the families of inmates attempted to circumvent its much-touted program of institutionally managed discretionary release by applying for pardons, even before the reformatory began to orient its management toward profit-making labor.[107] The sons of well-to-do families were the most favored among applicants. After Joseph O'Flanigan, a twenty-three-year-old employee of a Buffalo railroad company, forged documents relating to his employment to the tune of almost five hundred dollars, he was fortunate to have been convicted only of forgery in the third degree. In 1879, his family's and his supporters' bid for clemency began. Every official involved in O'Flanigan's prosecution, including the judge, the DA, and his employer, referred to the prisoner's "respectable and estimable family." His character was "well informed," petitioners stated, but he had fallen in with "a bad crowd." Aided by medical evidence that he suffered from a glandular disorder O'Flanigan managed to avoid the Board of Managers because Lucius Robinson pardoned him. Joseph Carroll's backers fought a tougher fight to win a pardon, as their application came before Republican governor Alonzo B. Cornell, late nineteenth-century New York's stingiest granter of pardons. Indicted for burglary, Carroll was well defended but convicted of larceny in the second degree after police caught him in a grocery store, having robbed the till. He had served only six months of his sentence when his attorney prepared a pardon application, but because Carroll, age nineteen, was imprisoned at Elmira, Governor Cornell's pardon clerk redirected the request to Brockway for his opinion.[108]

After the reformatory opened in 1876, the governor's office and the Elmira managers juggled two forms of discretionary justice when it came to the release of inmates prior to the expiration of their terms. In the Carroll case, Brockway took the lead, but Cornell made the final move. Brockway informed the governor that the prisoner was serving an indeterminate sentence "under the *law of 1877*" and he stated that Carroll could "earn his release" with continued good behavior in eight months. Brockway also wrote to the prosecuting DA to inform him he did "not think it best for [the prisoner] to be pardoned." But Carroll's attorney maneuvered around this institutional obstruction by presenting the case to State Senator Fowler, whose endorsement appears to have persuaded the governor that the prisoner was a fit subject for a pardon. One week after the Democratic senator assured the governor that "trustworthy friends" had vouched for Carroll, the young thief was pardoned without having to demonstrate, as Brockway had dictated, that he had "grown so strong in himself that he can resist" the influence of "bad company." Instead, as Carroll's lawyer had requested, the governor discharged him in "an act of mercy."[109]

This tango between Brockway and a governor, the former stating that prisoner may be released "if they reform" and the latter pardoning them on well-established grounds of previous good character, family hardship, or ill health, turned into a tangle of missteps and resentment by the end of the decade, when inmates began publicly to accuse Brockway of abusing his discretionary powers. James O'Connor, sentenced at seventeen to an indeterminate sentence for burglary in 1883, did not expect that his five-year maximum sentence at Elmira would almost double, or that it would include a spell in a state prison. After three years at Elmira O'Connor earned his parole, but reports alleging that he had violated the conditions imposed upon his liberty led the reformatory's parole agent to authorize his recapture in 1889. The Elmira managers sent the parole violator to Auburn State Prison, where the clerk reported that O'Connor was "on the verge of insanity." The prisoner considered himself sane enough to write the judge who had sentenced him. Brockway had treated him "unjustly," he charged, and he had "railroaded" him to Auburn. In 1892 O'Connor ended up back at Elmira, but this time he pled for mercy from the executive rather than front another parole review. Brockway was "trying to make an example of me," O'Connor protested to Governor Roswell P. Flower, and Brockway's correspondence with others involved in the cases suggests the prisoner may have been correct.[110]

In 1892, Brockway informed the district attorney who prosecuted the case that O'Connor was a prisoner in the "criminal class" (the lowest in the reformatory) and a youth "without ordinary moral susceptibility." To release such a man would be "an outrage." Brockway adopted a patronizing tone with a Mrs. M. J. Cameron, who took an interest in the long-serving prisoner. At first Brockway treated her with courtesy and explained that the release of the young man "rests with the board of managers." O'Connor could not be freed because he was a "desperate and bad man." When Mrs. Cameron pressed, Brockway commended her "kind interest in unfortunate humanity" but informed her that he had "no intention to continue the correspondence." Rebuffed by Elmira's chief agent, Mrs. Cameron turned to the state executive. On June 28, 1892, nine years after James O'Connor was sentenced to an indeterminate term not to exceed five years, Governor Flower commuted the once-paroled prisoner's sentence to time served. So began the most fractious period in the mixed marriage of pardoning and parole.

Roswell Pettibone Flower, the son of a mill owner in upstate New York, had a name worthy of an aristocrat, but his origins were far less illustrious, and his hardscrabble upbringing gave him a combative edge when fighting for the unfortunate.[111] The Democratic governor took office in 1892, just as complaints about Elmira's management began to multiply, and the Elmira managers' unjust treatment of inmates and parolees became a cause that motivated him to take action. In 1893, he began to identify cases such as O'Connor's as symptomatic of the Elmira board's abuse of its discretionary powers. Allegedly insane and desperate criminals were not the only ones who turned out to be suffering as a result of extra punishment heaped upon them after unfavorable parole reports. Flower commuted the sentence of Abraham Doblin, originally sent to Elmira in 1890 for a maximum of five years, after he was transferred to Auburn following a parole violation. "Doblin has now served a longer sentence than his crime deserved or the court intended," Flower announced, "and further imprisonment would be unjust." In Frank O'Reilly's case, the governor's criticism of Elmira was more pointed. After he heard from the judge who had sentenced the young offender to the reformatory, under the assumption O'Reilly would be subjected to "such mild restraint as the prisoner's youth and previous character and the nature of the act to which he pleaded guilty seemed to require," Governor Flower concluded that Brockway had treated the prisoner as if he were a dangerous criminal, not a young man who had admitted he received stolen goods. "But, by his transfer from the reformatory to the prison, the sentence is practically converted into the severest penalty prescribed for his offense. This is manifestly unjust." Flower exercised executive discretion to outplay institutional discretion, and he pronounced the term O'Connor had served as "punishment enough."[112]

It was customary for prisoners and their supporters to claim in pardon applications that an inmate's punishment was sufficient, or that his or her treatment was excessive or unduly stiff. Elmira inmates' complaints were different, since they exposed systematic problems with the management of indeterminate sentencing and discretionary release. Beginning in July 1893, the *New York World* began a crusade on behalf of ex-inmates and set the word of inmates against the reformatory's boasts. Numerous former "Elmira boys" described a regime based on beatings, lashings, and extended periods of isolation. The brutality of the keepers made for shocking headlines, but the case that convinced Governor Flower to launch a full-scale inquiry was that of John Gilmore, an Elmira parolee who defied the reformatory's authority to declare him a parole violator. Although his employer alleged he had stolen watches while serving his parole, Gilmore was not indicted, let alone convicted. Unlike O'Reilly and O'Connor, Gilmore came from a family that could afford to hire a lawyer to contest the parole agent's authority to return him on the mere suspicion of wrongdoing. But the two legal appeals argued before the state supreme court and the U.S. circuit court failed, and Gilmore ended back at Elmira in December 1893.[113]

The public outcry that ensued over the reformatory's treatment of youth and minor offenders led Governor Flower to call upon the State Board of Charities to investigate Elmira's management. Hearings held between October 1893 and March 1894 revealed that Brockway and his staff were guilty of "cruel, brutal, excessive, degrading and unusual punishment of the inmates." The reformatory also failed by its own standard of success—to fulfill the aim of indeterminate sentencing by encouraging "the young culprit" through mild punishment. Elmira managers' transfer of parole violators to the state prisons to serve out their sentences exposed young men to serious felons and punishment beyond what the offense called for. The reformatory report concluded by indicting Brockway: "all this autocratic power is wielded by one man, the general superintendent."[114] This one man's power and the laws that allowed him to abuse it must come to end, but would the scandal spell the end of New York's experiment with institutional discretion?

In 1895, Governor Flower exercised his authority to pardon John Gilmore, but he was powerless under the state constitution to remove Zebulon Brockway from his post or to dismiss his kowtowing Board of Managers.[115] After the charity board released its report, Brockway and his supporters fought back by rolling out a publicity juggernaut that painted the inquiry as biased in favor of criminals peddling false allegations. The face-saving campaign was sufficiently persuasive that Flower ordered a second inquiry. On this occasion the majority reported that Elmira's use of corporal punishment to instill discipline and maintain order was legal and within acceptable limits. Pisciotta rightly criticizes Flower for meekly accepting the second report and allowing the abuse he knew to exist at Elmira to continue. However, the governor did endorse the minority report, authored by the second commission's chairman, Judge W. L. Learned, recently a state supreme court judge. Learned determined that by transferring reformatory inmates to state prisons Brockway and the managers had improperly subjected them to punishment beyond that set out in the Penal Code. This finding turned out to be a prophetic statement on the greater capacity for the abuse of discretionary authority behind institutional walls, far from the highly exposed governor's office. As the judge had warned, "'The managers ought not to be clothed with the arbitrary power of committing to prison for long terms persons sent by the courts to the reformatory for purposes of reformation.'"[116]

Conclusion

Governors in the second half of the nineteenth century openly admitted that they pardoned on the basis of age (youth and old age), gender (reduced severity for women), infirmity (physical and mental), the suffering of family members (emotional and financial), and claims of previous good character. Without such bases on which to appeal for clemency, prisoners such as Victoria Moniqurial might, indeed, have died in prison. But servants and day laborers with friends in high places had a far greater chance of prompting a pardon than those whose families and associates lacked the resources to launch formal applications for mercy. Each time a governor received a file from his pardon clerk, New York's chief executive assumed a role more akin to an early modern monarch than a bureaucrat in a modern government office. In democracies, however, any case could become bound up in party politics, election cycles, and negative press commentary, and governors weighed their decisions in light of their political survival, all the moreso in rare cases, such as Frank Walworth's. The records of governors' pardoning practice, including the preserved clemency case files, confirm that white New Yorkers, the very young and old, and prisoners guilty of property offenses were favored in pardon deliberations. Nevertheless, the details of any case and its timing could disrupt those patterns, as the close reading of clemency case files confirms. Pardon petitioners such as Anthony Mahn, who submitted numerous appeals to several governors, appreciated another factor that shaped the outcome of clemency appeals, and which many delegates at the 1846 constitutional convention had decried: the idiosyncratic nature of executive clemency.

The reports into pardoning practice, conducted in 1846 and 1859, proved beyond a doubt that governors' use of their discretion varied within terms and not just between them. But fluctuating pardon rates did not lead to charges of corruption or malfeasance in mid-nineteenth century New York. Insufficient transparency in the exercise of clemency was the greatest bone of contention. Governors who reported at length on the factors involved in their decisions, men like Morgan and Hoffman, conveyed the impression that they took their responsibility seriously, while a governor such as Cornell had only to point to the minuscule number of pardons he granted to demonstrate that the chief executive respected the rule of law, using mercy sparingly and with reason.

Governor Flower pardoned several Elmira boys on this basis in the state executive's first confrontation with unchecked discretionary power operating behind the reformatory's walls. The final governor of the nineteenth century, Theodore Roosevelt, made a bolder attack on Elmira's management shortly after he assumed office in 1899. The anodyne second report on the reformatory in 1894 failed to reassure the *New York World*, which continued to report the frequent use of paddling abuses into the late 1890s.[117] Roosevelt charged at the Board of Managers, since they patently failed to operate at a standard he expected of official appointees. Before he began to break up trusts as president, Governor Roosevelt successfully broke Zebulon Brockway's hold on the state's landmark reformatory in 1900, and new men took the place of Elmira's original agent and physician. Despite this dramatic change of personnel, New York's penal authorities were convinced that indeterminate sentencing and parole as pioneered at Elmira deserved wider application and greater state support. Pardons merely released inmates from prison and relieved them from penalties; by the turn of the century, reformatory treatment and parole became the means to make men over.

6

The Entanglement of Parole and Pardoning in the Progressive Era

The Prison Association of New York (PANY) decided that its 1910 annual report deserved a title: "Making Men Over."[1] Comments on pardoning are sparse in this volume, while statistics, opinions, and theories concerning parole fill page after page. The association was proud of its long history of aiding and monitoring discharged prisoners, numbering in the thousands since it began operating in 1845, and it claimed credit for persuading New York legislators to establish the Elmira Reformatory and to introduce indeterminate sentencing in conjunction with state-administered parole. The landscape of released inmate supervision was considerably more crowded than it had been in the 1840s, and PANY now worked in company with charitable organizations and a state parole board.[2] Criminologists hailed these reforms, and they pressed the state to enlist more properly trained professionals to evaluate criminals' psychological, mental, and physical fitness for normal social relations. In Thomas Eddy's day the notion of making men over meant "converting them from vicious habits to virtuous ones"; a century later Progressives overlaid this earlier religious meaning with faith in the "scientific treatment" required to cure criminals of their "psycho-physical and moral maladies."[3]

The contrast between the first generation of prison advocates' objectives of penitence and retribution and penal scientists' ambition to diagnose criminality and cure criminals has captivated historians since Progressives first chronicled their triumphs. Since the 1970s most scholars have questioned the costs and failings of the changes they introduced.[4] Through the modern "treatment" of criminals, new modes of discipline and new categories of deviance developed.[5] Tests for mental and psychological abnormalities produced "defective delinquents" and the so-called feebleminded. Experts siphoned off "incurables" from the correctional system into long-term custodial institutions, subjecting them to permanent segregation and in some states (including New York, for a short time), eugenic sterilization.[6] By concentrating on the Progressives' grandiose and costly penal experiments historians have neglected one of the greatest challenges penal managers faced by the early twentieth century: the need to release the vast majority of incarcerated men and women back into society.[7]

Parole, aided by indeterminate sentencing, was the Progressives' answer to this problem, which became most pressing in the state with the nation's most diverse population and its highest number of prisoners.[8] In some of New York's carceral institutions, such as the Bedford Hills Reformatory for Women and the Elmira Reformatory for young male offenders, social scientists and medical experts assessed parole eligibility and internal managers exercised discretion over the release of inmates.[9] But the large state prisons, which held over 80 percent of prisoners, also produced the greatest number of applications for parole in the state, and the Board of Parole processed their files after 1901.[10] Minutes of the board's interviews of prospective parolees—in some years, verbatim accounts—indicate that its members' chief concern was that men would make good and that women would "behave" if released. With little attention to diagnosing deviance or calculating the likelihood of recidivism, the board made moralistic judgments of character and used plain talk, more patronizing than professional in tone. Applicants' responses to questions appear in these records as well, ranging from contrite acceptance to puzzlement and belligerence. The men governors appointed as parole's gatekeepers in the board's first decades of the twentieth century had more in common with Isaac Hopper, the Quaker who pioneered prisoners aid, than they did with the experts who delivered papers at international prison congresses, and who tower in Progressive penal historiography.

As the Board of Parole expanded the reach of administrative discretion, the number of prisoners released through pardons dropped sharply; however the Board of Parole was established to work with the governor's office, not to replace executive discretion. Governors reviewed applications for clemency aware that refusing a request or delaying a decision left open the prospect of parole, and the sample of preserved clemency files lodged between 1901 and 1920 (109) confirms this change of approach.[11] The board considered parole for prisoners sentenced to indeterminate terms, but it was also authorized to recommend individuals ineligible for parole for gubernatorial clemency—in effect, to act as internal petitioners for pardon. In turn, governors began to commute sentences rather than grant pardons, and they required released inmates to submit to the authority of the parole board. A century of protest against pardoning's interference in efforts to reform inmates through penal discipline resolved into a modus vivendi between two modes of discretionary release, one ancient and personal, the other modern and administrative. Nevertheless, the custom of petitioning the governor, and the conduct of gubernatorial discretion, remained more personal and more easily scrutinized than the administration of parole. Pardon clerks' growing assumption of responsibility for corresponding with prisoners and their advocates did not change the fact the governor was still the man who attached his name to annual reports of pardons, commutations, and reprieves, who signed the statements that sent prisoners to the electric chair, and who carried the power of life and death on his shoulders.[12]

Rudimentary State Parole and Indeterminate Sentencing

From the earliest phase of parole's implementation, its backers asserted that indeterminate sentencing was critical to its success. A sentence without a fixed terminal point was one "which the prisoner himself can terminate by good conduct."[13] New York's state prisoners had been able, since the 1860s, to earn remission time as a reward for obedience and the acceptable performance of work. Indeterminate sentencing laws differed because they granted institutional agents, starting with the Elmira Reformatory's Board of Managers, considerably more discretion in determining when and whether an inmate might be released; in addition, they opened up the prospect for prison superintendents to devise a wider range of criteria for parole eligibility. In 1889, the legislatures of New York, Minnesota, and Michigan each passed laws that allowed judges to sentence convicted criminals to ranges of periods of incarceration. Although Massachusetts and Ohio preceded New York in linking indeterminate sentencing to parole assessment and supervision, the state caught up by authorizing institutional parole boards to operate in each of the state prisons.[14] Over the 1890s, the Elmira Reformatory's system of graded imprisonment and monitored release began to spread system-wide.

New York's 1889 indeterminate sentencing law provided courts the option to sentence any convicted felon to an indeterminate sentence within the minimum and maximum terms set by law, and it set up a Board of Commissioners of Paroled Prisoners, made up of the warden, chaplain, physician, and principal keeper, plus the state superintendent of prisons.[15] Once prisoners completed their minimum sentences they were eligible to apply for release on parole, subject to reincarceration if they violated the conditions imposed on their liberty. In 1891, the National Conference of Charities and Correction warmly endorsed the 1889 law, pronouncing it "doubtless the most scientific code of prison law that has yet been enacted on either side of the Atlantic."[16] Delegates also predicted, correctly, that judges would resist the reform.[17] From 1889 to 1901, over which time courts committed 13,000 convicts to New York's prisons, judges handed down just 115 indeterminate sentences.[18] The vast majority of inmates in the state prisons who left prison prior to the expiration of their sentences did so because they earned "good time" remissions.[19]

The great exception was Elmira. Its inmates, young men mainly in their late teens and early twenties, had to navigate their way through Zebulon Brockway's classifications and pass the prison physician's appraisals before the reformatory's managers pronounced them suitable for parole. Managers classified each inmate from his reception on the basis of his offense and criminal history; more significantly, prison managers probed inmates' "antecedents," which entailed looking for evidence of insanity, epilepsy, dissipation, education, pecuniary condition, occupation and "pauper or criminal" status. Brockway worked closely with reformatory physician Dr. Hamilton Wey, who subscribed to biological theories of inheritable criminal tendencies. They agreed that more than one-third of Elmira's inmates were "dullards," "defective," or "degenerate," which left them unable to "keep pace with the moderate requirements of the educational, mechanical, and disciplinary" regime within the reformatory, let alone the wider world. Reformatory prisoners required "treatment prescriptions," according to Brockway. For most inmates treatment consisted of industrial training, school instruction, organized sports and physical training, and military drills and parades.[20]

Brockway knew from the start of his tenure that his reputation as a penal visionary and the fate of the rehabilitative ideal would hinge on the reformatory's success in turning criminals into successfully paroled men. When the *New York World* attacked the reformatory in the early 1890s, alleging that it brutalized inmates, Brockway fought back with records showing that Elmira's Board of Managers had paroled 3,723 inmates between 1877 and 1893, and that 81.9 percent of parolees "had not returned to crime." A favorable English review of Elmira in 1891 commended the reformatory's capacity to spark "the instinctive striving" of the individual: "it is indeed astonishing what striking results are thereby attained, no matter with how much indolence, and intellectual and physical inactivity the subject may have hitherto been afflicted." As long as an inmate's faculties were not "too defective and debased, or too dwarfed to be capable of being effectively awakened," the reformatory successfully prepared criminals for supervised liberty.[21]

The Prison Association of New York provided critical support for Elmira's model of discretionary institutional release. Whether or not its members privately believed prisoners' allegations of Brockway's cruelty and Elmira's arbitrary rule, they stood squarely behind the ideals of rehabilitation and reintegration. PANY's own credibility was on the line, since most of the inmates paroled from Elmira reported to the association's headquarters in New York City for job and housing assistance and to register for supervision.[22] The state also relied on PANY's assistance, because the state's Agency for Discharged Convicts, formed in 1877 to assist released inmates, simply handed them a few dollars after the prison gate closed and sent them on their way. In contrast, PANY's Discharged Prisoners Committee could report in 1895 that its own agents had registered 2,300 young men from Elmira since 1877 and settled approximately half of them into homes and jobs in Manhattan and Brooklyn. PANY's parole agents regularly admitted that a number of men had violated their parole, requiring their return to Elmira; yet the association's annual reports consistently stated that fewer than 10 percent fell into that category.[23] Frederick Wines, son of the founder of the American Prison Association and an authority on penology in his own right, declared in 1905 that the "percentage of cures already obtained" at Elmira, "still in the experimental stage, warrants its retention and extension."[24] Such positive evaluations, illustrated with compelling tales of wayward men who returned to the straight and narrow, elevated public confidence in the principles of indeterminate sentencing and monitored, earned release.

Manning the First Board of Parole

Zebulon Brockway and Dr. Wey both resigned from Elmira in 1900 after Governor Theodore Roosevelt stripped them of their authority by appointing new men to serve on the reformatory's Board of Managers.[25] But greater changes were underway after the turn of the century. In 1901 New York extended to all felons in the state prison system the opportunity to apply for parole as long as their crimes carried a maximum sentence of five years or less.[26] The new State Board of Commissioners of Paroled Prisoners was to work, for the first time, with salaried parole officers installed in Sing Sing, Auburn, and Clinton state prisons.[27] A more profound change occurred in 1907, when indeterminate sentencing applied to all first-time felonies, with the exception of murder in the first degree.[28] To manage this "materially enlarged" cohort of prospective parolees New York formed a new State Board of Parole, which included the superintendent of state prisons as chair plus two appointees.[29] The impact of the 1907 statute was profound: in just three years the number of inmates applying for parole rose by 400 percent.[30]

The first men appointed to the State Board of Parole carried experience in policing, criminal law, sentencing, and punishment to their new positions, not social scientific or medical training.[31] Cornelius V. Collins was the superintendent of prisons, which automatically qualified him to head the first Commission for Parole, and a string of Republican governors kept him on after the new Board of Parole formed in 1907.[32] Democrat John A. Dix, elected in 1910, put an end to the superintendent's tenure in 1911, but the other men of the board remained until their terms expired.[33] George A. Lewis, appointed in 1907 on a five-year term, began his career in criminal justice in 1886 as a municipal court judge in Buffalo. He then served as a manager of the Western House of Refuge (which operated under the State Board of Charities), followed by the New York State Training School for Girls north of New York City. Commodore Albina Verette Wadhams, a man with extensive experience of discipline and punishment, was the third member of the first separate Parole Board, and he joined after serving forty-three years in the U.S. Navy.[34] Despite the Prison Association's advocacy of professional penal administration, it was assured by "the independence of judgment, enlightened zeal and devotion which the members of the new Board are bringing to their task."[35]

Ex-judge Lewis was so confident in the board's work that he published a popular account of parole procedure in New York in 1911. Lewis provided figures to back his story of success. From 1907 to 1910, the board granted parole to two thousand state prisoners who had "made good" by becoming "useful members of society." Lewis believed that grants of parole had spread "the hope of early and favorable action" throughout the state system and saved New York considerable expense in the process. When he spoke of hope Lewis referred to a state of mind distinct from anticipating a pardon. To be granted parole, an applicant had to build up hope by attending classes, undertaking training, and following rules. Male prisoners had to secure "suitable offers of employment," and women as well as men needed to provide proof that their release would lead them to a "proper place of abode." Whenever board members came across reports that indicated "the interest of good people generally to lend a helping hand" they were doubly assured that an inmate would succeed.[36] Lewis did not frame his article as an assault on gubernatorial clemency, but the account he provided of the board's work set out the specific criteria involved in this administrative mode of discretion, in contrast to the broad principles and specific circumstances typically mentioned in governors' pardon reports.

Applying for parole required the generation of reports—many, many reports—before an inmate could be released under supervision. To be eligible prisoners had to complete a written test of thirty-five questions concerning their "criminal history", their "family relations," an account of their crime, and their work history. Applicants also had to appear before the board on one of its periodic visits (generally one or two days per month) to each prison. In these rushed hearings uniformed inmates sat in front of a desk facing a trio of suited white men. Between them lay the prisoner's "dossier," which included reports from the warden, the principal keeper, the prison clerk, the chaplain, the school principal, and the prison physician, "as to the convict's physical and mental condition." Finally, the district attorney of the jurisdiction in which the trial had occurred was asked to state whether he thought there was any reason why an inmate should *not* be paroled.[37] Well-educated prisoners and native speakers of English likely had an inkling of the information in their dossiers, but no prisoner could have doubted the power behind the documents in the hands of these men. As one Parole Board member lectured a prospective parolee: "our records do not lie but individuals do . . . you can't get away from the records."[38]

Do You Understand the Nature of Parole?

In the Parole Board's first decade, deciding whom to parole involved snap character appraisals rather than examinations of the prognosis of delinquency; in seeking truth in prisoners' dossiers the members' gaze was moral and tied to practicalities, not clinical. The board members' determination of parole eligibility was steeped in middle-class Protestant values, their notions of racial and ethnic hierarchies, and their fixed belief in men's and women's distinct natures. The parole hearing records provide a vivid picture of this form of discretion in action. In a visit to Auburn State Prison in 1908 Superintendent Collins gave the male parolees a speech that explained what restricted liberty entailed: "you [have] an opportunity to do just what you have said you would do numberless times since you have been in prison—that if you only had one more opportunity you could make good. The State assumes that you mean what you say." Collins ended his exhortation with a dollop of fatherly advice. "It is up to you to make good, and I hope each one of you will do so. Good luck, boys, and God bless you."[39]

Because Auburn also contained a prison for female felons, repurposed from the former prison for criminal "lunatics" in 1893, women's parole requests were processed by the all-male board. Man-to-woman exchanges differed from man-to-man talk.[40] At the conclusion of the board's hearings on its September 1908 trip to Auburn, the superintendent gave female parolees what he claimed to be "the same advice that applies to the men." Yet he made no reference to their honor or their "word," treating them more as children: "You are given your liberty on your promise to behave yourself . . . you are not to keep evil associations. You are not to frequent disorderly places. You are not to drink liquor in any form. You are to behave yourself as each one of you know[s] you ought to." Despite his warning to avoid "dissolute characters" and his observation of "the tendency for a woman if she becomes stranded . . . to start soliciting on the streets," Collins believed that women were more likely than men to leave prison life behind.[41] Women were naturally drawn to home, according to the board, whereas men had to be prodded to return to domestic life, to find steady jobs, and to support their dependents.

Female and male inmates in the state prisons received the same parole booklet, which spelled out the requirements for applications and told prisoners what the board expected of them. In short, prisoners had to show they understood their liberty, if granted, was conditional. Most of the board's interviews ended with questions concerning candidates' capacity to understand the rules for release. For many this meant abstaining from alcohol, with only the small number of inmates serving drug offence sentences quizzed about their use.[42] When inmates pledged to become teetotalers if released, board members peppered them with questions concerning their drinking history. Commodore Wadhams and his fellow members were favorably disposed toward Walter Jones's application, but they worried about the drunken state he was in when he committed the robbery that landed him in prison: "Q- Drunk when you committed this crime? A- Yes, Sir. Q- Been on a drunk for any length of time? A- Wouldn't call it being on a drunk. Had been drinking for 4 or 5 days." Jones's admission raised concerns about his capacity to resist temptation if released. Before they were prepared to place him with a Buffalo building firm, one member asked: "Do you understand the nature of parole?" The prisoner replied by paraphrasing the parole application handbook: "Lead a correct and abstemious life, and not visit saloons, or go with bad characters, or hang out where bad characters are known to be." The rote answer failed to satisfy the board, which ribbed Jones over his fall from respectability. Lewis and Wadhams were surprised to read in Jones's dossier that he had served in the army with an honorable discharge. "I see here letters from the Army people giving you all kinds of recommendations for bravery, etc.," Lewis commented, flicking through the prisoner's file. Then the superintendent weighed in: "Q- Don't you feel cheap in those [prison] clothes?" Collins's emasculating question is a reminder that class and race were not the only distinctions reinforced through parole interrogations. The man's response to the board chairman's question was possibly tearful: "A- Feel ashamed of myself. Cried many a night over it."[43]

Chaplains hired to work in prisons, visiting clerics, and representatives of charitable prisoner aid associations, particularly the Volunteers of America, which included a New York City–based Prisoners' League, helped inmates with their applications and pledged to assist them on release. Edward Oliver had a promise of work painting and decorating, and he told the board he would, if paroled, "go out and be a gentleman." Walter Comfort declared he would follow a simple plan: "To keep away from bad habits, and keep steady at work." When board members felt sympathetic toward a prisoner, they encouraged them toward the right answer. Robert J. Foreman, imprisoned for stabbing a man in a drunken fight, attracted Collins' concern about the prisoner's future prospects: "You would feel pretty humiliated if you were brought back for drinking rum. You have got it in you to make something for yourself if you want to, but you can't drink rum and keep out of prison." Before he left the hearing room, Foreman assured the board he was a man made over: "There is no danger of my drinking. I am a new man, physically, morally and mentally." Men with wives and children, such as convicted burglar Howard Hubble, won the board's favor with a pledge to become responsible providers. This prisoner declared that parole "means for me to live an upright life, to report to you each month, attend my work, take care of my family." And if he failed? "Would be brought back here."[44]

Prisoners with a poor command of English were at a considerable disadvantage in hearing interviews, which were conducted without translation, but the board was prepared to parole foreign-born offenders if they abided by rules and worked to the satisfaction of prison overseers. The most important matter was the promise of a job. The interview process was bewildering for inmates who struggled to understand English as they sat facing board members who raced through questions and showed little patience toward inmates who failed to keep up. Interpreters could be hired but the costs fell on the inmate, which left most with limited English struggling to understand questions or provide satisfactory answers. Massimilino Ferrato enlisted an interpreter when he appeared before the board, who recommended him for parole after an exchange that could have taken no more than a minute. When the board asked Antonio Bono if he could read and write in English, he replied, "little bit." In response to a demand that he define parole his answer was accurate but brief: "Parole has no job can no go out." The board tried to explain that it would take much more to go straight after his conviction for larceny: no drinking beer, no stealing, they warned Bono. Then the Italian replied to their question about what would happen if he failed to heed this warning: "I come back." The clerk summed up the board's negative decision: "NO WORK. LACK OF APPRECIATION OF WHAT PAROLE MEANS."[45]

The indices of the Parole Board's prison visits in the early twentieth century show a preponderance of applicants with Anglo-Celtic names; nevertheless, the range of ethnicities evident is far greater than it is among clemency petitioners from the same period. Italian names dominate in the parole records, but Russian, German, and Polish names appear regularly, along with those of Jews.[46] On the board's September 1908 visit to Auburn, for instance, thirty-three men and two women received parole, and nine were granted an absolute discharge after serving out their parole. Of that number, the board released fifteen prisoners who were recent immigrants, or whose first language was not English. Indeed, the parole of inmates who had learned in prison how to read and write and to "obtain an honest livelihood" confirmed for the board, and Progressive penologists broadly, that prisons, properly run, could educate men, train them, instill regular habits, and make them employable. The Prison Association's Discharged Prisoners Committee put the challenge bluntly in its 1910 report: "inmates on release either amalgamate with society and become part of its army of workers, or else they continue their life of crime."[47]

Although African Americans appeared before the board in far smaller numbers than European immigrants did, those who managed to gain respect in the racist penal regime could impress the board.[48] When applicants had solid references in their dossiers from prison foremen and teachers, all white, they stood a fair chance at parole, even when the crimes they committed threatened the white community. Like all offenders, African Americans' crimes typically occurred within their own communities, but Clarence Gayton's sexual assault in 1906 was a dramatic exception. The court gave the twenty-three-year-old tanner the maximum sentence of twenty years for rape after he admitted he had dragged a local white woman out of bed and into a field, where he attacked her. The sentencing judge underscored the racial threat Gayton posed by describing him as a "'brutal negro,'" and he stated further that "he found no adequate punishment for so serious a crime . . . the law does not contain a punishment commensurate with his crime." When Gayton appeared before the Parole Board after serving just half of his sentence (the minimum time required of prisoners serving definite sentences before they could apply for parole), he could not provide a clear answer when asked if he understood the conditions he would be expected to uphold. Curiously, the board granted him parole, perhaps because his father, a law-abiding constable, was willing to vouch for his son and secure him work.[49] Despite the positive outcome for this man, the fact remains that African American prisoners were significantly underrepresented among those whom keepers and wardens were willing to recommend for consideration.[50] The opposite was true of prisoners who suffered the extreme penalty: 24 of the 202 people executed between 1900 and 1920 were black men.[51]

The early Parole Board members were considerably more patronizing toward female applicants, especially African American women, who made up a disproportionate number of Auburn's separate prison for women.[52] Nellie Smith, "colored," was brought up from solitary confinement to appear before the board on its January 1909 visit to Auburn, even though the "D" on her uniform (to denote her delinquent status) disqualified her for parole. Lewis

opened with a taunt: "Q- What is that 'D' on your sleeve? You like it here better than outside? A- No." Smith admitted she had worked "on the street," and
that she was living with "a colored man in a furnished room" when arrested.
Collins followed with a scolding: "Q- You want to get that letter 'D' off of your
sleeve. You don't want to go out in disgrace? A- No, I will work if I go out."
Smith admitted that drink was the cause of her troubles, and she made the
usual pledge to avoid alcohol if released. Whether or not they believed her the
interviewers emphasized that she must first prove she could behave on the inside: "Q- Will you promise the Board you will behave long enough to get that
letter off of your sleeve before you come before the Board again? A- Yes, sir."[53]
   White women given to "smart" remarks could also try the board's patience.
Ethel Clayborne attempted to convince the board she had been a "lady's maid"
before her arrest for larceny. Pressed, she admitted she had a prior arrest for
soliciting. "Practice prostitution besides [being] a lady's maid?," Lewis jabbed,
to which she replied: "I didn't practice it." Infuriated, he drilled her when she
refused to itemize her prostitution arrests: "You know I want to know just exactly the times. Once, twice or a hundred." At this point Clayborne appeared
cowed, and she confessed to more than three arrests. The truth extracted,
the board decided to parole the woman, whose prison record was clean.[54]
Appearing before the board, inmates were needled for the truth. In contrast,
pardon petitioners could craft accounts of previous good character without
having to deliver a convincing live performance.
   Inmates who defied the board's authority or gave cheeky replies provoked
sarcastic barbs, not the cold, clinical response of the penal professional. Win-
nie Towhey, a repeat applicant for parole, came up before the board in February 1908. When asked why she could not qualify for parole, she spat back: "I
have got a temper. That is the only trouble." African American women were
especially vulnerable to internal disciplinary measures but recalcitrant white
women, such as Towhey, were sent to Auburn's dungeon (officially "refractory
cells") for similar reasons. When Collins scolded Towhey over her bad behavior record, she lashed out: "When punished for nothing what can I do? I don't
care if I don't get out until my time is up. I am punished for nothing, and sent
down in that dark hole for nothing." The board clearly believed the records,
not the prisoner, and Towhey vented her frustration: "I don't care. You can
kill me if you want to, I will stay here . . . I can stay until [the expiration of my
sentence], and I will die here." "Then you will stay here," Collins shot back:
"Don't get disrespectful or I will have to order you punished." Months later,
Towhey gave the men cheek a second time, after Collins pointed to the "D" on
her sleeve: "I don't look any the worse, do I?" Again, the board's stenographer
typed, "DENIED" at the bottom of the hearing transcript.[55]

Unlike confrontational women, who complained of cruel punishment for trivial offenses, such as talking or laughing, assertive men frequently referred to their rights under the law.[56] "I have been up 7 times for parole," Thomas Clark stated, in an effort to ensure that his application would be reviewed fairly. Then he told the board he deserved to be paroled: "Now I think I might get a chance. I ain't been punished since I have been here, and I intend to do what is right if I get out . . . Judge told me they would let me out in a year." Another male re-applicant demanded to know "what was I held back for last time?" When Collins refused to respond to George Stanley he became insistent:

> If there is anything wrong in the reason I don't make this parole, I wish the Board would state it. I have tried my utmost. I have done everything possible, and I can't see any reason. I have done my very best. I have done more in this institution than I would do outside I have worked myself like a slave in that shop.

As a white man, the convicted burglar had no experience of slavery, but he had a clear sense that the board's refusal to justify its decision was undemocratic. "I would like to have a reason," Stanley repeated: "I am merely asking my rights. I am only asking for justice."[57] Parolees who violated the conditions imposed on their liberty had the right to appear again, but in William Bell's case Collins informed the prisoner that the board would refuse his request for reconsideration. Defiant, Bell replied: "I am going to keep my word pretty good, even if you didn't yours." Another parole violator, James Williams, told the board he had served his maximum sentence; on top of that, by his calculation, he had earned seventeen months for good behavior while a prisoner. "They kept me in for 5 years that ain't justice."[58] Inmates who seized the opportunity to speak their minds may have left hearings with a modicum of self-respect, but confrontational candor and discretionary parole did not mix.

Fitness for Release

Beyond the walls of parole hearings penal politics in New York were shifting profoundly over the 1910s, but few of the changes they wrought influenced the Parole Board's exercise of its discretion. Male prisoners' references to rights may have owed their inspiration to the appointment of Thomas Mott Osborne as warden of Sing Sing in 1911, and his support for the idea of self-governance as the best means to build offenders' capacity for social adjustment and responsible citizenship. In other avenues of Progressive penology, experts lobbied for greater attention to the "menace" of feebleminded offenders and inmates with medical and psychological defects, which clogged the system with people incapable of improvement. In 1911, PANY hired Dr. George M. Parker as its "psychiatric examiner" and sent him into the state prisons and reformatories to comb for mental defectives. Allowing that "'defectiveness, mental inferiority, early psychoses and psychopathies [sic] are not easy to detect even by the trained man,'" Parker nonetheless reported that the state's prisons and reformatories held thirteen hundred "defectives"—roughly one in seven inmates.[59]

The Prison Association of New York was one of the first organizations in the world to investigate the hereditary nature of criminality, beginning in 1875 with its publication of Association executive officer Robert Dugdale's study of the Jukes, the fictitious name he gave to an upstate New York family filled with generations of paupers, insane individuals, and criminals.[60] The redis-covery of his work by eugenically minded policy makers in the Progressive Era was instrumental in persuading New York to adopt legislation in 1912 to authorize the sterilization of the "unfit" in its state institutions.[61] The Board of Parole appeared impervious to these eugenic fears, however, and aloof from the state's growing investment in medico-penal expertise.

As far as Cornelius Collins and his fellow men of the Parole Board were concerned, career criminals and callous recidivists posed the greatest threat to the law-abiding citizenry, not the "unfit." Commodore Wadhams, speaking in 1911, was acerbic in his assessment of habitual offenders: "'They are the mad dogs of society. They should be imprisoned for life or chloroformed and then buried in lime, they are so dangerous." Wadhams delivered his speech to a church audience in Bedford, only months after researchers up the road at the Bedford Hills Reformatory for Women had started to study feebleminded-ness in the new Bureau of Social Hygiene.[62] Wadhams worked for the same cutting-edge penal system, but for him, the feebleminded deserved pity. In his speech he identified the prisoners most worthy of assistance in finding work and charitable support after their release as "the class of feeble-minded, lazy or ignorant criminals, many of whom have never had a chance to live straight lives." Although the board frequently denied such prisoners parole, this was due to their poor job prospects, not because they posed a menace to society.[63] Parole hearing records also reveal that Wadhams and his fellow members (unlike Progressive experts) considered sexual offenders credible candidates for reform, content that the pains of imprisonment were likely sufficient to teach such men a stern lesson. The board approved parole for men guilty of rape, incest, and sodomy with minimal fuss.

Apprehension over nonconsensual and nonnormative sexual conduct escalated over the late nineteenth and early twentieth centuries across industrialized countries as coalitions of suffragists and social purity advocates succeeded in lobbying for laws that policed men's as well as women's conduct, and human scientists studied, diagnosed, and attempted to cure deviance and sexual pathologies.[64] The Parole Board's fixation in the early 1900s on female prisoners' history of "solicitation" was one expression of the attention to "vice." When they dealt with men charged with sexual offenses, however, their attitude differed radically. Their interview of Edward Thompson in 1907 provides a flavor of their approach with rapists: stern but matter-of-fact. The thirty-four-year old teamster from upstate New York was convicted of rape in the second degree in 1902 and sentenced to serve at least five years, up to a maximum of nineteen.[65] The victim was his niece, who had boarded with her aunt and uncle. At his trial, she testified that Thompson had attacked her, leaving her pregnant. Subsequently, the victim died in childbirth. All of this information sat in the prisoner's dossier, and it came out during the parole interview, with no condemnatory or sarcastic questions from the board. When Lewis asked the convicted rapist if he knew what conditions he would need to observe if paroled Thompson admitted he had no idea, and the next moments of the hearing demonstrated the all-male board's readiness to give male sexual offenders the benefit of the doubt. Lewis helpfully read out the rules (and Thompson obediently stated he would follow them). Then he questioned the credibility of the evidence against the prisoner: "was there any physician who testified at your trial?" Collins stepped in to ask Thompson to confirm whether the medical witness had testified against him. "Yes," he replied. This damning admission did not lead to a referral to a prison psychiatric clinic; instead, the board gave Thompson supportive advice, man-to-man: "Do you realize Edward that you are the kind of man that might occasionally be tempted to assault a girl?" The prisoner thought not, since he told the board that the incident had occurred only because he had drunk "a few beers" while he was "alone in the house" with his niece.[66]

The board's focus on Thompson's use of alcohol suggests that they regarded inebriation rather than psychopathology as the explanation for the offence. And then there was the question of the victim's possible culpability. The board bent over backward to help him out: "Was she a girl that was extraordinarily developed . . . ?" Again, Thompson admitted she was "not big for her age." Lewis, the ex-judge, leafed through the man's trial records. "I see by the papers that you said she excited you." When Thompson denied this statement the ex-judge simply ended the interview on a note of encouragement: "Q- You have quite a great inducement to leave the girls alone? A- Yes sir." With a promise to return to his wife ("a good respectable woman") and a job offer from his former employer, Thompson joined the seventeen men paroled from Auburn after the board's November 1907 visit.[67]

The minimal concern of the Parole Board toward sexual violence involving female victims is not surprising at a time when encrusted attitudes toward heterosexual men's inability to resist temptation retained their hold. Despite psychology's and sexology's contributions of new categories of diagnosis, the board operated under the persistent belief that men's sexual urges were natural, that witnesses were duplicitous, and that females, particularly working-class women, used sex to ensnare men.[68] These men of the Parole Board, it bears underscoring, deliberated over the fate of convicted sex offenders who had been prosecuted by a male attorney, convicted by an all-male jury, and sentenced to a term of imprisonment by a male judge for a felonious sexual act. After serving a portion of prison sentences of up to twenty years, these offenders appeared before another cohort of male authorities, a board with the power to deny parole and the freedom to censure them in pre-release interviews, as they did with other prisoners; yet, sex offender parole applicants in New York's state prisons discovered they had little to fear from the board, even men convicted for victimizing males.

If the men on the Parole Board in the early twentieth century shared the Progressives' concern about the problem of homosexuality as a pathological condition, their relaxed approach to sodomy cases suggests not. Until 1796 sodomy was a capital crime in New York, and in the early twentieth century the Penal Code still specified a stiff maximum penalty—twenty years. As George Chauncey notes, the prosecution of homosexual acts increased significantly in the late nineteenth century, largely at the urging of the Society for the Prevention of Cruelty toward Children, an influential New York City–based lobby group. After a long period of casual policing, the rate of arrests rose sharply after the 1890s. In New York City alone police arrested approximately fifty men for sodomy each year during the 1910s.[69] Judges took advantage of their option to sentence men accused of same-sex contact to the maximum term allowable under the law, and they did so with the weight of religious and moral support, plus the new findings of psychologists and medical doctors who interpreted homosexual acts as signs of pathological personality disorders.[70] In the Elmira Reformatory, Dr. Wey routinely examined all young men for signs of "degeneracy," irrespective of their crimes, and Dr. John E. Gerin of Auburn always made note of deviant sexual behavior in the form of homosexual activities when he prepared reports for parole applicants. Yet, each time the board considered a convicted sodomite a viable parolee they sidelined such expertise.

In Charles Elder's case the board's questioning revealed a past studded with signs of abnormality by the psychological standards of the day; nevertheless the members and the applicant before them treated the evidence in a low-key manner. Elder's mother had died when he was young, he stated, and because his father was a drinker, he spent his boyhood in a children's refuge. Elder's arrest record indicated he was charged with theft after stealing undergarments from a clothesline, and Collins asked what had prompted the theft. "That's one on me. I don't know," was all the prisoner had to say. In contrast to the grilling Collins gave Ethel Clayborne over her prior solicitation arrests, he appeared satisfied with the prisoner's brief explanation that he was imprisoned for "sodomy on boy . . . about 13 or 14 I reckon." Elder also admitted he had been punished twice in the ten years he had spent in prison on a twenty-year maximum term. Unconcerned over those infractions, the board was satisfied that a man from upstate New York had offered to hire him on a farm: "Q- Think you could behave yourself if paroled? A- Yes, sir." If Dr. Gerin's report on Elder's sexual impulses appeared in the prisoner's dossier, the board made no reference to it in the hearing. Their roster of applicants was particularly full on their July visit to Auburn. None of the members even asked Elder if he understood what parole meant.[71]

Pardoning despite Parole

In the first decades of its existence, the Board of Parole's exercise of administrative discretion shared much with the practice of executive discretion: both modes of releasing prisoners before their terms of imprisonment expired were governed by broad statutory and constitutional criteria, not formal rules. Further similarities between gubernatorial clemency and parole assessment emerged as governors began to impose conditions on pardons and sentence commutations, newly enforceable thanks to the introduction of statewide parole. "To be placed under the authority of the Parole Board" became a standard rider on governors' commutations of sentences by the 1910s; in contrast, the unconditional pardon became a rarity, reserved most often for sick or elderly prisoners.

There were two respects, however, in which these dual forms of discretionary justice remained distinct. First, the governor's constitutional powers still exceeded the statutory authority of the Parole Board, although the chief executive's use of his discretion could land him in hot water, as Governor Dix discovered during his term in office in the early 1910s. Second, the governor's greater discretionary authority came with closer scrutiny over his actions. The Parole Board reported annual figures on its activities without providing explanations for its decisions in individual cases, as numerous prisoners complained. Similarly, governors were not obliged to publicize their justifi-cations for pardons, commutations, and reprieves. Yet most found it wise to do so, following a tradition of openness established in the mid-nineteenth century, when critics of the executive privilege began to keep a close watch on the chief executive's use of his prerogative. Ironically, the constitutional convention delegates whose trust in executive discretion kept New York in the slow lane of reform predicted correctly that one man, holding the power to pardon, was more accountable than any board.

In the early 1890s, when Governor Flower pardoned Elmira inmates who appeared to suffer excessively through the Board of Managers' manipulation of the reformatory's internal parole system, he followed the traditional prac-tice of granting clemency on the basis of mental or physical affliction. At the same time, he anticipated subsequent governors' use of the prerogative to release prisoners who could not qualify for parole but who nonetheless deserved to be freed. In 6 percent of the 109 clemency files sampled be-tween 1901 and 1920, the prisoner's illness or impending death was stressed as grounds for clemency.[72] The number of inmates who died in prison, al-though it had lowered from the rates seen in New York's first penitentiaries, was far greater than the number released through executive discretion. In the early twentieth century, governors show they regarded extreme suffering in prison a legitimate basis for a clemency bid. In contrast, board members frequently advised prisoners with serious medical conditions that they must remain in prison to receive medical care. And for the good of the public, men and women diagnosed with venereal disease were forced to submit to prison physicians' treatment. The Parole Board regarded this medical status on par with the "D" on the sleeves of delinquents, but they often found that males were unconcerned about their infections. In hearings held over the 1910s sev-eral men openly admitted they had had "the clap," usually claiming they had been cured. When Arthur Murray appeared before the board with a job lined up, they advised him they could not parole him unless the doctor deemed him cured.[73] The records, as board chairman Collins reminded prisoners, did not lie.

Prisons were dangerous places where communicable diseases could fell weakened and poorly nourished inmates. Prisoners and their supporters solicited governors' compassion when they petitioned on the grounds that further imprisonment of an injured inmate would be cruel. When death was imminent, the executive office was more nimble than the Board of Parole. Governor Odell's secretary worked with the Erie County Penitentiary to arrange a swift end to John Darwin's sentence after he was diagnosed with "quick consumption." On February 6, 1901, the superintendent raised his concern; on February 8 Darwin's wife filed the application for clemency; on February 13 Odell pardoned Darwin; and on February 18 Mrs. Darwin wrote to thank the governor for his kindness. The whole process occurred in less time than it would have taken for the board to return on its monthly round, and besides, the state's local penitentiaries were not on the state board's roster. The pressure of time also prompted the district attorney of Suffolk County to write the governor's office in support of a commutation of sentence for convicted burglar Henry Hedger, since the prisoner "has a great desire to go home to die." Three days later Governor Hughes acted on the recommendation. The controversial superintendent of Sing Sing State Prison, Thomas Mott Osborne, used more emotive language to address the governor on behalf of murderer John Murphy: despite the prisoner having "the very worst of records . . . he has the stamp of death upon his face." Governor Charles S. Whitman, a former DA with a tough-on-crime reputation, pardoned the prisoner the following day.[74]

Prisons were also factories and workshops, which exposed inmates to risks of injury. An injury made it difficult for a prisoner to fulfill work expectations, one of the prime concerns of prison keepers and a key criterion for parole consideration. After a printing press badly mauled Charles F. Keyes' hand at Sing Sing prison, leaving him with only two fingers and damaged tendons, he felt he had become "a cripple." In May 1917, he faced almost two years before he could apply for parole, according to his indeterminate sentence of six to ten years, and so he applied for gubernatorial clemency, supported by his mother and sister. When Governor Whitman reported his decision to commute Keyes' sentence for sodomy he noted that the sentencing judge approved of the prisoner's release "in view of his injury, and for that reason only."[75] Whitman did not refer to the other letters in Keyes's clemency file, written by the prisoner's female relatives, including one his mother had sent to Whitman's wife, Olive, imploring her, as a fellow mother, to induce her husband to act mercifully. Keyes's sister wrote the governor as well, to say that their mother was on death's door, and this worry, on top of her brother's injury, meant her brother was "more punished than he deserves."[76] Whether or not these womanly emotional appeals or a word from his wife tipped Whitman in favor of commutation, the judge's endorsement gave the governor permission to act compassionately.

Although mental deficiency provided grounds in the Progressive Era for eugenicists and psychiatrists to advise the sterilization and custodial confinement of prisoners and patients, particularly those whose offenses were sexual, such evidence could also work in a prisoner's favor, particularly in the early years of the century. In 1901, when parole was introduced for state prisoners, it came with rules, forms, and hearings, which "dull" or "weak mentally" prisoners found incomprehensible. Yet their dullness was not a liability in the eyes of sympathetic governors. Benjamin B. Odell, governor during the first four years of the Parole Board's existence, granted clemency to prisoners *because* they were subnormal. In 1903, for instance, he pardoned William Mulligan— convicted for burglary and sentenced in 1901 to a maximum of five years— with the endorsement of the district attorney and sentencing judge. In this case, the DA responded favorably, saying "'I do not think he is exactly right in his mind. My judgment is that [Mulligan] has been punished enough.'" Odell clearly stated the reason he used his discretion to shorten Mulligan's sentence: "It is not at all likely that Mulligan could ever earn a parole." Odell's successor, Governor Frank W. Higgins, expressed similar motives when he pardoned George Cameron, convicted for sodomy in 1896 and sentenced to twenty years' imprisonment. Reports on his behavior, in addition to his offense, indicated he was "deficient mentally," and on these grounds Higgins believed the prisoner "probably could never obtain a parole. He has been more than sufficiently punished."[77] Governors' declarations that inmates had suffered "enough" were not part of the lexicon of parole evaluations, but they chimed with customs of executive discretion favoring youth and infirmity.

Pardoning to Parole

Petitions on behalf of prisoners sentenced to life and those serving long mandatory sentences made up a growing proportion of the executive office's business in the early twentieth century. One-sixth of the clemency files registered from 1901 to 1920 concerned charges of murder or manslaughter, and there were 106 cases in which prisoners were convicted of rape in the first degree or sodomy, both of which carried maximum sentences of twenty years. The reduction of the mandatory minimum sentence for murder in the second degree from life to twenty years first occurred in 1897, but that left prisoners convicted before that date still serving life sentences.[78] A statute passed in 1907 rectified this inequity by extending the twenty-year maximum sentence to prisoners previously sentenced to life for second-degree murder.[79] As a result, governors encountered a jump in cases from lifers.[80] The Parole Board could grant such prisoners parole, but only after they served the minimum term, whereas the executive could intervene at any point. Despite the wide latitude of their powers, most governors commuted long-term prisoners' sentences only after they completed at least half of their minimum time, conforming to the spirit if not the letter of indeterminate sentencing.

Most significantly, the advent of parole allowed governors to develop a new mode of discretionary justice by commuting the sentences of state prisoners ineligible for parole, subject to the approval and supervision of the Parole Board. "Governors' Special Commutation" cases added to the board's monthly caseload of parole applications. As gubernatorial appointees the members were unlikely to reject cases sent through the governor's pardon clerk; however, the board subjected the individuals recommended for clemency to rigorous interrogations, making up for the thinness of their dossiers. Through these procedures, the settlement ultimately reached in 1930, when the Parole Board assumed responsibility for vetting all clemency petitions, was previewed a generation earlier, as administrative and executive decision making overlapped and began to interconnect.

The mandatory death sentence for murder conveyed the gravity of the offense in the catalog of crime. By the early 20th century murder in the first degree was the only crime aside from treason that carried the death penalty in New York, and the state's execution tally topped the nation, with more than ten offenders on average put to death in the electric chair each year in the first two decades. Compared to this horrific end, a life sentence could appear merciful at the moment of its declaration, but the passage of years and decades could change hearts and minds, not just judges' and district attorneys' but also jurors'. A review of Joseph Heidt's case began in 1903 when the men on the jury who found the twenty-two-year-old guilty of murdering his uncle in 1892 wrote to Governor Odell to urge the prisoner's release. Despite having taught in common schools in Sullivan County, Heidt appeared to be a man of a "low order of intelligence," in the jury's opinion. Another petitioner believed Heidt's "mind was not right." With no objections from the prosecutor or judge to deter him from releasing the prisoner, Odell decided in 1904 that Heidt, now thirty-three, had been "punished enough."[81] Prisoners sentenced to life as far back as the 1880s presented even more compelling cases for clemency, particularly in light of the 1907 law. In his last act of clemency before leaving office on December 31, 1910, Governor Horace White commuted John Clark's life sentence for murder in the second degree, received in 1889, to time served: twenty-one years, fifteen days. No family members, jurors, or benevolent supporters petitioned the governor in this instance; instead, the Parole Board recommended that the governor pardon Clark, since it had no authority to discharge "life men."[82]

When prisoners who had served at least twenty years for murder became eligible to apply for gubernatorial clemency they did so—through the Board of Parole, which vetted applications for the governor's consideration. Sixty-four-year-old William McNeil decided to try his chances at applying for parole shortly after the 1907 law was passed. For several years leading up to his request he had worked in Auburn's storeroom, and he kept a clean prison record, but back in 1879 McNeil had brutally murdered his wife, whose threat to leave him and take their child enraged him. The Board of Parole recommended that the governor approve his release, but they made freedom sound like a mixed blessing for a man who had spent decades in captivity. Could he "live up to the parole," they asked him? As a "life man," they warned him, "you would be a paroled man for the balance of your life, although you would have your liberty." The board suggested that McNeil apply for a full pardon once his parole was granted, to relieve him of the obligations of abiding by conditions and the risk of re-imprisonment for parole violations:

> Now you have got a better means of earning your pardon than heretofore, because a pardon will be based largely on [your] actions subsequent to [your] parole and the recommendations made by the Parole Board as to how [you are] living . . . the law gives the Board the right to recommend these things.

Having done their part to steer McNeil toward a new life, the board closed with a final measure of moralizing: "you have got to work out your own salvation."[83]

Despite the board's suggestion that McNeil seek a pardon, governors preferred to commute the sentences of life men to effect their release rather than pardon them. There were rare exceptions to this trend, but they appear to have been prompted by evidence of inappropriate sentences or dubious convictions. Governor Hughes, highly cautious in the use of his discretionary powers, commuted the sentence of Bernard Hahn, sentenced to seventy years in 1880 for burglary and assault. Twenty-seven years on, the penalty appeared "too severe" in Hughes's opinion, and Hahn's continued imprisonment "exceedingly unjust."[84] In William H. Parker's case the board recommended that his sentence be commuted to time served, and the file made its way to the executive office. After Parker's death sentence for murder in the first degree was commuted to life in 1892, he made numerous petitions for mercy over the years, each unsuccessful. Then, in 1907, the law allowed him to apply as an applicant for clemency subject to board review.[85] In December 1907 the board held a special hearing that included the chaplain; Dr. Gerin, Auburn's physician, also attended. The verdict had been dubious from the start, since Parker was one of several men caught up in "an affray" between Polish and African American tunnel workers in Niagara Falls, which left one man dead and everyone arrested pointing fingers. Parker, one of the African Americans, took the fall. His dossier showed he was born in the South to parents who were slaves. After emancipation he migrated northward with thousands of others for opportunity and freedom, only to discover that New York offered no haven from racism.[86] Dr. Gerin stated the inmate had no prior arrests, a perfect prison record and excellent results in his prison schooling. On a more personal level he found Parker "a good fellow, and is always willing and obedient to the rules." In a word, he was "a gentleman."[87]

But could Parker, an excellent worker in prison, support himself if released? African American parole applicants for parole tended to have fewer connections than recent immigrants from Europe to prospective employers, and the board's review of Parker's bid for clemency focused on this question, which generally determined the outcome of parole applications. Wadhams, the Navy man, accused Parker of being too stout to work a real job, and this remark flipped the prisoner from polite to assertive: "The work that I am doing every day [in the prison kitchen] is harder than a pick and shovel [because] you . . . handle a 14 foot paddle, and stir hash and lift kettles. . . . It is no child's play. No boy can do what is done there." Fortunately for Parker, speaking up manfully did not harm his cause. Seven months after the board hearing Governor Hughes commuted the life sentence, as he "deemed it just to modify the sentence so that a parole may be granted if the Board think proper."[88]

"Sing Sing's Oldest Inmate Free" was the headline that announced the pardon of Joel C. Rundle in June 1916.[89] His release at the age of seventy-five, sanctioned by Governor Whitman, confirmed that gubernatorial pardoning provided a means of release for prisoners unable to meet the requirements of parole. Rundle, who shot and killed a neighbor in 1900, had a friend in a Yonkers Alderman, who supported a clemency bid because they had fought together in the Civil War. Numerous Grand Army Posts in the state also lent their support to a veteran now paralyzed and confined to a wheelchair.[90] Another aged prisoner, Howard Burt, was a decade younger than Rundle, but his petitioners urged it would be unjust to require that he serve his full twenty-year minimum sentence for murder in the second degree. By that point, they predicted, "[Burt] will be an old man, too old and infirm to successfully assume the responsibilities of a free man." In support of the aged prisoner, a modern coalition of male functionaries, different from the array of religious authorities, politicians, businessmen, and legal personages who had traditionally supported clemency petitions, urged Burt's release. Over the time he spent in New York's state prison system, Burt managed to earn the respect of the state superintendent of prisons, former Superintendent Collins, six wardens, three prison clerks, and five Parole Board members, including former members Lewis and Wadhams. Old age alone did not ensure a pardon, but persuasive petitioners and supportive functionaries could make executive wheels turn on these grounds.[91]

Recommendations for release prior to the completion of mandatory minimum sentences did not just travel from the board to the executive office: they also came from the governor. In such instances, which the board called "special Governor's commutations," members were not obliged to approve the governor's request, but it was typical for them to do so. When the pardon clerk informed the board of such a request, the exchanges were respectful and its authority to approve and administer parole was duly noted. Yet, both parties knew the governor could pardon or grant clemency without board approval if he so wished. Requests for clemency were most likely to proceed smoothly when accompanied by positive recommendations in the file from judges and DAs, and when there was credible proof of a prisoner's capacity to support him or herself, or to receive support from others.

In Leonard Darling's file the board encountered a story of moral reformation that could have been lifted from one of Isaac Hopper's prodigal tales from the middle of the previous century. Darling's wife stuck by her husband after his conviction in 1909 on a charge of arson, committed to cover up the burglary of a wealthy actress's home. According to a Dutch Reformed minister, the former carpenter experienced a religious conversion in 1912, and from that point the cleric coordinated the clemency campaign to cut short the prisoner's maximum sentence of nine years. Governor Glynn granted the pastor (who had served for six years at Sing Sing as a "Christian worker") two personal visits. On these occasions he pressed Darling's case and told Glynn this was "the first time I have come to ask for a pardon for any man at the hands of the Chief Magistrate of our State." The zealous campaigner also lobbied the DA, who sent his approval for clemency with a peevish note to the pardon clerk, complaining that he had "answered inquiries in reference to the pardon of Leonard Darling about five times, and I am somewhat tired of it."[92] Persistence paid off, however. On January 14, 1914, Governor Glynn commuted Darling's sentence to time served, subject to the Board of Parole's approval and jurisdiction. A man made over through faith got out.

Pardoning under Fire

The 1910s were the most volatile years in New York penal politics since the 1820s. Scandals over corruption in prisons and mounting outrage over outmoded conditions in prisons built a century earlier competed with public concern over pardoning.[93] The Prison Association of New York fully supported the attempt made by Thomas Mott Osborne, one of its vice presidents, to introduce "a really scientific" approach to the management of Sing Sing and to make men responsible for making themselves over.[94] Before his appointment as its warden in 1914 he posed as an undercover prisoner at Auburn, where he gained "first hand" knowledge of the cruelty and futility of harsh discipline. Osborne's Mutual Welfare League aimed to "redeem men to society by making the prison a society in which they learn to govern themselves and thus become fit to live under government."[95] Unlike the long-serving Brockway, Osborne lost his position just two years after his appointment, because Republican Governor Charles S. Whitman dismissed him.[96] Pardons of notable individuals had always drawn accusations of favoritism, as Francis Lieber had charged decades before, but in the 1910s, particularly during Democrat Governor John Alden Dix's administration (1911–12), accusations of outright malfeasance appeared in the press. Consequently, when Whitman came to office in 1915, on the back of the reputation he earned as a prosecutor so fearless that he dared to take on the New York City police, the stern-faced governor was equally determined to shake up executive discretion, to make it more transparent and to make greater use of parole over pardoning.[97]

With considerably less drama, the constitutional convention of 1915 also aired grievances over New York's retention of gubernatorial clemency. But claims of its awkward place in a modern criminal justice system merely replayed arguments aired in nineteenth-century debates over the advisability of establishing a state board of pardons.[98] What distinguished the Republican-dominated convention (111 of 164 delegates) was its timing, coming just three years after Governor Dix's use of the pardoning prerogative fed concerns that executive discretion must go.[99] During the course of debating the matter, the convention ordered the governor's office to provide a report concerning the numbers of pardons and commutations granted and denied, from 1900 up to March 1915. Both the number of inmates who benefitted from Dix's acts of clemency and the notoriety of those he pardoned strongly suggested he may have responded to influence, if not bribes.

No progress on revising the pardon power took place as a result of the 1915 convention, but its inquiry into the pardon record provided a sharp reminder that Dix's use of his prerogative had eroded public confidence in executive discretion. In one respect he was the victim of timing. Dix had the disadvantage of following Charles Evans Hughes, who granted a miserly annual average of seventeen commutations and pardons between 1907 and 1910. In contrast, Dix issued fifty-five grants of clemency in his first year as governor, one of which led to the release of William McNeil, the lifer Hughes had refused to pardon in 1907.[100] In Dix's second year in office, seventy-eight prisoners were recipients of his clemency.[101] This total was tiny compared to the hundreds of prisoners governors pardoned in the 1870s, or even the 1810s, when the prison population was a fraction of current levels. Nevertheless, papers such as the *New York Tribune* decided that Dix deserved to be added to the list of the nation's most irresponsible and possibly corrupt governors.[102] Critics who claimed, unfairly, that Dix was as free with his pardons as his southern counterparts also chose to disregard the high number of executions over his governorship. Had they had the chance to join the debate, the thirty-five men Dix declined to reprieve would undoubtedly have contradicted the critics' portrayal of the governor as a man of "excessive leniency."[103]

The Dix pardon that generated nationwide press was his merciful treatment of Albert Patrick, convicted in 1902 of the murder by poisoning of his millionaire employer.[104] A Chicago legal commentator, suspicious of the timing of Dix's decision in his last month in office in 1912, pronounced the pardon "one of the most striking abuses of executive clemency in recent times." The only good that could come of it, he projected, would be "legislation doing away with the power of any executive, after a secret hearing, to set aside the decision of an established court of law." Surely New Yorkers must follow other states and establish a board of pardons to work openly, and solely in response to newly discovered evidence.[105] Ironically, Dix agreed with his critics, political and legal, that the governor's constitutional prerogative to pardon must come to an end.[106] Two weeks before he left office he grumbled that he had suffered the "cavil and criticism of an unlicensed press," despite having devoted "earnest consideration to all the circumstances and data on file" in every case he had "investigated" during his governorship. Furthermore, he reached his decisions concerning clemency in "the best interests of justice"—on behalf of the people, the "prisoner and his relatives who, I regret to say, are usually the chief sufferers." In consideration of the governor's onerous duties, Dix advised it would be wise to amend the state constitution to introduce a "Pardoning Board." Such a body could consider "all applications for pardon, commutation of sentence, restoration to citizenship and parole." And because it could devote its energy to one duty, rather than handle the many tasks the governor was forced to juggle, a pardon board could review petitions thoroughly, beyond the glare of the partisan press.[107] Despite the nationwide scope of critical commentary during Dix's governorship, the convention of 1915 came and went without changing a word to the 1846 constitution's definition of the executive's discretionary power and authority.[108]

Neither Dix nor his naysayers were burdened by the responsibility of executive discretion after 1915: the man charged with that duty was newly elected governor Charles Seymour Whitman. Because the convention held that year failed to amend the constitution, the new governor decided to revamp the

Governor Charles S. Whitman's inauguration, 1915. Source: Library of Congress, image 2003668187, retrieved from https://www.loc.gov.

administration of executive justice himself. First, he introduced open hearings to allow petitioners with appointments to present evidence in support of clemency; second, he relied more heavily than previous governors on the Parole Board to investigate petitions for clemency addressed to the executive office. Whitman's third innovation concerned his reporting style. In granular detail, he set out the factors he weighed before he granted or denied reprieves, commutations or pardons, and he documented that evidence by publishing the full text of letters submitted by judges, DAs, prison officials, medical authorities, and, on occasion, the individuals and organizations that pressed for clemency.

Governor Whitman's public papers do not disclose prisoners' own accounts of their deservedness for clemency, but their claims appear in clemency files. In Ninifia Funari's case, her own and her family's letters provide a fuller picture than the one Whitman subsequently published, giving the grounds on which he decided to commute her ten-year minimum sentence to just over three years. In his public papers, Whitman briefly stated the sentencing judge's support for commutation, on the basis that Funari had given birth while at Auburn and that it would be "in the best interests of the child" to remain with its mother.[109] The woman expressed her plight with considerably more emotion, stating it would "break my heart" to lose the baby. The judge's response to the pardon clerk's first request for his opinion provided Whitman a strong reminder that this was a criminal who had conspired to kidnap a five-year-old boy, held for ransom on the threat of killing him. It was "premature" to grant clemency since she had served just two years, the judge urged, considering the need to set an example "of persons who kidnap children and extort money." But after Funari made a deal with the DA to provide evidence against her co-conspirators, her sister was granted an appointment to appear before Whitman at his regular monthly hearing. Days later the prisoner reunited with her daughter, whom she had described as "the last tie which has indeed helped to comfort me in my sad time of separation from my husband and children and other loved ones."[110]

A hearing with Whitman scheduled by his pardon clerk after he completed the standard paperwork was no guarantee that the governor would grant mercy, but this practice did transpose petition reviews into a version of parole hearings. Simultaneously, Whitman's reliance on the Parole Board to examine special clemency cases offloaded executive responsibility onto parole administrators. With the exception of cases involving prisoners who had come close to serving their minimum sentence, or elderly life-sentenced offenders who had spent decades in prison, Whitman typically ended his commutation statements with: "so that he may be released under and subject to the jurisdiction of the Parole Board," or "so that the Parole Board may take the matter up." These codas in executive decisions blurred the distinction between the governor's personal prerogative and the parole board's administrative discretion. However, Whitman's use of the Board of Parole to look into clemency petitions essentially contradicted his policy of open clemency hearings. Whenever petitions for mercy transformed into "governor's special commutation" cases, they fell under the authority of an agency with no obligation to justify their decisions or to provide reports beyond aggregate numbers.

Despite these shifts in the gears of discretionary justice, the business of clemency petitioning motored on in the Progressive Era. Governors continued to respond to long-established ploys to induce clemency. Prisoners with friends in high places still had reason to anticipate clemency, and when grants of mercy were issued unconditionally, released prisoners were not obliged to meet the criteria the Board of Parole imposed on applicants or prisoners released conditionally under the board's control. The petitioners who wrote to Governor Whitman on behalf of William J. Cummins, convicted for defraud-

ing trust companies of millions of dollars, included state officials and governors, federal politicians, and businessmen from "every state in the Union."
Whitman openly acknowledged their influence, since they expressed confidence in Cummins's character. The governor even considered it appropriate
to publish a long letter from Andrew Carnegie, one of the trust owners, who
vouched for the prisoner's good character and the suffering of his family. In a
case such as this, Whitman declared, "the Executive must regard the opinions
and feeling of those men whose good faith cannot be questioned."[111]

Whitman's statement could easily be read to confirm that prisoners with
no capacity to draw on a network of influential backers, or those whose supporters' motivations could be questioned, were shut out from the prospect of
discretionary release. Had that actually been the case gubernatorial pardons
and commutations of sentences would have numbered in the ones and twos,
since wealthy white prisoners, such as Cummins, were rarities. Nevertheless,
by the end of the 1910s the number of pardons issued did shrink, the proportion of sentence commutations to time served grew, and it became a standard
practice for governors to allow the bulk of petitions received each year—three
to four hundred—to gather dust in pigeon holes. No great design was at work
in these trends, certainly not a constitutional amendment. Governors simply
could not keep up with the growing flow of clemency applications, and they
were more than willing to share the load, and their authority over discretionary justice, with the Board of Parole.[112]

Conclusion

In the early twentieth century New York's system of discretionary justice
dragged along at the rear of the march toward penal modernization. The
state's hiring of medical and psychiatric personnel in reformatories and state
prisons, its introduction of a psychometric screening laboratory in Sing Sing,
and the legislature's decision to transform an existing juvenile reformatory
into an institution for defective delinquents were all signs that politicians
and the electorate supported Progressives' ambition to apply modern "scientific" theories of detecting and treating delinquency to captive populations.
The use of indeterminate sentencing, first restricted to the flexible punishment of juveniles and first offenders and then extended widely to a broad
range of criminals, marked a departure from the earning of good time as
the principal way for prisoners to shorten preset periods of incarceration.
Accompanied by a new statewide system of parole, sentences with minimums
and maximums opened up scope for parole assessors to judge inmates' release
eligibility and impose intrusive conditions on released inmates, under threat

of reincarceration. Yet, the board appointees of the early twentieth century were not the social scientific experts Progressive penologists envisioned. Nor did they consider it inappropriate to judge men and women according to their prejudices, personal beliefs, and moral values. The procedures governing the discretionary release of prisoners in the state prisons became more bureaucratic over the 1910s, but the nature of decision making remained informal and the scope of appointees' discretion considerable. And as prisoners with the wrong attitude learned the hard way, the board was under no obligation to justify its decisions.

The governors' use of their pardoning power was considerably more politically sensitive in the first decades of the century than was parole. But when executive clemency became most controversial the focus was on individual governors' use of their power to pardon, not the question of sovereign authority. At the 1915 constitutional convention, delegates made no headway in trying to implement the reforms Francis Lieber and the Prison Association of New York had lobbied for in the previous century.[113] Although New Yorkers were stuck with the 1846 constitution's definition of the pardon power, Governor Whitman used executive privilege to innovate administratively without abandoning traditional pardoning principles. New procedures did not erase old customs, and Whitman's voluminous reports of pardons, commutations, and reprieves show that even an ex-DA was responsive to traditional grounds for clemency, sensitive to the hardships imprisonment imposed on inmates' family members, to prisoners' previous good characters, and to the word of high-status supporters. And perhaps he was also prompted by compassion when he heard the stories of prisoners such as James Thompson, aged eighty-four. One of many elderly inmates released before his sentence expired, Thompson was otherwise a typical clemency recipient of the late 1910s, his sentence commuted to time served and his release to be managed "under the authority of the Parole Board."[114]

Gubernatorial discretion transformed over the 1910s to a default pattern of commuting sentences, a practice that entangled executive discretion in the work of the Parole Board. Yet petitioners did not stop seeking mercy; rather, they began to forum shop, seeking relief wherever they might best find it. As more and more inmates left prison on parole without serving their maximum sentences, public concern gravitated toward the work of the Parole Board. In the age of Prohibition and gangsterism, scandals involving crimes committed by parolees made embarrassing headlines, as newspaper editors and conservative politicians persuaded New Yorkers that penologists' experiment with parole and indeterminate sentencing had been a dangerous failure. Against this pressure, executive and administrative discretion transformed but endured.

The Crime Wave and the War against Discretionary Justice in the 1920s

In 1927, Harold W. Stoke, a young political scientist, published a law journal article titled "A Review of the Pardoning Power." Following in the footsteps of Francis Lieber, he stated that "it seems strange to us that this power judicial in character should have been allowed to remain in the hands of the executive almost unquestioned." Stoke discovered that twenty-three states had established advisory boards by the mid-1920s, and a further five had replaced the governor's prerogative power with the authority of a board.[1] Records of gubernatorial pardoning and prisoner release through parole indicated that some governors (most notoriously Miriam "Ma" Fergusson of Texas, who granted close to four thousand pardons in two years in office) had pardoned "lavishly" in recent years; however, Stoke was surprised to find that the overall number of pardons had declined in the early twentieth century.[2] Evidently, governors were "cautious and conservative" in granting pardons, and he deemed that most used their prerogative with "virtue and restraint." The discretionary justice problem of the 1920s, Stoke concluded, was not pardoning, but parole: "silently, continuously, unknown, the parole system has poured its masses of criminals upon us to murder and pillage."[3]

Stokes's distrust of "obscure and unknown board[s] working in the shadows of the prisons" was widely shared in the Prohibition Era, when most Americans were convinced that a crime wave had hit the country. Spikes in crime had occurred in the post-Revolutionary period, after the War of 1812, and during Reconstruction, in each instance leading to crackdowns against disorder and lawlessness.[4] The Volstead Act, which all but prohibited the consumption and sale and distribution of alcohol after 1919, added momentum to this latest wave.[5] The proliferation of guns and the wider availability of automobiles over the 1920s left law enforcement authorities playing a mugs game of catch-up.[6] Most observers believed that parole boards were stacking the odds in favor of criminals by setting gangsters and gun molls free from prison on flimsy evidence of reformation, possibly at the behest of criminals and corrupt officials. Newspaper exposés and official inquiries prized open the internal workings of discretionary release and no one, including Progressive penologists, liked what they saw. In New York the governors who held office in the 1920s faced intense pressure to abolish the board, but they defended it on condition that it set higher standards of accountability and screen parole applicants more rigorously. In New York it was not just parole on the line in the 1920s: it was discretionary justice more broadly.

Histories of discretionary justice in the latter years of the Progressive Era have focused overwhelmingly on the net-widening impact of penal expertise, which has produced a skewed image of parole's rocky history.[7] From the opening session of the American Prison Association meetings in the 1870s, reformers envisioned a medical model of correctional justice, dependent upon reformatory managers and allied experts with the skills to determine how to treat inmates and cure them of their criminal tendencies.[8] Their wishes came true fifty years later in many states but most vividly in New York, where experts in psychiatry and criminology were installed in its network of reformatories and prisons.[9] David J. Rothman's analysis of Progressive justice exposed how "broad and unfettered official discretion and expanded treatment options" worked to expand the carceral state, and most subsequent studies have followed this analytical tack, emphasizing that medical and psychiatric diagnoses created new categories of offenders and closed off earlier avenues for release.[10] However, the intensity of public dissatisfaction with parole in this period, combined with evidence of the Board of Parole's practice, calls for a reassessment of penal Progressivism's impact. By focusing on parole's struggle to maintain legitimacy against criticism of its governance of inmates' release we can better appreciate why New York became the first state to constrict the scope of indeterminate sentencing and constrain the Parole Board's discretionary authority.

The people most affected by New York's volatile penal politics in the lead-up to the Depression were the prisoners who sought early release. Parole case files from Auburn State Prison show that medical and psychiatric evaluations of prisoners, a rarity in dossiers of the early twentieth century, began to appear by the 1920s. Nevertheless, expert assessments of fitness for release were not nearly as authoritative as most historians of Progressive expertise have claimed. Indeed, the sex offender and psychopath posed no special concern to the men who served on the State Board of Parole.[11] Its hearing records confirm that customary character appraisal, with its attendant gender, ethnic, racial and class presumptions, as well as religious and moral judgments, held sway. In 1926, when the board approved the release of Izzy Presser, infamous gun bandit, the sloppy standards of parole screening grabbed public attention. In contrast, the prejudices that built higher walls against the early release of African Americans and poorly resourced whites did not garner headlines.[12]

Parole became the standard route for inmates who managed to exit the prison gate prior to the expiration of their sentences. Executive discretion became more restrained under pressure to appear tough on crime, but some stories of suffering still cut through and mercy still had a place in the hands of the governor. Accounts of gubernatorial pardoning practice, recorded in governors' published papers and clemency case files from the early 1920s, confirm that petitioners appealed for mercy on the same grounds that earlier governors had favored. Democrat Alfred E. Smith, who held office for eight years over four terms, gained a reputation for pardoning on the basis of hard-luck stories. Although he pardoned at a higher rate than Republican Nathan Miller, governor from 1921 to 1922, both men continued to exercise clemency principally by commuting sentences and assigning prisoners to the Board of Parole for discretionary release. After 1926, New York's mandatory sentencing laws created a steely backdrop for the personal dynamics of executive discretion: for law-and-order advocates, the pardon power became the safety net for any prisoner unjustly detained; for inmates facing life sentences without the right to apply for parole, the governor's prerogative power became the only straw of hope to clutch. The story of every inmate who lost hope, who died in prison, or who lacked the support required to make a compelling case for mercy will never be fully known.[13]

A hybrid system of discretionary justice emerged in New York, produced through a crisis of faith in parole combined with a loss of confidence in the state's capacity to hold back the crime wave. A statute orchestrated by Governor Franklin D. Roosevelt in 1929 brought pardon and parole under the executive branch of government, and this arrangement included the creation of a Division of Parole, charged with oversight of pardon petitions in addition to applications for parole. The appointment of Frederick A. Moran as executive director of the new enterprise in 1930 symbolized the professionalization of parole in New York. With his two degrees in sociology and psychology, Moran turned his division into a storehouse of statistics, tables, and graphs. The amalgamation of discretionary release processing meant that the "special governor's commutation" cases were no longer special, but it did not remove the governor's exclusive authority to pardon, reprieve or commute sentences. By the Depression's onset, discretionary justice had acquired the look of science.

The Crime Wave and the Postwar Politics of Clemency

When Governor Al Smith took office in January 1919, he marked the event with a public reception in the governor's suite in New York's City Hall. Common folk lined up in hope of an opportunity to meet the chief executive, a son of the tenements. One man, wearing a frayed shirt, worn shoes, and "stubby growth on his face," told Smith's secretary he had a "'pal in Sing Sing who is dying from tuberculosis. I want to see if I can get a pardon for him.'" True to his word the governor gave the man three minutes of his time, the *Tribune* reported.[14] Had the paper followed up on the case it would have discovered that Smith did not pardon the pleader's Sing Sing pal. In fact, the number of pardons granted in the postwar era was minuscule, as governors began to reserve the pardon almost exclusively to restore former prisoners' rights. In his first term of office (1919–20) Smith granted only three pardons, none of them prompted by claims of illness or hardship, or on account of likely innocence.[15] His successor, Nathan L. Miller, was no more generous. Like Smith, he granted only three pardons while in office (1921–22), but when it came to commuting sentences he was stingier: during his administration, Miller commuted the sentences of just thirty-four inmates. As governors both men upheld the use of the death penalty for murder, as the number of postwar executions confirms. Between 1919 and 1922 forty-six men were executed in New York.[16] So why did the public believe that gubernatorial clemency was lax?

In 1921, the Prison Association of New York (PANY) celebrated the fact that "modern efforts in the solution of the treatment of crime and delinquency" were underway in the state after the war. "Side by side with the warden and superintendent is coming to sit the scientist as a consulting colleague whose field is the study of abnormal behavior." However, PANY predicted that postwar fears of a "crime wave" might undo this progress. Property crimes with violence appeared to have increased, committed with growing "brutality and daring," and the press had cranked up "a loud clamor for a reversion to more punitive forms of treatment for law breakers." Orlando Lewis, the Association's secretary, reminded readers that a similar atmosphere had prevailed in the 1820s when a "brutally rigid" form of discipline derailed the first penitentiary movement. History showed that reviving draconian punishments would not solve the crime problem, so PANY demanded that the state treat crime as a matter for "wise, dispassionate study." Above all, politicians must not be seduced by "apparent 'crime waves,' or by a hysterical reaction of the public mind."[17] Governor Al Smith was one step ahead of PANY. In 1919, he commissioned a survey of New York's prison system, principally to root out the nagging problem of graft in prisons and to modernize the "archaic" institutions within the system.[18] No prison or reformatory was to be spared. As a peripheral matter, the governor asked the commissioners to review the Parole Board's operations, but Smith's commissioners went much further. Their final report, published in 1920, would foreshadow the problems and solutions ahead for a discretionary justice system in which the public was fast losing confidence.

The Prison Survey Committee (as the appointees called themselves) was composed of businessmen, philanthropists, and civic-minded New Yorkers led by Adolph A. Lewisohn, acting as chairman. A mining magnate who became a prominent philanthropist, Lewisohn encouraged his fellow members to think of the state's prison system as a kind of industry that could be run more efficiently and effectively to maximize its potential to benefit the state and the offender. By following this principle, taken from "the business world," the state would see the wisdom of investing heavily in parole. Board members must receive higher pay for full-time work, and they must base their decisions on "reliable data," calculated by the marks inmates received for good behavior and educational improvement.[19] From a managerial point of view this model of discretionary justice made good sense.

Delegating discretion was critical in a state where the governor was confronted by copious numbers of petitions. In 1919 alone five hundred new applications for pardon arrived in the executive office. No well-run business would expect its chairman to review a similar volume of petitions from employees each year, so the governor should not shoulder the burden of assessing so many of them. Furthermore, the committee noted that the state constitution authorized the legislature to determine the manner in which governors exercised their discretion, which meant that politicians could authorize a board of pardon and parole to "examine applications for pardon and mak[e] recommendations to the Governor as to whether or not executive clemency should be exercised."[20] According to Lewisohn, governors shared the committee's concern over the clemency bottleneck, with one of its chief executives recently remarking, "two Governors are needed in the state, one to conduct the business of the state, the other to hear pleas for pardon."[21]

The survey report advised the establishment of a combined system of pardon and parole review, and it laid the groundwork for the system New York would put into place a decade later. In contrast, the committee supported discretionary justice in spongey terms that quickly became indefensible. The committee believed that prisoners, including those guilty of the most serious offenses, should be able to demonstrate through their conduct in prison "their ability to live in harmony with a free community, if their freedom were restored." Inmates who have "really reformed" should be helped to "make appropriate application for parole or for pardon." At present, the application process was "entirely informal," and hearings did not permit "full discussion of all the facts, pro and con." The committee's interviews with pardoned and paroled prisoners who had made a successful transition to freedom stated what every inmate knew: "a prisoner undergoing a long sentence without friends who may assist him has little chance of release."[22] In these business-oriented prison surveyors' estimation, the formula to improve the efficiency and effectiveness of discretionary justice could be found in streamlined administrative efficiency, laced with compassion.

When Governor Smith received the committee's report he rejected its recommendation that a combined board be established. Perhaps Lewisohn had quoted a different chief executive when he made the "two governors" remark. In any case, Smith resented the committee's inference that he failed to cope with pardon applications: "I have never shirked the responsibility of giving a fair hearing in every deserving case." He considered himself "no sentimentalist," but his clemency calculus allowed for benevolent errors: "better one failure out of 200 men returned to useful lives than injustice to dependent wives and children of 199 and needless expense to the state."[23] If anyone doubted his willingness to see the full power of the law enforced they need only refer to the number of men put to death under Smith's watch. In his first term in office the state sent eighteen men to the electric chair.

Execution statistics were the last thing on petitioners' minds when they attempted to craft appeals for mercy; stirring the governor's sympathy was uppermost. Female relatives of male prisoners cued in to Smith's reputation for kindliness and touched on his image as a loving husband and father. Some even granted him regal status. In the fall of 1920, a thirteen-year-old girl wrote to "your Majesty Governor Smith, dear sir," and explained: "I am taking the freedom to write because I know you will grant my wish." Fanni Rost sought a pardon for her "poor father," who was serving a five- to ten-year sentence at Sing Sing for receiving stolen property. His imprisonment left Fanni, her siblings, and their mother "destitute" and dependent on the charity of the League of Child Welfare.[24] The pardon clerk recorded that the governor granted the girl a meeting at the Biltmore Hotel in Manhattan on the eve of the 1920 election, but staff prevented her from seeing him. Smith did not commute Rost's sentence before he left office in December 1920 (having lost the election to Nathan Miller); nevertheless, he preferred a hands-on approach to clemency, and kept it up in his later terms. "I . . . discouraged the idea of retaining attorneys to plead for pardons or commutations," Smith later wrote in his autobiography: "I had a feeling that it was not strictly legal work."[25] The human touch of clemency, enshrined since New York's first constitution, still mattered.

The Press and the Crime Wave

The man who inherited the Rost family's petition and thousands of others, crammed into the pardon clerk's pigeonholes, was Nathan L. Miller, a Republican endorsed by former governor Hughes.[26] Miller had formerly served as a judge on the state supreme court and court of appeals, and he followed in his backer's footsteps by exercising executive discretion cautiously. In January 1922, he presented his first annual report on the same day a Republican assemblyman introduced a bill in favor of a constitutional amendment to replace the governor's pardon privilege with a court of appeal for pardons.[27] Reviewing the governor's record of just two pardons and twelve commutations dispensed in 1921, the New York Times said of Miller: "He has been very sparing, indeed, some have called him niggardly." A Times reporter asked the governor whether he intended that his report be read "as a deterrent to crime." Miller dodged the question, preferring to proclaim that granting mercy sparingly was critical in an age of permissiveness:

> I understand I have a reputation for being hard-hearted. I am sorry. I have
> certain views with reference to the exercise of the pardoning power which, I be-
> lieve, have penetrated the walls of the prisons. . . . [It] is a power to be exercised
> very sparingly, with "very" underscored. . . . It is a power in which sentiment
> and sympathy should be very carefully controlled.[28]

Miller considered his restraint a corrective for the policies set by earlier governors, most of all by Smith, whom he accused of having "let a good many people out of prison." Although he did not believe his predecessors had caused the crime wave, Miller thought that high pardon rates sent the wrong message: "word spreads pretty rapidly through the institutions as to whether a Governor is soft-hearted or not."[29]

Highbrow magazines such as the Nation questioned the veracity of crime wave claims, and associations of judges, law enforcement agencies, and criminologists began to rake through official records to correct headlines that appeared in the metropolitan press. As one academic griped, the real problem was the "crime news wave."[30] Undeterred, newspaper editors, the Brooklyn Eagle's in particular, ratcheted up the number of stories asserting that crime was out of control: criminals knew they could anticipate easy parole in the off-chance they were caught. During Nathan Miller's governorship the press heaped blame on the State Board of Parole for releasing felons who slipped straight back into lives of crime. When their victims were vocal and well-heeled, politicians listened.

In the Jazz Age, many of Manhattan's and the nation's wealthiest families kept opulent summer residences on Long Island, and these residences were tempting treasure troves for break-in artists.[31] In the summer of 1921 a gang of thieves broke into the Sands Point home of Commodore Frank S. Hastings, a yachtsman, ranchman, and financier. Their loot included jewels, gold coins, and a safe holding forty thousand dollars' of stock certificates. After the men were convicted, one of the robbers boasted he had "'political influence,' which would enable him to get a speedy release from prison." On top of this, the "thug" vowed to return to Long Island to rob the residents and kill Hastings as soon as the board granted him parole. While experts debated the definition of a crime wave the citizenry prepared to take action against discretionary release.[32]

Brimming with "intense indignation," Hastings wrote to Governor Miller on January 11, 1922, to inform him that he and his fellow residents had hired a lawyer to protest the paroling of dangerous criminals "on the slightest pretext." One repeat offender, African American Luther Boddy, had recently shot and killed two white police officers. Yet, as dangerous as such "arch fiends" were, Hastings believed,

> we are in greater danger from that [parole] board than we are from the thugs themselves. We can kill the thugs, and are prepared to do so; but we seem to have no redress against the action of the Parole Board, which all agree is a menace to public safety.[33]

Perhaps fearful that Commodore Hastings and his fellow enraged Long Islanders might make good on their threat to take the law into their own hands, Governor Miller publicly backed the board with some diffidence.[34] The members were "not responsible for the crime wave," Miller stated, but he added a drop of doubt: inevitably, parole and the indeterminate sentence required that "we have to take chances on men."[35]

The relationship between gubernatorial and administrative discretion called for careful management in the 1920s. The headlines granted to hot-tempered influential citizens corroded confidence in the entire apparatus of indeterminate sentencing and parole that had been constructed over the previous half century. Governor Miller's internal communications and his own report on pardons, issued just days after his lukewarm defense of the board, conveyed his intention that the board act with greater restraint. Miller wrote to the board and put it on notice that it should rarely, if ever, parole "life men" or repeat offenders, and that exceptional cases should be referred to the executive. "These are merely suggestions," the governor ended politely, but his message was clear.[36] Both he and the press demanded that the board maintain a better record to appease the public. This four-ball juggling act, in which the governor exercised his own discretionary authority, monitored the board's, attempted to uphold the principles of reform, and tried to appear tough on thugs was difficult for any chief executive to carry off. Nathan Miller managed to do so, but he was a one-term governor who lost the election of 1922 to the man he had earlier defeated. As Al Smith made his way back to Albany the alarmist press went on a warpath, gunning for discretionary justice.

The Deplorable Parole System

Some of the harshest critics of discretionary justice in New York were the experts and lobby groups that had helped make the state's parole system one of the most comprehensive in the nation. Progressive penologists' idealism and high expectations of making men over heightened their disappointment in the failures of a system meant to be modern and scientific.[37] Men and women trained in social work, sociology, political science, and law were frustrated that untrained amateurs were steering parole into troubled waters and threatening to run hope-laden penal programs aground.[38] The purpose of parole was to prepare the criminal to "live an honest, industrious and self-supporting life." In 1916, when PANY conducted its first evaluation of New York's parole system it judged it "deplorable."[39]

It was also confusing. From the 1910s New York actually had three parole systems. The State Board of Parole had jurisdiction over inmates in the state prisons (Auburn, Sing Sing, Clinton, and Great Meadow) and its two hospitals for the criminally insane, Dannemora and Matteawan. Reformatories for juveniles, plus the Elmira and Bedford reformatories, operated under their own institutional systems of discretionary release. As of 1915, New York City established a separate Parole Commission to handle inmates discharged from its local penitentiaries in addition to Elmira parolees from the city. This local commission, which handled half the parolees in the state, was the best run in PANY's opinion, since it employed three full-time salaried members and a large staff who met regularly; in contrast, the state board members, responsible for about 3,500 state prison inmates in 1916, received half the salary of their New York City counterparts and worked only several days per month. This meant that the Board of Parole had no choice but to render decisions in six to eight minutes, even though the inmates it considered for parole were the most serious felons in the state. Parole had become "practically an automatic process, taking place at the expiration of the minimum sentence of the prisoner, and regarded by him as a right." As long as New York allowed this imperfect system to exist, it wasted its investment in training and education facilities in prisons.[40]

The establishment of a psychiatric clinic at Sing Sing State Prison in 1916 was a sign of progress in PANY's estimation, but New York still had much work to do on its state parole system. Nothing had changed by 1921, when

Edward R. Cass, PANY's assistant general secretary, conducted an ambitious study of "Parole Laws and Methods in the United States." In the tradition of Lieber and Dwight, he tried to produce a snapshot of "present procedure" by questioning authorities about their administration of parole. Cass discovered that no prison or state department kept credible statistics on recidivism, and there was no standard methodology for determining the effectiveness of selection or supervision. In the current climate of public fear, and in light of advances in social sciences, such failings were inexcusable:

> in these days, when an increasing number of accusations are made that the indeterminate sentence and parole are failures, and that a more repressive system, together with materially lengthened sentences, should be instituted, it is not only desirable but necessary that we know frankly, and with reasonable certainty, where we stand.[41]

In every state, parole authorities deserved "the severest reproach" because they had neglected to prove the worth of their work with credible data. In some ways New York was the worst offender, since the Elmira Reformatory scandal of the early 1890s had shown that bloated success figures provided ammunition for enemies. The time was ripe for "scientifically presented and candid parole statistics."[42]

To the members of the Prison Association and their fellow Progressives, the worth of parole could be measured by the number of inmates who reformed after being granted parole. Historians and socio-legal scholars have judged their efforts less favorably, viewing parole as the means through which offenders were normalized. "The real work of reform," Jonathan Simon writes, "had to take place in the community," where private employers, local law enforcers, and a shoestring staff of parole officers extracted labor and enforced order.[43] However, an even wider array of agents—families and neighbors, as well as religious and charitable agencies—had a hand in endorsing applications. As parole applicants' dossiers indicate, the board was inclined more to value the promise of support and supervision through community agents than to gear parole eligibility according to expert psychiatric classifications.

Seeking Support and Measuring Up

Community aid made Howard Eugene Smith a promising prospect for parole in the eyes of the board. The experts differed. Convicted of rape in upstate New York in June 1917 and sentenced to a minimum of eight years and maximum of sixteen for rape in the first degree, Smith was paroled in 1923 after he served his mandatory minimum. As PANY complained, this pattern of approval had become typical by the 1920s. However, Smith was an African American man, and the victim was a twelve-year-old white girl. There was no reference to race in the report of Auburn's prison physician, Dr. Frank Haecox, but he did provide a negative appraisal: the prisoner had contracted gonorrhea at twenty years of age; his IQ was only 65.6, with a mental age of 10.6; and he was an alcoholic. Although Haecox did not label Smith a psychopath (a common diagnosis of sex "deviants" by this period), he classified him as a mentally deficient moron with an "unfavorable outlook" who might, at best, be suited for farm work. Auburn's chaplain shared the doctor's ambivalence, using social work discourse to express his doubts. Smith had a good behavior and work record in prison, he acknowledged, but he lacked a well-formed "life plan."[44]

There were others in the prisoner's ring in this instance, and they were prepared to stand behind Smith if the Parole Board would grant him a second chance. Lynchings of men such as Smith appeared almost daily in the metropolitan press, and none of the men involved in his parole application could have been unaware that mob violence occurred in the North as well as in southern states.[45] This made external proof of Smith's support critical. To criminologists, the Parole Board's reliance on religious and volunteer agencies and surveillance services was a sign of its unprofessionalism, but these workers provided a lifeline for inmates such as Smith, who could ill afford legal representation. The Volunteers of America, one of the foremost philanthropic prisoners' aid organizations in the state, took great interest in the case, and they managed to find Smith a job in Syracuse, working as a car washer. The Parole Board registered no concerns about the prisoner's sexual impulses, but they did want to ensure that his job offer was sound. A motorcar agency manager wrote in to say he was prepared to offer the prisoner "honest employment." "From what I know of his case," Charles H. Cross told the board, "I firmly believe that he has been the unfortunate victim of circumstances, and if he is paroled I shall endeavor to help him."[46]

Most applicants who lacked family support or established religious ties were paroled to the Volunteers of America, headed by Maud Ballington-Booth, the "Little Mother" of the Prisoners, as her letterhead stated.[47] One of her lieutenants general, George Duquette, wrote State Prison Superintendent Charles F. Rattigan to assure him that one Edward Moore, "paroled into my custody," had become a "straightforward, steady working, Law abiding citizen." After the parolee had reported dutifully for one year, Duquette advised the state he would "make no mistake in giving this man a conditional discharge."[48] A state parole system that failed to provide a full staff of parole officers trained in casework management could ill afford to contest the word of a parole charity. Trusted agencies run by amateurs with real-world experience removed men of dubious mental and psychological makeup from the prison system's books.[49]

When inmates made formal applications for parole they were told to provide the names of six to eight "reputable citizens" who knew "something of [the prisoner's] past career" as well as "his history, habits and general reputation." The Syracuse car dealer was one of eight "reputable people" who had responded on Smith's behalf, including an African Methodist Episcopal Church pastor.[50] One local man believed Smith was not guilty of rape. In his view, "the trouble he got into was not because the boy was bad and willful, but he made a mistake of the head, and not the heart." In 1923, Smith left for Syracuse, and he dutifully submitted monthly reports to the board until 1927, when it granted him his final discharge.[51] What appeared to professionals to be an amateurish chain of impressions was a mode of discretionary release that boosted the board's success rate and released men whose likelihood of formulating a life plan was meager.

By the 1920s every prisoner in the state system was photographed, measured up and down and back to front, and subjected to a battery of medical and psychological tests, and the results found their way into parole application dossiers. Not even the most educated or literate prisoner could challenge such data. But other matters interested the Parole Board. The perfunctory style of reportage its stenographers adopted by the late 1910s gives a less robust sense of the application encounter than the earlier verbatim records provide; still, they allow us to question the pictures provided in Progressives' theories and newspaper exposés. Even this fragmentary evidence indicates how much inmates' respectful demeanor and deference mattered once parole applicants faced the board. Sarcasm and defiance remained of greater concern than signs of defectiveness.

Little changed after Dr. Larkin joined the Board in 1917, and he was as interested as his fellow members in the character of prisoners who appeared before them.[52] Most applicants seem to have been well coached in conforming to expectations. When asked if he knew what parole meant, Frederick Corprew got straight to the point: "Do good and make good." For women, promises of right living could make the difference between rejection and acceptance. Dianna Butts, imprisoned for wounding her husband, was denied parole because the board found her "very insolent and vengeful in answering questions. Showing a defiant manner." But Anna Susi told the men what they wanted to hear when they asked her what parole meant: "behave myself and be a dutiful wife to my husband."[53]

Occasionally, inmates were unwilling to play this game of promise and reward, knowing that they would face months or years of uncertain freedom, which could easily be revoked. One inmate, John Fronce, told the board he preferred to serve out his sentence minus earned compensation rather than leave under the restrictions of parole. When he appeared at the Parole Board's November 1919 Auburn Prison visit members decided that he exhibited "systematized delusions of persecution." But these were psychological terms that cloaked their disapproval of the man's assertiveness. "[D]ischarge me for the merit and good work I have done since coming here, and also my good conduct," Fronce defied the board, adding "I prefer to stay right here." Dr. Larkin took the lead after they dismissed Fronce from the room to deliberate. With no medical assessment to support his opinion, he declared that the prisoner conveyed a sense of "revenge" and ought not to be paroled against his will. Fronce made his point, but so did the board.[54]

The fate of men like Fronce, who ended up serving his full maximum sentence in prison, did not concern the public, but paroled men of Hugo Reisinger's ilk did. His father was a judge, he claimed, but his record indicated he had followed an unlawful life. Reisinger had spent a year's stretch at Illinois' Joliet Prison in 1913, and he followed that with a five- to ten-year sentence for grand larceny in New York in 1918. The man's record at Auburn was checkered: striking at an officer with a fork; gambling with cards; shirking his work; disobeying orders; having a razor and fork in his cell; arguing with guards; fighting with other inmates. Despite this unpromising record, and possibly due to the influence of his father, Reisinger was paroled in October 1926 to the Jewish Board of Guardians, a charitable organization that operated principally in New York City.[55] As a released man Reisinger was no less belligerent, however. Mr. Reingold, the Jewish Board's parole monitor, informed Auburn that the man had reported to him "in a defiant mood" and complained about the need to fill out reports. Reisinger refused to divulge what he did for work and stated that "all officials are grafters," and that communism was the only way to do away with corruption. But neither the Board of Parole nor the warden of Auburn had the power to impose "the rules and regulations as laid down by the society," and the Jewish Board soon lost track of him. Reisinger was prepared to accept parole, but expressing a "spirit of cooperation" in dealing with his overseers was too great a concession to religious and state authority.[56]

From the public's point of view, this was the great problem of parole, probation, and the indeterminate sentence, the tools of modern criminal justice that allowed thugs and thieves to defy the rules. If parole authorities and religious sob sisters were on the side of the Reisingers of the world, who was on the side of the law-abiding citizenry?

Discretionary Justice on the Defensive

When Al Smith returned to the governor's office in January 1923, the press declared open season on discretionary justice in all its forms. The beating he received from editors peaked in 1925. According to the Prison Association of New York, the public mind was "enflamed" with fear and growing anger at "the institutional methods of parole procedure." Every time a paroled prisoner robs a store, PANY complained, "the columns of the press are ablaze," whereas stories of released prisoners who made good never appeared.[57] Headline after headline exposed the Parole Board's incompetence, and many editors devoted columns that covered Governor Smith's pardon practice as well. The *Brooklyn Eagle's* editor, Herbert F. Gunnison, led a campaign in 1925 to overhaul the penal system and rid New York of its pampered prisoners, its indeterminate sentences, and its one-man pardon.[58] Smith's clemency record and the board's proceedings became front-page news, month after month, and the paper made sure that no one forgot the sitting governor's previous acts of clemency, as well as his current exercise of his prerogative powers.

The first of Smith's controversial acts of clemency, several days after he returned to Albany in January 1923, was his pardon of James "Big Jim" Larkin. Larkin was an agitator for Irish independence who was instrumental in founding the Communist Labor Party. A victim of the postwar Red Scare, Larkin was convicted under the state's criminal anarchy law in 1920 for distributing literature advocating the overthrow of the government.[59] Smith denounced Larkin's ideology, but he stood up for his right of free speech. Four other "anarchists," two women and two men, received pardons from Smith several weeks later, but there was a sting in the tail of the governor's mercy: Larkin and the quartet, none of them naturalized citizens, were deported by federal authorities soon after Smith's decision released them from their sentences.[60] Nevertheless, state Republicans accused the Democratic governor of using his clemency power to undermine the law.[61] Fresh from his surprise election victory, Smith described the objections as "pure politics," and he dismissed their accusation with a cocksure quip: "every time a Democratic governor is elected these Republican leaders seem to think it is a crime."[62]

The Red Scare began to subside by the mid-1920s, but fear of the state's criminals kept escalating, and Smith fell under greater pressure to show he placed more stock in public safety than the treatment of criminals. The *Brooklyn Eagle* kept its eye on Smith and the Parole Board, and its attack intensified at the close of 1925: "Time Now for the Public to Act and Demand Stiff Laws to Throw Fear into the Hearts of Criminals" was the three-line banner headline on December 27. The full-page story devoted six columns to the pardon power, which it called a "menace." Similar objections to executive discretion had been voiced for decades in constitutional conventions, but these appeared with exclamation points and bold type: the pardon power allowed governors to release "the MOST DANGEROUS CRIMINAL by a mere SWISH of the GUBERNATORIAL PEN!"[63]

Two weeks before the *Eagle* grilled Smith on his clemency record, the governor courted criticism over another overtly political pardon. This time it was Benjamin Gitlow, an associate of Larkin's and one of the men arrested for criminal anarchy in 1919.[64] Smith declared that he pardoned the radical publisher because he had "meekly submitted to the sovereign power of the State," and in light of the fact that he had been punished sufficiently for a non-violent crime.[65] But Gitlow's pardon gave the *Eagle* one more reason to hold up Smith's pardon rate against Miller's. Over an equal period of two years the Republican governor had granted 26 pardons, 32 commutations, and 20 reprieves, while Smith, the Democrat, had pardoned 156, commuted 138, and reprieved 26. The *Eagle* offered a simple solution: "Take Pardon Power from Governor and Remove Political Temptation."[66]

The message appeared on every newsstand: confidence in discretionary justice, both executive and administrative, had reached a low ebb and a political solution appeared elusive. In the summer of 1925 big business took the initiative to come up with a workable solution with the Chairman of the Board of U.S. Steel, the largest corporation in the nation in the 1920s, taking the lead. Elbert H. Gary invited Governor Smith and other "noted men" to unite with "big business" and law enforcement agencies to mount "a citizens' anti-crime crusade" to combat fears that had become "terrifying beyond all expression."[67] Galvanized by this meeting the men agreed to wage "a war on crime." Starting in New York their work could provide a model for the nation to follow.[68]

"To Subdue Crime We Must Have a Whale of Shakeup!"

Calling themselves the National Crime Commission, the coalition of big business crime fighters had no official powers when it formed in August 1925, but they did have the resources to place large advertisements to promote the message that they "mean[t] business." As they set about lobbying for policy change and attempting to inform the public on the most up-to-date anticrime measures, Governor Smith urged the legislature to grant more resources to its existing committees on criminal procedure.[69] His idea of establishing a formal crime commission for New York state, with greatly enhanced powers, pleased Republicans, the party that aligned itself with a tougher approach to crime during Smith's tenure.[70] As one Republican who endorsed the

Crime wave concerns in press, December 25, 1925. Source: *Brooklyn Daily Eagle*, December 25, 1927 (clipping from Papers of Alfred E. Smith, box 65, file 506, part 1).

governor's suggestion complained: "the laws are too lax, the parole board is—well—rotten, and the judges are too lax in imposing sentences under the laws we now have."[71] Smith's maneuver was successful on two fronts: it inspired President Calvin Coolidge to establish a National Crime Commission in November 1925 (with rising New York Democrat Franklin Roosevelt on the executive), and it tossed a bone to the Republican-dominated legislature, which passed the governor's plan into legislation.[72] But the governor's maneuver would come at a cost, as the state's crime commission went after the principles of indeterminate sentences and parole.

Glamorous World War I aviator and Republican assemblyman F. Trubee Davison was the sponsor of the bill that led New York to authorize the state commission in 1926.[73] Davison was the son of a millionaire financier; his fellow notables chose him as chairman of the first National Crime Commission, and President Coolidge followed suit.[74] Because the task of reducing "the appalling number of crimes of violence" was so daunting, Davison declared that the prospective commission's powers must be great.[75] However, while the bill was in preparation, Senator Baumes stole the spotlight from Davison when he presented a report from the innocuous-sounding Joint Legislative Committee on the Co-ordination of Civil and Criminal Practice Acts. In January 1925, this body had been charged to study crime and its prevention, and Baumes used the opportunity to come up with a clutch of bills designed to stiffen penalties and restrict criminals' rights.[76] In the first two weeks of April 1926, the assembly backed Baumes's proposals and rushed through a series of anticrime bills.[77] One month later Baumes was appointed head of the new Crime Commission of New York State.[78] The intimidating state senator warmed to the challenge.[79]

Despite the intensity of anticrime legislative maneuvering early in 1926, the Parole Board, a gangster, and the governor managed to overshadow action in Albany's political corridors. In a special message to the legislature on March 1, 1926, Smith declared he was in "perfect accord" with politicians concerned about the "appalling" rate of violent crime in the state, and he hoped the new commission would examine its "prisons, reformatories, parole and probation systems" and "disclose defects, if any, in the existing methods."[80] Several days prior to the governor's announcement, former governor Charles Evans Hughes had tabled a report produced by the state's Reorganization Commission, which worked to tame and trim New York's inefficient multidepartment system of government. One of Hughes's key recommendations was the abolition of the current Board of Parole and the establishment of a new correction commission to supervise tighter parole procedures for the entire prison and reformatory system.[81] A "shakeup" of New York's criminal justice system was overdue, not just in the opinion of the press but in accordance with Governor Smith's plans to modernize state administration.[82]

But before the government could be reorganized the parole of Izzy Presser grabbed headlines across the country. In 1915, Presser was indicted for murder in the first degree, and the New York County DA allowed him to plead guilty to manslaughter to avoid the possibility of a capital conviction for slaying a fellow gangster. Sentenced to serve twelve years, the stickup man bounced from prison to prison, racking up misconduct charges, until he escaped while working on a road gang in 1921. Recaptured in 1925, he came up for parole in the spring of 1926 because the State Superintendent of Prisons directed Sing Sing warden Lewis E. Laws to restore Presser's "good time" without penalizing him for his escape, as the law required. The board complied, and on April 29 the Jewish Board of Guardians took charge of Presser's parole. The actions of both the prison authorities and the Parole Board gave off a whiff of corruption at worst, and incompetence at best.

In an echo of Governor Flower's intervention in the Elmira Reformatory's manipulation of parole provisions in the 1890s, Governor Smith asserted executive authority to undo the problems caused by administrative discretion. His letter to the Parole Board conveyed none of the niceties common in commutation requests: "you are hereby directed . . . to revoke the action . . . in extending parole to Izzy Presser, pending an investigation by me into the whole matter."[83] The *Brooklyn Daily Eagle*, frequently Smith's nemesis, crowed with self-congratulation at the board's anticipated demise.[84] But the controversy swirling around parole since the start of his second term gave Smith an opportunity to conduct a more thoroughgoing study of parole in light of the recommendations in Hughes's report. The man Smith chose to head the review, George W. Alger, was perfectly suited to the task: a Republican; a lawyer and legal reformer; the counsel to the Prison Investigation Committee in 1919; a member of PANY's Prison Committee; and a longtime advocate of the parole system's overhaul.[85] Smith's choice suggests he was well aware that Progressives, not just the scandal-mongering press, believed the administration of parole had reached a crisis. When Alger's appointment was announced, the president of the American Institute of Criminal Law and Criminology, George W. Kirchwey, congratulated the governor: "it shows a rare degree of statesmanship."[86] As with all inquiries, its merits would be tested by its capacity to change business as usual.

George W. Alger could easily have stepped from the pages of *The Search for Order*. According to Robert H. Wiebe's classic account of Progressivism, middle-class white Americans sought out a "new core" after the Civil War to replace the old certainties of agrarian-centered life. What they developed through that yearning were impersonal rules designed to produce efficiency and procedural regularity.[87] New York's parole system exhibited none of these virtues, as Alger knew before he stepped into his job. But he was no Gitlow, intent on uprooting established institutions; instead he tried to determine how parole could be reformed.[88] As much as he believed that officials who failed in their duties must be replaced he was equally certain that innovative theories of justice must be properly tested before they were discarded.[89] Expectations were high when Alger presented his report to the governor early in December 1926 and he more than met them.[90] As expected, the report found that Superintendent Long had committed an error of judgment, which prison and parole authorities had compounded. But Alger used a broader brush to paint the sitting Board of Parole as a failed body whose time had ended.

Alger advised that the current members be dismissed and the board itself be abolished in the interest of "organized society." In the same breath he urged the state to retain this modern mode of discretionary justice.[91] Alger interviewed numerous officials in the course of his inquiry, including individuals involved in the board's general operations.[92] The star witness was board chairman George W. Benham, former warden of Auburn Prison (1905–1913) and a retired town banker.[93] Under Governor Miller he became the board's chairman in 1921, after having been appointed by Governor Whitman in 1917.[94] Benham's replies were frank and remarkably consistent with the Board of Parole hearing records: the scrutiny of applicants was a matter of character assessment, not the appraisal of expert assessments. According to the chairman the reports of experts in prisoners' dossiers were not especially significant; rather, board members relied on "the appearance of the man, the answers he gives to the questions, and also our experience with men of that type. . . . The papers are handed to us, but they are not conclusive at all." Alger was dismayed. Even if, as Benham proudly claimed, the percentage of applicants whose time in prison exceeded their minimum sentence was increasing (from a low of 3 percent in 1920 to 14 percent in the previous year), it was evident that the Parole Board still based its decisions on quick impressions, and that inmates still considered parole a right. As currently practiced, Alger concluded, parole in New York was "an underfinanced moral gesture." The only way to evaluate parole's merits was to place it "on a different basis in wise hands."[95]

The Baumes Laws and the War on Discretionary Justice

The Hughes's committee's recommendation early in 1926 that government agencies be consolidated meshed well with Alger's report, which advised the state to assume jurisdiction of the paroling of inmates from all state institutions, including reformatories, refuges, and workhouses. These recommendations led that year to the establishment of a new body, called the Commission of Correction, which inherited responsibility for the oversight of probation, prisons, and parole.[96] A further sign of New York's endorsement of Progressive penology was Governor Smith's appointment of a doctor with psychiatric expertise to head the consolidated operations.

Dr. Raymond F. C. Kieb, who took charge of the consolidated operations in February 1927, had earlier superintended the Matteawan State Hospital for the Criminally Insane.[97] In 1913 the institution had made news for all the wrong reasons when Harry Thaw, the millionaire murderer of architect Stanford White, made a blazing escape from the hospital in a car driven by accomplices.[98] Allegations of a "pardon ring" operating at Matteawan preceded this escape, and the management was also mired in claims that staff accepted kickbacks.[99] After the Thaw debacle, the doctor's fortunes rebounded. Kieb became a member of the American Psychiatric Association and the American Prison Association, and in 1925 President Coolidge selected him as a national delegate to the International Prison Congress. The rebranded board and its new chairman fit the Progressive penological bill perfectly.[100] The Prison Association of New York declared its support for the governor's choice and his proven commitment to "penal improvement."[101] Yet, less than two years after his appointment, Kieb's honeymoon as chairman was over. Scandal seemed to follow Kieb, and in 1929 it would come with far greater violence and broader consequences for discretionary justice.

The Crime Commission of New York State had a very different mission, and a far more formidable head. The war on discretionary justice intensified as Caleb H. Baumes and his ten fellow commissioners began to flex their muscle, confident that the public was behind the Republican-led campaign to build higher and more secure walls against discretionary release. The senator branded his name on the measures the state introduced to knock back indeterminate sentencing and bind the discretion of the Board of Parole, and Baumes took credit for inspiring the country to follow New York's lead in putting an end to "the protection of the law-breaker, particularly the professional criminal."[102] In the weeks leading up to the commission's launch on May 18 1926, the legislature passed ten bills, including An Act to Amend the Prison Law, in Relation to Paroles and Commutation. This law made it compulsory that the Parole Board "examine into the previous life and record of those appearing for parole." More pointedly it prohibited the commutation of life sentences and the capacity of lifers to earn compensation. Two other acts focused on four-time felony offenders. Such prisoners became subject to mandatory sentences of twenty-five years to life, with no right to release until they served their full terms. In addition, these inmates were ineligible for parole until they served the maximum penalty set for their particular fourth offense. The Crime Commission's sole concession to discretion concerned gubernatorial clemency, as defined by the state constitution.[103] The governor could still modify mandatory sentences by granting commutations or pardons, but by the mid 1920s he did so with the knowledge that any act of clemency would make him look soft on crime.

It appeared at first that the board and its beleaguered members, not the governor, would bear the full brunt of the commission's attack. Indeed, one recently appointed member resented the fact that public commentators confused the powers of pardoning and parole. Alexander Konta, a Manhattan banker appointed to the Parole Board in 1925, became testy during George Alger's interrogation. The board did not rubber-stamp applications, Konta asserted; he further declared that he and his fellow members treated inmates' medical reports seriously, especially when evidence of "mental defects" made prisoners poor prospects for parole. In his opinion it was unfair for the board to bear the blame for authorizing the release of prisoners serving definite terms, since the governor was responsible for recommending their paroles. Feeling the heat of public disapproval, he protested, "I think that the parole board should have some kind of protection, some greater power to be able to carry out its work, without being subjected to insult, prevarications, misstatements." The board operated within the rules, "yet we have to stand all the criticism." Alger regained the upper hand when he revealed Konta's apparent misunderstanding of the rule that granted the board authority to keep prisoners locked up, even those whom the governor recommended for clemency; additionally, the board had the power to set strict conditions for those whom they released.[104] If any improper exercise of discretionary power had occurred, it was not through the governor's hand. Nevertheless, there was one matter on which Konta made a valid point: the public had come to confuse parole with gubernatorial clemency.

The weapons Governor Smith chose to fend off criticism of his executive actions were more effective than board attempts to justify their actions, and he used them deftly. After the Presser parole controversy in the lead-up to the state elections of 1926, he maintained his open criticism of the Parole Board's sloppy procedures, and once he regained the governorship at the end of November he decided to address the state's crime commission as Alger prepared his report.[105] Flushed from his reelection victory, Smith not only threw his support behind a tighter parole system but also attempted to outdo Baumes with a proposal that judges be stripped of their sentencing discretion. The establishment of a sentencing board, Smith projected, would allow experts to assess inmates' mental and physical fitness after their incarceration, prescribe sentences and determine release prospects.[106]

But once again, a parole violator, John J. "Bum" Rodgers, arrested late in November 1926 after a murderous holdup spree, deflated Smith's credibility as an authority on discretionary release.[107] Back in 1920, during his first term in office, Smith had granted Rodgers clemency, and Republicans used the governor's act of clemency to renew their charge that Smith was an irresponsible pardoner.[108] The metropolitan press ignored Smith's post-election plan for sentencing reform, but it granted ample coverage to the Republican Party's scrutiny of the governor's exercise of executive discretion. It found that the governor had granted 1,789 acts of clemency over his past two terms. Because the report ignored distinctions between pardons and sentence commutation, and conflated minor and serious offences, it allowed the press to portray Smith as the pot calling the Board of Parole black over its ill-judged releases of dangerous criminals. On the same day that Rodgers was sentenced to life imprisonment in accordance with the state's mandatory fourth-offense act, Smith was forced once again to counter the "grossly absurd" allegations that made their way to the press.[109]

The Commission of Correction's establishment in 1926 and the appointment of Dr. Kieb provided only a temporary lull in the clamor against discretionary justice. By March 1927, accusations of mismanagement flared again, thanks to a series of articles published by a Progressive reformer who had built a national profile over the mid-1920s as a pest on parole matters.[110] Lawrence Veiller's first encounter with crime management came through his work with the Charity Organization Society of New York, whose committee on criminal courts he chaired from 1911.[111] As the Presser affair unfolded, Veiller published hard-hitting articles in a middle-brow review magazine, *The World's Work*, with provocative titles: "The Menace of Paroled Convicts," "How the Law Saves the Criminal," and "Shall Parole be Abolished?"[112] After the magazine published Veiller's fourth article, "Turning the Criminals Loose," which claimed the governor had pardoned notorious criminals without just cause, Smith was incensed, and for good reason. In fact, he had recommended Rodgers's parole on the "express recommendation of the judge" who had tried his case, and with the approval of the DA who had prosecuted it.[113] Smith fired off an angry response to the magazine and the writer. "It is about as complete a crackpot article as I ever read in any publication in my career."[114] The *Brooklyn Eagle*, whose editor, Thomas S. Rice, was a member of the crime commission, publicized the spat and predictably took Veiller's side: "If the Governor keeps it up the first news you know 'PA' SMITH will be Running Neck-and-Neck with 'Ma Ferguson.'"[115]

THE SERENADERS—"WE AIN'T GWINA STEAL NO MO'."
And the sentimental, tearful parole board actually believes it and will release them.

Parole Board "sob sisters," in *The World's Work*. Source: Lawrence Veiller, "The Menace of Paroled Convicts," *The World's Work* 51, no. 3 (February 1926): 363–75, 367.

Sending prickly letters and appearing before the Crime Commission was not the most potent means the governor had at his disposal to fend off cheap shots that he was overly generous toward criminals. Like Governor Hill before him, deliberating over the fate of Roxalana Druse while he planned a run at the White House, the case of a woman facing the death penalty landed on Smith's desk as he groomed himself for the Democratic nomination to contest the 1928 presidential election. In 1927 Ruth Snyder, a glamorous Queens housewife, was convicted with her paramour, Judd Gray, for the staged murder of her husband. Legal appeals prolonged speculation that her sentence might be commuted since almost twenty years had passed since a woman had been executed in New York.[116] "Pa" Smith's friends, as well as his political enemies, assumed the governor would shy away from sending a woman to the electric chair under his watch.[117] After the New York Court of Appeals upheld the lovers' conviction on November 22, 1927, Snyder's lawyers requested that Smith issue a reprieve long enough to permit psychiatrists to assess her sanity, and the governor agreed.[118] Since Smith made a practice of granting personal hearings to petitioners in all capital cases (the only element of Governor Whitman's practice Smith retained), he also agreed to meet with Snyder's counsel several days before the rescheduled execution.

Newspapers reporting on this meeting stated that the governor held little stock in psychiatric expertise. As he lectured the lawyers, he "did not think very much of 'this psychosis stuff' and 'this twilight zone business.'"[119] Public sentiment made a stronger impression on him, Smith later disclosed in his autobiography. "The volume of correspondence on both sides of the Snyder case that poured into the Executive Chamber was amazing," and he recalled that on January 13, 1928, the day set for her electrocution, he "sat at an open telephone wire" connecting him to Sing Sing prison up to an hour before the switch was pulled.[120] On that night Snyder and Gray clung to the hope of a last-minute reprieve while Smith's mind may have drifted to the prospect of his election to the White House. He allowed the sentence to stand. As it transpired, Herbert Hoover won the presidential election of 1928 and another Democrat, Franklin Delano Roosevelt, took over as New York's governor in 1929, only to confront new challenges, compounded by the 1926 restructuring of parole, the hiring of Kieb and the Baumes laws.

FDR, Baumes, and the Amalgamation of Pardoning and Parole

Bum Rodgers was just the sort of felon the mandatory sentencing laws were designed to punish: the "bandits, burglars and killers" who terrorized the public and cast doubt on the integrity of the Parole Board whenever one was released before serving his full sentence. But the Baumes laws cast a net so wide that it snagged smaller fish and snared them with life sentences. The first person so sentenced was twenty-one-year-old Clifford Hanson, convicted in the summer of 1926 for holding up a Brooklyn delicatessen at gunpoint.[121] More men and women began to follow, and by November 1927 there were forty-nine Baumes lifers in Sing Sing alone.[122] Defenders of indeterminate sentencing and judicial discretion—including prosecutors—began to complain that few repeat offenders fit the profile of the murderous gangster.

The case of the first woman to be sentenced to life for shoplifting under the Baumes laws became a rallying point for critics of mandatory sentencing.[123] With five prior convictions for stealing coats and dresses, twenty-nine-year-old Ruth St. Clair was sent to prison for life in January 1930 by a dissident judge who promptly declared he would petition the governor for mercy.[124] Although judges led the call for the repeal of the 1926 statutes everyone knew that the chief executive was the only man authorized to intervene mercifully in St. Clair's case or that of any other offender unfairly punished.[125] Scanning the political landscape, Roosevelt was mindful of his experience as a former executive member of the National Crime Commission, his Tammany Hall detractors in the Democratic Party, and his opponents in the Republican-dominated legislature, headed by an anticrime senator. The governor decided to tread lightly.[126]

Studies of Franklin Roosevelt's presidency greatly outnumber histories of his tenure at Albany, where he worked out his preference for consolidated executive power.[127] FDR's approach to the governance of discretionary justice in New York's penal system is a perfect illustration. In the decade leading up to his governorship, biographer Frank Freidel notes, Roosevelt cultivated a reputation as a crime fighter seeking greater efficiencies in the criminal justice system.[128] Years before he set up his White House Brain Trust, Roosevelt turned to experts to devise policy rather than plod through the state legislative process or debate constitutional amendments that never came to fruition. Columbia University professor of law and fellow National Crime Commission member Raymond Moley was one of FDR's closest advisors during his governorship.[129] Samuel Lewisohn, the author of *The New Leadership in Industry* (1926), was another. Having inherited his father Adolph's interest in crime prevention in addition to his business talent, the younger Lewisohn had served as an advisory member of State Commission of Correction under Governor Smith.[130] Roosevelt maintained Smith's practice of recruiting women to his inner circle, notably Jane Hoey. One of the new breed of female professionals, she was the only woman member of the Crime Commission of New York and she held a master's degree in social work.[131] These were the bearers of practical and professional wisdom to whom Roosevelt turned as he shifted from caution to action late in 1929. Indeed, he had little choice but to act after a different cohort of men voiced protest from the state's pressure cooker prisons.

Within months of Roosevelt's election, New York's antiquated prison system, the problem of prison overcrowding, and the troubles produced through mandatory sentencing created a perfect storm in New York's criminal justice system. Over the 1920s the rise in the state's prison population greatly outstripped the state's growth rate.[132] The number of men in Auburn Prison rose by fifty percent, from 1127 in 1920 to 1759 in 1929, and Sing Sing's population spurt was greater, rising from 1179 to 1936 over the same period. Altogether, the state prison system, over which the Corrections Department exercised jurisdiction in regard to parole, shot from 6672 inmates to 10,929, and the pace quickened in the years following the introduction of mandatory sentencing and restricted parole.[133]

In December 1927, Governor Smith's testimony before the Crime Commission of New York included a warning that long definite sentences posed a danger to the prisoner and to the state: "a man loses hope. It is hard to do anything with him when hope goes out of his heart, and he knows that he is never going to see the world again. You have a pretty despondent man. A man hard to handle."[134] Within two years, inmates at Clinton and Auburn confirmed Smith's prediction.[135] Three riots took place in July and December, causing death, destruction, and a vivid sense of crisis in penal management.[136] New Yorkers were deeply divided: supporters of the Baumes laws considered the disturbances proof that tough laws were necessary; opponents of mandatory sentencing and restricted parole urged that the laws be repealed to restore men's hope. With the help of his advisors, Roosevelt struck a middle path that restructured the administration of parole and pardoning.

Roosevelt reached this conclusion at the end of an eventful year. Late in July 1929 Auburn State Prison erupted in a riot, and the governor vowed to get to the base of the problem. "Governor Orders Jail Riot Inquiry" announced his intention. Several months later a less favorable headline described Roosevelt's decision to commute a four-time felony offender's sentence: "Governor Wrong on Baumes Law."[137] Roosevelt's grant of clemency made Bert N. Garstin in September 1929 the first inmate to escape the noose of the Baumes laws. In the course of announcing his decision Roosevelt took a swipe at the state's tough sentencing laws:

> The circumstances in this case show the possibility of a grave injustice being committed under the mandatory statute providing life sentence [sic] for all

fourth felony offenders. . . . While the Baumes laws, as a whole, were absolutely necessary as a salutary deterrent to crime, I believe that, in a few isolated cases to which they apply . . . the result reached is unjust.[138]

Roosevelt put right what the law had made wrong in Garstin's case. A serial "paper hanger" with just enough previous convictions for passing worthless checks to be punished under the life sentence statute was not a man who deserved to spend the remainder of his life in prison. But Roosevelt also used the case to underline that discretion was vital to justice. Once he shrank Garstin's sentence from life down to time served—just over two years—the battle lines with Baumes and his fellow travelers were drawn.

Newspaper editors across the country sent Roosevelt letters accusing him of trying to repeal New York's stiff sentencing laws, but Republicans came up with a craftier response. They effectively twisted Garstin's commuted sentence into an endorsement of mandatory sentencing, since the statutes of 1926 had been passed with the knowledge that the governor's prerogative could sort out exceptional cases. A just outcome was unlikely in 100 percent of cases, members of the Crime Commission conceded. Since Smith and Roosevelt had, between them, commuted just one life sentence for fourth offenders, out of the 160 imposed since 1926, the laws were evidently just. The Baumes laws were "All Right" and Roosevelt was "All Wrong."[139]

The tables began to turn, however. The most dramatic of the year's prison riots, in December 1929, left Auburn's chief keeper dead at the hands of a prisoner, and public support for the Baumes laws began to slacken. This debacle opened up space for Roosevelt to outmaneuver his Republican opponents on the crime question.[140] "Desperate prisoners" had made their grievances clear: there was something deeply wrong with statutes that doomed recidivists to life in prison with no prospect of parole and only the slimmest chance of gubernatorial clemency.[141] The chief executive could respond to individual cases, but turning back to the early nineteenth-century practice of wholesale pardoning as a release valve was not an option. State Supreme Court Justice James B. Hill said as much in his letter to Roosevelt after the Garstin commutation: "the power reposed in the Executive to pardon in no wise corrects the harshness of these statutes."[142]

Constructing a Professional Board on a Business Model

In the background of the political skirmishes over discretionary justice, the Commission of Correction persisted with the business of parole. When Raymond C. Kieb took over the entire correctional system, he did so without the legislature providing him with full-time board members. Benham finally retired as the chairman of the Board of Parole in July of 1927, but Alexander Konta remained a member, acutely aware that the public expected fewer prisoners to be released. As a result of the board's new commitment to restraint, the Baumes laws were not the only cause of prison overcrowding. Within months of Kieb's appointment, the *New York Times* observed that the trend toward fewer paroles had produced "a serious problem in the State of New York."[143]

Under the new Commission, the Board of Parole could not win: reducing paroles elevated prison numbers without translating to greater public confidence in parole or the Commission's head. With three major prison riots in the state within one year, the clock on Dr. Kieb's tenure began to tick. Republican Senator John Knight called for the Commissioner's removal from office, charging that he had bungled prisoner transfers and allowed Auburn to become critically overcrowded. The Prison Association of New York also lost faith in Kieb, albeit for different reasons. "He allows his own attitudes, too frequently, to dominate in the determination of the fitness of a prisoner for parole," PANY claimed. "In short, the parole board is very much of a one man board."[144] Dr. Kieb's time was up. Roosevelt decided to sacrifice him to make way for a bold plan to organize discretionary justice on a business model of efficiency.

Roosevelt could have sought advice from a criminologist (plenty were eager to advise), but he preferred a businessman. Unlike Smith, who had responded to industrialist Elbert H. Gary's invitation to wage war against crime, FDR took the lead by enlisting his friend Sam Lewisohn. The governor began by sending a draft five-year plan to update the prison system by investing in modern prisons and replacing the state's century-old penal infrastructure. Roosevelt's plan included a new mode of discretionary justice. In his mind, he saw a "parole court" that would process applications for gubernatorial clemency as well as parole applications.[145] The Republicans had come up with a scheme of their own, a three-person parole board to be manned by laymen and backed by a bolstered corps of parole officers, but FDR told Lewisohn it was inferior: "the Baumes plan for a revamped parole board is silly." Once he had Lewisohn on board, the governor asked the business leader to work out the details: "Don't you want to sit down and let me have a two or three page memorandum showing the kind of set-up which this court should have?"[146]

Roosevelt's intention to reformulate discretionary justice received its first public airing in his annual message to the legislature, delivered on January 2, 1930. This change would first require a "very careful study" of prison management and the parole system, and two weeks later, in enemy territory, Roosevelt informed the Republican Club of New York City that he had appointed a panel of experts to conduct such an investigation. In particular his Special Committee on the Parole Problem was charged to advise the government on the replacement of the parole board by a parole court. Lewisohn set to work on January 24 as the chairman, with Jane Hoey, Raymond Moley, George W. Alger, and two other advisers to assist him. Setting a standard of business efficiency, the committee presented its report to the governor on February 5, complete with draft legislation.[147]

Roosevelt's "blue-ribbon panel" delivered what David J. Rothman describes as a "damning report" of a parole system that manifestly failed prisoners as well as society; however, the criticism was constructive, and its recommendations restructured the administration of executive clemency as well as parole.[148] In fact, Lewisohn recommended that the state establish a board of pardon and parole, to "apply scientific methods" to "re-establish" prisoners in "organized society." The terminology was modern, but the argument was familiar: neither the governor nor the parole board could possibly cope with the volume of applications for discretionary release. As of January 1 1930, there were 1,350 pardon applications on file, 507 of which were lodged in 1929; 425 former prisoners had applied for citizenship restoration, and 50 aliens had applied to secure naturalization papers. A total of 1,825 applications awaited the governor's decision. In 1929, Roosevelt had pardoned only six inmates and granted twenty-eight commutations of sentence. The committee read these figures as evidence that the chief executive could devote "only a modicum of attention to the very important questions involved in the pardon power." But Roosevelt's advisers stopped short of recommending an end to executive discretion. The prerogative to pardon and grant commutations and reprieves must remain an executive privilege. To aid the governor, it suggested that a well-staffed board, acting in an advisory capacity, could assess clemency petitions with greater efficiency, by carefully examining "the accumulation of data involving the facts and reasons for or against the application." This new blended board, nested in the executive branch of government, could help New York's prisons fulfill their objective, to serve as "a means of discipline, reformation and rehabilitation."[149]

Roosevelt was clearly anxious over the public response to the proposal, especially after his commutation of Garstin had provoked such an angry reaction. He ordered his staff to collect editorials published in the state's principal papers, and they turned out to be surprisingly favorable. Twelve newspapers, including the irascible *Brooklyn Eagle*, gave Lewisohn's report lengthy coverage, and it pledged support for a board of pardon and parole.[150] The proposed changes to discretionary justice rationalized decision making (the assessment of parole and pardon applications by one body) and eliminated the duplica-tion of effort caused by prisoners' forum shopping for release. Most editors hoped that Baumes and his commissioners would soon reach a compromise with the governor in the interest of averting greater unrest among the prison population and in separating the running of prisons from the operation of parole.

After the report's release, and armed with its positive response, Roosevelt sought a truce with Senator Baumes. The Joint Legislative Committee had already declared its support for the governor's attempt to devise "an adequate modern prison policy," so this left Baumes the only impediment to the pas-sage of the legislation needed to put it into effect. With a little diplomacy Roosevelt managed to persuade Baumes to drop his party's proposal (which would have left pardoning separate from parole, and kept the Parole Board within the Department of Correction). The governor sent his lieutenant, Lewisohn, to begin negotiations prior to the report's release, and Roosevelt followed with a bipartisan appeal. The tactic worked, and Baumes gave in, on the basis that "saving men and women from lives of crime" should not be drawn into "the maelstrom of politics, nor can it be in any ways a mat-ter on which either political party can have anything but a desire to bring it about as speedily as possible."[151] The senator quickly brokered a deal with his Republican colleagues to scrap their bill and support the governor's, which the legislature passed into law on April 25, 1930. After a century of criticism of the one-man pardon, followed by a half-century of controversy over the administration of parole, a gentlemen's agreement led to a blended system of discretionary release.

Fiscal concern, which deepened from the autumn of 1929, was equally sig-nificant, and it turned financial distress into a handmaiden for parole reform in 1930. Locking up prisoners and keeping them in prison with narrowed op-tions for release was clearly explosive, but it was also expensive. The prison-building program already underway in New York, including construction on the newest state prison at Attica, came with a price tag of thirty-eight mil-lion dollars, which threatened to break the state budget.[152] As the Depression began to grip, there were 9,106 inmates in the state's prisons, reformatories, and institutions for the insane and "defective," with no sign of reduced num-bers in sight. Parole was meant only for the fit, the Parole Problem Committee advised: "we have many men in prison today of such low or abnormal mental or physical qualifications that they never will be useful in the community again, and in many cases, if released would constitute a renewed menace."[153] Committee member George W. Alger predicted that the legislature would support the governor's scheme, if only because "budgetary implications ought to be enough to alarm the voters and taxpayers."[154] Parole's economy, in contrast to the unaffordable costs of imprisonment, was the trump card advocates of discretionary release had played since the late nineteenth century. The darkening days of economic decline and the prospect of further prison outbreaks sealed the deal for the Division of Parole.

Conclusion

In 1930, Chapter 824 of the Laws of New York defined the "powers and duties" of New York's modernized Board of Parole as an aid to executive direction, not as its replacement. At the governor's request, the board was authorized to investigate petitions sent to the chief executive "as to pardon or commutation of sentence and of applicants for restoration of citizenship." In the discourse of social science the statute spelled out casework methodology as the basis for decision making. Prisoners were to be interviewed, analyzed, and diagnosed, and plans for their "treatment" devised; in addition, individuals and agents were to be correlated according to the best "methods of influencing human behavior." No reference to religion or morality appeared in the text of the statute. A behavioral and social scientific library became scripture, and the executive director of the new division was expected to provide his staff with "the leading books on parole . . . together with reports and other documents on correlated topics of criminology and social work." From July 1930, the date the new division began to operate, the law required all parole officers to keep "complete social, physical, mental psychiatric and criminal records" of each offender under their jurisdiction.[155] The fact that crime was the last-mentioned factor in this list demonstrates just how far the Enlightenment and utilitarian ideal of punishment as proportional to the crime had traveled in 150 years of penal modernization. By the Depression, it was secondary, and in the case of "subnormal" prisoners, irrelevant.

The integration of executive and administrative discretion in New York left the governor less busy but he remained the dominant partner, as the power of life and death lay where it had been since 1821, in the governor's hands. Prior to Sam Lewisohn's meeting with his fellow committee members, the captain of industry sent Roosevelt a long letter to spell out his proposal, in which he portrayed the members of the new Board of Parole as company directors, headed by the governor as CEO. "To get good men" for the board he advised it would be necessary to grant them latitude. "Some real discretion and power in its best sense is necessary, and if such a body is hampered . . . it will be distasteful to forceful men."[156] Discretion was not just compatible with case-study method and social scientific research: it was essential to the success of parole. However, Lewisohn warned the state to steer clear of the path other states had blazed by granting boards full responsibility for discretionary release.[157]

The apocryphal crime wave, whipped up in the torrent of alarming headlines and partisan jousting, led to criticism of Al Smith, and it came close to undoing New York's investment in parole, initiated in the 1870s. Enemies of indeterminate sentencing and parole also massed in New York during the Prohibition era. President Herbert Hoover commissioned a nationwide study in 1929 to examine the breakdown of law and order, which exposed, among other things, the American public's loss of faith in the Progressive vision of criminal treatment and cure.[158] Despite the pall cast over parole and pardoning in the 1920s, it was the stiff Baumes laws that were clipped in the 1930s, not executive discretion.

Epilogue

Mercy, Parole, and the Failed Search for Penal Certainty

The social scientists, businessmen, and politicians who supported the Parole Board of New York's assumption of responsibility for clemency petitions in addition to parole applications could look back at the change as inevitable and long overdue. Administrative approaches to discretionary justice emerged in advanced industrial democracies from the early nineteenth century.[1] New York made its first move in this direction by establishing a reformatory for juvenile delinquents in the 1820s; it leapt forward with the Elmira Reformatory's establishment in the 1870s, and the introduction of indeterminate sentencing in the 1880s expanded the reach of bureaucratic discretion. The formal establishment of a State Parole Board in 1901 and, in 1926, a Commission of Correction, were two further steps New York took, well before other states, in the trek toward a recognizably modern, bureaucratic means of discretionary justice. This disciplinary apparatus conformed to case management methods, and it folded into a Fordist drive toward efficiency. In his gubernatorial reelection campaign speech in the autumn of 1930, Franklin Roosevelt stated that the revised Board of Parole offered each prisoner "the best that modern thought and modern social science could provide so that his individual case can be studied with a view toward rehabilitating him to good citizenship."[2]

Using graphs and tables, newly hired parole authorities tabulated offender statistics at an industrial scale to analyze the time inmates served in relation to the crimes they committed, their intelligence quotients, mental ages, sexual habits, hereditary defects, and psychological pathologies. Researchers set out to disprove the contention that predicting prisoners' fortunes on parole was impossible, given the variability of their social and economic environments and the imponderables of human nature. William F. Lanne's "Parole Prediction as Science," published in the *Journal of Criminal Law and Criminology* in 1935, claimed scholars could test for significant correlations between inmate characteristics and parole outcomes using sophisticated statistical formulae. One of a growing cohort of actuarialists, Lanne included "church attendance" as a relevant factor but made no mention of contrition or human sympathy, the key ingredients of successful reintegration in the minds of the philanthropists who founded discharged prisoner aid a century earlier.[3]

Most supporters of parole were less sanguine about the notion of predictive perfection by the 1930s. Edward R. Cass, author of PANY's 1921 critical review of poor record keeping and sloppy parole reviews, grew to believe that administrative release under supervision was the most advanced, cost-effective, and socially responsible means of encouraging prisoners and rewarding reform. New York had shown this when the entire edifice of Progressive penology came close to collapsing in the late 1920s. Caleb Baumes and his band of law and order zealots imposed nondiscretionary punishment to correct parole's failures, but governors risked their political fortunes to prop up parole long enough for it to be rescued. A financial crisis at the onset of the Depression, and most significantly a cluster of prisoners in the state prisons who turned their desperation into violent action, ultimately pulled New York back from the brink of abandoning parole. Cass chose a more modest title than Lanne's for his 1938 retrospective—"Parole Can be Successful." Nevertheless, he was proud to claim it most successful in New York.[4]

As president, Franklin D. Roosevelt brought his crime fighting agenda, cultivated in the early 1920s, into office.[5] Partly in response to FBI Director J. Edgar Hoover, who used his high profile as a crime fighter to lead a federal campaign against "easy and speedy parole,"[6] Roosevelt decided a large-scale review of probation, parole, and pardoning was needed. Attorney General Homer Cummings launched the survey in 1935, and over the next two years researchers, many of them out-of-work college men and women, fanned across the country to collect data on each state's handling of discretionary release. Their five-volume report dwarfed PANY's study of the penitentiary system in North America, a landmark of social scientific study when it appeared in 1867.[7] In states with rudimentary penal systems and staff without training in statistics, the agents' work was heavy going, but New York was the exception. When contacted in 1936 for details of the state's system of discretionary release the Division's executive director, Frederick A. Moran, simply handed over the latest annual report, stacked with statistics. In return Moran received a compliment from the survey's administrator: "yours is perhaps the best organized and administered of all the various parole departments."[8]

The division's reports included accounts of its review of clemency petitions. Not surprisingly, petitioners continued to send applications to the governor's office, but from July 1930 the new administrators began to process them, using a different model of case management:

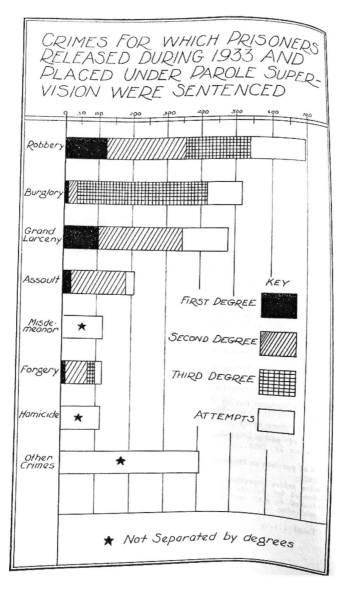

New York State Division of Parole, *Sixth Annual Report of the Division of Parole of the Executive Department*, 1936, 48.

Applicants and their relatives [are informed] that the intervention of an attorney does not assist the application, nor does the advocacy of any politician, for only the facts of the case as revealed in the investigation by the Parole Board and by correspondence, are given weight by the Governor.

Bureaucratic processes overtook personal clemency. If desk officers considered a case had "sufficient merit to warrant an investigation," they requested reports from the sentencing judge, the DA, and the warden. If these "data" were favorable, the board authorized "an executive field investigation [to be] made by an official representative of the Division of Parole." The end product in this clemency assembly line was "a synopsis of the case" and a recommendation for the governor's consideration.[9] Samuel Lewisohn's business model of discretionary justice was in place. In a speech he made at Governor Herbert Lehman's 1935 conference on crime, Lewisohn proudly reported that New York's Division of Parole employed a staff of twenty-one, including "executive clemency investigators and parole employment officers in the field."[10]

The 1930 statute solemnized the mixed marriage of pardon and parole without formally assigning capital cases to the governor's office as a reserve pocket of executive authority. Roosevelt and his band of advisors simply took for granted that the chief executive's historic authority to reprieve from execution would continue. The thread that connected the ancient prerogative power of kings, the privilege of colonial governors, and the discretionary power of chief executives in the democratic republic had not frayed. Frederick Moran appeared clear that his division had authority over "all applications for executive clemency with the exception of capital cases."[11] For Lewisohn and Roosevelt, there were some decisions so grave that only the CEO should make them. When considering the possible reprieve of prisoners sentenced to death, or the commutation of death sentences to terms of imprisonment, Governor Roosevelt conducted "open hearings in the Executive Chamber," a tradition Al Smith established in his time in office. Over the following decades subsequent governors kept up the practice of dealing with capital cases themselves, in consultation with their counsel, until state legislators greatly restricted the death penalty's scope in 1967.[12] In 1958, Governor Averell Harriman described for the Saturday Evening Post "what it's like to hold the fearful power to reprieve a condemned man or let him go to the electric chair." "Mercy is a Lonely Business," was the article's title.[13]

Despite the weight of sovereign tradition, the chief executive's life-and-death powers faced considerable criticism that could have, at numerous junctures, weaned New York from its reliance upon gubernatorial discretion. From the 1820s, opponents of the one-man pardon argued for a model of discretion more in keeping with a republic. At constitutional conventions, in philosophical treatises, and in penal reformers' studies based on surveys of gubernatorial practice and statistics of pardoning, the balance of thinking on executive discretion favored the idea that Francis Lieber promoted through-out his career—that the governor be divested of his prerogative to pardon. Yet in New York, conservative arguments in support of the gubernatorial discretion proved more persuasive. Even in 1930, the merger of pardon and parole management occurred through a statute, not a constitutional amendment.

The experts who prepared the federal Survey Release report on discretionary release imagined executive discretion as the elderly "father" of parole: "the principles of parole and probation are children of the aging concept, which shrinks to make way for its new and growing offshoots." This metaphor of penal succession was based on the history of states such as New York, which joined others in 1930 when it belatedly set up an administrative body to review clemency requests. Like a doddering parent, the pardoning power could be granted a special place at the table of modern criminal justice, even if it had "unfortunate attributes," most notably the temptation to use gubernatorial authority indiscriminately or corruptly. While they never doubted administrative means of modifying criminal sentences to be superior, the authors of the report on pardons admitted they had a soft spot for clemency: "When we weigh the abuses and errors of pardon against its social benefits the scale tips definitely in favor of this old and ever-young institution."[14]

Quaint statements of this nature on the virtues of executive discretion appear naïve next to statistical tables on parole predictability. But practitioners of administrative discretion turned out to be more realistic than actuarial criminologists. At the 1935 Crime Conference hosted by New York's Governor Lehman, a psychiatrist who headed New York City's Parole Commission presented a paper that asked, "What should be the prerequisites for release from prison?" The doctor, Joseph W. Moore, answered his question in an unclinical fashion, admitting that his board members' feelings guided their decisions, and that they often acted on a "hunch" about a prisoner's likelihood of making good. These hunches developed "subconsciously" through "accumulated experiences." Parole could never be an "exact science," Moore discovered: "I personally have little confidence in the predictability of human behavior to the extent of being able to decide on a parole risk by a calculation of plus and minus factors."[15] William Lanne was more confident in his formulas, perhaps because his real name was Nathan Leopold, convicted along with Richard Loeb in 1924 for a murder that became known as the "crime of the century." During his life sentence at Joliet State Prison, Leopold worked in the prison library, which allowed him to read the latest criminological texts and participate in studies sponsored by Northwestern University.[16] Earlier in his life Leopold had been obsessed with the philosophy of Friedrich Nietzsche, especially his notion of the *Übermensch*, or "superman."[17]

Mere mortals such as George W. Alger and Francis Lieber could see shades of gray in modern forms of discretionary justice, for all their harsh commentary on parole's imperfections. Alger, who flayed the Board of Parole members in 1926 over their poor decision-making practice, published an article in the *Atlantic Monthly* a decade later about the current state of parole across the nation. He agreed with Cass that New York's improved system had come to set the standard for other states by the mid-1930s, even if it had not yet reached the "pinnacle of perfection." No matter how well funded or staffed or administered parole might become, Alger conceded that it is "at best an administrative problem of extreme complexity."[18] The simple fact that prisoners must be released at some point rendered that problem unavoidable. For Alger it went without saying that the governor's authority to pardon, reprieve, and commute sentences should persist. In contrast, Lieber's reading of pardoning's sovereign nature was more personal, since in 1841 he had sought his own pardon from the King of Prussia, whom he addressed as "Most illustrious and most mighty King, Most merciful King and Lord."[19] Citizens pleading for mercy in a democratic republic were different: they were not obliged to pay such obeisance to the men they elected to govern them, although many thought it best to do so.

The constitution of New York has retained the chief executive's authority to pardon, as Governor John Yates did in 1823, and as John Young did in the midst of the anti-rent crisis of the 1840s, in both instances to release prisoners who paid the price of hard-line penal policies. Prison abolitionists, critics of the racial disparities of imprisonment produced through the so-called war on drugs, and opponents of the Baumes-like mandatory sentencing wave of the 1980s and '90s remind us that popular punitiveness produces injustice today no less than it did in the eighteenth and nineteenth centuries, when governors made considerably greater use of their discretionary authority to mitigate punishment.[20] The Great Seal of New York is an apt reminder that "Liberty's" kick of the crown left sovereign power in the picture and intact.

NOTE ON SOURCES

Many of the primary sources used in this book are published and previously underutilized by criminal justice historians. Charles Zebina Lincoln's *Messages from the Governors of New York*, published in full in 1909, cover the period from 1693 to 1906[1] Lincoln's notes add context to the messages, which frequently conveyed governors' concerns over their prerogative to pardon (including responses to criticism). They also cite penal and political conditions (such as the anti-rent agitation that peaked in the 1830s and '40s), which influenced their policies and practices. Most governors provided an annual report of their pardons, commutations, and reprieves in their messages to the legislature, due to a new constitutional requirement in 1846. Many governors also chose to include these reports when they published their public papers. Chief executives supplemented statistics with references to individual cases, often quoting from correspondence received from district attorneys, judges, prominent citizens and, by the late nineteenth century, medical and psychiatric authorities. These published records alone provide far greater insight into the history of executive clemency than the records historians of mercy in most other jurisdictions have relied upon. In Britain, for instance, neither the monarch nor her or his ministers published pardoning statistics, and the Home Office, which acted effectively as a civil servant pardon board by the mid-nineteenth century, did not divulge its decision-making rationales beyond the privileged circle of government ministers.[2]

The Prison Association of New York (PANY) produced a long unbroken record of its work as a watchdog on penal practice, and a key player in the state's shifting approach to discretionary justice. Consequently, this study draws on every PANY report, from 1844 to 1940. From its inception, the association's Discharged Prisoners Committee assisted released prisoners and monitored their behavior, creating a proto-parole system that previous historians have overlooked. PANY also produced influential investigative reports on the performance of the penal innovations it backed, including indeterminate sentencing and parole. Well before the state was forced to review its delivery of Progressive justice in the mid-1920s, PANY's studies, conducted by national and international leaders in penology, exposed problems and promoted solutions within and beyond New York.

Evidence of gubernatorial discretion in practice lies in two archival sources. From 1799 to 1931, executive pardon registers (ten volumes in total) document the names of pardoned prisoners, their offenses and sentences, and the conditions governors sometimes imposed on their liberty.[3] This source is particularly valuable in the first sixty years of New York's statehood, before governors began regularly to report the number of pardons they granted, and prior to the keeping of clemency files. The open prejudices of the past are inked on register pages that refer to "slave," "color'd," and "Indian" prisoners, distinguishing them from the white majority. However, these markings also make it possible to map patterns of clemency over time in relation to the gender, ethnicity, and status of offenders. After 1858, fifty-eight volumes of the journals of governors' actions and decisions produced between 1859 and 1916 make it possible to supplement gaps in governors' reports of executive discretion.[4]

As a result of a change in archival access policy in 2009, researchers now have access to the 8,121 clemency case files that have survived from 1859 to 1926.[5] Some files, particularly in the early period, contain little more than a jacket with minimal information aside from the inmate's name and offense. Others fill several standard archival boxes; these are typically capital cases and, toward the twentieth century, cases in which appeal court proceedings protracted the pardon process. The typical file includes correspondence that flags the grounds on which petitioners pled for mercy and officials considered the prospect of clemency.[6] Letters from prosecutors and sentencing judges appear in all but a few files, which supports the claims governor often made, that they reached their decisions in light of advice from officials. However, the rise of statewide parole in the early twentieth century shows the turn governors took to relying upon the parole application process to handle prisoners seeking early release. The files of this period, dealing principally with prisoners serving indeterminate sentences, show a higher proportion of unsuccessful clemency applications and cases with unclear outcomes. These later files also reveal the factors that impeded applicants' chances at clemency, as discretionary justice acquired a more administrative character.

Because the collection of clemency files was too vast to read in full, I adopted a sampling technique that favored the second half of the nineteenth century, when petitioning the governor was the only hope of most petitioners. Legal appeals were rare in this period, and parole was only in its rudimentary phase. All but a few of the preserved files come from the post–Civil War period. For the late nineteenth century, I undertook a 10 percent semi-random sample of the 2,644 files preserved from 1859 to 1900. I chose the tenth file after the first file of 1860, but because some files held minimal information the number of cases with considerable correspondence totaled 252, just under 10 percent (9.53%). I also examined several fat files, most involving capital cases that generated intense public debate and protracted internal deliberations over the governor's prerogative powers. Since a purely random sample ran the risk of turning up no cases involving women, I oversampled for women's cases by looking, after every twentieth case, for a case involving a female offender in the next or previous ten. This method produced only a slightly disproportionate number of women's cases in the 252-case sample at 6.3 percent.[7]

Beginning with files registered in 1901, the year New York introduced a statewide parole system, I switched to a five-files-per-year sample, which yielded a further 139 cases. I selected cases from the register of petition filing dates (without knowing the offense or gender of the petitioner or the outcome) to cover five points in the calendar year: April, June, September, October and December. This selection is also based on governors' published reports of their pardons and commutations of sentences, which show that governors often processed requests in batches, between legislative sessions, in the summer, and at the end of calendar years (often in the last weeks in office). Again, I oversampled for women's cases, which produced a 5 percent subset for the period from 1901–1926.[8] Unlike the files from the pre-parole era, application records from this period typically fail to indicate the final result. Very few "unknown outcome" case files belonged to successful petitioners, which I determined by cross-checking petitioners' names against the published reports of petitions granted. By the 1910s, governors began to reserve pardons for former prisoners seeking the restoration of rights, and they switched to commuting sentences (often to time served) as standard practice.[9]

In the course of processing this massive collection of clemency case files, the state archives produced a database, which I supplemented with data from the sampled cases (391 in total), as well information in the Espy file of executions and Daniel Hearn's study of capital punishment in New York.[10] Using this method I produced an enhanced database, which includes, for my sampled cases, each offender's name, prison, year in which the application was lodged, sex, and crime. Where possible I supplemented these data with information concerning the offender's age, ethnicity, religion, and family status. I also took systematic account of the relationship of offenders to the victim (in property crimes, violent crimes, and morals offenses), the petitioner's relationship to the prisoner, and the grounds on which petitioners urged the governor to grant clemency.

Historian Peter King has used a "factor-mentions" method to analyze clemency patterns in late eighteenth-century England, based on judges' reports and petitions against or in favor of mercy.[11] By comparing the factors mentioned in these documents to the outcomes, he set out to determine which case characteristics appeared most commonly in successful and unsuccessful petitions. Unfortunately, the preponderance of successful outcomes in the clemency files that have survived in New York made it impossible to conduct this test. However, these files are considerably richer than the records King used. They include letters from a variety of petitioners, organizations, medical authorities, external officials, and family members, and this evidence made it possible to tabulate the principal grounds for clemency presented to governors. Such pleas indicate "the writer's sense" of the criteria they considered most germane to clemency-decision making.[12] Table 1 shows that many of the factors mentioned in petitions from the Hanoverian period appear in the late nineteenth and early twentieth century clemency files. More significantly, the factors that appeared most frequently in the positive petitions King studied appear with comparable frequency in the New York files from the mid-nineteenth and early twentieth century.[13]

The rise of administrative discretionary justice in New York is documented officially in the Board of Parole's annual reports, from 1901 onward (published as part of the State Superintendent of Prisons' annual reports), and in the board's hearing records, which include prisoner's voices. As the three-man board traveled to each of the state prisons one or two days per month to conduct hurried interviews with prospective parolees, stenographers transcribed their interviews with applicants, some of them verbatim. I took most detailed notes on hearings held in April and September, when large numbers of applications tended to be reviewed. In addition, I read parole case files for male and female inmates at Auburn State Prison over the same period. I reviewed two cases per year (for men), randomly selected from the two hearing visits, and I examined the file of each female applicant, as the number of these files was small (filling just two letter-size boxes for cases between 1920 and 1930). Together these parole records reveal the growing network of disciplinary managers involved in discretionary decision making, including prison officers, wardens, teachers, workshop supervisors, and psychiatrists.

This combination of archival and published primary sources provides the groundwork for a new understanding of the relationship between pardoning and parole, correcting the consensus that the latter replaced the former. Significantly, these records also provide a springboard for further studies that can train on specific governors, shorter periods of history, specific subsets of offenders and offenses, and different regions of the state. Furthermore, historians may find similar evidence in other states, and build a state-by-state analysis of discretionary justice across the nation.

GOVERNORS OF NEW YORK, 1777–1942

Governor	Terms of Office
George Clinton	July 1777–April 1795
John Jay	April 1795–April 1801
George Clinton	April 1801–April 1804
Morgan Lewis	April 1804–April 1807
Daniel D. Tompkins	April 1807–February 1817
John Tayler	February 24, 1817–July 1, 1817
DeWitt Clinton	July 1, 1817–1822
Joseph C. Yates	1823–1824
DeWitt Clinton	1825–February 11, 1828
Nathaniel Pitcher	February 11–December 31, 1828
Martin Van Buren	January 1–March 12, 1829
Enos T. Throop	March 12, 1829–1832
William L. Marcy	1833–1838
William H. Seward	1839–1842
William C. Bouck	1843–1844
Silas Wright	1845–1846
John Young	1847–1848
Hamilton Fish	1849–1850
Washington Hunt	1851–1852
Horatio Seymour	1853–1854
Myron H. Clark	1855–1856
John A. King	1857–1858
Edwin D. Morgan	1859–1862
Horatio Seymour	1863–1864
Reuben E. Fenton	1865–1868
John T. Hoffman	1869–1872
John Adams Dix	1873–1874
Samuel J. Tilden	1875–1876
Lucius Robinson	1877–1879
Alonzo B. Cornell	1880–1882

Governor	Terms of Office
Grover Cleveland	1883–1884
David B. Hill	1885–1891
Roswell P. Flower	1892–1894
Levi P. Morton	1895–1896
Frank S. Black	1897–1898
Theodore Roosevelt	1899–1900
Benjamin B. Odell	1901–1904
Frank W. Higgins	1905–1906
Charles E. Hughes	1907–October 6, 1910
Horace White	October 6–December 31, 1910
John Alden Dix	1911–1912
William Sulzer	January 1–October 17, 1913
Martin H. Glynn	October 17, 1913–1914
Charles S. Whitman	1915–1918
Alfred E. Smith	1919–1920
Nathan L. Miller	1921–1922
Alfred E. Smith	1923–1928
Franklin D. Roosevelt	1929–1932
Herbert H. Lehman	1933–1942

Source: Governors of New York State [including New Netherland, New Belgium, and New-York Proprietary and Royal Colony], Patchogue-Medford Library; http://history.pmlib.org.

TABLES

TABLE 1. Factors Mentioned as Grounds for Clemency in Case Files

Grounds for clemency cited in petitions	Frequency
1859–1879	
Innocence/lesser culpability	36
Family hardship	29
Excessively severe sentence	21
Illness (physical)	18
Previous good character	15
Trial irregularities/inadequate counsel	13
Sufficiently punished/reformed	11
Insanity	4
Youth	2
1880–1900	
Excessively severe sentence	40
Family hardship	24
Innocence/lesser culpability	21
Illness (physical)	16
Sufficiently punished/reformed	8
Previous good character	6
Trial irregularities/inadequate counsel	4
Youth	4
Insanity	3
1901–1926	
Family hardship	59
Innocence/lesser culpability	36
Illness (physical)	24
Trial irregularities/inadequate counsel	18
Sufficiently punished/reformed	17
Excessive	14
Previous good character	13
Youth	5
Insanity	2

Source: NYSA, executive clemency and pardon case files, A0597 (n=391).
Note: See "Note on Sources" for the categorization of grounds.

TABLE 2. Clemency Rates in File Sample by Period and Type of Disposition

	1859–1879	1880–1900	1901–1926
Pardoned after first application	48	16	9
Commuted after subsequent application	40	95	37
Pardoned or commuted after one or more refusal	31	9	0
Refused	2	0	33
Paroled	0	0	6
Unknown	6	5	54
Totals:	127	125	139

Source: NYSA, executive clemency and pardon case files, A0597 (n=391).

TABLE 3. Crime Categories in Sample and in NYSA Database of Clemency Files

Crime category	Percentage in sample (n=391)	Percentage in NYSA clemency file database (n=8121)
Larceny	16.8	17.5
Burglary	14.3	14.8
Assault	11.0	10.9
Robbery	8.9	10.0
Rape	6.4	5.0
Sexual morality	7.1	4.9
Forgery	5.1	5.1
Manslaughter	5.1	7.1
Murder	4.8	8.6
Public order	4.8	2.2
Other violence	4.8	3.8
Petty larceny	4.3	2.6
Fraud	3.3	3.8
Receiving	2.8	3.0
Other	0.5	0.7
Total	100	100

Source: NYSA, executive clemency and pardon case files, A0597 (n=391).
Note: Because 62 percent of the 644 clemency applications filed on behalf of prisoners convicted of murder between 1859 and 1926 come from the 1901–1926 period, the lower sampling rate adopted for this period under-represents murder cases. Similarly, 78 percent of the 552 clemency applications filed on behalf of prisoners convicted of manslaughter between 1859 and 1926 come from the 1901–1926 period.

TABLE 4. Gender in Sample and in NYSA Database of Clemency Files by Period

Period	Males in sample	Males in NYSA clemency file database	Females in sample	Females in NYSA clemency file database
1859–1879	117	1,168	10	63
1880–1900	118	1,368	6	46
1901–1926	133	5,305	7	171
Total	368 (94.1%)	7,841 (96.6%)	23 (5.9%)	280 (3.4%)

Source: NYSA, executive clemency and pardon case files, A0597 and NYSA index (database) of executive clemency records, retrieved from http://www.archives.nysed.gov.

Notes: Sample n=391; database n=8121. See "Note on Sources" for explanation of sampling technique.

NOTES

INTRODUCTION

1 This image replaced the first seal, produced in haste in April 1777. The second closely resembled the final version adopted as the official Arms and Seals in 1882. Edgar A. Werner, *Civil List and Constitutional History of the Colony and State of New York* (Albany, NY: Weed, Parsons and Co., 1888), 148.

2 Norval Morris and David J. Rothman, eds., *The Oxford History of the Prison* (New York: Oxford University Press, 1995); Terance D. Miethe and Hong Lu, *Punishment: A Comparative Historical Perspective* (Cambridge, UK: Cambridge University Press, 2005); Mary Gibson, "Global Perspectives on the Birth of the Prison," *American Historical Review* 116, no. 4 (2011): 1040–63.

3 On Philadelphia's early leadership see Meranze, *Laboratories of Virtue*; Lewis, *From Newgate to Dannemora*, 2–5, 9; Kann, *Punishment, Prisons and Patriarchy*, 55–60, 92–111.

4 Nir Shafir, "The International Congress as Scientific and Diplomatic Technology: Global Intellectual Exchange in the International Prison Congress, 1860–90," *Journal of Global History* 9 (2014): 72–93. The first meeting was held in London in 1872, organized by Enoch Cobb Wines. Evelyn Ruggles-Brise, *Prison Reform at Home and Abroad: A Short History of the International Movement Since the London Congress, 1872* (London: Macmillan, 1924).

5 Pisciotta, *Benevolent Repression: Social Control and the American Reformatory-Prison Movement*; Mark Colvin, *Penitentiaries, Reformatories, and Chain Gangs: Social Theory and the History of Punishment in Nineteenth-Century America* (New York: Macmillan, 1997); Anthony Platt, "The Triumph of Benevolence," 177–96. Hereafter, the prison will be referred to as the Elmira Reformatory.

6 One of the last institutions to integrate Progressive-inspired designs was the New York State Vocational Institute at Coxsackie, opened in 1935.

7 Jensen, *The Pardoning Power in the American States*, 11–16; Dinan, "The Pardon Power and the American State Constitutional Tradition," 398–99.

8 David Garland, *Punishment and Modern Society* (Chicago: University of Chicago Press, 1990), 193.

9 Monica Chowdry and Charles Mitchell, "Responding to Historic Wrongs: Practical and Theoretical Problems," *Oxford Journal of Legal Studies*, 27, no. 2 (2007): 339–54; Sarat and Hussain. "On Lawful Lawlessness: George Ryan, Executive Clemency, and the Rhetoric of Sparing Life," 1307–44.

10 For early exceptions see Messinger, Berecochea, Rauma, and Berk, "The Foundations of Parole in California," 69–106; A. Keith Bottomley, "Parole in Transition: A Comparative Study of Origins, Developments, and Prospects for the 1990s," *Crime and Justice* 12 (1990): 319–74. For recent exceptions see Blue, *Doing Time in the Depression*; Miller, *Crime, Sexual Violence, and Clemency*.

11 Dowling, *Clemency and Cruelty in the Roman World*, 271, 146.

12 Natalie Zemon Davis, *Fiction in the Archives*, 58.

13 Hay, "Property, Authority and Criminal Law," 17–63, 50. On the political context in which this landmark publication appeared, see Robert R. Sullivan, *Liberalism and Crime: The British Experience* (Lanham, MD: Lexington Books, 2000), 113–14.

14 For an outstanding example, see Andrew Novak, *Comparative Executive Clemency: The Constitutional Pardon Power and the Prerogative of Mercy in Global Perspective* (New York: Routledge, 2016). I am grateful to Andrew for providing me with an advance copy of his book.

15 Miller, *Crime, Sexual Violence, and Clemency*, 6.

16 Some presidential scholars argue that state constitutions provide models of discretionary justice that could be adopted at the federal level. Love, "Reinventing the President's Pardon Power," 5–15.

17 Scheuerman, "American Kingship? Monarchical Origins of Modern Presidentialism," 50. Dowling notes that the civil wars of the Late Roman Republic "brought clemency more into political vocabulary." *Clemency and Cruelty*, 2.

18 Kathleen Dean Moore, *Pardons: Justice, Mercy and the Public Interest* (New York: Oxford University Press, 1989); Paul J. Haase, "Oh My Darling Clemency: Existing or Possible Limitations on the Use of the Presidential Pardon Power," *American Criminal Law Review* 39, no. 3 (Summer 2002): 1287–1307; Jonathan T. Menitove, "The Problematic Presidential Pardon: A Proposal for Reforming Federal Clemency," *Harvard Law and Policy Review* 3, no. 2 (2009): 447–60; P. S. Ruckman Jr., "Executive Clemency in the United States: Origins, Development, and Analysis (1900–1993), *Presidential Studies Quarterly* 27, no. 2 (Spring 1997): 251–71.

19 Jeffrey Crouch, *The Presidential Pardon Power* (Lawrence: University Press of Kansas, 2009); Margaret Colgate Love, "The Twilight of the Pardon Power," *Journal of Criminal Law and Criminology* 100, no. 3 (2010): 1169–218.

20 Marie Gottschalk, *The Prison and the Gallows: The Politics of Mass Incarceration in America* (Cambridge, UK: Cambridge University Press, 2006); Nicola Lacey, "Punishment, (Neo)Liberalism and Social Democracy," in *The Sage Handbook of Punishment and Society*, ed. Jonathan Simon and Richard Sparks (Thousand Oaks, CA: Sage, 2013): 260–80.

21 Hamm, *Murder, Honor and Law*; Friedland, *The Death of Old Man Rice*; Arpey, *The William Freeman Murder Trial*; Baatz, *For the Thrill of It*; Robert Asher, Lawrence B. Goodheart, and Alan Rogers, eds., *Murder on Trial: 1620–2002* (Albany: State University of New York Press, 2005).

22 The film dramatized the life and death of Barbara Graham, convicted of murder and executed in 1955. Kathleen A. Cairns, *Proof of Guilt: Barbara Graham and the Politics of Executing Women in America* (Lincoln: University of Nebraska Press, 2013).

23 Rothman, "The Pardoning Power," 149–220.

24 In addition to this scholarship, see Petersilia, *When Prisoners Come Home*; Robert Melvin Carter, Daniel Glaser, and Leslie T. Wilkins, eds., *Probation, Parole, and Community Corrections* (New York: John Wiley and Sons, 1984); Bernard E. Harcourt, "From the Ne'er-Do-Well to the Criminal History Category: The Refinement Of The Actuarial Model In Criminal Law," *Law and Contemporary Problems* 66, no. 3 (2003): 99–151; A. Keith Bottomley, "Parole in Transition: A Comparative Study of Origins, Developments, and Prospects for the 1990s," in *Crime and Justice a Review of Research, Volume 12*, ed. Michael Tonry and Norval Morris (Chicago: Chicago University Press, 1990), 319–74.

25 Simon, *Poor Discipline*, 3, 6–7, 108.

26 Messinger et al., "The Foundations of Parole," 95.

27 Harvey C. Mansfield, *Taming the Prince: The Ambivalence of Modern Executive Power* (Baltimore, MD: Johns Hopkins University Press, 1993); Samuel Walker, *Taming the System: The Control of Discretion in Criminal Justice, 1950–1990* (New York: Oxford University Press, 1993).

28 Miller, *Crime, Sexual Violence, and Clemency*, 10, 172.

29 Blue, *Doing Time in the Depression*, 217, 234–35.

30 In 1930, the population of the state of Texas was 5,824,715. *United States and Texas State Populations, 1850–2014*, Texas State Library and Archives Commission. https://www.tsl.texas.gov, accessed 29 June 2015.

31 "Table 14. Nativity of the Population, for Regions, Divisions, and States: 1850 to 2000," in Campbell Gibson and Kay Young, *Historical Census Statistics on the Foreign-Born Population of the United States: 1850–2000* (Washington, DC: U.S. Census Bureau Population Division, 2006).

32 Sebouh David Aslanian, Joyce E. Chaplin, Kristin Mann, and Ann McGrath, "How Size Matters: The Question of Scale in History," *AHR* Conversation, *American Historical Review* 118, no. 5 (December 2013): 1431–72; Jo Guldi and David Armitage, *The History Manifesto* (Cambridge, UK: Cambridge University Press, 2014). This provocative piece was published first online and was updated in February 2015 at http://historymanifesto.cambridge.org, accessed June 28, 2015. For a response that calls for the articulation of scale to questions, see Deborah Cohen and Peter Mandler, "*The History Manifesto*: A Critique," *American Historical Review* 120, no. 2 (April 2015): 530–42.

33 Friedman, *Crime and Punishment in American History*; Elizabeth Dale, *Criminal Justice in the United States, 1789–1939* (New York: Cambridge University Press, 2011).

34 David J. Rothman, *The Discovery of the Asylum*; David J. Rothman, *Conscience and Convenience*. Rothman's books do not fully cover the period from the mid- to late nineteenth century.

35 Stanley Cohen, "The Archaeology of Power," *Contemporary Sociology* 7, no. 5 (September 1978): 568. Cohen also praised *Discipline and Punish* as "the most stimulating and revealing history of prisons and punishment ever written" (568).

36 Christianson, *With Liberty for Some*, 25–26; Louis P. Masur, "The Revision of the Criminal Law in Post-Revolutionary America," *Criminal Justice History* 8 (January 1987): 21–36.

37 Fisher, *Plea Bargaining's Triumph*; William Francis Kuntz, *Criminal Sentencing in Three Nineteenth-Century Cities: Social History of Punishment in New York, Boston, and Philadelphia, 1830–1880* (New York: Garland, 1988), 124–25.

38 For a full account of the published and unpublished sources used in this book, see "Note on Sources."

39 A list of governors and their terms appears in the appendix.

40 Colonial governors could also recommend pardons in capital cases, but their decisions required royal approval.

41 The president's power is greater, since he may pardon without conviction. McDonald, *The American Presidency*, 132–34.

42 Moore, *Pardons*, 7.

43 John Young to Isaac T. Hooper, n.d. (ca. 1846), quoted in Child, *Isaac T. Hooper*, 413.

44 The term "fancy" referred in the nineteenth century to high-status white offenders, and ones who expected preferential treatment. Gilfoyle, *A Pickpocket's Tale*, 131.

45 Alexander, *The Girl Problem*; Odem, *Delinquent*; Hicks, *Talk with You Like a Woman*; Anne E. Bowler, Chrysanthi S. Leon, and Terry G. Lilley, "'What Shall We Do with the Young Prostitute? Reform Her or Neglect Her?': Domestication as Reform at the New York State Reformatory for Women at Bedford, 1901–1913," *Journal of Social History* 47, no. 2 (Winter 2013): 458–81; Pisciotta, *Benevolent Repression*.

46 Henry Weihofen, "Legislative Pardons," *California Law Review* 27, no. 4 (May 1939): 371–86. Weihofen described arguments that pardoning was inherently an executive power as "historically untrue, politically unsound and socially a nuisance," 371.

47 Potter, *War on Crime*.

48 United States Attorney General, *The Attorney General's Survey of Release Procedures*. Volume 3 covers pardoning and volume 4 covers parole.

49 Bryan Stevenson, *Just Mercy: A Story of Justice and Redemption* (New York: Penguin Random House, 2014). An activist lawyer who established the Equal Justice Initiative, Stevenson focuses on the systemic racial and class biases that lead to wrongful convictions and sentencing disparities.

CHAPTER 1. GOVERNING MERCY IN THE EMERGING REPUBLIC

1 Riker, *"Evacuation Day" 1783*, 3, 18.

2 Galie, *Ordered Liberty: A Constitutional History of New York* (New York: Fordham University Press, 1996). Eric Nelson goes so far as to define the Revolution as a "rebellion in favor of royal power." Nelson, *The Royalist Revolution*, 4.

3 Tiedemann, *Reluctant Revolutionaries*; De Pauw, *The Eleventh Pillar*. Kammen notes that the powerful Whigs of New York became "nervously reluctant" to rebel by the mid-1770s. Kammen, *Colonial New York*, 337.

4 Betsy Knight, "Prisoner Exchange and Parole in the American Revolution," 202.

5 Harcourt, "Beccaria's 'On Crimes and Punishments': A Mirror on the History of the Foundations of Modern Criminal Law."

6 Ritchie, *The Duke's Province*.

7 Hay, "Property, Authority and Criminal Law," 17–63. For the United States, see Blue, *Doing Time in the Depression*; Miller, *Crime, Sexual Violence, and Clemency*.

8 Tomlins, *Freedom Bound*, 325. On British possession as conquest, see Pagden, "Law, Colonization, Legitimation, and the European Background," 25.

9 Goebel, "The Courts and the Law in Colonial New York," 6–7.

10 Slavery was institutionally established by 1664, but the codification of slaves' distinct legal status occurred after the British conquest of New Netherland. Goodfriend, *Before the Melting Pot*, 111.

11 "An Act for Preventing Suppressing and Punishing the Conspiracy and Insurrection of Negroes and other Slaves," Chapter 250, passed December 10, 1712, in Lincoln, Johnson, and Judd, *The Colonial Laws of New York from the year 1664 to the Revolution*, 761. In 1708, the Provincial Assembly determined that slaves accused of murder or conspiracy to murder could be tried summarily, thereby excluding them from the right to trial by jury after indictment.

12 Lepore, *New York Burning*, 59. I have used Lepore's appendix of trials and outcomes. Kammen claims that eighteen slaves and four whites were hanged, and thirteen slaves were burned. Kammen, *Colonial New York*, 285.

13 Whites were eligible for a reward of one hundred pounds and a pardon; slaves, twenty pounds and freedom; and free Blacks forty-five pounds. Lepore, *New York Burning*, 88, 175, 191, 248–60

14 For an exegesis of persuasive coercion see Tomlins, *Freedom Bound*, 258–60.

15 Goebel and Naughton, *Law Enforcement in Colonial New York*, 759.

16 Bonomi, *A Factious People*.

17 Hearn, *Legal Executions in New York*, 14–19.

18 William E. Nelson, "Legal Turmoil in a Factious Colony," 212.

19 Letters and Papers of Cadwallader Colden, quoted in Goebel and Naughton, *Law Enforcement in Colonial New York*, 749.

20 For further detail see Historical Society of the New York Courts, "Colonial New York Under British Rule, The Supreme Court of Judicature of the Province of New York: 1674–1776," retrieved from http://www.nycourts.gov, accessed June 29, 2015.

21 Ross, "Legal Communications and Imperial Governance," 104–5.

22 Lincoln, *The Constitutional History of New York*, 34.

23 Quoted in Countryman, *A People in Revolution*, 15.

24 Judges also took the law into their own hands by substituting whipping for the death penalty. Goebel and Naughton, *Law Enforcement in Colonial New York*, 704.

25 Nelson, *William Tryon and the Course of Empire*, 177.

26 The occupation was established by late 1776, and territory included the colonial capital plus Staten Island, Long Island, and Manhattan Island, as well as portions of Westchester County and territory in the current borough of the Bronx.

27 Nelson, *William Tryon and the Course of Empire*, 164–65.

28 Cornog, *The Birth of Empire*, 13.

29 This state-federal contrast is of long standing. See, for instance, Bryce, *The American Commonwealth*.

30 Jensen, *The Pardoning Power in the American States*, 10–11.

31 Pennsylvania's first constitution, of 1776, assigned legislators to elect governors from the membership of the Supreme Executive Council, and the governor cast only one vote among twelve when determining pardons. As in most other states, the governor's term was limited to one year. Holcolme, *State Government in the United States*, 56–57.

32 Hulsebosch, *Constituting Empire*, 175. The governor was also commander in chief of the state militia and navy, and he could prorogue and convene the legislature.

33 McDonald, *The American Presidency*, 132; Scheuerman, "American Kingship? Monarchical Origins of Modern Presidentialism," 40.

34 Delaware, Maryland, New Hampshire, New Jersey, North Carolina, Pennsylvania, South Carolina, and Virginia wrote constitutions in 1776. New York and Georgia followed in 1777, and Massachusetts in 1780. Connecticut and Rhode Island retained their previous charters, striking out references to royalty and its representatives and substituting elected officials.

35 Maier, *From Resistance to Revolution*.

36 Smith moved to Quebec, where he became Chief Justice of Lower Canada. Chopra, *Unnatural Rebellion*.

37 Countryman, *A People in Revolution*, 37.

38 The core members of the drafting committee came from the landlord class: James Duane was raised in Livingston Manor and later married into the Livingston family; Jay's maternal grandfather, Jacobus Van Cortlandt, established a large estate, and he married Sarah Livingston and was nephew by marriage to Philip Livingston; Gouverneur Morris grew up in the Morris Manor home in Westchester on an estate of two thousand acres; and Robert R. Livingston was a scion of Clermont Manor. Ibid., 166–67.

39 Edward Rutledge to John Jay, November 24, 1776, quoted in Haw, *John and Edward Rutledge of South Carolina*, 97.

40 In a speech to the Constitutional Convention on June 18, 1787, Hamilton went so far as to advocate that the nation's chief executive be an elected monarch for life, subject to recall. Chernow, *Alexander Hamilton*, 230, 259. On the wide appeal of kingship in eighteenth-century America see Brendan McConnville, *The King's Three Faces: The Rise and Fall of Royal America, 1688-1776* (Chapel Hill: University of North Carolina Press for the Omohundro Institute of Early American History and Culture, 2006).

41 Adams, *Gouverneur Morris: An Independent Life*, 85; Eric Nelson, *The Royalist Revolution*, 167.

42 Kaminski, *George Clinton*, 25. Male adults with twenty pounds freehold could vote for assembly members. Lincoln, *Messages from the Governors*, 171–72 (hereafter Lincoln, *Messages*).

43 Gerlach, *Proud Patriot*.

44 Philip Schuyler to John Jay, July 14 1777, in Johnston, *The Correspondence and Public Papers of John Jay, vol. 1*, 147.

45 Tiedemann, *Reluctant Revolutionaries*, 39–40. On the rise of "new men" more broadly in this period see Richard Alan Ryerson, *The Revolution is Now Begun: The Radical Committees of Philadelphia, 1765–1776* (Philadelphia: University of Pennsylvania Press, 1978), 4–6.

46 Patricia U. Bonomi, "Constitution Making in a Time of Troubles," in *Essays on the Genesis of the Empire State*, ed. Thomas E. Felt (Albany: New York State Bicentennial Commission, 1979), 51–56.

47 Kaminski, *George Clinton*, 20. Clinton attempted to resign his commission as brigadier general of the New York militia on May 9, 1777. Hugh Hastings, ed., *Public Papers of George Clinton, First Governor New York, 1777–1795–1801–1804, vol. 1, Military* (New York and Albany: Wynkoop Hallenbeck Crawford, 1899), 809–10 (hereafter Hastings, *Public Papers of George Clinton*).

48 George Washington to the Council of Safety of New York, August 4, 1777, in Sparks, *The Writings of George Washington*, 20.

49 Before it could pass any laws, the legislative session was broken up in early October, as the British rapidly advanced toward Albany.

50 On July 16, an Ordinance of the New York Convention resolved that the establishment of an independent civil government be postponed, with the exception of the judicial proceedings. Hastings, *Public Papers of George Clinton, vol. 1*, 253.

51 The Council of Safety fulfilled the executive functions of government from May to September 1777. State of New York, *New York in the Revolution as Colony and State*, 149.

52 New York, Convention of the Representatives, A Declaration, or Ordinance, of the Convention of the State of New-York, passed May 10, 1777, Offering Free Pardon to Such of the Subjects of the said State, as, Having Committed Treasonable Acts Against the Same, Shall Return to their Allegiance (Fishkill, NY: Samuel Loudon, 1777).

53 Louis Fisher, *Military Tribunals and Presidential Power*.

54 Hastings, *Public Papers of George Clinton, vol. 1*, 274.

55 Hastings, *Public Papers of George Clinton, vol. 1*, 502, 569. The ensign submitted his petition on November 6 and escaped his holding place on December 12, 1777.

56 Edward Countryman, *The American Revolution* (New York: Hill and Wang, 1985), 152.

57 In February 1777 the Convention disbanded the committee and established the commission. Hunt, *The Provincial Committees of Safety of the American Revolution*, 73–75.

58 May 17, 1777. *Minutes of the Committee and of the First Commission For Detecting and Defeating Conspiracies in the State Of New York*, 295. Board members were to be "persons of known probity and attachment to the American cause, who reside in and are well acquainted with the characters and conduct of the inhabitants thereof." Ibid., 2.

59 Edward Countryman, "Consolidating Power in Revolutionary America: The Case of New York, 1775–1783," *Journal of Interdisciplinary History* 6, no. 4 (Spring 1976): 645–77.

60 Hulsebosch, *Constituting Empire*, 165–66.

61 Louis Fisher, *Military Tribunals and Presidential Power*, 4–5. By 1776, the jurisdiction of federal military courts was expanded to civilians. Morgan, "Court Martial Jurisdiction over Non-Military Persons under the Articles of War," 99.

62 Andre was a British intelligence officer who was captured behind American lines wearing civilian clothing. He was hanged in Rockland County, New York, on October 2, 1780, in accordance with the Congressional Resolution of August 21, 1776, which stated that foreign spies found "lurking" were to suffer death or other punishment "according to the law and usage of nations, by sentence of a court-martial." Carso, *Whom Can We Trust Now?*, 162.

63 George Clinton to the President of the Convention of the State of New York, February 25, 1777, in Hastings, *Public Papers of George Clinton*, vol. 1, 632.

64 George Clinton to Colonel Hathorn, November 14, 1778, in ibid., 252.

65 Ibid., 749.

66 Countryman, "Consolidating Power in New York," 662–64.

67 Hastings, *Public Papers of George Clinton*, vol. 2, 632, 783–84, 791–92.

68 Calhoon, *The Loyalists in Revolutionary America, 1760–1781*, 411. When civilians were sentenced to death by military courts, their ultimate punishment was a matter for the Council of Safety's discretion.

69 The full text of the resolution of April 1, 1777 is: "Whereas from the want of Courts properly instituted for the Trial of Treasons and other Offenses against this State, the Resolutions heretofore passed for the Punishment of the same have not been executed." Hastings, *Public Papers of George Clinton*, vol. 1, 690.

70 Chapin, "Colonial and Revolutionary Origins of the American Law of Treason," 12–13.

71 A former student of William Smith's, Peter Van Schaack, considered the Conspiracies Commission's use of undefined and extraordinary power scandalous. Thompson, "Anti-Loyalist Legislation during the American Revolution," 152.

72 State of New York, *New York in the Revolution as Colony and State*, 227–35.

73 Hulsebosch, *Constituting Empire*, 35–42.

74 Clinton to the Chairman of the Albany Committee of Safety, March 8, 1778. Hastings, *Public Papers of George Clinton*, vol. 2, 878.

75 Ibid., 684. Clinton's refusal to reprieve the men and his reprieve of Augur appear in the same letter of January 19, 1779 to Sheriff Isaac Nicholl. Harry M. Ward identifies Smith as one of the foremost revolutionary "banditti." See Ward, *The War for Independence and the Transformation of American Society*, 71–72.

76 Clinton referred to the case in the course of delivering his annual message to the legislature, on January 30, 1779. He justified his decision on the basis of the recommendation to mercy from the judges who presided over the trial in Orange County. Lincoln, *Messages*, 67.

77 *An Act for Pardoning Amy Auger, for the Felony Therein Mentioned. Laws of New York*, chapter 9, February 17, 1779. The legislature cited the nonattendance of material witnesses at her trial as a justification for the pardon.

78 *"Duely and Constantly Kept": A History of the New York Supreme Court, 1691–1847 and an Inventory of its Records (Albany, Utica, and Geneva Offices), 1797–1847* (Albany: New York State Court of Appeals and The New York State Archives and Records Administration, 1991), 55–56. General Sessions courts were not empowered to try cases for which sentences of life imprisonment applied, which effectively pushed most felonies up to the Supreme Court after 1796.

79 *The Remembrancer, or, Impartial Repository of Public Events*, 97.

80 Hastings, *Public Papers of George Clinton*, vol. 3, 181–82. The second man, Jonathan Ackerly, was also convicted on two counts of burglary. Neither his nor Smith's name appears in Hearn's *Legal Executions in New York State* nor in the Espy file (they list two "unknowns"). However, their executions are mentioned in the revolutionary war pension application of Private James Vanderburgh, file number S.28, 919, Series A1193, New York State Archives.

81 Hastings, *Public Papers of George Clinton*, vol. 3, 240–42.

82 In addition, piracy, grand larceny, arson, rape, abduction, buggery and theft from churches were capital offenses. Second-time offenders convicted of lesser offenses, such as petty larceny and attempted rape, were also subject to the death penalty without benefit of clergy. "An Act for Punishing Treasons and Felonies, and for the Better Regulating the Proceedings in Cases of Felony," *Laws of New York*, chap. 37 (passed February 1788).

83 By combining data in the Espy file with the account of executions in Daniel Allen Hearn's *Legal Executions in New York State*, and cross-checking them with legislative pardons, the published papers of governors, and newspaper accounts, I traced a total of 119 executions between 1777 and 1796, during which George Clinton was governor for all but the final year. Of that number, all but three were convicted of murder, and only one, Joseph Bettys (or Bettis), was executed for treason, in Albany on April 1, 1782.

84 Forty-five were convicted of these offences. Two men were convicted of treason and seven of espionage. Hearn lists three African Americans, hanged in White Plains in October 1788, with "crimes unknown." Hearn, *Legal Executions in New York State*, 25.

85 Preyer, "Penal Measures in the American Colonies," 327. In 1775 New York City's population was 22,000, compared to London's 900,000 at the same time.

86 Hastings, *Public Papers of George Clinton*, vol. 3, 334–35, May 20, 1778. The "benevolent" citizens included prominent and influential men, such as Abraham Yates Jr., a member of the Council of Safety and a state senator.

87 Gould, "Remembering Metacom," 115.

88 Hastings, *Public Papers of George Clinton*, vol. 5, 207, 257.

89 Greenleaf, *Laws of the State of New York*, vol. 1, 338, 336.

90 Ibid., 336–37.

91 Young, *The Democratic Republicans of New York*, 526–27.

92 Cesare Beccaria's treatise on crime and punishment, originally published in Italian in 1764, and its English translation circulated widely among leading Revolutionary leaders, including George Washington and John Adams. Banner, *The Death Penalty*, 91, 149.

93 "Annual Message to the Legislature," January 7, 1794, in Lincoln, *Messages, Volume 2*, 335–36.

94 Jack D. Marietta and Gail S. Rowe, *Troubled Experiment: Crime and Justice in Pennsylvania, 1682–1800* (Philadelphia: University of Pennsylvania Press, 2006), 213. Other states also beat New York. Masur, *Rites of Execution*, 76.

95 "Annual Message to the Legislature," January 3, 1795, in Lincoln, *Governors' Messages to the Legislature, Volume 2*, 350.

96 Lewis, *From Newgate to Dannemora*, 2–5. The statute was written by a former Tory, Samuel Jones, who had served as the Recorder (a judicial position) for the City of New York from 1789 to 1797. Countryman, *A People in Revolution*, 267–68.

97 "To the justices and selectmen of the town of Norwalk, Conn.," July 2, 1798, in William Jay, *The Life of John Jay with Selections from his Correspondence and Papers by his Son William Jay*, 399. The recipients had petitioned for mercy for a Connecticut man imprisoned in New York.

98 Rothman, *The Discovery of the Asylum*, 60–61; Banner, *The Death Penalty*, 97–98; Lewis, *From Newgate to Dannemora*, 27–28; Christianson, *With Liberty for Some*, 93–95; Friedman, *Crime and Punishment in American History*, 73–74, 94.

99 *Laws of the State of New York*, Chapter 30, 1796, "An Act making Alterations in the Criminal Law of this State and for erecting State Prisons."

CHAPTER 2. MERCY AND DIVERSITY

1 Eddy's name choice illustrates the transatlantic dynamics of penal reform. In London, Newgate was the name of the city's new jail in 1783. Lewis, *From Newgate to Dannemora*, 5.

2 Rebecca McLennan argues that faith in "truly Christian and republican penal practice" evaporated by the 1810s. *The Crisis of Imprisonment*, 3.

3 Orlando F. Lewis, *The Development of American Prisons and Prison Customs*, 38–39.

4 McClennan, *The Crisis of Imprisonment*, 46; Christianson, *With Liberty for Some*, 100, 114; Lewis, *From Newgate to Dannemora*, 42–43.

5 *Journals of Executive Pardons, 1799–1846, 1856–1931*, vols. 1–10, New York State Archives, B0042–79. See "Note on Sources" for a detailed discussion of primary sources.

6 On railroad time see Bartky, *Selling the True Time*. Jonathan Simon states that industrial society's time management regime was "the predominant influence on prison management, not the other way around." Simon, *Poor Discipline*, 44. On Foucault's analysis of discipline through time see *Discipline and Punish*, 118–28.

7 Missionaries were among the few whites who questioned state as well as private land negotiations involving the Brothertown and Stockbridge Indians. Hauptman, *Conspiracy of Interests*, 72.

8 "An Act Declaring the Jurisdiction of the Courts of this State, and Pardoning Soo-non-gize, Otherwise Called Tommy Jemmy," *Laws of New York*, 1822, Chapter 204, passed April 12, 1822.

9 Katz, *In the Shadow of the Poorhouse*. Katz criticizes earlier works that overlook the involvement of the state in addressing poverty, but many state actors, including governors, belonged to charitable organizations. For a full list of voluntary associations in this period see Mohl, *Poverty in New York*, 20.

10 Beccaria, *An Essay on Crimes and Punishment*, 107–8, 83.

11 For excellent analyses of penal servitude's ideological foundations see McLennan, *The Crisis of Imprisonment*, 16–46; Christianson, *With Liberty for Some*, 103–32. The classic text on the slavelike conditions imposed on prisoners is Sellin, *Slavery and the Penal System*.

12 Inmates mutinied in 1799, and scores of prisoners seized guards, who resorted to the use of firearms. A riot in 1800 left guards and inmates seriously wounded. Meranze, *Laboratories of Virtue*, 203; Lewis, *From Newgate to Dannemora*, 42–43, 69.

13 Lewis, *From Newgate to Dannemora*, 46.

14 Beccaria, *An Essay on Crimes and Punishment*, 175.

15 Eddy, *An Account of the State Prison*, 66–67.

16 Ibid., 68.

17 Foucault, *Discipline and Punish*, 177–94.

18 Eddy, *An Account of the State Prison*, 67, 66.

19 Eddy, *An Account of the State Prison*, 79. Eddy reported 344 inmates in Newgate as of December 31, 1801. Twenty percent were black—57 men and 14 women. Later in his report he estimated (p. 86) that blacks "form nearly one third of the whole number of convicts."

20 Lewis, *From Newgate to Dannemora*, 42.

21 *Journals of Executive Pardons*, vol. 2, November 7, 1814, 200.

22 Tompkins to Hon. E. Sage, June 15, 1812. The governor explained why he declined Sage's request that he pardon a Dr. Howell: "The judges, Inspectors, Attorney General, Mayor, Recorder and District Attorney, were I believe unanimous in their opinion of the impropriety of his being pardoned, which is, in some measurement, though not absolutely, binding upon me." Hugh Hastings, *Public Papers of Daniel D. Tompkins, Governor of New York, 1807–1817*, vol. 2 (Albany,

NY: J. B. Lyon, 1902), 425 (hereafter Hastings, *Public Papers of Daniel D. Tompkins*).

23 Lewis, *From Newgate to Dannemora*, 44.

24 *Journal of the Senate of the State of New York at their Fortieth Session*, 1816–17 (Albany, NY: J. Buel, 1816–17), 167.

25 Lincoln, *Messages from the Governors*, vol. 2, 855, February 2, 1816 (hereafter Lincoln, *Messages*). Tompkins added that his former colleagues on the state supreme court agreed.

26 Rothman, "Perfecting the Prison," 111–30, 115.

27 Lincoln, *Messages*, 583, January 28, 1806; 634, November 1, 1808.

28 "An Act Declaring the Punishment of Certain Crimes, and for Other Purposes," *Laws of New York*, 1808, Chapter 155, passed April 8, 1808. The punishment of whipping was optional and set at a maximum of 39 lashes under § 12 of the Act, which was repealed in 1813.

29 Lincoln, *Messages*, 634, November 1, 1808.

30 In George Clinton's second term (1801–4) he pardoned 128, an average of 42 per annum. Lewis pardoned 214 between July 4, 1804 and June 1807 (an annual average of 71). Figures compiled from *Journals of Executive Pardons*, vols. 1 and 2.

31 Between 1817 and 1822, DeWitt Clinton pardoned 1,515 offenders, an average of 250 per year. *Journals of Executive Pardons*, vols. 3 and 4.

32 Lincoln, *Messages*, vol. 2, 982, 981, January 6, 1819.

33 Jay retired from public life in 1801. Gardiner's was one of the last pardons he granted. *Journals of Executive Pardons*, vol. 1, 93–95.

34 On March 29, 1799, the legislature passed an "Act Relative to the Civil Relations of Persons Sentenced to Imprisonment for Life," which declared felons sentenced to imprisonment for life civilly dead. Lincoln, *Messages*, vol. 2, 427.

35 David Roediger provides a broader analysis of republican citizenship's racial foundations in the early national period. *The Wages of Whiteness: Race and the Making of the American Working Class*, rev. ed. (New York: Verso, 1999).

36 The act was passed on March 20, 1799, on the approval of the Council of Revision. All children born of bonded slaved mothers after July 4, 1799, were to be free, but only after serving masters until the age of twenty-eight for males and twenty-five for females. Zilversmit, *The First Emancipation*; Nash and Soderlund, *Freedom by Degrees*.

37 McManus, *A History of Negro Slavery in New York*, 178. Slave marriages were recognized, and children born of married slaves were declared legitimate in 1809; slaves were permitted to own and transfer property by will in 1809; slaves were permitted to testify against whites and to be tried by jury in 1814.

38 Mason, *Slavery and Politics in the Early American Republic*, 142–43.

39 The merchants of New York City and Albany, plus the state's greatest landlords, including the chancellor of New York and Philip Schuyler, were the largest owners of slaves in this period. Young, *The Democratic Republicans of New York*, 252.

40 Gellman, *Emancipating New York*, 202–5; Zilversmit, *The First Emancipation*, 208–9. Neither Gellman nor Zilversmit considers pardoning in their analysis of discretionary transportation.

41 Simon Devereaux, "Transportation, Penal Practices and the English State, 1770–1830," in *Qualities of Mercy: Justice, Punishment and Discretion*, ed. Carolyn Strange (Vancouver: University of British Columbia Press, 1996), 52–76.

42 "An Act Concerning Pardons," *Laws of New York*, 1794, Chapter 29, enacted March 13, 1794. Greenleaf, *Laws of the State of New*, vol. 3, 113.

43 Figures compiled from *Journals of Executive Pardons*, vols. 1 and 2.

44 "An Act to Amend the Act concerning Slaves," *Laws of New York*, Chapter 28, enacted 22 March 1790. Greenleaf, *Laws of the State of New York*, vol. 2, 312.

45 John Jay to Lewis A. Scott, October 26, 1797, Papers of John Jay. Scott was New York's Secretary of State from 1794–98 and his office was responsible for the preparation of pardons. http://wwwapp.cc.columbia.edu.

46 *Journals of Executive Pardons*, vol. 1, 97–98. Sarah was pardoned on July 8, 1801, four months after her conviction.

47 On July 14, 1806 Kay, "a Black girl" sentenced to life at hard labor for arson in Queen's county in September 1805, was pardoned on condition that she be transported out of the United States. *Journals of Executive Pardons*, vol. 2, 21.

48 Shane White, "The Death of James Johnson," 782, 786. Johnson had court-appointed counsel, which White regards as poor.

49 Tompkins to Samuel Hopkins and George Griffin, January 8, 1811, in Hastings, *Public Papers of Daniel D. Tompkins*, vol. 2, 315–20.

50 Ibid., 446–47. Tompkins's bold pronouncement against slavery appears in numerous accounts of gradual abolition, which do not consider his critique and use of transportation. See, for instance, Gellman, *Emancipating New York*, 205; Zilversmit, *The First Emancipation*, 211.

51 *Journals of Executive Pardons*, vol. 2, 206.

52 *Journals of Executive Pardons*, vol. 3, 283.

53 Greenberg, *Crime and Law Enforcement in the Colony of New York*, 130–31.

54 Tompkins aspired to this ideal in his January 28, 1812 message to the legislature. Lincoln, *Messages*, vol. 2, 692.

55 Lincoln, *Messages*, vol. 2, January 28, 1812, 693.

56 Hauptman, *Conspiracy of Interests*; Rosen, *American Indians and State Law*.

57 Richard White, *The Middle Ground*.

58 Alan Taylor, *The Divided Ground*, 10.

59 Bethany R. Berger, "Red: Racism and the American Indian," *UCLA Law Review* 56, no. 3 (2009): 591–656, 611–18.

60 Anderson and Cayton, *The Dominion of War*, 39–41; Richter, *The Ordeal of the Longhouse*, 236–54.

61 Graymont, *The Iroquois in the American Revolution*, 204–6.

62 George Washington to Major General John Sullivan, May 31, 1779, in Lengel, *The Papers of George Washington*, 716–19.

63 Banner, *How the Indians Lost their Land*, 127–28.

64 "Treaty with the Six Nations, 1789," in Kappler, *Indian Affairs: Laws and Treaties*, 23–25, 25.

65 Taylor, *Divided Ground*, 29–31.

66 Ford, *Settler Sovereignty*, 174–77.

67 Timothy Pickering to George Washington, September 5, 1790, in Twohig, *The Papers of George Washington, Presidential Series*, 401–3, 401.

68 *Ontario Gazette*, August 10, 1802. Red Jacket further noted that five Indians had been murdered by whites in the recent past, in each case resulting in reparations not demands for prosecution.

69 Ganter, *The Collected Speeches of Sagoyewatha*, 118.

70 Hauptman, *Conspiracy of Interests*, 64.

71 Densmore, *Red Jacket*, 61–62.

72 Dennis, *Seneca Possessed*, 294, n58.

73 Dearborn to Jefferson, September 3, 1802; Dearborn to Clinton, February 14, 1803, in Oberg, *The Papers of Thomas Jefferson*, 273–74. The trial took place on February 23, 1803.

74 Dennis, "Sorcery and Sovereignty," 193.

75 No witnesses were called at the trial, and Stiff-Armed George's counsel presented no case; instead, Red Jacket addressed the court, using arguments similar to those presented at the August 1802 council. *New York Evening Post*, March 15, 1803.

76 "An Act Concerning the Rights of Citizens of this State," passed on January 26, 1787, recast rights set out in the 1683 Charter of Liberties as rights befitting citizens rather than subjects. Conley and Kaminski, *The Bill of Rights and the States*, 238.

77 "An Act to Pardon George, a Seneca Indian, Otherwise Called Stiff-Armed George, Convicted of Murder," *Laws of New York*, 1803, Chapter 31, passed March 12, 1803.

78 Jarvis, "Preserving the Brothertown Nation of Indians," 203.

79 Lincoln, *Messages*, vol. 2, 514–15, January 30, 1802. The appointment of a superintendent for the Brothertown (and also for the Stockbridge and later Oneida) was ostensibly for their "care and protection." Lincoln, *Messages*, vol. 2, 1076, February 7, 1821.

80 Patrick Frazier, *The Mohicans of Stockbridge* (Lincoln: University of Nebraska Press, 1992).

81 Whitney Luna M. Hammond, *History of Madison County*, 156–57, 707. There is no evidence in Governor Tompkins's papers to indicate that he recommended a reprieve.

82 Three years later John Tuhi, a Brothertown Indian, was tried for the murder of his brother, committed in a drunken haze. He was convicted on June 20, 1817, and executed five days later before an "immense" but orderly crowd at Utica, New York. *Utica Patriot*, July 29, 1817.

83 Lisa Ford analyzes how the Jemmy trial provided impetus for the wider turn toward inter se prosecutions in other settler jurisdictions in the 1820s. Ford, *Settler Sovereignty*, 2. Sydney L. Harring traces its impact in subsequent appeals. Harring,

Crow Dog's Case, 38–39, 44–45. Kaius Tuor examines the case in light of the move away from legal pluralism in his *Lawyers and Savages: Ancient History and Legal Realism in the Making of Legal Anthropology* (New York: Routledge, 2015), 40–41.

84 Hauptman, *The Tonawanda Senecas' Heroic Battle*, 19; Rosen, *American Indians and State Law*, 26.

85 The supreme court's review and inaction were reported in the *New York Gazette*, August 1, 1821, and the *Ithaca Republican Chronicle*, August 1, 1821. Hauptman, *The Tonawanda Senecas' Heroic Battle*, 138, n. 26.

86 Rosen, *American Indians and the State*, 27.

87 In January 1821 Red Jacket had successfully lobbied the New York legislature to pass an act that prohibited the further intrusion of non-natives on Seneca land. Ganter, *Collected Speeches*, 227.

88 "Singular Law Case," *Niles Weekly Register*, August 4, 1821. The *Washington Gazette's* headline of August 3, 1821 was more damning: "Glorious Uncertainty of the Law." I am grateful to Alyssa Mt. Pleasant for these references.

89 Quoted in Governor DeWitt Clinton, "Special Message to the Legislature," February 26, 1822, in Lincoln, *Messages*, vol. 2, 1119–20.

90 New York State, *The Speeches of the Different Governors to the Legislature of the State of New York, Commencing with those of George Clinton and Continued Down to the Present Time* (Albany, NY: J. V. Van Steenbergh, 1825), 114, January 28, 1812.

91 Quoted in Lincoln, *Messages*, vol. 2, 1120, February 26, 1822.

92 Dennis, *Seneca Possessed*, 214. Dennis concludes that the state recognized Seneca sovereignty "after a fashion" in this effort to extinguish it.

93 DeWitt Clinton, Message to the Legislature, February 7, 1821, in Lincoln, *Messages*, vol. 2, 1076.

94 Lewis, *From Newgate to Dannemora*, 61.

95 "Remarks on the Present State of our Prisons by Thomas Eddy," November 17, 1818, DeWitt Clinton Papers, vol. 24, mfm reel 6, Columbia University Library.

96 Galie, *Ordered Liberty*, 61.

CHAPTER 3. DEBATING THE PARDON IN ANTEBELLUM NEW YORK

1 The canal flowed between Buffalo and Albany, allowing goods to travel from the western reaches of the Great Lakes to New York City via the Hudson River. Shaw, *Erie Water West*, (Lexington: University Press of Kentucky, 2013).

2 Eddy was treasurer (and Philip Schuyler was president) of the Western Inland Lock Navigation Company, established after the passage of the Inland Navigation Act of 1792. Shaw, *Erie Water West*, 21.

3 Gellman and Quigley, *Jim Crow New York*, 90.

4 Thereafter, the legislature could pardon only in cases of treason or impeachment. The second state constitution did not expressly grant governors the power to commute a sentence of death to imprisonment for life.

5 Other states moved in the opposite direction beginning in the 1840s, when fifteen state constitutional conventions took place. Galie, *Ordered Liberty*, 99.

6 Klein, *The Empire State*, 257.

7 Graber, *The Furnace of Affliction*, 66–70.

8 The second constitutional convention, held in 1801, clarified the terms for constitutional revision but it did not lead to a revised constitution. The third constitutional convention, in 1821, led to the adoption of the second constitution.

9 Henretta, "The Slow Triumph of Liberal Individualism," 87–106, 101–2. Although conservatives were in the minority, many were landed oligarchs and prominent men of law.

10 Carter and Stone, *Reports*. Free men "of color" could vote only if they owned $250 worth of real property, free and clear, on which taxes had been paid. Consequently, only 5 percent of adult male free black voters were enfranchised under the second constitution. Galie and Bopst, *The New York State Constitution*, 11.

11 Peterson, *Democracy, Liberty, and Property*, 190; Volk, *Moral Minorities and the Making of American Democracy*, 22–23.

12 Hulsebosch, *Constituting Empire*, 261. On the Bucktails' pressure to revise the constitutions see also Cole, *Martin Van Buren and the American Political System*, 67–71.

13 Klein, *The Empire State*, 371.

14 Carter and Stone, 1821 *Reports*, 131. On Livingston's lineage, see Livingston, *The Livingstons of Livingston Manor*, 277–78.

15 Carter and Stone, 1821 *Reports*, 133, 128. Williams had recently served as district attorney of Oneida County. Platt was a Federalist and fellow Oneida County man, who served with Justices Kent and Spencer on the state supreme court.

16 Ibid., 131. Root also accused Quakers in the legislature of voting as a block against bills that ordered executions to proceed.

17 Ibid., 125. For Edwards's role in provoking the Convention, see Zimmerman, *The Government and Politics of New York*, 138–39. On the Convention as a Bucktail showdown, see Hanyan with Hanyan, *DeWitt Clinton and the Rise of the People's Men*, 62–74.

18 Carter and Stone, 1821 *Reports*, 128, 125. Platt claimed that more murderers would have been executed in the recent past had decision making been the responsibility of one man (129).

19 Ibid., Edwards, 125; Livingston, 127.

20 Scheuerman, "American Kingship? Monarchical Origins of Modern Presidentialism," 24–53, 41.

21 The fourth constitutional convention was held in 1846. Nunez, "New York State Constitutional Reform—Past Political Battles in Constitutional Language," 366–77, 367.

22 The Society for the Prevention of Pauperism in the City of New York published the commission's report as an appendix (pp. 90–107) in its own review. Society for the Prevention of Pauperism in the City of New York, *Report on the penitentiary system in the United States, prepared under a resolution of the Society for the Prevention of Pauperism, in the City of New York* (New York: Mahlon, 1822; hereafter Society, *Report*).

23 Lincoln, *Messages*, 22, n5. Chapter 253, passed April 12, 1821, appointed Stephen Allen, Samuel M. Hopkins, and George Tibbits commissioners to visit the state prisons at New York and Auburn. Allen was a former mayor of New York; Hopkins was a Federalist assemblyman; Tibbits was a former state senator.

24 Senate Commission Report, in Society, *Report*, 90–107, 96.

25 The society included Massachusetts and Pennsylvania as equally blighted by the "pernicious evil" of pardoning to reduce prison overcrowding. Society, *Report*, 33.

26 Haskell, *The Emergence of Professional Social Science*; Theodore M. Porter, *Trust in Numbers: The Pursuit of Objectivity in Science and Public Life* (Princeton, NJ: Princeton University Press, 1995).

27 Senate Commission Report in Society, *Report*, 91, 97.

28 Society, *Report on the Penitentiary System, 1822*, 36.

29 Senate Commission Report in Society, *Report*, 93–95, 97.

30 *New York Evening Post*, May 10, 1822.

31 Society, *Report*, 19, 35, 36

32 Lewis, *From Newgate to Dannemora*, 51.

33 W. David Lewis notes that New York's support for the introduction of solitary punishment overlooked evidence of similar problems at Philadelphia's Walnut Street Jail. Ibid, 65.

34 The commissioners' report to the senate urging the adoption of solitary punishment was tabled on March 5, 1822, and the act that implemented the recommendation was passed on April 15, 1822. Lincoln, *Messages*, vol. 3, 10, n. 5.

35 Society, *Report*, 52, 58.

36 Senate Commission Report in Society, *Report on the Penitentiary System, 1822*, 99.

37 Lincoln, *Messages*, vol. 3, 9.

38 Society, *Report*, 82.

39 Ibid., 51.

40 McLennan, *The Crisis of Imprisonment*, 57.

41 Agent Elam Lynds's report to the legislature, January 17, 1824, in *Journal of the Assembly of the State of New York at their Forty-Seventh Session* (Albany, NY: Leake and Croswell, 1824), 95.

42 Powers, *Report of Gershom Powers*, 81–82.

43 Lincoln, *Messages*, vol. 3, 22.

44 Subsequent investigation revealed that many men released from solitary confinement reoffended, some immediately upon release. Powers, *Report of Gershom Powers*, 83.

45 Lewis, *From Newgate to Dannemora*, 68–71; Christianson, *With Liberty for Some*, 113–17; McClennan, *The Crisis of Imprisonment*, 56–63; Schneider and Barnes, *The Rise of Humane Institutions*, 281–82.

46 Quoted in Orlando F. Lewis, *The Development of American Prisons and Prison Customs, 1776–1845*, 81.

47 William Jay, *The Life of John Jay with Selections from his Correspondence and Papers by his son William Jay*, vol. 1, 400.

48 McIntosh, *Ontario Co., New York*, 39. The chronicle stated that Thompson was "ably defended" by two local counselors.

49 Journals of Executive Pardons, vol. 2, B0042–79, New York State Archives (NYSA), 449–50. Yates made this statement public on January 11, 1823.

50 Silverberg, *Gender and American Social Science.*

51 On declining severity toward women who killed infants in the early national period see Gilje, "Infant Abandonment in Early Nineteenth-Century New York City: Three Cases," 580–90.

52 Carroll Smith-Rosenberg, "The Republican Gentleman: The Race to Rhetorical Stability in the New United States," in *Masculinities in Politics and War: Gendering Modern History*, ed. Stefan Dudink, Karen Hagemann, and John Tosh (Manchester, UK: University of Manchester Press, 2004), 61–76, 65.

53 When de Beaumont and de Tocqueville conducted their survey of imprisonment in the United States, they confined their tour to the northern states and focused on Pennsylvania, Massachusetts, and New York. Mancini, *Alexis de Tocqueville and American Intellectuals*, 29–45.

54 Perry, *The Life and Letters of Francis Lieber*, 91.

55 Meranze, *Laboratories of Virtue*, 261.

56 Beaumont and Tocqueville, *On the Penitentiary System*, 13.

57 Beaumont and Tocqueville, *On the Penitentiary System*, 57. Both men were councilors in the Royal Court at Paris.

58 Beaumont and Tocqueville, *On the Penitentiary System*, 57 n. 8.

59 Francis Lieber, preface to de Beaumont and de Tocqueville, *On the Penitentiary System*, xxxi, xxix, xx, xxxii.

60 The heading for this section plays on a phrase in Porter's *The Rise of Statistical Thinking, 1820–1900*, 18. Most historians trace the root of the study of "social numbers" to the seventeenth century and the scientific revolution.

61 Cohen, *A Calculating People*, 170, ix.

62 *Laws of New York*, 1839, Chapter 259, passed April 26, 1839.

63 Carey, *Thoughts on Penitentiaries and Prison Discipline*, 60, 59. Carey's most up-to-date figures for Auburn, from 1828, were collected for his 1829 publication, *Essays on Penitentiary Discipline* (Philadelphia: M. Carey, 1829).

64 Lieber criticized Carey for failing to take the prospect of gubernatorial impeachment into account. Beaumont and Tocqueville, *On the Penitentiary System*, 237.

65 Jenkins, *Lives of the Governors of the State of New York*, 519–40.

66 Lincoln, *Messages*, vol. 3, 230, 285, 342.

67 Throop stated in his January 3, 1832, address to the legislature that he had pardoned seventy-three criminals in 1831 (in contrast to 24 in 1829, his first year in office), and he claimed that most pardons had been granted "without the intervention of friends, for many of them had none." Lincoln, *Messages*, vol. 3, 384; 284.

68 Spencer, *The Victor and the Spoils*. Throop did not contest the election. Marcy was a Van Burenite who later became U.S. secretary of war and secretary of state.

69 Journals of Executive Pardons show that in Marcy's first year in office he pardoned fifty-nine offenders. In 1837 he reported to the legislature that his pardon rate had decreased over the previous four years but he did not provide full statistics. Lincoln, *Messages*, vol. 3, 402, 617.

70 Alexander, *A Political History of the State of New York*, 31–35.

71 Bancroft, *The Life of William H. Seward, in Two Volumes*, vol. 1, 120.

72 Seward also maintained full records of pardon requests received and granted. Reels 166–172, Manuscript Series S514, Papers of William H. Seward, New York State Library.

73 The *Argus* published its attack on July 7, 1840, and on September 10 the *Albany Evening Journal* responded. The influential national magazine *Niles Register* supported Seward in a September 26, 1840, summary report, which included a table of the statistics. On Seward's concerns regarding his reputation for pardoning, see Bancroft, *The Life of William H. Seward*, vol. 1, 124–25.

74 "Governor's Message," *New York Herald*, January 6, 1841.

75 Lincoln, *Messages*, vol. 3, 862.

76 Comstock was found to be pregnant at the time of her sentencing, and Throop commuted her sentence to three years on September 27, 1830, after she delivered her child. Journals of Executive Pardons, vol. 5, B0042–79.

77 *Journal of the Assembly of the State of New York at Their Fifty-Fifth Session*, 1832 (Albany: E. Croswell, 1832), 17; Lincoln, *Messages*, vol. 3, 340.

78 Lincoln, *Messages*, vol. 3, 862.

79 The greatest number of individuals executed between 1829 and 1839 in any single year was four (in 1829). Although Marcy did not speak against the death penalty in his messages, only six men were executed in his six years in office. Lincoln, *Messages*, vol. 3, 402; Journals of Executive Pardons, vol. 5, 485–566; vol. 6, 1–178.

80 Sarat, *Gruesome Spectacles*, 17. Revulsion over the behavior of crowds at executions, particularly in New York City, was the principal impetus for this reform, which occurred in other northeastern states in the same period.

81 In Seward's four years in office thirteen men were executed—eleven white and two black. Journals of Executive Pardons, vol. 6, 179–326.

82 Banner, *The Death Penalty*, 132–33.

83 O'Sullivan, *Report in Favor of the Abolition of the Punishment of Death*, 131.

84 Sampson, *John L. O'Sullivan and His Times*, 101.

85 Benjamin, *The Oxford Handbook of New York State Government and Politics*, 324.

86 Galie, *Ordered Liberty*, 95.

87 This amendment to the constitution did not occur until April 13, 1860, when the legislature passed "An Act to Perfect an Amendment to the Constitution Abolishing the Property Qualification of People of Color," *Laws of New York*, Chapter 349, passed April 13, 1860.

88 Chester and Williams, *Courts and Lawyers of New York*, 666–68.

89 New York Department of State, *Third Constitution of the State of New York* (hereafter *Third Constitution*).

90 Henretta, "Foreword: Rethinking the State Constitutional Tradition," 819–40, 823.

91 Lubert, "The New York Constitution," 126–45, 127. Lubert claims that New York's enduring "preference for a strong executive" came to "define American constitutional politics."

92 Several petitions in favor of woman suffrage were presented at the Convention. One signed by "six ladies of Jefferson County" appeared in the published version of the proceedings. Cogan and Ginzberg, "1846 Petition for Woman's Suffrage, New York State Constitutional Convention," 427–439, 429.

93 McCurdy, *The Anti-rent Era in New York Law and Politics, 1839–1865*, 275.

94 Galie, *Ordered Liberty*, 99.

95 Croswell and Sutton, *Debates and Proceedings in the New York State Constitutional Convention*, 278, 235, 234 (hereafter 1846 *Proceedings*).

96 Henretta, "The Rise and Decline of 'Democratic-Republicanism': Political Rights in New York and the Several States, 1800–1915," 50–90, 50.

97 Chatfield proposed that the governor be authorized to pardon "according to law," rather than on grounds "he may think proper." 1846 *Proceedings*, 278, 235, 234.

98 1846 *Proceedings*, 277.

99 Ibid., 236. On other matters, notably racial equality, Tallmadge was considerably more progressive. In the 1821 Convention he attempted to accelerate abolition. Gellman, *Emancipating New York*, 212.

100 1846 *Proceedings*, 236.

101 Ibid., 239–40. Shepard, a Hunker Democrat, shot to prominence late in the 1840s as the Grand Sachem of Tammany Hall and U.S. attorney for New York City. *New York Times*, September 20, 1856.

102 1846 *Proceedings*, 232, 279.

103 Ibid., 233; 278. Bascom was a Whig lawyer and a supporter of abolition and women's suffrage.

104 Ibid., 706.

105 William E. Nelson, "Legal Turmoil in a Factious Colony," 69–162, 154–55; Huston, *Land and Freedom*, 33–34; Carp, *Defiance of the Patriots*, 141–60.

106 The anti-rent movement also gained the support of powerful editors, notably Horace Greeley of the *New York Tribune* and Thomas Devyr of the *Freeholder*, in addition to Henry George's National Reform Association. Huston, *Land and Freedom*, 82–83.

107 Huston, *Land and Freedom*, 253–56. Even the judge who presided over the anti-renter leader's trial in 1845 used this language. Edmonds, "The People v. Smith Boughton," 140–75.

108 *New York Tribune*, December 26, 1844. William Cullen Bryant's *New York Evening Post*, and the Whig paper the *Albany Argus* all recommended that the perpetrators ought to be punished to the full extent of the law.

109 The Anti-Rent Party asserted that Smith Boughton and others had been given disproportionately severe sentences. McCurdy, *The Anti-Rent Era*, 251.

110 Thomas Summerhill contends that Young made this promise. Summerhill, *Harvest of Dissent*, 84. This supposition has also been cited in Peter Knight, *Conspiracy Theories in American History*, 68–69. McCurdy considers the pardon more an outcome of radical Whig support for the anti-rent cause. McCurdy, *The Anti-Rent Era*, 271.

111 Executive Orders for Commutations, Pardons, Respites, Reprieves, vol. 2, January 27, 1847, B0049–78. Through Hamilton's lobbying, the president was vested with supreme authority to pardon, especially to "restore tranquility to the commonwealth." Shapiro, *The Federalist Papers*, 371.

112 *New York Evening Post*, February 28, 1847. The *Post*, the *New York Sunday Times*, and the *New York Express* all condemned Young and his pardon. Charles McCurdy contends that Alexander G. Johnson, the editor of the anti-rent organ, the *Freeholder*, drafted the pardon. McCurdy, *The Anti-Rent Era*, 376, n22.

113 Brooke, *Columbia Rising*, 466.

114 Huston, "The Parties and 'The People': The New York Anti-Rent Wars and the Contours of Jacksonian Politics," 241–71, 246, 260.

115 Galie claims that "limiting the executive" and the power of the legislature were two key outcomes of the 1846 Convention. Galie, *Ordered Liberty*, 103–5. Stephen M. Feldman argues that "Benthamism" was prominent in constitutional debate in 1846, but he does not account for its absence in deliberation over the pardon power. Feldman, *American Legal Thought from Premodernism to Postmodernism*, 71.

116 This judgment, reached in *Strong and Gordon, Chiefs of the Seneca Nation of Indians v. Waterman* (1845), repudiated the earlier concept of limited autonomy, in *Goodell v. Jackson* (1822). Rosen, *American Indians and State Law*, 32–33.

117 This figure is taken from Daniel Allen Hearn's count in his *Legal Executions in New York State*, 39–49. It is likely that some executions are not accounted for, although that likelihood is less so for this period than in earlier years.

CHAPTER 4. THE PARDON AND THE PROGENESIS OF PAROLE IN THE
MID-NINETEENTH CENTURY

1 Edmonds (1799–1874) trained in law and served as a Democratic assemblyman and senator in the 1830s. He presided over Smith Boughton's trial as a circuit court judge of his home county of Columbia. Cephas Brainerd, "Memorial Sketch of Hon. John W. Edmonds," Prison Association of New York, *Thirty-Second Annual Report of 1876* (New York: Jerome B. Parmenter, 1877), 168–78. This report, with appropriate years, is hereafter referred to as PANY, *Report*.

2 Rothman, "Perfecting the Prison: United States, 1789–1865," 111–29.

3 PANY, *Report*, 1844, 23.

4 Ibid., 1844, 7, 11. On the association as a prototypical reform association of its era, see Heale, "The Formative Years of the New York Prison Association, 1844–1862," 320–47; Graber, *The Furnace of Affliction*, 135–57.

5 The organization is currently called the Correctional Association of New York, and its motto is "A Force for Progressive Change in the Criminal Justice System since 1844."

6 Petersilia, *When Prisoners Come Home*, 55–58.

7 On penal citizenship building see McBride, *Punishment and Political Order*, 127–46.

8 Kirkland, *The Helping Hand*, 38.

9 See Whitehead, Dodson, and Edwards, *Corrections*, 101–4. For a Progressive Era perspective, see Lindsey, "Historical Sketch of the Indeterminate Sentence and Parole System," 9–69.

10 Modern, *Secularism in Antebellum America*, 253. The turn toward a theological dialogue with Foucault's oeuvre began in English with Jeremy R. Carrette's edited collection, *Religion and Culture: Michel Foucault*.

11 Meranze, *Laboratories of Virtue*, 7–13. See also Kann, *Punishment, Prisons and Patriarchy*.

12 Pillsbury, "Understanding Penal Reform: The Dynamic of Change," 726–80, 37–8.

13 Industrial towns and larger cities still coped poorly with both disease-bearing sewage and poisonous effluent from factories in the 1840s, and campaigns to improve sanitation used forms of expression similar to those used by campaigners engaged in moral reform. Melosi, *Pollution and Reform in American Cities*; Gilfoyle, "Prostitutes in History," 117–41.

14 PANY, *Report*, 1846, 64, 66.

15 Kann, *Taming Passion for the Common Good*, 1–2.

16 PANY, *Report*, 1844, 29.

17 In 1822, New York legislated the removal of Stockbridge Mohican people to Wisconsin, eight years before the federal government endorsed a policy of Indian removal east of the Mississippi and fourteen years before the forced removal of the Cherokee from Georgia. Graymont, "New York Indian Policy after the Revolution," 438–74, 452; Tiro, *The People of the Standing Stone*, xiv.

18 Shane White, *Somewhat More Independent*, 84.

19 Ury, "American Society for Colonizing the Free People of Color of the United States," 187–97. On the split between converted Seneca and followers of Red Jacket, see Dennis, *Seneca Possessed*, 58–60.

20 Seward paid for Sing Sing's first library (at a cost of three hundred dollars) out of his own pocket. Luckey, *Life in Sing Sing State Prison*, 24–25. On the course of Luckey's early career at the prison, see Lewis, *From Newgate to Dannemora*, 216–18; Graber, *The Furnace of Affliction*, 168–77.

21 Luckey, *Life in Sing Sing State Prison*, 64–66.

22 PANY, *Report*, 1844, 63. For a picture of Hopper as a heroic, if flawed, character, see Bacon, *Lamb's Warrior*.

23 William Parker, *"Parole": Origins, Development, Current Practices, and Statutes* (College Park, MD: American Correctional Association, 1972); David Dressler,

Practice and Theory of Probation and Parole (New York: Columbia University Press, 1959); A. Keith Bottomley, "Parole in Transition: A Comparative Study of Origins, Developments, and Prospects for the 1990s," in *Crime and Justice: A Review of Research*, vol. 12, ed. Michael Tonry and Norval Morris (Chicago: University of Chicago Press, 1990), 319–74; Joseph F. Spillane and David B. Wolcott, *A History of Modern American Criminal Justice* (Los Angeles: Sage, 2013), 95–96.

24 McLennan, *The Crisis of Imprisonment*, 70. In 1837 a separate building was opened for Sing Sing's female felons.

25 PANY, *Report*, 1845, 45. Two matrons were assigned to the home, which PANY referred to as a "place of resort." The home was later recognized as "the first halfway house in the world." Bacon, *Abby Hopper Gibbons*, 55.

26 The eighth article of PANY's constitution referred to the formation of a female department within the "Society," to be composed of "females" interested in the "welfare of prisoners of their sex." PANY, *Report*, 1844, 6. Abby Hopper Gibbons (1801–1893) became an active member of the department's Executive Committee. Bacon, *Abby Hopper Gibbons*, 55–58.

27 "The Penal Code of America," 2.

28 PANY, *Report*, 1854, 128.

29 Second Report of the Female Department, in PANY, *Report*, 1846, 128.

30 Kirkland, *The Helping Hand*, 31.

31 In the home's first six months of operation, it found service positions for thirty-one of seventy-five women received in service, with twenty-one remaining "in the house." Second Report of the Female Department, in PANY, *Report*, 1846, 132; PANY, *Report*, 1850, 234.

32 PANY, *Report*, 1846, 93; PANY, *Report*, 1852, 53; PANY, *Report*, 1849, 174, 178.

33 Female rates of imprisonment rose significantly in the 1840s and '50s, particularly in New York City, where many Irish famine refugees settled. Freedman, *Their Sisters' Keepers: Women's Prison Reform in America*, 12–13.

34 PANY, *Report*, 1853, 32–33.

35 Freedman, *Their Sisters' Keepers: Women's Prison Reform in America*, 33. Similar splits occurred in the antislavery and temperance movements in this period. Ginzberg, *Women and the Work of Benevolence*, 125–29.

36 Rafter, *Partial Justice*, 43–47. The House of Refuge was renamed the Isaac T. Hopper House.

37 PANY, *Report*, 1855, 20. On the racist residue in emancipation rhetoric, see Marcus Wood, *The Horrible Gift of Freedom*.

38 The international correspondents included Beaumont and Tocqueville, Dr. Julius of Berlin and Professor Mittermaier of Heidelberg, both legal experts, and four prison inspectors from England.

39 PANY, *Report*, 1846, 38–41. The text of the report closely follows page 236–37 of Lieber's note in his 1833 translation of *On the Penitentiary System*.

40 PANY, *Report*, 1849, 94.

41 Chapter 310, enacted April 10, 1849, in *Statutes of the State of New York, of a Public and General Character, Passed from 1829 to 1851*, 750.

42 Corning, *Hamilton Fish*, 23–40.

43 Lincoln, *Messages from the Governors*, vol. 4, 435. Fish made this bid for pardon reform in his maiden address to the legislature on January 2, 1850.

44 Both the *Sun* and the *Argus* are searchable online through the Old Fulton NY Post Cards website: http://fultonhistory.com. Further searches were conducted using the Library of Congress's Chronicling America: Historical American Newspapers: http://chroniclingamerica.loc.gov/.

45 *Brooklyn Daily Eagle*, June 2, 1849, and July 18, 1849. Myers's notices continued to appear until mid-August 1849.

46 Fish to George A. Cornell, October 25, 1849; Fish to James E. Tyler, November 2, 1849, Papers of Hamilton Fish, container 183, letterbook H.

47 Volume 6 of the Executive Pardon registers ends in 1846 and volume 7 picks up with Myron H. Clark's governorship in 1856. For the missing decade, I referred to volumes 1–3 of the Executive Orders for Commutations, Pardons, Respites, Reprieves, New York State Archives, B0049–78, 1847–1854.

48 John Edmonds also supported pardons, not just recommending them in his judicial role but on an ex parte basis. PANY, *Report*, 1846, 65, 95.

49 PANY, *Report*, 1846, 107.

50 PANY, *Report*, 1846, Part II, 29, 41. The pardon statistics were not broken down by year in this report, but over 1845–46, 120 men and women were pardoned from Sing Sing.

51 Quoted in Child, *Isaac Hopper*, 413. Child lived and worked with the Hoppers in New York, and she dedicated her book to Hopper's widow, Hannah Attmore Hopper. Karcher, *The First Woman in the Republic*, 271, 373.

52 Quoted in Child, *Isaac Hopper*, 413. Child's citation of Young's letter does not provide the date, but it was likely written in 1846 or 1847.

53 PANY, *Report*, 1857. Beal was born in 1803 and worked with ex-prisoners' temperance in London before arriving in New York City in 1848, where he became involved with PANY's work.

54 Lewis, *From Newgate to Dannemora*, 277.

55 Rafter, *The Criminal Brain*, 4–5.

56 *Argument of William H. Seward, in Defence of William Freeman, on His Trial for Murder, at Auburn, July 21st and 22nd, 1846. Reported by S. Blatchford* (Auburn, NY: J. C. Derby and Company, 1846). This version went through multiple editions and other publishers picked it up. Horace Greeley's *New York Tribune* also gave it saturation coverage.

57 The case is analyzed in depth in Arpey, *The William Freeman Murder Trial*. Seward appealed for a pardon on the theory that Freeman was a "lunatic" and "hopelessly insane." (125).

58 Wright to Seward, September 7, 1846, quoted in Arpey, *The William Freeman Murder Trial*, 126.

59 Hopper followed this observation with two pages of stories concerning inmates reformed through hope, aid, and encouragement. PANY, *Report*, 1850, 169.

60 Stephen White, "Alexander Maconochie and the Development of Parole," 72–88. White's is one of the few studies to combine a critical analysis of Maconochie's failings and achievements with an appreciation for his system's impact on later parole programs.

61 PANY, *Report*, 1854, 44, 83.

62 Ibid., 62. The appendix appeared on pages 68 to 121.

63 Carpenter, *Reformatory Prison Discipline as Developed by the Rt. Hon. Sir Walter Crofton*, 10, xiv, 73, 9, 99, 95. The system was introduced after penal servitude became a substitute for transportation, and by 1857 the Third International Prison Congress endorsed Crofton's methods. Goldman, *Science, Reform, and Politics in Victorian Britain*, 155–61.

64 Bartrip, "Public Opinion and Law Enforcement," 150–81.

65 Mahoney, *Politics and Progress*, 5–7. Lieber held the first professorship in political science in the United States.

66 Graber, *The Furnace of Affliction*, 180–81.

67 Witt, *Lincoln's Code*, 229–31. General Henry W. Halleck and Secretary of War Edward Stanton formally requested Lieber to draft "'a code of regulation'" drawn from "'the laws and usages of war'" (quoted, 229).

68 Articles 119 to 134 in section seven of Lieber's code concerned parole.

69 The presidential use of pardoning during the War and Reconstruction was controversial at the time and remains so among historians. See Dorris, *Pardon and Amnesty under Lincoln and Johnson*; Foner, *Reconstruction*, 183–93.

70 PANY, *Report*, 1864, 30, 123.

71 Article V, §10 of New Jersey's 1844 constitution stated that the governor and six judges of the Court of Errors and Appeals had the power to grant pardons. This history is overlooked in Jensen, *The Pardoning Power in the American States*. However, Jensen correctly identifies the other states listed, most of which had boards by the mid-1860s.

72 The survey was sent only to former governors of states that had remained loyal during the Civil War, so it was biased toward the opinions of governors in northern states.

73 Wines and Dwight, *Report on the Prisons*, 368.

74 For an exception see Travis, *But They All Come Back*, 9–10. Most historians focus on the *Report*'s indictment of profit-driven inmate labor extraction. See, especially, McLennan, *The Crisis of Imprisonment*, 92. Nicole Hahn Rafter underlines that the lower profits extracted from female labor compounded belief in their lower likelihood of reform in *Partial Justice*, 12–13. For a foundational analysis in this vein, see Sellin, *Slavery and the Penal System*, 141–43.

75 Wines and Dwight, *Report on the Prisons*, 306.

76 Ibid., 370, 381, 382, 379.

77 "It is a profound and masterly exposition of the principles which belong to free government. All its discriminations are not only philosophical but eminently practical, and in harmony with the teaching of experience, ancient and modern." Hunt to Lieber, April 29, 1860. Papers of Francis Lieber, box 12.

78 Wines and Dwight, *Report on the Prisons*, 379–80.

79 Galie, *Ordered Liberty*, 117. The legislature took over a year to put the revised constitution to the electorate. In 1869, New Yorkers accepted only one section of the proposed constitution (concerning the judiciary) and rejected all others. Ibid., 131.

80 On June 6, 1867, Lieber's "Reflections on the Changes which may seem Necessary in the Present Constitution of the State of New York" was presented at the convention and endorsed by the *New York Times*.

81 Fenton stated that the "pardoning power should be delegated to a co-operative bureau." *New York Times*, January 2, 1867.

82 *Proceedings and Debates of the Constitutional Convention of the State of New York, Held in 1867 and 1868, vol. 2*, 1209 (hereafter 1867 *Proceedings*).

83 Ibid., 1184, 1187–88.

84 Ibid., 1200, 1186, 1188–89.

85 "Report of the Committee on the Pardoning Power," *New York Tribune*, August 19, 1867. Horace Greeley, the *Tribune*'s publisher, who was also a delegate to the convention, proposed that ex-governors compose a "council" to advise sitting governors.

86 Bergeron, *The Papers of Andrew Johnson*, vol. 13, 41–42.

87 Without the constitutional obligation to do so, Seward kept a record of pardon "judgments" during his governorship. William Henry Seward Papers, University of Rochester, boxes 48–58.

88 Witt, *Lincoln's Code*, 317–18. Late in 1865 Seward invited former Confederate senator Robert M. T. Hunter to dinner and placed a formal pardon beneath his dinner plate. Frederick W. Seward, *Seward at Washington as Secretary of State*, 295–96.

89 "Amnesty and Pardon," *Chicago Times*, September 7, 1867.

90 Francis Lieber to King Wilhelm Friedrich IV, November 4, 1841. Papers of Francis Lieber, box 18. The original is written in German. I am grateful to Hilary Howes for her translation.

91 The king pardoned Lieber on January 15, 1842: "Trusting in the veracity of the statements and assurances contained in your petition of 4 November last year, I am prepared to grant you clemency and have struck down by means of an order to the Minister of Justice the investigation that was imposed against you, so that there is no further obstacle to your return to the Fatherland from this side. [Signed] Friedrich Wilhelm."

92 1867 *Proceedings*, vol. 2, 1182.

CHAPTER 5. REFORMULATING DISCRETION IN THE MID- TO LATE
NINETEENTH CENTURY

1 Lieber, "A Paper on the Abuse of the Pardoning Power," 390–407, 401.

2 Florida's Pardon Board case files, which begin in 1887, show the board's role in reinforcing racial and gender hierarchies. Vivien M. L. Miller, *Crime, Sexual Violence, and Clemency.*

3 "An Act to Amend the Revised Statutes Concerning the Powers and Duties of the Governor, and to Fix the Compensation of Officers in the Executive Department," *Laws of New York*, 1858, passed April 1, 1858.

4 For works that make excellent use of official correspondence see Hay, "Property, Authority and the Criminal Law," 17–63; Chadwick, *Bureaucratic Mercy*; King, *Crime, Justice and Discretion in England, 1740–1820.* Messinger and his colleagues drew on governors' pardon papers (1880–1914) in their analysis of the origins of parole in California: Messinger, Berecochea, Rauma, and Berk, "The Foundations of Parole in California," 69–106. The records of the Texas Board of Pardon are richly explored in Ethan Blue's *Doing Time in the Depression.*

5 For a full explanation of the records and the sampling technique, see "Note on Sources."

6 Rebecca McLennan's book was published one year prior to the opening of the case files to researchers. *The Crisis of Imprisonment*, 341, n56.

7 Davis, *Fiction in the Archives.*

8 See table 1.

9 Some historians place the dawn of the Progressive Era in 1900. However, historians of punishment generally identify the establishment of the national and international prison associations and the opening of the Elmira Reformatory as Progressive penology's formative moments. Blomberg and Lucken, *American Penology.*

10 State of New York, "Report of the Secretary of State in Relation to Pardons Granted Since January 1, 1840." The study was ordered by an assembly resolution of March 21, 1846.

11 "Table CLXXIX—State Prisons and Penitentiaries, 1850," in DeBow, *Statistical View of the United States*, 166–67. In 1850, there were only 70 women in the state prison system, of whom 21 were "colored," making up 5 percent of the state prison population.

12 Unfortunately, no references to race or place of birth appear in these statistics. It is unlikely that none but whites were pardoned from 1840 to 1845, especially during Seward's tenure. Although a substantial of proportion have names that are likely of Irish origin, the precise number of Irish offenders pardoned is difficult to track.

13 "An Act to Amend the Revised Statutes," § 1.

14 State of New York, *Report of the Secretary of State, in Answer to a Resolution Relative to Pardons*, 1. State prisoners, plus those held at penitentiaries (most incarcerated at New York City's Blackwell's Penitentiary), county prisons and jails,

and juvenile reformatories—one in Manhattan and the other Rochester's Western House of Refuge—appear in this report.

15 Figures and names taken from table B in State of New York, *Report of the Secretary of State in Answer to a Resolution Relative to Pardons*, 4–16.

16 Governor Edwin D. Morgan made this claim in a special address to the assembly on February 17, 1859. Lincoln, *Messages from the Governors*, vol. 5, 116–17 (hereafter Lincoln, *Messages*).

17 Kennedy, "'The Burglar's Friend.'"

18 "Scenes from the Rogue World," *Harper's Weekly* 2, no. 57 (January 30, 1858), 80.

19 "The Pardoning Business," *Harper's Weekly* 2, no. 101 (December 4, 1858), 770–71.

20 Lewis, *From Newgate to Dannemora*, 273–75. Serious unrest began in 1855, including several attempts on the life of Auburn's warden.

21 The records of executive pardons confirm that 47 percent of the prisoners King pardoned over 1857 and 1858 (180 of 382) were minor offenders held in local jails, county prisons, and the New York Penitentiary. Governor Myron H. Clark, who preceded him, pardoned only 135 prisoners in 1856, almost two-thirds (62 percent) of whom were serious offenders. *Journals of Executive Pardons*, vol. 7, B0042–79.

22 The 1859 pardon report recognized the special gravity of forgery by assigning it a column in its tables separate from "property" offenses.

23 King was deluged with petitions to exonerate convicted rapist Joseph Jackson, whom he pardoned on November 25. *Albany Journal*, November 27, 1858.

24 Lewis, *From Newgate to Dannemora*, 273–75; McLennan, *The Crisis of Imprisonment*, 82–83.

25 "Another Murderer to be Pardoned?," *Harper's Weekly* 2, no. 72 (May 15, 1858), 306.

26 Maurice O'Connell, aged sixteen, was convicted of murder, with the jury's strong recommendation of mercy, on February 2, 1858. The sentencing judge and DA also supported the commutation of the sentence on the grounds of youth and lack of intent to murder. *New York Times*, May 15, 1858.

27 Peck, *History of Rochester and Monroe County, New York*, 171–72.

28 Secretary of State, *Report of the Secretary of State, in Answer to a Resolution Relative to Pardons*, table B, 4.

29 Martin, *Devil of the Domestic Sphere*. The illicit trade in alcohol and tobacco was exposed in numerous reviews of prison disorder and corruption at mid-century. McLennan, *The Crisis of Imprisonment*, 71.

30 State of New York, *Report of the Secretary of State, in Answer to a Resolution Relative to Pardons*, table B, 4, 9. In 1857–58, just under 6 percent of pardons were conditional. In 1846, the percentage was higher (8.3). The earlier report included only felony offenders, most of whom were pardoned on condition of leaving the locality, state, or country.

31 "The Conditional Liberation of Prisoners," 125–26.

32 Morgan was elected to the New York State Senate in 1850 as a Whig, then switched in 1855 to the newly formed Republican Party. From 1856 to 1864 he served as chairman of the Republican National Committee. Rawley, *Edwin D. Morgan*.

33 Lincoln, *Messages*, vol. 5, 170.

34 Lincoln, *Messages*, vol. 5, 169, 170. During the Civil War Morgan served as a major general of volunteers for the state.

35 *Albany Statesman*, May 20, 1859.

36 Wines and Dwight, *Report on the Prisons and Reformatories of the United States and Canada*, 570.

37 Lincoln, *Messages*, vol. 5, 169, 171, 172. O'Brien was hanged in Albany. *Troy Times*, June 3, 1859.

38 The decision of John Brown's defense to enter a plea of insanity for his attack at Harpers Ferry and Daniel Sickle's murder trial, both in 1859, brought national attention to the question of criminal motivation and culpability. Mohr, *Doctors and the Law*, 92–93. New York became the epicenter of medico-legal expertise by the late 1860s. Tighe, "The New York Medico-legal Society," 231–43.

39 Segrave, *Women and Capital Punishment in America, 1840–1899*, 35–36; "Mrs. Hartung's Case," *New York Times*, April 28, 1859.

40 "The Poughkeepsie Executions," *Brooklyn Eagle*, August 3, 1852. Hoag made a full confession. Pitts, Waldo, Barculo, and Walker, *Life and Confessions of Lucy Ann Hoag*.

41 Chester and Williams, *Courts and Lawyers of New York*, 1017.

42 Arpey, *The William Freeman Murder Trial*, 55–56.

43 "Executive Clemency Denied in the Case of Mrs. Hartung—The Governor's Letter," *New York Times*, April 6, 1859.

44 "Executive Clemency," *New York Times*, April 6, 1859. The *Times* published the letter in full.

45 The Hartung case enhanced Hadley's reputation as a criminal defense specialist, which received a further boost when he represented cuckolded Major General George Cole for the murder of constitutional delegate L. Harris Hiscock in 1867. Hartog, "Lawyering, Husbands' Rights, and the Unwritten Law in Nineteenth-Century America," 67–96, 78, 88, 89.

46 Horowitz, *The Transformation of American Law*, 10.

47 The initial law was passed on April 14, 1860, and amended in 1861 to clarify that hanging was the punishment for first-degree murder. In *Hartung v. People*, 1863, both acts were declared unconstitutional, and Hartung was released on March 26, 1863. For the full judgment, see https://casetext.com. For the wider import of the ruling, see Chester, *Legal and Judicial History of New York*, vol. 3, 37–43.

48 "Mrs. Hartung," *Brooklyn Eagle*, April 1, 1859. The *Eagle* backed the equal application of the law and supported Morgan's refusal to pardon.

49 In Morgan's 1861 message to the legislature, he urged the amendment of the poorly drafted 1860 statute, contrasting it to the pardon power: "a delicate and necessary one, the proper exercise of which involves patient research and the most careful discrimination." Lincoln, *Messages*, vol. 5, January 2, 1861, 266.

50 See table 3 for a comparison of the sampled case files and information provided in the State Archives' database.

51 See table 2.

52 Hoffman made this statement in his January 3, 1871 address to the legislature. Lincoln, *Messages*, vol. 6, 268.

53 Bernstein, *The New York City Draft Riots*, 190.

54 Wines and Dwight, *Report on the Prisons and Reformatories of the United States and Canada*, 304.

55 Tullack, "Humanity and Humanitarianism with Special Reference to the Prison Systems of Great Britain and the United States," 204–18, 207.

56 Hartog, "Lawyering, Husbands' Rights, and the 'Unwritten Law' in Nineteenth-Century America," 67–96.

57 Lande, *The Abraham Man*, 79–86.

58 See table 4. Because the State Archives' database included first and last names, it was possible to provide a reliable indication of prisoners' gender. Information on race and ethnicity is far patchier.

59 "Henry Alexander," Executive Clemency and Pardon Case Files, 1859–1926, box 10, file 27, 1873 (hereafter Clemency Files). The dates refer to the year in which clemency pleas were first officially registered.

60 Journals of Governors' Actions and Decisions, vol. 16, February 21, 1874, A0607, NYSA, 89.

61 Clemency Files, "Henry Alexander."

62 Clemency Files, "Victoria Moniqurial," 1873, box 11, file 1.

63 Clemency Files, "Margaret Caveran," 1875, box 15, file 75.

64 In his study of judges' reports and petitions for mercy in 136 cases from 1789 and 1790, Peter King found previous good character the most frequently mentioned, followed by "sympathy for the young, the old, or the weak," and family destitution. King, *Crime, Justice and Discretion in England, 1740–1820*, 299.

65 Platt, "The Triumph of Benevolence," 177–96.

66 Grant, *The Boy Problem*, 1–3.

67 "A Murderer Sentenced to Prison For Life," *New York Times*, May 18, 1867.

68 Clemency Files, "Anthony Mahn," 1870, box 5, file 7.

69 The law of murder was unclear in the aftermath of the statutes passed in response to the Hartung case. On April 2, 1862, the legislature repealed the law that had been declared unconstitutional, but courts continued to recognize the distinction between first- and second-degree murder.

70 State of New York, *Public Papers of Grover Cleveland, 1883–1884*, vol. 2, 832. Although he commuted Mahn's sentence to thirty years, Cleveland set the release date at the expiration of eighteen years, owing to the good time Mahn had earned.

71 Numerous letters in Mahn's file underlined the issue of his family's distress. On the announcement of the commutation, the *Auburn (NY) Weekly News and Democrat* credited Cleveland's approach as "humane" and "closer in consonance with the constitution" than the approach of his predecessor, Governor Cornell. "Cleveland's Pardons," February 28, 1884.

72 Thomas, "Elizabeth Cady Stanton and the Notion of a Legal Class of Gender," 139–55, 146–48.

73 *New York Sun*, January 2, 1876. On the ring, see Teaford, *The Unheralded Triumph*, 181–86.

74 Clemency Files, "Owen Tully," 1876, box 18, file 6.

75 Lee, *American Journalism 1690–1940*, vol. 4, 586–87.

76 For the press's portrayal of the Walworth trial as a melodrama see O'Brien, *Fall of the House of Walworth*.

77 Walworth was the first person in New York to be convicted of murder in the second degree, shortly after the legislature finally sorted out the statute covering degrees of murder in 1873. Strange, "The Unwritten Law of Executive Justice," 891–930.

78 Papers of Samuel J. Tilden, box 32.

79 Clemency Files, "Frank Walworth," 1873, box 10, folders 34–37.

80 Numerous papers published the declaration in full, and most regarded Walworth's mental state as a legitimate basis for clemency. "The public, as a whole, will acquiesce in rather than approve of the pardon," stated the *Brooklyn Eagle*, August 2, 1877.

81 Baker, *The Moral Frameworks of Public Life*.

82 *Auburn (NY) Daily Bulletin*, August 2, 1877.

83 "F. H. Walworth Pardoned," *New York Times*, August 2, 1877. The *Times* published the governor's statement without comment.

84 Smith-Rosenberg and Rosenberg, "The Female Animal," 332–56; Theriot, *Mothers and Daughters in Nineteenth-Century America*.

85 Table 2 in United States Bureau of the Census, *Prisoners and Juvenile Delinquents in the United States 1910*, 16.

86 Ramsey, "Intimate Homicide," 101–91.

87 Freedman, *Their Sisters' Keepers: Women's Prison Reform in America, 1830–1930*, 46–57.

88 Basch, *Framing American Divorce*, 68; Ireland, "The Libertine Must Die," 27–44.

89 Pleck, *Domestic Tyranny*, 88–107.

90 Streib, "Rare and Inconsistent," 101–32, 112–13.

91 Clemency Files, "Roxalana Druse," 1886, box 35, folders 17–32, folder 17.

92 State of New York, *Public Papers of Grover Cleveland, 1883–1884*, vol. 2, April 11, 1884, 317–17.

93 "Two Months More of Life," *New York Times*, December 23, 1886. After her legal appeals failed, Druse's execution date was set for December 29, 1886. Hill's respite rescheduled it to February 28, 1887.

94 On the virilization of masculine ideals in the 1880s see Rotundo, *American Manhood*, 222–46.

95 "Women and the Death Penalty," *New York Herald*, January 1, 1887.

96 State of New York, *Public Papers of David B. Hill, Governor, 1885–1891*, vol. 2, 322–23, 325–26.

97 Clemency Files, "Roxalana Druse," folder 18. This is one of the few capital files in which an entire folder of letters urging execution has been preserved.

98 The public did not hear about this decision until February 26, which suggests that Hill preferred to sit on the medical report until the fate of the legislative bill was determined. The appointed doctors were Judson B. Andrews of the Buffalo Insane Asylum, Carlos Macdonald of the Asylum for Insane Criminal at Auburn, and Lewis Balch, Secretary of the State Board of Health.

99 "Refusing to Intervene to Save Mrs. Druse from the Gallows," *New York Sun*, February 19, 1887.

100 A member of the Albany General Democratic Committee accused Hill of being "'very weak in respect to that great essential for a leader—backbone.'" "Plucky Dave Hill," *New York Herald*, 23 January 1887.

101 Hill, "The Pardoning Power," 50–83, 57, 56. Jensen's *The Pardoning Power in the American States* (1922) cited Hill's work as an authoritative source.

102 "An Act in Relation to the State Reformatory," *Laws of New York*, 1870, Chapter 427, passed April 27, 1870. It permitted any criminal court to apply an indeterminate sentence "at its discretion" (§ 9).

103 "An Act Relating to State Prisons and for Other Purposes," *Laws of New York*, Chapter 382, passed June 6, 1889.

104 Eugene Smith, *Prison Science with Special Reference to Recent New York Legislation*. Smith was secretary of the Prison Association of New York and praised the state's expansion of indeterminate sentencing provisions in 1889.

105 Pisciotta, *Benevolent Repression*, 26.

106 Hinkle and Whitmarsh, *Images of Elmira Reformatory*, 8–9.

107 McLennan, *The Crisis of Imprisonment*, 177–78. McClennan disagrees with Pisciotta's view that Brockway ruled Elmira to make machines of men from the reformatory's opening. Pisciotta, *Benevolent Repression*, 22.

108 Clemency Files, "O'Flanigan," 1879, box 26, file 4; "Carroll," 1880, box 28, file 23.

109 Clemency Files, "Carroll."

110 Clemency Files, "O'Connor," 1889, box 40, file 23.

111 The *New York Times* published an overview of Flower's career on his death on May 12, 1899: "Roswell P. Flower Dies Suddenly," May 13, 1899.

112 State of New York, *Public Papers of Roswell P. Flower, Governor, 1893*, vol. 2, 462–3, 471.

113 Pisciotta, *Benevolent Repression*, 65–66.

114 State of New York, *Report and Proceedings of the State Board of Charities Relative to the Management of the State Reformatory at Elmira*, vol. 1, xxxiii, xxxi.

115 Clemency Files, "Gilmore," 1895, box 54, file 22.

116 "Brockway Is Vindicated," *New York Times*, December 11, 1894. Flower quoted Learned's statement in his acceptance of the second report.

117 More conservative papers also reported on the reformatory's questionable use of physical discipline. See "Brockway's Paddle Barred Out," *New York Times*, November 18, 1899. This article quoted Roosevelt's policy: "'I am firmly opposed to paddling . . . it will not be tolerated.'"

CHAPTER 6. THE ENTANGLEMENT OF PAROLE AND PARDONING IN
THE PROGRESSIVE ERA

1 Prison Association of New York, *Making Men Over, Being the Sixty-Fifth Annual Report of the Prison Association of New York, 1910* (Albany: J. B. Lyon, 1910) (hereafter PANY, *Report*).

2 The New York State Parole Board reported in 1919 that in the previous year 842 of 1,181 prisoners were released to the Catholic Protective Society, the Jewish Protectory and Aid Society, the Salvation Army, the Christian Science Church, and the Volunteers of America, in addition to the Prison Association of New York. "State Parole Board freed 1,181 Convicts During Past Year," *Brooklyn Eagle*, February 19, 1919.

3 Paley, *Of the Direct Historical Evidence of Christianity* vol. 1, 36–37; Speranza, "What Are We Doing for the Criminal?," 215–20; 219. Speranza drew heavily on Wines, "The Treatment of the Criminal," 422–34 (hereafter Charities *Proceedings*).

4 Lewis, *The Development of American Prisons and Prison Customs*; Barnes, "Some Leading Phases of the Evolution of Modern Penology," 251–80. For subsequent critiques see, in particular, Rafter, *Creating Born Criminals*; Rothman, *Conscience and Convenience*; and McLennan, *The Crisis of Imprisonment*, chapters 8 and 9. On the wider international context of Progressive penology see Becker and Wetzell, *Criminals and their Scientists*.

5 On the "invention" and treatment of juvenile delinquency see Schlossman, *Transforming Juvenile Justice*; Schneider, *In the Web of Class*; Platt, *The Child Savers*; Tanenhaus, *Juvenile Justice in the Making*; Ward, *The Black Child Savers*.

6 Forty-one sterilizations took place exclusively on females in asylums between 1912 and 1918 (when the state's sterilization law was ruled unconstitutional). Paul, *"Three Generations of Imbeciles Are Enough": State Eugenic Sterilization Laws in American Thought and Practice*, 560–63.

7 Wines, "The Treatment of the Criminal," 422–34, 434.

8 The nation's total prison population in 1910 was 136,472. New York's alone was 16,082, and the next highest incarcerator was Pennsylvania, at 10,313. United States Bureau of the Census, *Prisoners and Juvenile Delinquents in the United States 1910*, 27.

9 On the Progressives' approach to female delinquency, see Freedman, *Their Sisters' Keepers, 1830–1930*, chapter 6, 109–25; Alexander, *The Girl Problem*; Odem, *Delinquent Daughters*; Hicks, *Talk With You Like a Woman*.

10 "Report of the Board of Parole for State Prisons," in New York, *Annual Report of the Superintendent of State Prisons*, 1908 (Albany: J. B. Lyon, 1908): 25–32, 27 (hereafter Parole Report).

11 See "Note on Sources" for an explanation of the sampling technique adopted for this period.

12 The Espy file lists 184 executions in New York between 1901 and 1920, the highest number of any state in this period. Espy and Smykla, *Executions in the United States, 1608–2002: The Espy File.* On August 12, 1912, seven men were electrocuted at Sing Sing state prison in just over one hour. *Brooklyn Eagle*, August 12, 1912.

13 National Prison Association, "Report of the Standing Committee on Criminal Law Reform," *Proceedings of the Annual Congress of the National Prison Association*, 17.

14 Wolin, "After Release: The Parolee in Society," 1–41, 4, n11.

15 "An Act Relating to State Prisons and for Other Purposes," *Laws of New York*, Chapter 382, passed June 6, 1889. An amendment to this law, passed in 1892, increased the number of crimes punishable by indeterminate sentences. *Laws of New York*, Chapter 662.

16 Eugene Smith, Collin, and Lewis, "Report of the Committee on Penal and Reformatory Systems," 202, 207.

17 Lindsey, "Historical Sketch of the Indeterminate Sentence and Parole System," 9–69, 36.

18 Lewis, "Golden Rule of 'Try Again' for Penitent Convicts."

19 Inmates in local jails could not earn "good time." As of 1910, more than twice as many prisoners served time in the four state prisons, compared to the inmates in reformatories, principally Elmira, Napanoch, and Bedford Hills (4,652 versus 2,421). United States Bureau of the Census, *Prisoners and Juvenile Delinquents in the United States 1910*, 24.

20 Brockway, *Fifty Years of Prison Service*, 301, 218–19, 362.

21 Winter, *The New York State Reformatory in Elmira*, 26–27.

22 PANY acted as Elmira's parole agency from 1877 until 1912, when the Reformatory assumed full management of its parole system.

23 The success rate reported in 1898 was typical. Of 256 Elmira parolees registered, PANY claimed it returned only 17 for violations. PANY, *Report*, 1898, 147.

24 Wines, "The Treatment of the Criminal," 431.

25 "Brockway Out at Last," *New York Tribune*, August 1, 1900. Brockway resigned officially on the basis of "advanced age." His memoirs attribute his retirement to "interference" with his management. Brockway, *Fifty Years of Prison Service*, 363.

26 "An Act Constituting the State Prison Commission, a State Board of Parole, and Authorizing it to Parole the Prisoners in State Prisons," *Laws of New York*, 1901, Chapter 260, passed April 4, 1901.

27 Kirk, *The Laws of New York Relating to the State Prisons*. In 1901, Governor O'Dell reduced the earlier-constituted commission to three members, in concert with the passage of the parole law. "New Prison Commission," *New York Times*, February 15, 1901.

28 "An Act to Amend the Revised Statutes Relative to the Parole of Prisoners from State Prisons," *Laws of New York*, 1907, Chapter 467, passed June 16, 1907. This law also expanded the scope of New York's Probation Commission, established in

1905. New York State Probation Commission, *Report of the New York State Probation Commission*, vol. 7 (New York: J. B. Lyon, 1914), 414.

29 Parole Report, 1908, 29.

30 Gault, "The New York State Board of Parole," 791–95, 794.

31 Governor Charles S. Whitman appointed Dr. Elmer E. Larkin, its first medical professional, to the board in 1917.

32 Collins became superintendent of state prisons in 1898. Republican governor Frank Black appointed him after he served as an executive member of Republican State Committee. Collins resigned on April 25, 1911.

33 Dix complained in his first message to the legislature that parole board appointees had gone from earning $10 per day of service in 1901 to an annual salary of $3,600 plus expenses as of 1910. "It is Time for Drastic Reform and Retrenchment, Says Governor Dix in First Message to Legislature," *Brooklyn Daily Eagle*, January 4, 1911.

34 Lewis served as a board member from 1907 until 1911. Severance, *Publications of the Buffalo Historical Society*, vol. 22, 408. Wadhams's last active service occurred during the war with Spain. Harriet Weeks Wadhams Stevens, *Wadhams Genealogy, Preceded by a Sketch of the Wadham Family in England, With Illustrations* (New York: Frank Allaben Genealogical Company, 1913), 413–15.

35 PANY, *Report*, 1908, 13.

36 Lewis, "Golden Rule."

37 As of 1917 at least, wardens of the state prisons sent district attorneys a form that asked them to report "any reason why [the applicant] should not receive favorable consideration." New York State Board of Parole, Inmate Case Files, February 27, 1917, B0076–77, vol. 1 (1913–21), State Archives of New York (hereafter Parole Hearings).

38 Superintendent Cornelius V. Collins to Henry McGovern, in Parole Hearings, February 7, 1911. Born in 1856, Collins was a Troy lawyer who served as sheriff of Rensselaer County from 1888 to 1894.

39 Parole Hearings, July 15, 1908, 14–16.

40 Alexander, *The Girl Problem*, 123–48. Alexander focuses on Bedford Hills and the Albion institution for female delinquents.

41 Cheryl D. Hicks argues that Collins and other state parole officials had lower expectations of African American women and the communities to which they returned. Hicks, *Talk With You Like a Woman*, 239.

42 The association of drugs with criminality did not begin until the late 1910s. Spillane, "Did Drug Prohibition Work? Reflections on the End of the First Cocaine Experience in the United States, 1910–45," 517–38, 521–2.

43 Parole Hearings, January 1909, 13. On self-control as a masculine ideal in this period, see Bederman, *Manliness and Civilization*, 96–97.

44 Parole Hearings, January 6, 1910, 2, 9; n.d. April 1909, 16.

45 Parole Hearings, July 22, 1910, 26; October 13, 1910, 42.

46 The Jewish Protectory and Aid Society operated in New York City from 1902 to 1921, after which it became the Jewish Board of Guardians. Walkowitz, *Working with Class*, 71–72.

47 Parole Hearings, n.d. September 1908, 39–40; PANY, *Report*, 1910, 20.

48 Muhammad, *The Condemnation of Blackness*, 4–6. Muhammad isolates the Progressive Era as the point when links between blackness and criminality hardened in the urban North.

49 "Gayton Gets the Extreme Penalty. Negro Assailant of Olean Woman Will Serve Twenty Years at Auburn," *Buffalo Express*, March 21, 1906. Gayton fled town but later pled guilty to first-degree rape after his father turned him in. "Clarence Gayton Sentenced to Auburn for Twenty Years," *Rochester Democrat Chronicle*, March 21, 1906. Board of Parole, Minutes, February 21, 1916.

50 Without photographs in board records it is difficult to estimate the number of people of color who appeared before the board, but rare references to "color" and the use of "negro" to describe inmates signal that members regarded the appearance of African American applicants as exceptional.

51 In contrast, black men made up a minority in the male prison population in this period. Of 34,300 prisoners committed to penal institutions in New York in 1910, 2,145 were classified as "Negro," and another 56 were listed as "Other Colored." "Table 13, Prisoners and Juvenile Delinquents Committed to Penal or Reformatory Institutions," in United States Bureau of the Census, *Prisoners and Delinquents in the United States 1910* (Washington, DC: United States Printing Office, 1918), 326.

52 In 1910, half of the 128 women incarcerated at Auburn were listed as "colored." "Table 1, Prisoners and Juvenile Delinquents," in United States Bureau of the Census, *Prisoners and Delinquents*, 264. This disproportionate rate persisted in the 1920s. Hicks, *Talk with You Like a Woman*, 305.

53 Parole Hearings, January 20, 1909, 16.

54 Parole Hearings, June 15, 1909, 40. This pattern of intrusive moral questions and evasive answers is also common in the parole hearing records of Bedford Hills. Alexander, *The Girl Problem*; Hicks, *Talk with You Like a Woman*.

55 Parole Hearings, n.d. February 1908, n.d. April 1909, 57.

56 Hicks, *Talk with You Like a Woman*, 123; Alexander, *The Girl Problem*, 94–95.

57 Parole Hearings, January 6, 1910, 32; n.d. October 1910, 60.

58 Parole Hearings, January 20, 1909, 16; January 6, 1910, 41.

59 "The Treatment of the Feeble-Minded Delinquent," PANY, *Report*, 1912, 47–51.

60 Dugdale, *The Jukes*. In 1916, Arthur H. Estabrook, a researcher in the Eugenics Research Office at Cold Spring, Long Island, published an updated version of the book, calling it *The Jukes in 1915*. On the resurgence of interest in Dugdale's work and its influence in spurring sterilization statutes, see Stern, *Eugenic Nation*; Rafter, *White Trash*.

61 "An Act to Amend the Public Health Law, in Relation to Operations for the Prevention of Procreation," *Laws of New York*, 1912, Chapter X, passed April 16,

1912. It applied to inmates of state institutions, including asylums, work houses, jails, reformatories, and state prisons. The law was repealed in 1920.

62 Garton, "Criminal Propensities," 79–97.

63 "Why Young Men Go Wrong," *Brooklyn Daily Eagle*, December 22, 1911. The Bureau of Social Hygiene set up operation at Bedford Hills in March 1911. Rafter, *Partial Justice*.

64 Bulmer, "Knowledge for the Public Good," 16–39; Pivar, *Purity and Hygiene*; Donovan, *White Slave Crusades*; Luker, "Sex, Social Hygiene, and the State," 601–34.

65 Due to privacy regulations concerning juvenile victims of sexual offences I have anonymized the offender's name. He was convicted in an upstate New York town.

66 Parole Board, Hearings, November 11–12, 1907, 3–6.

67 Ibid., 18–19.

68 Wood, *The Freedom of the Streets*; Robertson, *Crimes Against Children*.

69 Chauncey, *Gay New York*, 140–41.

70 Greenberg, *The Construction of Homosexuality*, 397–433. Although I found no references to female same-sex crimes or prison activities in parole hearing records, these issues greatly concerned prison superintendents and in-house medical and psychiatric experts by the 1910s. Freedman, "The Prison Lesbian," 397–423.

71 Parole Hearings, July 25, 1910, 25–26.

72 Of the 109 sampled clemency files registered between 1901 and 1920, 7 petitioned the governor on the basis of illnesses (mental and physical) acquired in prison, or on account of the prisoner's imminent death. For further information on factors mentioned in clemency petitions see table 1.

73 Parole Hearings, February 7, 1911, 24–25.

74 John Darwin, Clemency Files, 1901, box 63, file 23; Henry Hedger, Clemency Files, 1907, box 70, file 34; John Murphy, Clemency Files, 1915, box 131, file 36.

75 State of New York, *Public Papers of Charles Seymour Whitman, Governor*, 1917, vol. 3, 576–77.

76 Charles Keyes, Clemency Files, box 133, file 48.

77 State of New York, *Public Papers of Benjamin B. Odell, Jr., Governor for 1903*, vol. 3, 162; State of New York, *Public Papers of Frank W. Higgins, Governor, 1905*, vol. 1, 217.

78 New York State, *Public Papers of Charles Seymour Whitman, 1918*, vol. 4, 348.

79 "An Act to Amend the Penal Code, relative to the Punishment for Murder, *Laws of New York*, 1907, Chapter 738, passed July 25, 1907.

80 The sentences of prisoners serving life sentences for murder in the second degree became indeterminate sentences, with a maximum term of life. State of New York, *Public Papers of Charles Evans Hughes, 1910*, vol. 3, 37.

81 The archival record indicates that Governor Odell commuted Heidt's sentence on May 19, 1904. He did not report it in his published papers, however.

82 Journals of Governors' Actions and Decisions, box 43, volume 2, 590.

83 Parole Hearings, August 12, 1907, 14–18. Hughes did not pardon McNeil.

84 State of New York, *Public Papers of Charles Evans Hughes, 1907*, vol. 1, 302–303. The recommendation that Hahn be released likely came from prison officials, as was often the case with lifers who had lost contact with their families.

85 Governor Flower commuted Parker's sentence on March 7, 1893. He referred to the judge's report that it was unclear which man had fired the fatal shot. In addition, "Most of the witnesses were ignorant and of a low moral standard." State of New York, *Public Papers of Governor Roswell P. Flower, Governor, 1893*, vol. 2, 468.

86 Wilkerson, *The Warmth of Other Suns*, 7–10, 460.

87 Parole Hearings, December 11, 1907, 1–22.

88 State of New York, *Public Papers of Charles Evans Hughes, 1908*, vol. 2, 224.

89 *New York Times*, June 24, 1916. The article also mentioned that Whitman had pardoned John E. Anhut, the lawyer convicted for assisting convicted murderer Harry Thaw escape from Matteawan Prison for the Criminally Insane.

90 State of New York, *Public Papers of Charles Seymour Whitman, 1916*, vol. 2, 359.

91 State of New York, *Public Papers of Charles Seymour Whitman, 1917*, vol. 3, 561–63.

92 Clemency Files, Leonard Darling, box 129, folder 52.

93 New York's Sing Sing State Prison became a national flashpoint for concern over corruption in prison management in the early twentieth century. McLennan, *The Crisis of Imprisonment*, 280–318.

94 PANY, *Report*, 1914, 76. In this year the association judged 1913 the most controversial in state penal politics since its foundation in 1844.

95 A. W. Taylor, review of *Society and Prisons*, 690–91, 691. Osborne posed as a prisoner after Governor William Sulzer appointed him to chair his Commission on Prison Reform in the summer of 1913.

96 For an excellent appraisal of Osborne's downfall in relation to contemporary anxieties over manliness, see Murphy, *Political Manhood*, 161–70.

97 Whitman successfully prosecuted Vice Squad officer Charles Becker in 1914 for his part in a murder tied to a gambling racket. Becker's death sentence was carried out at Sing Sing on July 30, 1915, and the execution remains controversial. Westervelt and Humphrey, *Wrongly Convicted*, 160–61.

98 Three proposed amendments were debated. The third one, for the creation of a state board and the "transfer to it of the pardoning power now vested in the governor," was modified on July 29 to make the proposed board's recommendations subject to the governor's approval, but this watered-down version failed to earn support from the majority of delegates. Proposed Amendments 82 (May 4, 1915), 237 (May 18, 1915), and 272 (May 20, 1915), in *Revised Record of the Constitutional Convention of the State of New York*.

99 Galie and Bopst, *The New York State Constitution*, 29–30. No members of the Progressive Party were delegates, although they helped to defeat the revised constitution when it came up for electoral approval in November 1915. Unfortunately, there is no published record of the debates for this convention.

100 Dix's successor, William Sulzer, investigated this and other "beneficiaries of Dix's Favor" in March 1913, but ultimately found no evidence of malfeasance. "13 Mysterious Cases On Dix's Pardon List," *New York Sun*, January 4, 1913.

101 These figures appeared in a report ordered by the Convention. "Document 12," in New York (State), *Documents of the Constitutional Convention of the State of New York, 1915*, 1–4, 3.

102 "Dix Rivals Blease in Breaking Record For Pardoning Convicts," *New York Tribune*, December 24, 1912. The story also framed Dix with Arkansas governor G. W. Donaghey, who pardoned 360 prisoners on December 23, 1912.

103 Figures from 1911 to 1912 taken from the Espy file.

104 The trial and the multiple appeals dragged the case through the courts for four years, before Governor Higgins commuted his death sentence to life in prison in 1906. Friedland, *The Death of Old Man Rice*.

105 Crossley, "The Pardon of Albert T. Patrick," 675. Former governor David B. Hill argued Patrick's case before the New York Court of Appeals. Papers of David Bennett Hill, box 2, folder 61M89.

106 "Dix Merciful to Many," *New York Tribune*, May 16, 1913.

107 State of New York, *Public Papers of John A. Dix, Governor, 1912*, vol. 2, 384–85.

108 Sulzer's Tammany enemies orchestrated his impeachment later that year over allegations of financial corruption. Lifflander, *The Impeachment of Governor Sulzer*.

109 State of New York, *Public Papers of Charles Seymour Whitman, 1917*, vol. 3, 575. Her name was given as Niva Funnera in this publication.

110 Clemency Files, Funari, 1916, box 137, file 29.

111 State of New York, *Public Papers of Charles Seymour Whitman, 1916*, vol. 2, 339.

112 In debating the responsibilities of the governor, Republican William S. Ostrander claimed Governor Whitman had 1,300 pardon petitions pending: "they are up in the pigeon holes. The Governor has never had time to look at them." *Revised Record of the Constitutional Convention*, vol. 3, 3360.

113 Henderson, *Prison Reform*, vol. 1, 145–49.

114 State of New York, *Public Papers of Charles Seymour Whitman, 1918*, vol. 4, 266–67.

CHAPTER 7. THE CRIME WAVE AND THE WAR AGAINST DISCRE-
TIONARY JUSTICE IN THE 1920S

1 Stoke, "A Review of the Pardoning Power," 34–37, 36. Stoke based his conclusion on data from Illinois, Indiana, Kentucky, Ohio, Missouri, and Tennessee.

2 P. S. Ruckman Jr. faults Stoke on his small sample size of states; however, Stoke's contemporaries agreed that parole was the greater problem by the late 1920s. See Ruckman, "The Study of Mercy," 783–837, 797–98.

3 Stoke, "A Review of the Pardoning Power," 36–37.

4 In New York City the postwar jump in homicides was greater after World War I than after any other. Monkkonen, *Murder in New York City*, 18–19.

5 "County Judge Deaf to Clemency Pleas; Imposes 25 Years," *Brooklyn Daily Eagle*, January 10, 1922. The term was used by Brooklyn Judge Reuben L. Haskell in sentencing hold-up men and violent robbers. On the rise of prohibition, see Hamm, *Shaping the Eighteenth Amendment*. On New York see Lerner, *Dry Manhattan*.

6 A lawyer who addressed the Medico-Legal Society of New York stated, "there is no crime wave," but simply an increase in young men's use of guns, "owing to the use of firearms in the army." "Measures Proposed to Check Crime Wave," *New York Times*, January 12, 1922.

7 Blomberg and Mestre, "Net-Widening," 573–77.

8 Lindsey, "Historical Sketch of the Indeterminate Sentence and Parole System," 1–69, 18–21.

9 A 1931 review of modern penal institutions in the United States referred to New York as a leader. Robinson, "Institutions for Defective Delinquents," 352–99.

10 Thomas G. Blomberg, foreword to Rothman, *Conscience and Convenience*, xi. For the most influential work in this vein see Rafter, *Creating Born Criminals*, 202–29. On the promise of parole on condition of sterilization see Kline, *Building a Better Race*, 81–85.

11 On psychiatric influence over parole decisions see Garton, "Criminal Propensities: Psychiatry, Classification and Imprisonment in New York State 1916–1940," 79–97.

12 Campbell, "African Americans and Parole in Depression-Era New York," 1065–86. The Division made concerted attempts to service African American parolees for the first time in the 1930s.

13 Hay, "Writing about the Death Penalty," 35–52, 47–8.

14 "Receives all Callers, Rich and Poor Alike," *New York Tribune*, January 12, 1919. On Smith's appeal to the humble, see Finan, *Alfred E. Smith*, 116–18. On Smith's own humble beginnings, see Pringle, *Alfred E. Smith*, 107–24.

15 See appendix, table 1.

16 Figures taken from the Espy file. Espy and Smykla, *Executions in the United States, 1608–2002*.

17 PANY, *Report*, 1921, 23; 24–5.

18 "Prisons Scandal is First Problem for Gov. Smith. Making Plans for Full Inquiry into System and 'Graft' Stories," *New York Evening World*, January 3, 1919.

19 State of New York, *Report of the Prison Survey Committee*, 256 (hereafter *Prison Survey Report*), 7, 250.

20 Ibid., 263.

21 *Rochester Democrat and Chronicle*, October 21, 1920.

22 *Prison Survey Report*, 256.

23 "Smith Defends his Pardon Record," *New York Evening World*, October 20, 1920.

24 "Michael Rost," Executive Clemency and Pardon Case Files, 1859–1926, NYSA, A0597, box 165, file 52, 1873 (hereafter Clemency Files). File dates refer to the year in which clemency pleas were first officially registered.

25 Smith, *Up to Now—An Autobiography*, 173.

26 Miller, born in 1868, was a lawyer from Cortland County who was appointed to the state supreme court in 1904, later serving on the New York Court of Appeals in 1913 for two years. Case, "Miller, Nathan L(ewis)," 985–86.

27 Republican assemblyman Charles H. Betts tabled two bills on January 19, 1922: one to transfer the power of clemency through a constitutional amendment and the other to abolish the death penalty.

28 "Governor Sees Crime Wave Due to 'Living Fast,'" *New York Times*, January 20, 1922.

29 The final statement was the reporter's, which elicited Miller's claim to hard-heartedness. Ibid.

30 Moley, *An Outline of the Cleveland Crime Survey*, 57. Within one month in 1919, Moley (who held a PhD in political science from Columbia University) found that the amount of crime coverage in Cleveland had increased sevenfold, while the rate of crime remained steady.

31 Miller, *Supreme City*.

32 Hastings to Miller, January 11, 1922; January 15, 1922, in Papers of Governor Nathan L. Miller (hereafter Miller Papers), box 14, file 150–586.

33 "Miller Defends Parole Board. Governors Says Commodore Hastings was Hasty in Criticizing Release of Criminals," *New York Times*, January 15, 1922.

34 Miller to George W. Benham, January 17, 1922, Miller Papers, box 14, file 150–586.

35 Ibid. The Parole Board's defense was published by the *Times* the day after Hastings sent his January 11 letter to the press. The *Times* published a verbatim excerpt in this report on Miller's response.

36 Miller to George W. Benham, January 17, 1922, Miller Papers. Benham was the board's chairman and a fellow Republican.

37 Rothman, *Conscience and Convenience*.

38 Helen Leland Witmer, a social worker and statistician, published several land-mark articles on parole in this period when she was an assistant professor of sociology at the University of Minnesota: "The Development of Parole in the United States," "The History, Theory and Results of Parole," and "Some Factors in Success or Failure on Parole."

39 PANY, *Report*, 1917, 72.

40 PANY, *Report*, 1917, 136, 79.

41 Cass, *A Study of Parole Laws and Methods in the United States*, 3.

42 Ibid., 8.

43 Simon, *Poor Discipline*, 48.

44 Division of Parole, Auburn Prison Inmate Parole Files (hereafter Parole Files), box 2, Smith.

45 "Only 16 States Lynching-Free in Last Ten Years," *New York Herald*, February 6, 1923. The Federal Council of Churches of Christ carried out the report cited in the article. For a study of lynching directed against the historiographical focus on the South see Pfeifer, "Introduction," in *Lynching Beyond Dixie*, 1–12.

46 Parole Files, Smith, 1923.

47 Platt, "The Volunteers of America," 35–50. Booth was a member of Salvation Army's founding family. The Volunteers separated from the Army in 1896, but both organizations assisted prospective parolees.

48 Parole Hearing Records, October 25, 1921.

49 Reverend Thomas J. Lynch of the Catholic Protective Society of the Archdiocese of New York became supervisor of corrective work in the 1910s and was a trusted associate of the state system by the 1920s.

50 Referees were expected to attest that they had known an applicant for at least three years prior to his or her arrest.

51 Parole Files, box 2, no. 35830.

52 "Dr. Larkin on Parole Board," *Adirondack Record*, May 4, 1917. Larkin replaced sixty-eight-year-old William Townsend, a lawyer and Democratic ex-state senator who had been appointed by Governor Dix.

53 Parole Hearings, Corprew, October 29, 1920, 2; Butts, April 1920, 12; Susi, December 19, 1921, n.p.

54 Parole Hearings, Fronce, November 19, 1919, 2–3.

55 Parole Files, Reisinger, box 1.

56 Reisinger was apprehended in 1929, declared a delinquent, and made to serve out his maximum term at Sing Sing. Parole Files, Reisinger, box 1.

57 PANY, *Report*, 1926, 12.

58 "Would Fortify Stores and Oust Parole Board to Halt Crime Rise Here," *Brooklyn Daily Eagle*, January 11, 1925. This front-page story quoted County Court Judge Franklin Taylor, who considered the Parole Board "well-meaning but foolish."

59 Larkin, *James Larkin*.

60 "Smith Pardons Four Anarchists," *Kingston Daily Freeman*, February 13, 1923.

61 Lusk headed a joint committee of the legislature, established in 1919, to investigate individuals and organizations suspected of "seditious" activities. It used the criminal anarchy law, passed in 1902 after President McKinley's assassination, to prosecute left-wing groups and immigrants. Bennett, *The Party of Fear*, 193–96.

62 "Condemns Smith for Pardoning of Irish Agitator," *Times Herald*, January 18, 1923.

63 *Brooklyn Daily Eagle*, December 27, 1925.

64 Gitlow was a Bronx assemblyman, first elected as a Socialist in 1918. He was arrested in 1919 for publishing and distributing *The Revolutionary Age*.

65 Gitlow spent two years at Sing Sing, from 1920 to 1922, before his release on a writ of habeas corpus. When the Supreme Court upheld his conviction on June 8, 1925, he was sent back to prison. Gitlow, *I Confess*.

66 *Brooklyn Daily Eagle*, December 27, 1925.

67 "Gary in Body to Fight Crime. Leading Men Band to Study Situation—Are Alarmed at Existing Conditions," *New York Times*, July 29, 1925. Elbert H. Gary was also referred to as a judge, after having served two terms as a county court judge in the late nineteenth century. Olds, *Judge Elbert H. Gary (1846–1927)*.

68 Eric H. Monkkonen argues that the turn to crime commissions in the 1920s marked the origins of the rise of a "crime control" model of policing. *Crime, Justice, History*, 180.

69 At the time of Smith's meeting with Gary, Senator Baumes chaired the Joint Legislative Committee with oversight of the state's Penal Code.

70 On Smith's capacity to shepherd prison reform despite dealing with Republican majorities, see Colburn, "Governor Alfred E. Smith and Penal Reform," 315–27.

71 "Clayton Indorses Gov. Smith's Plan for a Crime Board," *Brooklyn Daily Eagle*, August 2, 1925. Like many Republicans, Clayton thought the Parole Board should be abolished or made to work "in favor of the average citizen instead of the criminal and law-breaker."

72 Twenty-nine of fifty-one senators in 1926 were Republicans. The legislature approved $50,000 to fund the commission's operation in May 1926. Stolberg, *Fighting Organized Crime*, 101–2.

73 The senate sponsor of the bill was John Knight, a former district attorney of Wyoming County, and sitting president of the state senate. In 1931 President Hoover appointed him to the U.S. District Court for the Western District of New York.

74 F. Trubee Davison Papers, series 1, box 6, folder 104. Davison chaired the President's Commission from 1925 to 1927. He was a Brooklyn assemblyman from 1922–26.

75 "State Senate gets Bill to End Bail Evil!" *Brooklyn Daily Eagle*, March 9, 1926.

76 Davison's bill was inspired, in part, by the work of the Missouri Association for Criminal Justice, formed in 1925. Moley, *The Administration of Justice in Missouri*.

77 On April 1 alone the state senate passed five bills recommended by the Baumes report, including increasing the term for burglary from ten to fifteen years and abolishing bail for second offenders and criminals who used firearms.

78 The Crime Commission was established through Chapter 460 of the Laws of 1926. The appointees were announced on May 18, 1926.

79 Contemporaries regarded the new commission and its head as models for the nation. Moley, *State Crime Commissions*. Baumes was appointed on May 21, 1926.

80 "The First Step in a United Move to Check Crime," *Oneonta Daily Star*, March 2, 1926.

81 Appointed in November 1925, Hughes assigned PANY executive member and former Attorney General George W. Wickersham to oversee recommendations concerning "correction." State of New York, *Report of the State Reorganization Commission*, 4, 57–61. On the wider context of administrative rationalization, see Maxwell, "The Executive Branch," 384–400, 392–93.

82 Colburn, "Governor Alfred E. Smith and Penal Reform," 315–27. A front-page editorial in the *Brooklyn Daily Eagle*, August 13, 1925, by the *Eagle's* Sunday magazine editor, Frederick Boyd Stevenson, called for a major overhaul of parole and pardoning. The heading of this section ("To subdue crime we must have a whale of shakeup!") was the title of Stevenson's editorial.

83 Smith quoted his letter verbatim in his public papers. State of New York, *Public Papers of Alfred E. Smith, Governor of New York, 1923–1928, 1926*, vol. 4 (Albany: J. B. Lyon, 1938), 514.

84 "Parole Board's Fall Seen as Smith Backs Eagle Presser Probe," *Brooklyn Daily Eagle*, May 1, 1926.

85 The Committee included Adolph Lewisohn, a member of the National Committee on Prisons and Prison Labor. Ingham, *Biographical Dictionary of American Business Leaders*, vol. 2, 792–93.

86 Kirchwey to Smith, May 18, 1926, in Papers of Alfred E. Smith, box 65. From 1901 to 1910 Kirchwey served as dean of the Columbia University Law School. He wrote to Smith on letterhead from the Department of Criminology, which at that time was within the university's School of Social Work.

87 Wiebe, *The Search for Order, 1877–1920*, foreword by David Herbert Donald, xiv. Wiebe's work was a riposte to Richard Hofstadter's view that reform was driven by status anxiety. See his *The Age of Reform, from Bryan to F.D.R.*

88 In 1913 Alger (1872–1967) published a call for judicial reform along business models of efficiency and accountability in *The Old Law and the New Order*. On Alger as a prototypical Progressive see Ross, *A Muted Fury*, 77–78.

89 Alger was also involved in the enforcement of anti-vice laws. Mackey, *Pursuing Johns*, 111–23.

90 Alger, *Report of George W. Alger Commissioner*.

91 Ibid., 18.

92 George Fisher, *Plea Bargaining's Triumph*, 186–89. Fisher focuses on the relation between probation, parole, indeterminate sentencing, and plea bargaining.

93 "Investigation of the Board of Parole and Prison Department of the State of New York, Stenographer's Minutes," June 11, 1926, Papers of Alfred E. Smith, box 65, file 13682–53A.

94 In 1910 Benham chaired the prison discipline committee of the American Prison Association and presented a paper on the improvement of prison conditions at the joint meeting of the American and International Prison Associations, held in Washington, DC. Brown, *History of the State of New York. Political and Governmental*, vol. 4, 313.

95 Alger, *Report of George W. Alger*, 9, 21.

96 New York City already had a Department of Correction supervised by its own commissioner of correction, appointed by the mayor. PANY, *Reports*, 1926, 103.

97 This prison opened in 1892, receiving inmates formerly held at the State Asylum for Insane Convicts at Auburn, where Frank Walworth was imprisoned.

98 For a superb study of the case, which involved a love triangle between prominent architect White, Thaw, a volatile millionaire, and Thaw's wife, chorus girl Evelyn Nesbit, see Umphrey, "The Trouble with Harry Thaw," 9–23.

99 "Saw Pardon Ring in Thaw Bribery," *New York Times*, February 25, 1913. See also Lifflander, *The Impeachment of Governor Sulzer*, 188–91.

100 "Dr. Raymond F. C. Kieb Appointed Head of Department of Correction," *Psychiatric Quarterly* 1, no. 2 (1927), 258.

101 PANY, *Annual Report,* 1928, 17. This report also congratulated Edward R. Cass for his election as president of the American Prison Association.

102 Nourse, "Rethinking Crime Legislation: History and Harshness," 925–39, 930. Between 1920 and 1945, more than twenty states passed life-sentence statutes for repeat felony offenders.

103 Cass, "Legislation in 1926," 92–99, 96–98. These laws came into effect in July 1926.

104 "Investigation of the Board of Parole," 410, 414–15.

105 The state election was held on November 2, 1926, and returned a majority of Republicans to the assembly and senate.

106 Leading criminologists favored this proposal. Glueck, "Principles of a Rational Penal Code," 453–82.

107 Police Department of New York, *Annual Report, 1927,* 59. The officers who arrested the "notorious criminal" were given a commendation.

108 Prior to the election the Republicans accused Smith of pardoning to secure votes. "Attacks Gov. Smith on Pardon Record. Morris says he restored 663 Criminals to Citizenship to Make Tammany Voters," *New York Times,* October 4, 1926. George K. Morris was chairman of the Republican State Committee. Rodgers began a life sentence as a repeat offender on December 7, 1926.

109 "Calls upon Morris to Make Known Who Is Responsible for 'Absurd' Attacks on his Policy," *Cornell Daily Sun,* December 8, 1926. Senator Lafayette B. Gleason, secretary of the Republican State Committee from 1906, led the partisan attack. "Gleason Disputes Smith on Pardons; Republican Data 'Not Absurd' He Says," *New York Times,* December 20, 1926.

110 Mackey, *Pursuing Johns,* 77, 157–69. From the 1910s, Veiller became a "propagandist and lobbyist" who advised Governor Hughes and submitted draft legislation on behalf of legislators. Wesser, *Charles Evans Hughes,* 160, 324.

111 David, *Spearheads for Reform,* 67–68.

112 Alfred E. Smith to Arthur W. Page, editor of *World's Work,* March 11, 1927, Papers of Alfred E. Smith, box 65.

113 State of New York, *Public Papers of Alfred E. Smith, Governor, 1919–1920,* vol. 2, 550.

114 Alfred E. Smith to Lawrence Veiller, March 11, 1927. Smith likely knew Veiller personally, and he appeared disappointed in him: "If you desired to write such an article, you knew where to get the right information." Papers of Alfred E. Smith, box 65.

115 Editorial, *Brooklyn Daily Eagle,* March 22, 1927.

116 Mary Farmer, an Irish immigrant, was convicted of murdering a female neighbor for gain. Gillespie, *Executed Women of the 20th and 21st Centuries,* 23–24.

117 Late in 1927 the tabloid press conducted polls and contests for proponents and opponents of the execution. The *New York Daily News* asked readers: "'What would *you* do if *you* were Governor?" MacKellar, *The "Double Indemnity" Murder,* 273.

118 Three lawyers attended the hearing on Snyder's behalf: Edgar F. Hazleton, Dana Wallace, and Joseph Lonardo.

119 "Looks Like Chair for Mrs. Snyder and Gray," *Olean Times Herald,* January 5, 1928.

120 Alfred E. Smith, *Up to Now—An Autobiography*, 310. Smith's conscience might have pricked after he lost the election to Herbert Hoover: "Probably the hardest time a governor has had in recent years came to me in the period of two weeks before and the night of the execution of Mrs. Snyder." Ibid.

121 "Gets Life Sentence under Baumes Law," *New York Times*, August 21, 1926. The subtitle referred to others in the same situation: "They Have No Hope of Parole, But Governor Can Pardon Them."

122 "49 Baumes 'Lifers' in Sing Sing," *Brooklyn Daily Eagle*, November 18, 1927. The prison received offenders from New York City, not New York State's western or northern regions.

123 Segrave, *Shoplifting*, 35. Segrave identifies department stores as leading supporters of harsher penalties for shoplifters in the 1920s.

124 "Shoplifter, Sentenced for Life, Tells Story," *Ogden (NY) Standard-Examiner*, February 23, 1930. St. Clair's case garnered nationwide coverage, aided by the fact that she fit the flapper image—white, bob-haired, attractive—and had worked in vaudeville.

125 One journalist who specialized in legal affairs commented that for judges the laws "virtually make justified leniency impossible." Levy, "Judges and the Legislature," 557–62, 559.

126 Kenneth Sydney Davis, *FDR: The Beckoning of Destiny, 1882–1928: A History*, vol. 1, 791–92.

127 Kenneth Sydney Davis, *FDR: The New York Years, 1928–1933*, vol. 2; Bellush, *Franklin D. Roosevelt as Governor of New York*.

128 Freidel, *Franklin Roosevelt*, 59–61.

129 Moley's *State Crime Commissions* (1926) was published by the National Crime Commission, but it focused on the formation of the New York commission that year.

130 Domhoff, *The Power Elite and the State*, 47. The journal *Prison World* honored Lewisohn at his death in 1951 for his contributions to "the field of correction." *Sam A. Lewisohn, 1884–1951* (Stamford, CT: Overbrook Press, 1951), 30–32, 30.

131 Leavitt, *American Women Managers*, 117. Another woman, Molly Dawson, was a superintendent of parole at the Massachusetts State Industrial School for Girls before becoming an operative in the Democratic Party. She served on FDR's reelection campaign in 1930. Davis, *FDR*, vol. 1, 65.

132 "State Prisons Reach Capacity. Longer Sentences and Fewer Paroles Have Filled the Institutions to Overflowing," *New York Times*, April 10, 1927.

133 "State of New York Department of Correction Report—Growth in Inmate Population, Proposed Additions, and Alterations. Correctional Institutions—November 1929. R. F. C. Kieb, M.D. Commissioner." Typescript report, Papers of Franklin Roosevelt, box, 59, New York State Archives.

134 New York State Crime Commission, Executive Chamber, December 7, 1927, Minutes, box 63, folder 200–506–1, Papers of Alfred E. Smith—Baumes Commission Part II. These typescript minutes record Smith's response to the commissioners' questions, which followed his prepared presentation.

135 McLennan, *The Crisis of Imprisonment*, 456.

136 One guard and an inmate were killed in this riot, with four guards shot. One convict serving a twenty-year term (Henry Sullivan) was also killed. In the first riot at Clinton on July 22, three prisoners were killed and twenty injured. On July 24, two prisoners were killed in the riot at Auburn.

137 *Albany Evening News*, July 29, 1929; *Brooklyn Daily Eagle*, September 23, 1929. The national press also covered the outbreak, connecting it to mandatory sentencing.

138 State of New York, *Public Papers of Franklin D. Roosevelt, Governor, Forty-eighth Governor of the State of New York, 1929–1932, 1930*, vol. 1, 470.

139 Frederick Boyd Stevenson, editorial, *Brooklyn Daily Eagle*, September 24, 1929. Stevenson claimed that not even former Governor Smith, "who was quite liberal with pardons and commutations," showed "executive clemency to fourth offenders."

140 Spillane, *Coxsackie*, 44.

141 Warden Jennings of Auburn, who resigned after the riot, blamed the Baumes laws for creating "desperate prisoners." "Jennings Foresaw Mutiny at Auburn," *New York Times*, January 31, 1930. Many news editors agreed. *Time* magazine referred to the "fierce despair" of "life-time felons." "Prisons and Power," *Time*, January 13, 1930.

142 James B. Hill, associate justice of the New York State Supreme Court, Appellate Division, to Roosevelt, September 24, 1929, Papers of Franklin D. Roosevelt, box 10.

143 "State Prisons Reach Capacity," *New York Times*, April 27, 1927. The article also pointed to the high cost of maintaining aging prisons.

144 PANY, *Report*, 1939, 40–41. On December 13 the board of directors of the National Society of Penal Information also called on Roosevelt to sack Kieb, on the grounds that he would be unable to carry out the governor's plans to modernize the prison system.

145 "Governor Proposes New Type of Prison," *New York Times*, November 13, 1929. Roosevelt made this announcement at the meeting of the New York State Federation of Women's Clubs meeting.

146 Franklin Roosevelt to Samuel A. Lewisohn, January 6, 1930. Lewisohn wrote to Roosevelt on December 31, to commend his proposal for a parole court and hoped it would be "prestigious and command the respect of prisoners and the public." Papers of Franklin D. Roosevelt, box 161.

147 Special Committee on Parole Problem, *Report of Special Committee on the Parole Problem* (New York, 1930). John S. Kennedy, a Republican telephone executive, was vice chairman of the State Commission of Correction; Edwin J. Cooley, chief probation officer of greater New York City, was the author of *Probation and Delinquency*.

148 Rothman, *Conscience and Convenience*, 181. Rothman incorrectly identifies the committee chair as Alfred Lewisohn.

149 Special Committee on Parole Problem, *Report*, 22, 24–25, 34.

150 Papers of Franklin D. Roosevelt, box 151.
151 Caleb Baumes to Sam Lewisohn, February 3, 1930; Franklin Roosevelt to Caleb Baumes, February 6, 1930, Papers of Franklin D. Roosevelt, box 151. Baumes indicated he was "anxious to meet [the governor] and go over the Parole Board matter with [him], face to face."
152 Special Committee on Parole Problem, *Report*, 10.
153 Ibid., 23, 36.
154 George W. Alger to Franklin Roosevelt, February 25, 1930, box 151, Papers of Franklin D. Roosevelt.
155 *Laws of New York* (1930), Chapter 824, §116.
156 Samuel A. Lewisohn to Franklin Roosevelt, January 13, 1930, Papers of Franklin D. Roosevelt, box 151.
157 On the same day that New York passed the new parole bill, University of Chicago sociologist Ernest W. Burgess published an article in which he advocated a "scientific board of pardons" made up of experts and "socially minded citizens." Burgess, "Cure for Parole Evils."
158 Walker, *Popular Justice*, 152–55.

EPILOGUE
1 Chadwick, *Bureaucratic Mercy*; Hall, *The Magic Mirror*, 211–35.
2 Campaign Address, Rochester, 21 October 1930, in Roosevelt and Rosenman, *The Public Papers and Addresses of Franklin D. Roosevelt*, vol. 1, *The Genesis of the New Deal*, 415.
3 Lanne, "Parole Prediction as Science," 377–400, 392. He coded church attendance simply as "regular" or "irregular."
4 Cass, "Parole Can be Successful (Five Year Study—New York)," 7–13. In 1962, the American Correctional Association named its highest award after Cass in recognition of his forty-year service as its general secretary.
5 The first federal review of law enforcement, known as the Wickersham Commission, reported in 1931 but had little influence over policy. Calder, "Between Brain and State," 1035–1108.
6 Hoover forwarded to Attorney General Cummings a clipping from a *Chicago Daily News* editorial of November 13, 1936, which made this claim. United States Attorney General, "Records of the Attorney General's Survey of Release Procedures—Correspondence with State Officials and Professional Organizations, Jan 1936–May 1938." National Archives and Records Administration, RG 60, Box 1 (hereafter Attorney General, *Records of Survey*).
7 United States Attorney General, *Attorney General's Survey of Release Procedures*. The volumes were published over three years, from 1938 to 1940.
8 Justin Miller to Frederick A. Moran, December 12, 1936, in Attorney General, *Records of Survey*, box 1. Miller was the first administrative director of the survey. He was also chairman of the federal Attorney General's Advisory Committee on Crime.

9 New York State, Division of Parole, *Annual Report of the Division of Parole of the Executive Department, 1931*, 13.

10 New York State, *New York State Governor's Conference on Crime, the Criminal and Society, Proceedings*, 201 (hereafter *Conference on Crime*).

11 Division of Parole, *Annual Report*, 1931, 13.

12 Heller, "Death Becomes the State," 589–615.

13 Harriman and Bloom, "Mercy Is a Lonely Business," 24, 25, 82, 83, 84.

14 United States Attorney General, *Survey of Release Procedures*, vol. 3 (1939), 52–53.

15 New York State, *Conference on Crime*, 262–64.

16 Baatz, *For the Thrill of It*, 507, n37. The pseudonym is likely a play on Ferris F. Laune, whom the Sociological Research Office at Joliet employed while he conducted his doctoral dissertation research on parole prediction in the mid-1930s. Leopold, *Life Plus 99 Years*, 252–160; 261.

17 Clarence Darrow successfully argued that Leopold's interpretation of the superman notion developed into a personality disorder, which likely saved him and his co-accused from the death penalty. Higdon, *Leopold and Loeb*, 209–12.

18 Alger, "What's the Matter with Parole?," 269–75, 273, 275.

19 Lieber, Petition to His Majesty the King of Prussia, November 10, 1841, Box 19, Papers of Francis Lieber, Huntington Library.

20 Most advocates of gubernatorial pardons to rectify unduly harsh punishment highlight the racialized impact of overincarceration. See, for instance, Martin, "Pardons Are One Remedy for our Excessively Punitive System." For a broader endorsement of mercy's capacity to enhance the credibility of criminal justice, see Austin Sarat, "When Can or Should Legal Judgment Be Merciful? An Introduction," in Sarat, *Merciful Judgments and Contemporary Society*, 1–18.

NOTE ON SOURCES

1 Lincoln, *State of New York, Messages from the Governors*. Lincoln, a lawyer, acted as legal adviser to Governors Morton, Black, and Theodore Roosevelt. Governor Higgins appointed him in 1905 to edit the messages. Brown, *History of the State of New York, Political and Governmental*, vol. 3, 407.

2 Chadwick, *Bureaucratic Mercy*.

3 There is a gap in the years the registers cover, from 1845–1855. For a full explanation of the record holdings (B0042–79) see the "Guide to Records of the Governor's Office," accessible at http://www.archives.nysed.gov.

4 Journals of governors' actions and decisions, NYSA, A0607. These ledgers contain daily entries, including decisions concerning clemency petitions.

5 NYSA, executive clemency and pardon case files, A0597.

6 I worked closely with two assistants, who read approximately half of the files (mainly from the nineteenth century) and took images of key documents in each case. We conducted regular meetings to review notes, and we developed a typology of grounds for commutation, based on the dominant justifications in the petitions. I reviewed all the document images in the assistants' files and standardized all notes.

7 The New York State Archives collection of petitions filed from 1859 to 1900 includes the cases of 109 women (4.1 percent of the total of 2,644 files). My sampling technique produced the files of 16 women (6.3 percent of the sampled files) over that period.

8 From 1901 to 1926 the collection includes 171 files pertaining to women's cases (3.1 percent of the total of 5,477). My sample includes 7 women's files (5 percent of the sampled files) over that period.

9 The governor's staff seems to have established a filing system in 1897 to track restorations of citizenship for prisoners earlier pardoned or offenders who had completed their sentences. From 1897 to 1923, governors granted 1,201 restorations of citizenship for offenses ranging from being a common gambler to manslaughter (57 cases) and murder (23 cases). NYSA, B2079. I am grateful to Monica Gray, who provided me with the database of the names of these offenders, the year of the restoration granted, the prison in which they served their sentence, their offense, and the county in which they were convicted.

10 The Espy file has been cleaned and updated but still contains flaws and gaps. Espy and Smykla, *Executions in the United States, 1608–2002*. On its shortcomings, see Blackman and McLaughlin, "The Espy File on American Executions: User Beware," 209–27. Daniel Allen Hearn provides short descriptions of cases, some of which do not appear in the Espy file, in his *Legal Executions in New York*. On the limitations that continue to hamper research on the death penalty's history see Allen and Clubb, with Lacey, *Race, Class and the Death Penalty*, 191–204.

11 King examined every judge's report and the accompanying petition in criminal cases from 1787–90, and "counted each occasion on which any factor is mentioned either in favor of or against the prisoner." King, "Decision-Makers and Decision-Making in the English Criminal Law, 1750–1800," 25–58, 44.

12 King, *Crime, Justice and Discretion in England, 1740–1820*, 297.

13 For another study that applies King's method, see Palk, *Gender Crime and Judicial Discretion*, 140–41. Most American historians have concentrated on the demographic status of offenders (race, age, gender), and victim-offender relations, to explain why certain cohorts have been denied clemency. See, for instance, Acker, Harmon, and Rivera, "Merciful Justice: Lessons from 50 Years of New York Death Penalty Commutations," 183–99.

SELECTED BIBLIOGRAPHY

UNPUBLISHED PRIMARY SOURCES AND DATABASES

Archival Records and Manuscript Collections

NEW YORK STATE ARCHIVES AND LIBRARY

B1201. Name Index to Executive Pardons, Respites, Commutations, Restorations of Citizenship and Certificates of Good Conduct, 1799–1930.

B0042–79. Journals of Executive Pardons, 1799–1846, 1856–1931.

B0049–78. Executive Orders for Commutations, Pardons, Restorations, and Respites, 1840–1920, 1924–1929.

B0048. Respites and Commutations, 1854–1931.

A0607. Journals of Governors' Actions and Decisions, 1859–1938.

A0597. Executive Clemency and Pardon Case Files, 1859–1926.

B0082–77. Division of Parole. Auburn Prison Inmate Parole Files, 1918–1930.

B0050. Division of Parole. Auburn Prison Female Inmate Case Files, 1920–1930.

B0076–77. Minutes of Meetings of the Board of Parole, 1905–1930.

B0075. Parole Board Register of Inmates Paroled, 1889–1926.

B0060. Register of Commutations for Female Inmates, 1920–1930.

B0064. Parole Board Ledgers of Applicants to be Considered for Parole, 1924–1935.

B0136–80. New York Reformatory Biographical Register of Parole Violators, 1913–1937.

Manuscript series 13682–53A, Papers of Alfred E. Smith.

Manuscript series 13683–82A, Papers of Franklin Roosevelt.

Manuscript series 13682–78B, Papers of Governor Nathan L. Miller.

Manuscript series S514, Papers of William H. Seward, New York State Library.

LIBRARY OF CONGRESS

Mss 20602, Papers of Hamilton Fish.

NEW YORK PUBLIC LIBRARY

MssCol 1396, Papers of David Bennett Hill.

MssCol 2993, Papers of Samuel J. Tilden.

HUNTINGTON LIBRARY

MssLI-5222. Papers of Francis Lieber.

COLUMBIA UNIVERSITY LIBRARY

Clinton, DeWitt. "DeWitt Clinton Papers." Microfilm, vol. 24, mfm. reel 6.

Jay, John. Papers of John Jay, Columbia University Libraries Digital Library Collections. https://dlc.library.columbia.edu.

YALE UNIVERSITY LIBRARY
MX601. F. Trubee Davison Papers.

UNIVERSITY OF ROCHESTER
A.S51. Seward, William Henry. "William Henry Seward Papers." University of Rochester, boxes 48–58.

PUBLISHED PRIMARY SOURCES
Laws of the State of New York, retrieved from *Manhattan Past*. http://www.manhattanpast.com.

Governors' Public Papers
Hastings, Hugh, ed. *Public Papers of George Clinton, First Governor of New York*. 10 vols. Albany Wynkoop Hallenbeck Crawford Co. 1899–1914.
Hastings, Hugh, ed., *Public Papers of Daniel D. Tompkins, Governor of New York, 1807–17: Military*, vols. 1–3. Albany: J. B. Lyon, 1904.
New York. *Public Papers of John T. Hoffman, Governor of New York, 1869–1872*. Albany: J. Munsell, 1872.
New York. *Public Papers of Lucius Robinson, Governor of the State of New York*, vols. 1–3. Albany: Jerome B. Parmenter, 1877.
New York. *Public Papers of Alonzo B. Cornell, Governor of the State of New York, 1880–1882*, vols. 1–3. Albany: E. H. Bender, 1882.
New York. *Public Papers of Grover Cleveland, Governor of New York, 1883–4*, vols. 1–2. Albany: Argus, 1884.
New York. *Public Papers of David B. Hill, Governor, 1885–91*, vols. 1–7. Albany: Argus, 1885–1891.
New York. *Public Papers of Roswell P. Flower, Governor, 1892–1894*, vols. 1–3. Albany: Argus, 1894.
New York. *Public Papers of Levi P. Morton, Governor, 1895–1896*, vols. 1–2. Albany: Weed-Parsons, 1896.
New York. *Public Papers of Frank S. Black, Governor, 1897–1898*, vols. 1–2. Albany: Brandow Printing, 1898.
New York. *Public Papers of Theodore Roosevelt, Governor*, vols. 1–2. Albany: Brandow Printing, 1900.
New York. *Public Papers of Benjamin B. Odell, Jr. Governor for 1901–1904*, vols. 1–4. Albany: J. B. Lyon, 1907.
New York. *Public Papers of Frank W. Higgins, Governor, 1905–6*, vols. 1–2. Albany: J. B. Lyon, 1907.
New York. *Public Papers of Charles E. Hughes, Governor of New York, 1907–1910*, vols. 1–4. Albany: J. B. Lyon, 1908–1910.
New York. *Public Papers of Horace White, Governor of New York, 1910*. Albany: J. B. Lyon, 1911.
New York. *Public Papers of John A. Dix, Governor, 1911–1912*, vols. 1–2. Albany: J. B. Lyon, 1912–13.

New York. *Public Papers of William Sulzer, Governor: January 1 to October 17, 1913.* Albany: 1914.

New York. *Public Papers of Martin H. Glynn, Governor, 1913–1914.* Albany: J. B. Lyon, 1925.

New York. *Public Papers of Charles Seymour Whitman, Governor, 1915–1918,* vols. 1–4. Albany: J. B. Lyon, 1916–1919.

New York. *Public Papers of Nathan L. Miller, Forty-Sixth Governor of the State of New York, 1921–1922,* vols. 1–2. Albany: J. B. Lyon, 1924.

New York. *Public Papers of Alfred E. Smith, Governor, 1919–1920,* vols. 1–2. Albany: J. B. Lyon, 1920.

New York. *Public Papers of Alfred E. Smith, Governor, Forty-seventh Governor of the State of New York, fourth term, 1928.* Albany: J. B. Lyon, 1938.

New York. *Public Papers of Franklin D. Roosevelt, Forty-eighth Governor of the State of New York, 1929–1932,* vols. 1–4. Albany: J. B. Lyon, 1932.

Newspaper Databases

Chronicling America: Historic American Newspapers, retrieved from http://chroniclingamerica.loc.gov.

Newspapers.com, retrieved from https://www.newspapers.com.

New York State Historic Newspapers, retrieved from http://nyshistoricnewspapers.org.

Nineteenth Century U.S. Newspapers (Gale Group).

Old Fulton NY Post Cards, retrieved from http://www.fultonhistory.com.

Proquest Historical Newspapers.

OTHER PUBLISHED PRIMARY SOURCES

Alger, George William. *The Old Law and the New Order.* New York: Houghton Mifflin, 1913.

Alger, George William. *Report of George W. Alger Commissioner under the Executive Law on the Board of Parole and Parole System and the State Prisons and State Reformatories of the State of New York.* Albany: J. B. Lyon, 1926.

Alger, George W. "What's the Matter with Parole?" *Atlantic Monthly* (March 1936): 269–75.

American Prison Association. *Proceedings of the Congress of the American Prison Association.* New York: American Prison Association, 1922.

Assembly of the State of New York. *Documents of the Assembly of the State of New-York, Seventy-Fifth Session. 1852. No. 81 to No. 125, Inclusive.* Albany: C. Van Benthuysen, 1852.

Assembly of the State of New York. *Journal of the Assembly of the State of New York at their Forty-Seventh Session.* Albany: Leake and Croswell, 1824.

Baillie, James. S. *The Hurly-Burly Pot.* New York: James Baillie, 1850.

Barnes, Harry Elmer. "Some Leading Phases of the Evolution of Modern Penology." *Political Science Quarterly* 37, no. 2 (June 1922): 251–80.

Barnett, James D. "The Grounds of Pardon." *Journal of Criminal Law and Criminology* 17, no. 4 (1927): 490–530.

Barrows, S. J. *The Reformatory System in the United States, Reports Prepared for the International Prison Commission.* Washington: U.S. Government Printing Office, 1900.

Bates, Sanford. *The Parole System. The Federal Prison Director Replies to Critics Who Condemn It.* Washington: U.S. Government Printing Office, 1936.

Beccaria, Cesare. *An Essay on Crimes and Punishment, Translated from the Italian with a Commentary Attributed to Mons. De Voltaire, Translated from the French.* London: J. Almon, 1767.

Bergeron, Paul H., ed. *The Papers of Andrew Johnson*, vol. 13, *September 1867–March 1868.* Knoxville: University of Tennessee Press, 1996.

Blatchford, S. *Argument of William H. Seward, in defence of William Freeman, on his trial for murder.* Auburn: J. C. Derby & Company, 1846.

Bonaparte, Charles J. "Punishment and Pardon," in *Proceedings of the Annual Congress of the National Prison Association of the United States.* Indianapolis: W. B. Burford, 1907: 194–205.

Brainerd, Cephas. "Memorial Sketch of Hon. John W. Edmonds." *Prison Association of New York, Thirty-Second Annual Report of 1876.* New York: Jerome B. Parmenter, 1877.

Brockett, L. P., ed. *Men of Our Day; or Biographical Sketches of Patriots, Orators, Statesmen, Generals, Reformers, Financiers and Merchants, Now on the State of Action: Including Those Who in Military, Political, Business and Social Life, Are the Prominent Leaders of the Time in This Country.* Philadelphia: Ziegler and McCurdy, 1872.

Brockway, Zebulon Reed. *Fifty Years of Prison Service. An Autobiography.* New York: Russell Sage Foundation, 1912.

Burgess, Ernest W. "Cure for Parole Evils." *Bode Bugle*, April 25, 1930.

Bye, Raymond T. "Recent History and Present Status of Punishment in the United States." *Journal of Criminal Law and Criminology* 17, no. 2 (August 1926): 234–435.

Carey, Matthew D. *Essays on Penitentiary Discipline.* Philadelphia: Matthew Carey, 1829.

Carey, Matthew D. *Thoughts on Penitentiaries and Prison Discipline.* Philadelphia: Clark and Raser, 1831.

Carpenter, Mary. *Reformatory Prison Discipline as Developed by the Rt. Hon. Sir Walter Crofton, in the Irish Convict Prisons.* London: Longman, Longman, Green, Longman, 1872.

Carter, Nathaniel H., and William L. Stone. *Reports of the Proceedings and Debates of the Convention of 1821 Assembled for the Purpose of Amending the Constitution of the State of New York.* Albany: E. and F. Hosford, 1821.

Cass, Edward R. "Legislation in 1926." *Journal of Criminal Law and Criminology* 18, no. 1 (Spring 1927): 92–99.

Cass, Edward R. "Parole Can Be Successful (Five Year Study—New York)." *Journal of Criminal Law and Criminology* 31, no. 1 (May–June 1940): 7–13.

Cass, Edward R. *A Study of Parole Laws and Methods in the United States.* Albany: Prison Association of New York, 1921.

Champlin, John Denison, ed. *Orations Addresses and Speeches of Chauncey M. Depew*, vol. 1, *Orations and Memorial Addresses.* New York: Privately printed, 1910.

Child, Lydia Maria. *Isaac T. Hooper. A True Life.* Boston: J. P. Jewett and Company, 1853.

Clinton, Henry L. "Defence of Insanity in Criminal Cases; Law of Murder; Writs of Error in Capital Cases." In *Law Trials and Speeches*, edited by John K. Porter, 1601–1666. New York: John K. Porter, 1873.

Coffey, William A. *Inside out, or an Interior View of the New-York State Prison, Together with Biographical Sketches of the Lives of Several of the Convicts*. New York: James Costigan, 1823.

Colden, Cadwallader. *The History of the Five Indian Nations of Canada, Which Are Dependent on the Province of New-York in America*. London: T. Osborne, 1747.

Committee on Indian Affairs. *Laws of the Colonial and State Governments, Relating to Indians and Indian Affairs, from 1663 to 1831, Inclusive, with an Appendix Containing the Proceedings of the Congress of the Confederation. And the Laws of Congress, from 1800 to 1830, on the Same Subject*. Washington: Committee on Indian Affairs, House of Representatives, 1832.

"The Conditional Liberation of Prisoners." *Science* 9, no. 210 (February 15, 1887): 125–26.

Cooley, Edwin J. *Probation and Delinquency*. New York: Catholic Charities of the Archdiocese of New York, 1927.

Crossley, Frederick. "The Pardon of Albert T. Patrick." *Journal of Criminal Law and Criminology* 3, no. 5 (1913): 675.

Croswell, S., and R. Sutton. *Debates and Proceedings of the New York State Constitutional Convention, 1846, for the Revision of the Constitution*. Albany: Argus, 1846.

Darrow, Clarence. *Crime: Its Causes and Treatment*. New York: Thomas Crowell Company, 1922.

De Beaumont, Gustave, and Alexis de Tocqueville. *On the Penitentiary System in the United States and Its Application in France; with an Appendix on Penal Colonies, and Also Statistical Notes*. Translated by Francis Lieber. Philadelphia: Carey, Lea, and Blanchard, 1833.

De Bow, J. D. B., ed. "Table CLXXIX—State Prisons and Penitentiaries, 1850." In *Statistical View of the United States*, 166–7. Washington: Beverley Tucker, Senate Printer, 1854.

Documents of the Constitutional Convention of the State of New York, 1915 Begun and Held at the Capitol in the City of Albany on Tuesday the Sixth Day of April. Albany: J. B. Lyon, 1915.

Dugdale, Richard L. *The Jukes: A Study in Crime, Pauperism, Disease and Heredity*. New York: G. P. Putnam's Sons, 1877.

Estabrook, Arthur H. *The Jukes in 1915*. Washington, DC: Carnegie Institution, 1916.

Eddy, Thomas. *An Account of the State Prison or Penitentiary House, in the City of New York*. New York: Isaac Collins and Son, 1801.

Edmonds, John W. "The People V. Smith Boughton." In *Reports of Select Cases Decided in the Courts of New York*, vol. 1, 140–75. New York: S. S. Peloubet and Company, 1883.

Federal Works Agency. *Prisoners' Case Records: A Manual for Developing Case Records of Prisoners Confined in State Prisons*. Washington: WPA Division of Research, 1939.

Ganter, Granville, ed. *The Collected Speeches of Sagoyewatha, Or Red Jacket.* Syracuse: Syracuse University Press, 2006.

Gault, Robert H. "The New York State Board of Parole." *Journal of the American Institute of Criminal Law and Criminology* 2, no. 5 (January 1912): 791–95.

Gerry, Elbridge T., Alfred P. Southwick, and Matthew Hale. *Report of the Commission to Investigate and Report the Most Humane and Practical Method of Carrying into Effect the Sentence of Death in Capital Cases.* Troy: Troy Press Co., 1888.

Gilman, Daniel Coit, ed. *The Miscellaneous Writings of Francis Lieber,* vol. 2. London: J. B. Lippincott and Co., 1881.

Gitlow, Benjamin. *I Confess: The Truth about American Communism.* New York: E. P. Dutton and Co., 1940.

Glueck, Sheldon. "Principles of a Rational Penal Code." *Harvard Law Review* 41, no. 4 (February 1928): 453–82.

Greenleaf, Thomas. *Laws of the State of New York, Comprising the Constitution, and the Acts of the Legislature, since the Revolution, from the First to the Twentieth Session,* vols. 1–3. New York: Thomas Greenleaf, 1792–97.

Hartung v. The People, 1863. https://casetext.com.

Hill, David B. "The Pardoning Power." *North American Review* 154, no. 422 (1892): 50–83.

Hillard, George Stillman. "Lieber's Essay on Penal Law." *North American Review* 47, no. 101 (1838): 452–64.

Hough, Franklin B. *The New-York Civil List Containing the Names and Origin of the Civil Divisions and the Names and Origin of the Civil Divisions, Names and Dates of Election or Appointment of the Principal State and County Officers, from the Revolution to the Present Time, Compiled from the Public Records in the Office of the Secretariate of State, and Other Authentic Sources.* Albany: Weed Parsons, 1858.

Jefferson, Thomas. *Notes on the State of Virginia.* Merrill D. Paterson, ed. New York: Library of America, 1782.

Jensen, Christen. *The Pardoning Power in the American States.* Chicago: University of Chicago, 1922.

Johnston, Henry P., ed. *The Correspondence and Public Papers of John Jay,* vol. 1, *1763–1781.* New York: Putnam's Sons, 1890.

Johnston, Henry P., ed. *The Correspondence and Public Papers of John Jay,* vol. 4, *1794–1826.* New York: Putnam's Sons, 1893.

Kappler, Charles J., ed. *Indian Affairs: Laws and Treaties,* vol. 2. Washington: Government Printing Office, 1904.

Kennedy, Robert C. "'The Burglar's Friend.'" Frank Bellew, artist. January 30, 1858. *Harpweek Cartoons.* Accessed February 11, 2015. http://www.harpweek.com.

Kettle, Thomas Prentice, ed. *Constitutional Reform in a Series of Articles Contributed to the Democratic Review Upon Constitutional Guarantees in Political Government, the Errors and Abuses to Which They Are Liable; the Proper Mode of Reforming Them; Political Patronage in Its Effects Upon the Freedom and Purity of Elections; Together with a History of Constitutional Reform in New Jersey, Louisiana, Texas, Missouri,*

Maryland, Iowa, Indiana, Illinois, Mississippi, and New York. New York: Democratic Review, 1846.

Kirk, James E. *The Laws of New York Relating to the State Prisons, Including the Provisions of the Constitution and Revised Statutes Applicable Thereto, and Miscellaneous Acts of the Legislature, as Amended to and in Force June 1, 1904.* Albany: 1904.

Kirkland, Caroline. *The Helping Hand: Comprising an Account of the Home for Discharged Female Convicts, and an Appeal in Behalf of That Institution.* New York: Scribner, 1853.

Lanne, William F. "Parole Prediction as Science." *Journal of Criminal Law and Criminology* 26, no. 3 (1935): 377–400.

Laughlin, Harry Hamilton. *Eugenical Sterilization in the United States.* Chicago: Psychopathic Laboratory of the Municipal Court of Chicago, 1922.

Levy, Newman. "Judges and the Legislature." *Journal of Criminal Law and Criminology* 19, no. 4 (February 1929): 557–62.

Lewis, George A. "Golden Rule of 'Try Again' for Penitent Convicts." *Washington Post,* June 25, 1911.

Lewis, Orlando C. Faulkland. *The Development of American Prisons and Prison Customs, 1776–1845. With Special Reference to Early Institutions in the State of New York.* New York: Prison Association of New York, 1922.

Lieber, Francis. *On Civil Liberty and Self-Government.* 2 vols. 3rd revised edition, edited by Theodore D. Woolsey. Philadelphia: J. B. Lippincott and Co., 1883.

Lieber, Francis. "A Paper on the Abuse of the Pardoning Power." *On Civil Liberty and Self Government.* London: Richard Bently, 1859.

Lieber, Francis. "The Pardoning Power and Its Abuses." *Stryker's American Register* 6 (1851): 552–53.

Lieber, Francis. "A Popular Essay on Subjects of Penal Law, and on Uninterrupted Solitary Confinement at Labor, as Contradistinguished to Solitary Confinement at Night and Joint Labor by Day, in a Letter to John Bacon, Esquire." Philadelphia: Philadelphia Society for Alleviating the Miseries of Public Prisons, 1838.

Lieber, Francis. *Reflections on the Changes Which May Seem Necessary in the Present Constitution of the State of New York, Elicited and Published by the New York Union League Club.* New York: Union League Club, 1867.

Lincoln, Charles Z., William H. Johnson, and A. Judd Northrup. *The Colonial Laws of New York from the Year 1664 to the Revolution Including the Charters to the Duke of York, the Commissions and Instructions to Colonial Governors, the Duke's Laws, the Laws of the Dongan and Leisler Assemblies, the Charters of Albany and New York and the Acts of the Colonial Legislatures from 1691 to 1775 Inclusive, Transmitted to the Legislature by the Commissioners of Statutory Revision, Pursuant to Chapter 125 of the Laws of 1891.* 5 vols. Albany: J. B. Lyon, 1894.

Lincoln, Charles Z. *The Constitutional History of New York, from the Beginning of the Colonial Period to the Year 1905, Showing the Origin, Development, and Judicial Construction of the Constitution,* vols. 1–4. Rochester: Lawyers' Co-Operative Publishing Company, 1905.

Lincoln, Charles Z., ed. *McKinney's Consolidated Laws of New. York Annotated.* Index to S*tate of New York, Messages from the Governors Comprising Executive Communications to the Legislature and Other Papers Relating to Legislation from the Organization of the First Colonial Assembly in 1683 to and Including the Year 1906 with Notes.* 11 vols. Albany: J. B. Lyon, 1909.

Lincoln, Charles Z., ed. *State of New York. Messages from the Governors Comprising Executive Communications to the Legislature and Other Papers Relating to Legislation from the Organization of the First Colonial Assembly in 1683 to and Including the Year 1906, With Notes.* 11 vols. Albany: J.B. Lyon, 1909.

Lindsey, Edward. "Historical Sketch of the Indeterminate Sentence and Parole System." *Journal of Criminal Law, Criminology, and Police Science* 16, no. 1 (1925): 9–69.

Locke, John. "Of Prerogative." In *Second Treatise on Government*, edited by C. B. Macpherson, vol. 2, 83–88. Indianapolis: Hackett Publishing, 1980 [1690].

Luckey, John. *Life in Sing Sing State Prison, as Seen in a Twelve Years' Chaplaincy.* New York: N. Tibbals and Co., 1860.

Lyon, F. Emory. "Review of *A Treatise Giving the History, Organization, and Administration of Parole* by John Philip Bramer [New York: Irving Press, 1926]." *Journal of Criminal Law and Criminology* 17, no. 4 (February 1927): 640–41.

Macomb, Alexander. *Treatise on Military Law and Courts Martial.* Charleston, SC: Hoff, 1809.

Manley, Henry S. *The Treaty of Fort Stanwix, 1784: Being the First Attempt to Collect from the Sources the Facts Leading up to and Covering the Peace Negotiated by the Congress of the United States and the Six Nations Indians after Britain Acknowledged the Freedom of Her Colonies.* Rome, NY: Daily Sentinel Co., 1932.

Marcosson, Isaac F. "Making Men Over. The Process by Which William Muldoon Rehabilitates the Weary and the Unfit." *Munsey's Magazine* 48, no. 1 (October 1912): 65–75.

Moley, Raymond. *State Crime Commissions. What They Are and How They Should Be Organized.* New York: National Crime Commission, 1926.

Moley, Raymond, ed. *The Administration of Justice in Missouri; A Summary of the Missouri Crime Survey.* St. Louis: Missouri Association for Criminal Justice, 1926.

Moley, Raymond Charles. *An Outline of the Cleveland Crime Survey.* Cleveland: Cleveland Foundation, 1922.

National Prison Association. "Report of the Standing Committee on Criminal Law Reform." *Proceedings of the Annual Congress of the National Prison Association, Boston, July 14–19, 1888* (Chicago: Knight and Leonard, 1888).

New York Prison Commission. *Investigation of the State Prisons and Report Thereon.* Albany: Weed, Parsons and Co., 1876.

New York State. *Annual Report of the Superintendent of State Prisons* (1878–1926).

New York State Committee for Detecting and Defeating Conspiracies. *Minutes of the Committee and of the First Commission for Detecting and Defeating Conspiracies in the State of New York, December 11, 1776 to September 23, 1778, April 2, 1777 to May 3, 1779, with Collateral Documents, to which is added Minutes of the Council of Appointment, Vol. 1.* New York: New York Historical Society, 1924.

New York State. Convention of the Representatives. "A Declaration, or Ordinance, of the Convention of the State of New-York, Passed May 10, 1777, Offering Free Pardon to Such of the Subjects of the Said State, as, Having Committed Treasonable Acts against the Same, Shall Return to Their Allegiance." New York Convention of the Representatives, 1776–1777. Fishkill: Samuel Loudon, 1777.

New York Department of State. *Constitutional Convention. Third Constitution of the State of New York.* Albany: Department of State, 1846.

New York State. "New York State Governor's Conference on Crime, the Criminal and Society." Albany: New York State, 1935.

New York State. *Report of the Joint Legislative Committee on the Co-Ordination of Civil and Criminal Practice Acts.* 1926.

New York State Division of Parole. *Annual Report of the Division of Parole of the Executive Department, 1931.* Albany: J. B. Lyon, 1932.

New York State Inspectors of State Prisons. *Annual Report of the Inspectors of State Prisons.* 1849–1871. Albany: s.n.

New York State Legislature. *Proceedings of the Legislature of the State of New York Relative to the Life and Public Services of David Bennett Hill.* Albany: s.n., 1911.

New York State Probation Commission. *Report of the New York State Probation Commission*, vol. 7. New York: J. B. Lyon, 1914.

Oberg, Barbara B., ed. *The Papers of Thomas Jefferson*, vol. 38, *1 July–12 November 1802.* Princeton, NJ: Princeton University Press, 2011.

Ordronaux, John. *Commentaries on the Lunacy Laws of New York, and on the Judicial Aspects of Insanity at Common Law and in Equity, Including Procedure, as Expounded in England and the United States.* Albany: John Parsons Jr., 1878.

O'Sullivan, John L. *Report in Favor of the Abolition of the Punishment of Death, Made to the Legislature of the State of New York.* 2nd ed. New York: J. and H. G. Langley, 1841.

Paley, William. *Of the Direct Historical Evidence of Christianity, in Three Parts.* Vol. 1, 9th ed. London: R. Falder, 1803.

Parker, Amasa J., George Wolford, and Edward Wade. *Revised Statutes of the State of New York, as Alerted by Subsequent Legislation.* 3 vols. Albany: Banks and Brothers, 1859.

"The Penal Code of America." *New York State Mechanic, A Journal of the Manual Arts, Trades and Manufacturers.* December 3, 1842.

Perry, Thomas Sergeant. *The Life and Letters of Francis Lieber.* Boston: James R. Osgood and Co., 1882.

Pitts, Ellis, L. F. Waldo, Seward Barculo, and S. L. Walker. *Life and Confessions of Lucy Ann Hoag, put upon her Trial, March 16th, 1852, for the Murder (by Poison) of her Husband, Nelson Hoag, in July 1851; Executed July 30th, 1852. Including the Evidence Adduced on the Trial, with the Charge to the Jury, &c.* Poughkeepsie, NY: The American Publishers, 1852.

Police Department of New York Annual Report, 1927. New York: Bureau of Printing, 1928.

Powers, Gershom. *Report of Gershom Powers, Agent and Keeper of the State Prison, at Auburn: Made to the Legislature, Jan. 7, 1828.* Albany: Croswell and Van Renthuysen, 1828.

Prison Association of New York. *Annual Reports of the Prison Association of New York* (1844–1940).

"Prisons and Power." *Time*, January 13, 1930.

Proceedings and Debates of the Constitutional Convention of the State of New York, Held in 1867 and 1868, in the City of Albany, vol. 1. Albany: Weed Parsons and Company, 1868.

Proceedings of the Court for the Trial of Impeachments. The People of the State of New York, by the Assembly Thereof, against William Sulzer as Governor: Held at the Capital in the City of Albany, New York, September 18, 1913, to October 17, 1913. Albany: J. B. Lyon, 1913.

The Remembrancer, or, Impartial Repository of Public Events, vol. 6, 3rd ed. London: J. Almon, 1778.

Revised Record of the Constitutional Convention of the State of New York, April Sixth to September Tenth, 1915. Vol 1. New York: J. B. Lyon, 1916.

Robinson, Governor L. "Frank Walworth Pardoned. Gov. Robinson States His Reasons for the Exercise of Executive Clemency." *Albany Weekly Times*, August 9, 1877.

Robinson, Louis N. "Institutions for Defective Delinquents." *Journal of Criminal Law and Criminology* 24, no. 2 (July–August 1931): 352–99.

Roosevelt, Franklin D., and Samuel Irving Rosenman. *The Public Papers and Addresses of Franklin D. Roosevelt*, vol. 1, *The genesis of the New Deal, 1928–1932: With a Special Introduction and Explanatory Notes by President Roosevelt*. New York: Random House, 1938.

Sanders, Barkev S. "The Way out of Prison." *Survey* 72, no. 11 (November 1936): 330–31.

Smith, Alfred E. *Up to Now—An Autobiography*. New York: Viking Press, 1929.

Smith, Beverley A. "Female Admissions and Paroles of the Western House of Refuge in the 1880s: An Historical Example of Community Corrections." *Journal of Research in Crime and Delinquency* 26, no. 1 (1898): 36–66.

Smith, Eugene. *Prison Science with Special Reference to Recent New York Legislation*. New York: New York Society for Political Education, 1903 [1890].

Smith, Eugene, Charles A. Collin, and Charlton T. Lewis. "Report of the Committee on Penal and Reformatory Systems." In *Proceedings of the National Conference of Charities and Correction, at the Eighteenth Annual Session, held in Indianapolis, Ind., May 13–20, 1891*. Boston: Press of George H. Ellis, 1891.

Smithers, William W. *Executive Clemency in Pennsylvania*. Philadelphia: International Print Co., 1909.

Society for the Prevention of Pauperism in the City of New York. *Report on the Penitentiary System in the United States, Prepared under a Resolution of the Society for the Prevention of Pauperism in the City of New York*. New York: Mahlon, 1822.

Spafford, Horatio Gates. *A Gazetteer of the State of New York: Embracing an Ample Survey and Description of Its Counties, Towns, Cities, Villages, Canals, Mountains, Lakes, Rivers, Creeks, and Natural Topography, Arranged in One Series Alphabetically*. 1824.

Sparks, Jared. *The Writings of George Washington; Being his Correspondence, Addresses, Messages, and other Papers, Official and Private.* Vol. 5. Boston: Ferdinand Andrews, 1840.

Special Committee on Parole Problem. *Report of Special Committee on the Parole Problem.* New York, 1930.

Speranza, Gino C. "What Are We Doing for the Criminal?" *American Law Register* 49 (April 1901): 215–20.

State of New York. *Report and Proceedings of the State Board of Charities Relative to the Management of the State Reformatory at Elmira. Transmitted to the Legislature, March 19, 1894.* Vol. 1. Albany: J. Lyons, 1894.

State of New York. *Report of the Prison Survey Committee.* Albany: J. B. Lyon, 1920.

State of New York. *Report of the Secretary of State, in Answer to a Resolution Relative to Pardons, and the Sentences which have been Abridged or Commuted in Consequence thereof, During the Years 1857 and 1858, Transmitted to the Legislature February 2, 1859.* Albany: Charles Van Benthuysen Printer, 1859.

State of New York. "Report of the Secretary of State in Relation to Pardons Granted Since January 1, 1840, Assembly Document 198, 27 March 1846."

State of New York. *Report of the State Reorganization Commission. February 26, 1926.* Albany: J. B. Lyon, 1926.

State of New York Department of Correction. *Parole Reports on Female Mental Defectives, New York State Reformatory for Women, Bedford Hills.* 1930–34.

State of New York Department of Correction. *Seventh Annual Report of the State Commission of Correction for the Year 1933.* Albany: State Department of Correction, 1934.

State of New York Department of Correction. *Sixth Annual Report of the Commissioner of Correction for the Year 1932.* Albany, 1933.

Statutes of the State of New York, of a Public and General Character, Passed from 1829 to 1851, Both Inclusive: With Notes, and References to Judicial Decisions, and the Constitution of 1846. Auburn: Derby and Miller, 1852.

Stoke, Harold W. "A Review of the Pardoning Power." *Kentucky Law Journal* 16, no. 1 (1927): 34–37.

Syrett, Harold C., ed. *The Papers of Alexander Hamilton.* Vol. 3, *1782–1786.* New York: Columbia University Press, 1962.

Taylor, A. W. "Review of *Society and Prisons* (New Haven: Yale University Press, 1916) by Thomas Mott Osborne." *American Journal of Sociology* 23 no. 5 (March 1918): 690–91.

Taylor, Floyd. *Parole.* Albany: State of New York, Executive Department Division of Parole, 1936.

Thayer, Walter N., Jr. "Criminal and the Napanoch Plan." *Journal of Criminal Law & Criminology* 16, no. 2 (1925): 278–89.

Titus, Mary V. *Index to the Reports of the National Prison Association, 1870, 1873, 1874, 1883–1904.* Introduction by Eugene Smith. Washington, DC: Government Printing Office, 1906.

Train, Arthur. *The Prisoner at the Bar: Sidelights on the Administration of Criminal Justice*, 2nd ed. New York: Scribner's Sons, 1908.

Tullack, William. "Humanity and Humanitarianism with Special Reference to the Prison Systems of Great Britain and the United States." In *Transactions of the National Congress on Penitentiary and Reformatory Discipline Held at Cincinnati, Ohio, October 12–18*. Edited by Enoch. C. Wines, 204–18. Albany: Argus, 1871.

Twohig, Dorothy, ed. *The Papers of George Washington, Presidential Series*, vol. 6, *1 July 1790–30 November 1790*. Charlottesville: University of Virginia Press, 1996.

United States Attorney General. *The Attorney General's Survey of Release Procedures*, vols. 1–4. Washington, DC: United States Printing Office, 1938–40.

United States Bureau of the Census. *Prisoners and Juvenile Delinquents in Institutions in 1904*. Washington, DC: United States Printing Office, 1907.

United States Bureau of the Census. *Prisoners and Juvenile Delinquents in the United States, 1910*. Washington, DC: United States Printing Office, 1918.

United States Census Bureau. *Prisoners in State and Federal Prisons and Reformatories: Statistics of Prisoners Received and Discharged During the Year, for State and Federal Penal Institutions*. Washington, DC: Government Printing Office, 1929.

Vaux, Roberts. *Notices of the Original, and Successive Efforts, to Improve the Discipline of the Prison at Philadelphia, and to Reform the Criminal Code of Pennsylvania: With a Few Observations on the Penitentiary System*. Philadelphia: Kimber and Sharpless, 1826.

Wilson, James. *The Works of the Honorable James Wilson, L. L. D.: Late One of the Associate Judges of the Supreme Court of the United States and Professor of Law in the College of Philadelphia*. Vol. 3. Edited by Bird Wilson. Philadelphia: Lorenzo, 1804.

Wines, Enoch C., and Theodore W. Dwight. *Report on the Prisons and Reformatories of the United States and Canada, Made to the Legislature of New York, January, 1867*. Albany: Van Benthuysen and Sons, 1867.

Wines, Enoch Cobb. *Transactions of the National Congress on Penitentiary and Reformatory Discipline Held at Cincinnati, Ohio, October 12–18, 1870*. Albany: Weed, Parsons and Co., 1871.

Wines, Frederick Howard. *Punishment and Reformation: A Study of the Penitentiary System*. New edition, revised and enlarged by Winthrop D. Lane. New York: Thomas Y. Crowell, 1919 [1910].

Wines, Frederick Howard. "The Treatment of the Criminal." *Proceedings of the National Conference of Charities and Correction at the Thirty-First Annual Session Held in the City of Portland, Maine, June 15–22* (1904): 422–34.

Winter, Alexander. *The New York State Reformatory in Elmira*. London: Swan Sonnenschein and Company, 1891.

Witmer, Helen Leland. "The Development of Parole in the United States." *Social Forces* 4, no. 2 (December 1925): 318–25.

Witmer, Helen Leland. "The History, Theory and Results of Parole." *Journal of the American Institute of Criminal Law and Criminology* 18, no. 1 (May 1927): 24–64.

Witmer, Helen Leland. "Some Factors in Success or Failure on Parole." *Journal of the Institute of Criminal Law and Criminology* 18, no. 3 (November 1927): 384–403.

SECONDARY SOURCES

Abadinsky, Howard. *Probation and Parole: Theory and Practice*, 12th ed. New York: Prentice Hall, 2013.

Abramowitz, Elkan, and David Paget. "Executive Clemency in Capital Cases." *New York University Law Review* 39, no. 1 (1964): 136–92.

Acker, James R. "New York's Proposed Death Penalty Legislation: Constitutional and Policy Perspectives." *Albany Law Review* 54 (1990): 515–616.

Acker, James R., Talia Harmon, and Craig Rivera. "Merciful Justice: Lessons from 50 Years of New York Death Penalty Commutations." *Criminal Justice Review* 35, no. 2 (2010): 183–99.

Adams, William Howard. *Gouverneur Morris: An Independent Life*. New Haven, CT: Yale University Press, 2003.

Adcock, Robert. *Liberalism and the Emergence of American Political Science: A Transatlantic Tale*. New York: Oxford University Press, 2014.

Adler, David Gray. "The President's Pardon Power." In *Inventing the American Presidency*, edited by Thomas E. Cronin, 119–53. Lawrence: University Press of Kansas, 1989.

Alexander, DeAlva Stanwood. *A Political History of the State of New York*, vols. 1–3. New York: Henry Holt, 1906 and 1909.

Alexander, Ruth M. *The Girl Problem: Female Sexual Delinquency in New York, 1900–1930*. Ithaca, NY: Cornell University Press, 1995.

Allen, Howard W., and Jerome M. Clubb, with assistance from Vincent A. Lacey. *Race, Class and the Death Penalty: Capital Punishment in American History*. Albany: State University of New York Press, 2008.

Anderson, Fred, and Andrew Robert Lee Cayton. *The Dominion of War: Empire and Liberty in North America, 1500–2000*. New York: Viking, 2005.

Appleby, Joyce Oldham. *Liberalism and Republicanism in the Historical Imagination*. Cambridge, MA: Harvard University Press, 1992.

Ariens, Michael. "Supreme Court Justices Benjamin N. Cardozo (1870–1938)." http://www.michaelariens.com.

Arpey, Andrew W. *The William Freeman Murder Trial: Insanity, Politics and Race*. Syracuse, NY: Syracuse University Press, 2003.

Baatz, Simon. *For the Thrill of It: Leopold, Loeb and the Crime that Shocked Chicago*. New York: HarperCollins, 2008.

Bacon, Margaret Hope. *Abby Hopper Gibbons: Prison Reformer and Social Activist*. Albany: State University of New York Press, 2012.

Bacon, Margaret Hope. *Lamb's Warrior: The Life of Isaac T. Hopper*. New York: Thomas Y. Crowell, 1970.

Baker, Paula. *The Moral Frameworks of Public Life: Gender, Politics, and the State in Rural New York, 1870–1930*. New York: Oxford University Press, 1991.

Bancroft, Frederick. *The Life of William H. Seward, with Portraits, in Two Volumes*. New York: Harper and Bros., 1900.

Banner, Stuart. *The Death Penalty: An American History*. Cambridge, MA: Harvard University Press, 2009.

Banner, Stuart. *How the Indians Lost their Land: Law and Power on the Frontier*. Cambridge, MA: Harvard University Press, 2007.

Banner, Stuart. "Reviewed Work: Daniel J. Hulsebosch, *Constituting Empire: New York and the Transformation of Constitutionalism in the Atlantic World, 1664–1830* (Chapel Hill: University of North Carolina Press, 2005)." *American Historical Review* 112, no. 2 (2007): 498–99.

Bartky, Ian R. *Selling the True Time: Nineteenth-Century Timekeeping in America*. Stanford, CA: Stanford University Press, 2000.

Bartrip, Peter W. J. "Public Opinion and Law Enforcement: The Ticket-Of-Leave Scares in Mid-Victorian Britain." In *Policing and Punishment in Nineteenth-Century Britain*, edited by Victor Bailey, 150–81. London: Croom Helm, 1981.

Basch, Norma. *Framing American Divorce: From the Revolutionary Generation to the Victorians*. Berkeley: University of California Press, 1999.

Becker, Peter, and Richard F. Wetzell, eds. *Criminals and Their Scientists: The History of Criminology in International Perspective*. New York: Cambridge University Press, 2009.

Bederman, Gail. *Manliness and Civilization: A Cultural History*. Chicago: Chicago University Press, 1995.

Bellush, Bernard. *Franklin D. Roosevelt as Governor of New York*. New York: Columbia University Press, 1955.

Benjamin, Gerald. *The Oxford Handbook of New York State Government and Politics*. New York: Oxford University Press, 2012.

Bennett, David Harry. *The Party of Fear: From Nativist Movements to the New Right in American History*. Chapel Hill: University of North Carolina Press, 1988.

Bernstein, Iver. *The New York City Draft Riots: Their Significance for American Society and Politics in the Age of the Civil War*. New York: Oxford University Press, 1990.

Bessler, John D. *Cruel and Unusual: The American Death Penalty and the Founders' Eighth Amendment*. Boston: Northeastern University Press, 2012.

Bienen, Leigh B., and Brandon Rottinghaus. "Criminal Law: Learning from the Past, Living in the Present: Understanding Homicide in Chicago, 1870–1930." *Journal of Criminal Law and Criminology* 92, no. 3 (Spring 2002): 437–54.

Blackman, Paul H., and Vance McLaughlin. "The Espy File on American Executions: User Beware." *Homicide Studies* 15, no. 3 (2011): 209–27.

Blomberg, Thomas G., and Julie Mestre. "Net-Widening: Past, Present and into the Future." In *The Encyclopedia of Theoretical Criminology*. Vol. 2, edited by J. Mitchell Miller, 573–77. New York: Wiley-Blackwell, 2014.

Blomberg, Thomas G., and Karol Lucken, eds. *American Penology: A History of Control*. Enlarged 2nd ed. New Brunswick, NJ: Transaction Publishers, 2011.

Blue, Ethan. *Doing Time in the Depression: Everyday Life in Texas and California Prisons*. New York: New York University Press, 2012.

Bonomi, Patricia U. *A Factious People: Politics and Society in Colonial New York*. New York: Columbia University Press, 1971.

Brooke, John L. *Columbia Rising: Civil Life on the Upper Hudson from the Revolution to the Age of Jackson.* Williamsburg, VA: Omohundro Institute of Early American History and Culture, 2010.

Brown, Roscoe C. E., ed. *History of the State of New York, Political and Governmental,* vol. 3, *1865–1896.* Syracuse, NY: Syracuse University Press, 1922.

Brown, Roscoe C. E., ed. *History of the State of New York. Political and Governmental,* vol. 4, *1896–1920.* Syracuse, NY: Syracuse University Press, 1922.

Bulmer, Martin. "Knowledge for the Public Good: The Emergence of Social Sciences and Social Reform in Late-Nineteenth- and Early-Twentieth-Century America, 1880–1940." In *Social Science and Policy-making: A Search for Relevance in the Twentieth Century,* edited by David L. Featherman and Maris A. Vinovskis, 16–39. Ann Arbor: University of Michigan Press, 2001.

Bryce, James. *The American Commonwealth, Abridged and Revised from the First Edition.* Philadelphia: John D. Morris and Company, 1888.

Calder, James D. "Between Brain and State: Herbert C. Hoover, George W. Wickersham, and the Commission That Grounded Social Scientific Investigations of American Crime and Justice, 1929–1931 and Beyond." *Marquette Law Review* 96, no. 4 (2013): 1035–108.

Calhoon, Robert McCluer. *The Loyalists in Revolutionary America, 1760–1781.* New York: Harcourt Brace Jovanovich, 1973.

Campbell, James. "African Americans and Parole in Depression-Era New York." *Historical Journal* 54, no. 4 (December 2011): 1065–86.

Cardozo, Benjamin N. "What Medicine Can Do for Law." In *Law, Literature and Other Essays,* 70–120. New York: Harcourt, Brace, 1931.

Carp, Benjamin L. *Defiance of the Patriots: The Boston Tea Party and the Making of America.* New Haven, CT: Yale University Press, 2010.

Carrington, Paul D. "Francis Lieber (1798–1872) Author, Professor, and Public Intellectual." In *Yale Dictionary of American Legal Biography,* edited by Roger K. Newman, 335–36. New Haven, CT: Yale University Press, 2005.

Carso, Brian F. Jr. *Whom Can We Trust Now? The Meaning of Treason in the United States, from the Revolution Through the Civil War.* Lanham, MD: Lexington Books, 2006.

Case, Dick. "Miller, Nathan L(ewis)." In *The Encyclopedia of New York State,* edited by Peter Eisenstadt, 985–86. Syracuse, NY: Syracuse University Press, 2005.

Chadwick, George Roger. *Bureaucratic Mercy: The Home Office and the Treatment of Capital Cases in Victorian Britain.* New York: Garland, 1992.

Chapin, Bradley. "Colonial and Revolutionary Origins of the American Law of Treason." *William and Mary Quarterly* 17, no. 1 (January 1960): 3–21.

Chauncey, George. *Gay New York: Gender, Urban Culture, and the Making of the Gay Male World, 1890–1940.* New York: Basic Books, 1994.

Chernow, Ron. *Alexander Hamilton.* New York: Penguin, 2004.

Chester, Alden. *Legal and Judicial History of New York,* vol. 3. New York: National Americana Society, 1911.

Chester, Alden, and E. Melvin Williams. *Courts and Lawyers of New York: A History, 1609–1925*, vols. 1–3. Clark, NJ: Law Book Exchange, 2005 [1925].

Chopra, Ruma. *Unnatural Rebellion: Loyalists in New York City during the Revolution.* Charlottesville: University of Virginia Press, 2011.

Christianson, Scott. "Bad Seed or Bad Science: The Story of the Notorious Jukes Family." *New York Times*, February 8, 2003.

Christianson, Scott. *With Liberty for Some: 500 Years of Imprisonment in America.* Boston: Northeastern University Press, 1998.

Cogan, Jacob Katz, and Lori D. Ginzberg, "1846 Petition for Woman's Suffrage, New York State Constitutional Convention." *Signs* 22, no. 2 (Winter 1997): 427–39.

Cohen, Patricia Cline. *A Calculating People: The Spread of Numeracy in Early America.* New York: Routledge, 1999 [1982].

Colburn, David R. "Governor Alfred E. Smith and Penal Reform." *Political Science Quarterly* 91 (1976): 315–27.

Cole, Donald B. *Martin Van Buren and the American Political System.* Princeton, NJ: Princeton University Press, 2005.

Conley, Carolyn. *The Unwritten Law: Criminal Justice in Victorian Kent.* Oxford: Oxford University Press, 1991.

Conley, Patrick T., and John P. Kaminski, eds. *The Bill of Rights and the States: The Colonial and Revolutionary Origins of American Liberties.* Madison, WI: Madison House, 1992.

Corning, A. Elwood. *Hamilton Fish.* New York: Lanmere Publishing Company, 1918.

Cornog, Evan. *The Birth of Empire: Dewitt Clinton and the American Experience, 1769–1988.* New York: Oxford University Press, 2000.

Countryman, Edward. *A People in Revolution: The American Revolution and Political Society in New York, 1760–1790.* Baltimore, MD: Johns Hopkins University Press, 1981.

Dale, Elizabeth. "AHR Forum: Getting Away with Murder?" *American Historical Review* 111 (February 2006): 95–103.

Dale, Elizabeth. *The Rule of Justice: The People of Chicago Versus Zephyr Davis.* Columbus: Ohio State University Press, 2001.

Dandridge, Danske. *American Prisoners of the Revolution.* Charlottesville: Michie Company, 1911.

David, Allen Freeman. *Spearheads for Reform: The Social Settlements and the Progressive Movement.* New Brunswick, NJ: Rutgers University Press, 1984 [1967].

Davis, Kathleen. *Periodization and Sovereignty: How Ideas of Feudalism and Secularization Govern the Politics of Time.* Philadelphia: University of Pennsylvania Press, 2008.

Davis, Kenneth Sydney. *FDR: The Beckoning of Destiny, 1882–1928: A History.* Vol. 1. New York: G. P. Putnam's Sons, 1972.

Davis, Kenneth Sydney. *FDR: The New York Years, 1928–1933.* Vol. 2. New York: Random House, 1985.

Davis, Natalie Zemon. *Fiction in the Archives: Pardon Tales and their Tellers in Sixteenth-Century France.* Stanford, CA: Stanford University Press, 1988.

Dennis, Matthew. "Murder! Or the Remarkable Trial of Tommy Jemmy, 19th-Century Seneca Witch-Hunter and Defender of Indian Sovereignty." *Redex Report 7*, no. 2 (2010). http://www.readex.com.

Dennis, Matthew. *Seneca Possessed: Indians, Witchcraft, and Power in the Early American Republic*. Philadelphia: University of Pennsylvania Press, 2010.

Dennis, Matthew. "Sorcery and Sovereignty: Senecas, Citizens, and the Contest for Power and Authority on the Frontiers of the Early American Republic." In *New World Orders: Violence, Sanction and Authority in the Colonial Americas*, edited by John Smolenski and Thomas J. Humphrey, 179–202. Philadelphia: University of Pennsylvania Press, 2005.

Densmore, Christopher. *Red Jacket: Iroquois Diplomat and Orator*. Syracuse, NY: Syracuse University Press, 1999.

De Pauw, Linda Grant. *The Eleventh Pillar: New York State and the Federal Constitution*. Ithaca, NY: Cornell University Press, 1966.

Derrida, Jacques. "The Century and the Pardon." http://fixion.sytes.net.

Derrida, Jacques. "To Forgive: The Unforgivable and the Imprescriptible." In *Questioning God*, edited by John D. Caputo, Mark Dooley and Michael J. Scanlon, 21–51. Bloomington: Indiana University Press, 2001.

Dinan, John J. "The Pardon Power and the American State Constitutional Tradition." *Polity* 35, no. 3 (April 2003): 389–418.

Domhoff, G. William. *The Power Elite and the State: How Policy is Made in America*. New York: Aldine de Gruyter, 1990.

Donovan, Byan. *White Slave Crusades: Race, Gender and Anti-vice Activism, 1888–1917*. Champaign: University of Illinois Press, 2005.

Dorris, Jonathan Truman. *Pardon and Amnesty under Lincoln and Johnson: The Restoration of the Confederates to Their Rights and Privileges, 1861–1898*. Chapel Hill: University of North Carolina Press, 1953.

Dowling, Marissa Barden. *Clemency and Cruelty in the Roman World*. Ann Arbor: University of Michigan Press, 2006.

Dressner, Richard B., and Glenn C. Altschuler. "Sentiment and Statistics in the Progressive Era: The Debate on Capital Punishment in New York." *New York History* 56, no. 2 (April 1975): 197–208.

"Duely and Constantly Kept": A History of the New York Supreme Court, 1691–1847 and an Inventory of its Records (Albany, Utica, and Geneva Offices), 1797–1847. Albany: New York State Court of Appeals and New York State Archives and Records Administration, 1991.

Eisenstadt, Peter, ed. *The Encyclopedia of New York State*. Syracuse, NY: Syracuse University Press, 2005.

Ellis, David Madwyn. *Landlords and Farmers in the Hudson-Mohawk Region, 1790–1850*. New York: Octagon Books, 1967 [1946].

Espy, M. Wyatt, and John Ortiz Smykla. "Executions by the State." In *Executions in the United States, 1608–1991: The Espy File* [computer file]. 3rd ed. Ann Arbor, MI: Inter-university Consortium for Political and Social Research, 1994.

Espy, M. Wyatt, and John Ortiz Smykla. *Executions in the United States, 1608–2002: The Espy File* [computer file]. 4th ed. Ann Arbor, MI: Inter-University Consortium for Political and Social Research, 2004.

Evers, John T. "Investigating New York: Governor Alfred E. Smith, the Moreland Act, and Reshaping New York State Government." PhD diss., State University of New York, 2013.

Feldman, Stephen M. *American Legal Thought, from Premodernism to Postmodernism: An Intellectual Voyage.* New York: Oxford University Press, 2000.

Finan, Christopher N. *Alfred E. Smith: The Happy Warrior.* New York: Hill and Wang, 2002.

Finkelman, Paul. *Slavery and the Founders: Race and Liberty in the Age of Jefferson.* 2nd ed. Armonk, NY: M. E. Sharpe, 2001.

Finkelman, Paul. "Slavery in the United States: Persons or Property?" In *The Legal Understanding of Slavery from the Historical to the Contemporary*, edited by Jean Allain, 105–34. Oxford: Oxford University Press, 2012.

Finkelman, Paul, and Stephen E. Gottlieb, eds. *Toward a Usable Past: Liberty under State Constitutions.* Athens: University of Georgia Press, 1991.

Fisher, George. *Plea Bargaining's Triumph: A History of Plea Bargaining in America.* Stanford, CA: Stanford University Press, 2003.

Fisher, Louis. *Military Tribunals and Presidential Power: American Revolution to the War on Terrorism.* Lawrence: University Press of Kansas, 2005.

Foner, Eric. *Reconstruction: The Unfinished Revolution.* New York: HarperCollins, 2002 [1988].

Ford, Lisa. "Indigenous Policy and Its Historical Occlusions: The North American and Global Contexts of Australian Settlement." *Australian Indigenous Law Review* 12, no. 1 (2008): 69–80.

Ford, Lisa. *Settler Sovereignty Jurisdiction and Indigenous People in America and Australia, 1788–1836.* Cambridge, MA: Harvard University Press, 2010.

Foucault, Michel. *Discipline and Punish: The Birth of the Prison.* Translated by Alan Sheridan. New York: Vintage, 1995 [1977].

Foucault, Michel. *Religion and Culture.* Ed. Jeremy R. Carrette. New York: Routledge, 1999.

Freedman, Estelle B. "The Prison Lesbian: Race, Class, and the Construction of the Aggressive Female Homosexual, 1915–1965." *Feminist Studies* 22, no. 2 (1996): 397–423.

Freedman, Estelle B. "Their Sisters' Keepers: An Historical Perspective on Female Correctional Institutions in the United State: 1870–1900." *Feminist Studies* 2, no. 1 (1974): 77–95.

Freedman, Estelle B. *Their Sisters' Keepers: Women's Prison Reform in America, 1830–1930.* Ann Arbor: University of Michigan Press, 1984.

Freidel, Frank. *Francis Lieber: Nineteenth Century Liberal.* Baton Rouge: Louisiana State University Press, 1947.

Freidel, Frank. *Franklin Roosevelt: A Rendezvous with Destiny.* New York: Little, Brown, 1990.

Freilich, Joshua D., and Craig J. Rivera. "Mercy, Death and Politics: An Analysis of Executions and Commutations in New York State, 1935–63." *American Journal of Criminal Justice* 24, no. 1 (1999): 15–29.

Friedland, Martin. *The Death of Old Man Rice: A True Story of Criminal Justice in America.* Toronto: University of Toronto Press, 1994.

Friedman, Lawrence M. *Crime and Punishment in American History.* New York: Basic Books, 1993.

Galie, Peter J. *Ordered Liberty: A Constitutional History of New York.* New York: Fordham University Press, 1996.

Galie, Peter J., and Christopher Bopst, eds. *The New York State Constitution.* 2nd ed. New York: Oxford University Press, 2012.

Garton, Stephen. "Criminal Propensities: Psychiatry, Classification and Imprisonment in New York State, 1916–1940." *Social History of Medicine* 23, no 1 (2010): 79–97.

Gellman, David N. *Emancipating New York: The Politics of Slavery and Freedom, 1777–1827.* Baton Rouge: Louisiana State University Press, 2006.

Gellman, David N., and David Quigley, eds. *Jim Crow New York: A Documentary History of Race and Citizenship, 1777–1877.* New York: New York University Press, 2003.

Gerlach, Don R. *Proud Patriot: Philip Schuyler and the War of Independence, 1775–1783.* Syracuse, NY: Syracuse University Press, 1987.

Gilfoyle, Timothy J. *A Pickpocket's Tale: The Underworld of Nineteenth-Century New York.* New York: W. W. Norton, 2006.

Gilfoyle, Timothy J. "Prostitutes in History: From Parables of Pornography to Metaphors of Modernity." *American Historical Review* 104, no. 1 (1999): 117–41.

Gilje, Paul A. "Infant Abandonment in Early Nineteenth-Century New York City: Three Cases." *Signs* 8, no. 3 (Spring 1983): 580–90.

Gillespie, L. Kay. *Executed Women of the 20th and 21st Centuries.* Lanham, MD: University Press of America, 2009.

Ginzberg, Lori. *Women and the Work of Benevolence: Morality, Politics and Class in the Nineteenth Century United States.* New Haven, CT: Yale University Press, 1990.

Goebel, Julius. "The Courts and the Law in Colonial New York." In *History of the State of New York*, edited by Alexander C. Flick, 1–44. New York: Columbia University Press, 1933.

Goebel, Julius Jr., and Thomas Raymond Naughton. *Law Enforcement in Colonial New York: A Study in Criminal Procedure (1664–1776).* New York: The Commonwealth Fund, 1944.

Goldman, Lawrence. *Science, Reform, and Politics in Victorian Britain: The Social Science Association, 1857–1886.* Cambridge, UK: Cambridge University Press, 2002.

Goodfriend, Joyce D. *Before the Melting Pot: Society and Culture in Colonial New York City, 1664–1730.* Princeton, NJ: Princeton University Press, 1992.

Goodnow, Frank Johnson. *Comparative Administrative Law: An Analysis of the Administrative Systems National and Local, of the United States, England, France and Germany*, vols. 1 and 2. New York: Putnam's Sons, 1893.

Gould, Philip. "Remembering Metacom: Historical Writing and the Cultures of Masculinity in Early Republican America." In *Sentimental Men: Masculinity and the Politics of Affect in American Culture*, edited by Mary Chapman and Glenn Hendler, 112–24. Berkeley: University of California Press, 1999.

Graber, Jennifer. *The Furnace of Affliction: Prisons and Religion in Antebellum America.* Chapel Hill: University of North Carolina Press, 2011.

Grant, Julia. *The Boy Problem: Educating Boys in Urban America, 1870–1970.* Baltimore, MD: Johns Hopkins University Press, 2014.

Graymont, Barbara. *The Iroquois in the American Revolution.* Syracuse, NY: Syracuse University Press, 1972.

Graymont, Barbara. "New York Indian Policy after the Revolution." *New York History* 57, no. 4 (October 1967): 438–74.

Greenberg, David F. *The Construction of Homosexuality.* Chicago: University of Chicago Press, 1988.

Greenberg, Douglas. *Crime and Law Enforcement in the Colony of New York, 1691–1776.* Ithaca, NY: Cornell University Press, 1974.

Grondahl, Paul. *I Rose Like a Rocket: The Political Education of Theodore Roosevelt.* Lincoln: University of Nebraska Press, 2004.

Guarneri, Carl J. "Reconstructing the Antebellum Communitarian Movement: Oneida and Fourierism." *Journal of the Early Republic* 16, no. 3 (Autumn 1996): 463–500.

Hagan, Edward A., and Mark Sullivan. *William C. Bouck, New York's Farmer Governor.* Edited by Lester Hendrix. Westminster, MD: Heritage Books, 2007.

Hall, Kermit L. *The Magic Mirror: Law in American History.* New York: Oxford University Press, 1989.

Hamm, Richard F. *Murder, Honor, and Law: Four Virginia Homicides between Reconstruction and the Great Depression.* Charlottesville: University of Virginia Press, 2003.

Hamm, Richard F. *Shaping the Eighteenth Amendment: Temperance Reform, Legal Culture and the Polity, 1880–1920.* Chapel Hill: University of North Carolina Press, 1995.

Hammond, Jabez Delano. *The History of Political Parties in the State of New York, from the Ratification of the Federal Constitution to December, 1840, in Two Volumes.* Albany: C. Van Benthuysen, 1842.

Hammond, Whitney Luna M. *History of Madison County, State of New York.* Syracuse, NY: Truair, Smith and Co., 1872.

Hanyan, Craig, with Mary L. Hanyan. *DeWitt Clinton and the Rise of the People's Men.* Montreal: McGill-Queens University Press, 1996.

Harcourt, Bernard E. *Against Prediction: Profiling, Policing, and Punishing in an Actuarial Age.* Chicago: University of Chicago Press, 2007.

Harcourt, Bernard E. "Beccaria's 'On Crimes and Punishments': A Mirror on the History of the Foundations of Modern Criminal Law." Coase-Sandor Institute for Law and Economics Working Paper no. 648 (2d Series). Public Law and Legal Theory Working Paper no. 433, July 22, 2013. http://chicagounbound.uchicago.edu.

Hare, John S. "Military Punishments." *Journal of the American Military Institute* 4, no. 4 (1940): 225–39.

Harley, Lewis R. *Francis Lieber. His Life, Times, and Political Philosophy.* New York: Macmillan, 1899.

Harmon, Talia Roitberg, James R. Acker, and Craig Rivera. "The Power to Be Lenient: Examining New York Governors' Capital Case Clemency Decisions." *Justice Quarterly* 27, no. 5 (October 2010): 742–64.

Harriman, Averell, and Murray Teigh Bloom. "Mercy Is a Lonely Business—New York's Chief Executive Reveals What It's Like to Hold the Fearful Power to Reprieve a Condemned Man or Let Him Go to the Electric Chair." *Saturday Evening Post,* March 22, 1958, 24–25; 82–84.

Harring, Sydney L. *Crow Dog's Case: American Indian Sovereignty, Tribal Law, and United States Law in the Nineteenth Century.* Cambridge, UK: Cambridge University Press, 1994.

Hartog, Hendrik. "Lawyering, Husbands' Rights, and the Unwritten Law in Nineteenth-Century America." *Journal of American History* 84, no. 1 (June 1997): 67–96.

Hartog, Hendrik. "Wives as Favorites." In *Law as Culture and Culture as Law: Essays in Honor of John Phillip Reid,* edited by Hendrik Hartog and William E. Nelson, 292–321. Madison, WI: Madison House, 2002.

Haskell, Thomas L. *The Emergence of Professional Social Science: The American Social Science Association and the Nineteenth-Century Crisis of Authority.* Urbana: University of Illinois Press, 1977.

Hauptman, Laurence M. *Conspiracy of Interests: Iroquois Dispossession and the Rise of New York State.* Syracuse, NY: Syracuse University Press, 1999.

Hauptman, Laurence M. *The Tonawanda Senecas' Heroic Battle against Removal: Conservative Activist Indians.* Albany: State University of New York Press, 2011.

Haw, James. *John and Edward Rutledge of South Carolina.* Athens: University of Georgia Press, 1997.

Hay, Douglas. "Property, Authority and the Criminal Law." In *Albion's Fatal Tree: Crime and Society in Eighteenth-Century England,* edited by E. P. Thompson, Douglas Hay, Peter Linebaugh, John G. Rule, and Cal Winslow, 17–63. New York: Pantheon, 1975.

Hay, Douglas. "Writing about the Death Penalty." *Legal History* 10, nos. 1 and 2 (2006): 35–52.

Heale, M. J. "The Formative Years of the New York Prison Association, 1844–1862." *New York Historical Society Quarterly* 59, no. 4 (October 1975): 320–47.

Hearn, Daniel Allen. *Legal Executions in New York State: A Comprehensive Reference.* Jefferson, NC: McFarland, 1997.

Heller, Deborah L. "Death Becomes the State: The Death Penalty in New York State—Past, Present and Future." *Pace Law Review* 28, no. 3 (Spring 2008): 589–615.

Henderson, Charles Richmond, ed. *Prison Reform: Correction and Prevention,* vol. 1. Philadelphia: Russell Sage Foundation, 1910.

Henretta, James A. "Foreword: Rethinking the State Constitutional Tradition." *Rutgers Law Journal* 22 (1990–1991): 819–40.

Henretta, James A. "The Rise and Decline of 'Democratic-Republicanism': Political Rights in New York and the Several States, 1800–1915." In *The Search for a Usable Past: Liberty under State Constitutions*, edited by Paul Finkelman and Stephen E. Gottlieb, 50–90. Athens: University of Georgia Press, 1991.

Henretta, James A. "The Slow Triumph of Liberal Individualism: Law and Politics in New York: 1780–1860." In *American Chameleon: Individualism in Trans-national Context*, edited by Richard Orr Curry and Lawrence B. Goodheart, 87–106. Kent, OH: Kent State University Press, 1991.

Henretta, James A. "The Strange Birth of Liberal America: Michael Hoffman and the New York Constitution of 1846." *New York History* 77, no. 2 (April 1996): 151–76.

Hicks, Cheryl D. *Talk with You Like a Woman: African American Women, Justice, and Reform in New York, 1890–1935*. Chapel Hill: University of North Carolina Press, 2010.

Higdon, Hal. *Leopold and Loeb: The Crime of the Century*. Champaign: University of Illinois Press, 1999 [1975].

Higginbotham, A. Leon. *In the Matter of Color: Race and the American Legal Process. The Colonial Period*. New York: Oxford University Press, 1978.

Hinkle, William G., and Bruce Whitmarsh. *Images of Elmira Reformatory*. Charleston, NC: Arcadia Publishing, 2014.

Hofstadter, Richard. *The Age of Reform, from Bryan to F.D.R.* New York: Vintage Books, 1955.

Holcolme, Arthur N. *State Government in the United States*. New York: Macmillan, 1918.

Horowitz, Morton J. *The Transformation of American Law, 1870–1960*. New York: Oxford University Press, 1992.

Hulsebosch, Daniel J. *Constituting Empire: New York and the Transformation of Constitutionalism in the Atlantic World, 1664–1830*. Chapel Hill: University of North Carolina Press, 2005.

Humbert, Willard H. *The Pardoning Power of the President*. Foreword by W. W. Willoughby. Washington, DC: American Council on Public Affairs, 1941.

Hunt, Agnes. *The Provincial Committees of Safety of the American Revolution*. Cleveland: Winn and Judson, 1904.

Huston, Reeve. *Land and Freedom: Rural Society, Popular Protest, and Party Politics in Antebellum New York*. New York: Oxford University Press, 2000.

Huston, Reeve. "The Parties and 'the People': The New York Anti-Rent Wars and the Contours of Jacksonian Politics." *Journal of the Early Republic* 20, no. 2 (2000): 241–71.

Ingham, John N. *Biographical Dictionary of American Business Leaders*. Vol. 2. Westport, CT: Greenwood, 1983.

Ireland, Robert M. "The Libertine Must Die: Sexual Dishonor and the Unwritten Law in the Nineteenth-Century United States." *Journal of Social History* 23, no. 3 (Fall 1989): 27–44.

Jarvis, Brad Devin Edward. "Preserving the Brothertown Nation of Indians: Exploring Relationships amongst Land, Sovereignty, and Identity, 1740–1840." PhD diss., University of Minnesota, 2006.

Jay, William. *The Life and Times of John Jay: With Selections from His Correspondence and Miscellaneous Papers*, vol. 2. New York: J. and J. Harper, 1833.

Jenkins, John Stilwell. *Lives of the Governors of New York*. Auburn: Derby and Miller, 1851.

Kaminski, John P. *George Clinton: Yeoman Politician of the New Republic*. Lanham, MD: Rowman and Littlefield, 1993.

Kammen, Michael. *Colonial New York: A History*. New York: Oxford University Press, 1996.

Kann, Mark E. *Punishment, Prisons, and Patriarchy: Liberty*. New York: New York University Press, 2005.

Kann, Mark E. *Taming Passion for the Common Good: Policing Sex in the Early Republic*. New York: New York University Press, 2013.

Karcher, Carolyn L. *The First Woman in the Republic: A Cultural Biography of Lydia Maria Child*. Durham, NC: Duke University Press, 1998.

Katz, Michael B. *In the Shadow of the Poorhouse: A Social History of Welfare in America*. New York: Basic Books, 1996 [1986].

Kent, Madelyn. "Erie Canal Who's Who." Graduate Center of the City University of New York. http://library.gc.cuny.edu.

Kerby, Robert L. "The Militia System and the State Militias in the War of 1812." *Indiana Magazine of History* 73, no. 2 (1977): 102–24.

King, Peter. *Crime, Justice and Discretion in England, 1740–1820*. Oxford: Oxford University Press, 2000.

King, Peter. "Decision-Makers and Decision-Making in the English Criminal Law, 1750–1800." *Historical Journal* 27, no. 1 (March 1994): 25–58.

Klein, Milton M., ed. *The Empire State: A History of New York*. Ithaca, NY: Cornell University Press, 2001.

Kline, Wendy. *Building a Better Race: Gender, Sexuality, and Eugenics from the Turn of the Century to the Baby Boom*. Berkeley: University of California Press, 2001.

Knight, Betsy. "Prisoner Exchange and Parole in the American Revolution." *William and Mary Quarterly* 48, no. 2 (April 1991): 201–22.

Knight, Peter. *Conspiracy Theories in American History: An Encyclopedia*. Santa Barbara, CA: ABC-Clio, 2003.

Lande, R. Gregory. *The Abraham Man: Madness, Malingering, and the Development of Medical Testimony*. New York: Algora Publishing, 2012.

Larkin, Emmet. *James Larkin: Irish Labor Leader, 1876–1947*. Cambridge, MA: MIT Press, 1965.

Leavitt, Judith A. *American Women Managers and Administrators: A Selective Biographical Dictionary of Twentieth-Century Leaders in Business, Education, and Government*. Westport, CT: Greenwood Press, 1985.

Lee, Alfred McClung. *American Journalism 1690–1940*. Vol. 4, *The Daily Newspaper in America II. The Evolution of a Social Instrument*. New York: Routledge, 2000.

Lengel, Edward G., ed. *The Papers of George Washington, Revolutionary War Series*, vol. 20, *8 April–31 May 1779*. Charlottesville: University of Virginia Press, 2010.

Leopold, Nathan. *Life Plus 99 Years*. New York: Doubleday, 1954.

Lepore, Jill. *New York Burning: Liberty, Slavery, and Conspiracy in Eighteenth-Century Manhattan*. New York: Vintage Books, 2006.

Lerner, Michael A. *Dry Manhattan: Prohibition in New York City*. Cambridge, MA: Harvard University Press, 2008.

Levinson, Sanford. *Framed: America's 51 Constitutions and the Crisis of Governance*. New York: Oxford University Press, 2012.

Lewis, W. David. *From Newgate to Dannemora: The Rise of the Penitentiary in New York, 1796–1848*. Ithaca, NY: Cornell University Press, 2009 [1965].

Lifflander, Matthew L. *The Impeachment of Governor Sulzer: A Story of American Politics*. Albany: State University of New York Press, 2012.

Lindsey, Edward. "Historical Sketch of the Indeterminate Sentence and Parole System." *Journal of Criminal Law, Criminology, and Police Science* 16, no. 1 (1925): 9–69.

Livingston, Edwin Brockholst. *The Livingstons of Livingston Manor*. New York: Knickerbocker Press, 1910.

Lossing, Benson John. *The Empire State: A Comprehensive History of the Commonwealth of New York*. Hartford, CT: American Publishing Company, 1968 [1888].

Love, Margaret Colgate. "Reinventing the President's Pardon Power." *Federal Sentencing Reporter* 20, no. 1 (October 2007): 5–15.

Lubert, Howard L. "The New York Constitution: Emerging Principles in American Constitutional Thought." In *The Constitutionalism of American States*, edited by George E. Connor and Christopher W. Hammons, 126–45. Columbia: University of Missouri Press, 2008.

Luker, Kristen. "Sex, Social Hygiene, and the State: The Double-Edged Sword of Social Reform." *Theory and Society* 27, no. 5 (1998): 601–34.

Lumer, Michael, and Nancy Tenney. "The Death Penalty in New York: A Historical Perspective." *Journal of Law and Policy* 4, no. 1 (1995): 81–142.

Lustig, Mary Lou. *Privilege and Prerogative: New York's Provincial Elite, 1710–1776*. Madison, NJ: Fairleigh Dickinson University Press, 1995.

Lustig, Mary Lou. *The Imperial Executive in America: Sir Edmund Andros, 1637–1714*. Cranbury, NJ: Rosemont, 2002.

Lynch, Mona. "Rehabilitation as Rhetoric: The Ideal of Reformation in Contemporary Parole Discourse and Practices." *Punishment and Society* 2, no. 1 (2000): 40–65.

MacKellar, Landis. *The "Double Indemnity" Murder: Ruth Snyder, Judd Gray, and New York's Crime of the Century*. Syracuse, NY: Syracuse University Press, 2006.

Mackey, Thomas C. *Pursuing Johns: Criminal Law Reform, Defending Character, and New York City's Committee of Fourteen, 1920–1930*. Columbus: Ohio State University Press, 2005.

Maguire, Peter. *Law and War*. New York: Columbia University Press, 2000.

Mahoney, Dennis J. *Politics and Progress: The Emergence of American Political Science.* Lanham, MD: Lexington Books, 2004.

Maier, Pauline. *From Resistance to Revolution: Colonial Radicals and the Development of American Opposition to Britain, 1765–1776.* New York: Alfred A. Knopf, 1972.

Maier, Pauline. *Ratification: The People Debate the Constitution, 1787–1788.* New York: Simon and Schuster, 2010.

Mancini, Mathew J. *Alexis de Tocqueville and American Intellectuals: From His Time to Ours.* Lanham, MD: Rowman and Littlefield, 2006.

Martin, Glenn E. "Pardons Are One Remedy for our Excessively Punitive System." *New York Times,* February 25, 2015.

Martin, Scott. *Devil of the Domestic Sphere: Temperance, Gender, and Middle-Class Ideology, 1900–1860.* DeKalb: Northern Illinois University Press, 2008.

Mason, Matthew. *Slavery and Politics in the Early American Republic.* Chapel Hill: University of North Carolina Press, 2006.

Masur, Louis P. *Rites of Execution: Capital Punishment and the Transformation of American Culture.* New York: Oxford University Press, 1989.

Maxwell, Terrence A. "The Executive Branch." In *The Oxford Handbook of New York State Government and Politics,* edited by Gerald Benjamin, 384–400. New York: Oxford University Press, 2012.

McBride, Kelly D. *Punishment and Political Order.* Ann Arbor: University of Michigan Press, 2007.

McCurdy, Charles W. *The Anti-Rent Era in New York Law and Politics, 1839–1865.* Chapel Hill: University of North Carolina Press, 2001.

McDonald, Forrest. *The American Presidency: An Intellectual History.* Lawrence: University Press of Kansas, 1994.

McElroy, William H., and Alexander McBride, eds. *Life Sketches of Executive Officer and Members of the Legislature of the State of New York for 1873, 1874, 1875.* Albany: Weed, Parsons and Company, 1873–1875.

McIntosh, W.H. *Ontario Co., New York: With Illustrations Descriptive of its Scenery, Palatial Residences, Public Buildings, Fine Blocks, and Important Manufactories.* Philadelphia: Everts, Ensign and Everts, 1876.

McLennan, Rebecca M. *The Crisis of Imprisonment: Protest, Politics, and the Making of the American Penal State, 1776–1941.* New York: Cambridge University Press, 2008.

McManus, Edgar J. *A History of Negro Slavery in New York.* Syracuse, NY: Syracuse University Press, 1966.

Melosi, Martin V. *Pollution and Reform in American Cities: 1870–1930.* Austin: University of Texas Press, 1980.

Meranze, Michael. *Laboratories of Virtue: Punishment, Revolution, and Authority in Philadelphia, 1760–1835.* Chapel Hill: University of North Carolina Press, 1996.

Messinger, Sheldon L., John T. Berecochea, David Rauma, and Richard A. Berk. "The Foundations of Parole in California." *Law and Society Review* 19, no. 1 (1985): 69–106.

Miller, Donald L. *Supreme City: How Jazz Age Manhattan Gave Birth to Modern America*. New York: Simon and Schuster, 2014.

Miller, Vivien M. L. *Crime, Sexual Violence, and Clemency: Florida's Pardon Board and Penal System in the Progressive Era*. Gainesville: University Press of Florida, 2000.

Modern, John Lardas. *Secularism in Antebellum America, with Reference to Ghosts, Protestant Subcultures, Machines and their Metaphors; Featuring Discussions of Mass Media, Moby Dick, Spirituality, Phrenology, Anthropology, Sing Sing State Penitentiary, and Sex with the New Motive Power*. Chicago: University of Chicago Press, 2011.

Mohl, Raymond A. *Poverty in New York, 1783–1825*. New York: Oxford University Press, 1971.

Mohr, James C. *Doctors and the Law: Medical Jurisprudence in Nineteenth-Century America*. New York: Oxford University Press, 1993.

Monkkonen, Eric. *Crime, Justice, History*. Columbus: Ohio State University Press, 2002.

Monkkonen, Eric. "Homicide: Explaining American Exceptionalism." *American Historical Review* 111, no. 1 (2006): 76–94.

Monkkonen, Eric H. *Murder in New York City*. Berkeley: University of California Press, 2001.

Moore, Sean T. "'Justifiable Provocation': Violence against Women in Essex County." *Journal of Social History* 35, no. 4 (2002): 889–918.

Morgan, Edward M. "Court Martial Jurisdiction over Non-Military Persons under the Articles of War." *Minnesota Law Review* 4, no. 2 (January 1920): 79–116.

Mt. Pleasant, Alyssa. "Reconsidering the Case of Tommy-Jemmy: Contexts for Criminal Prosecution in the Early Republic." Paper presented at the 29th Annual Meeting of the Society for Historians of the Early American Republic, Worcester, Massachusetts, July 21, 2007.

Muhammad, Khalil Gibran. *The Condemnation of Blackness: Race, Crime, and the Making of Modern Urban America*. Cambridge, MA: Harvard University Press, 2010.

Murphy, Kevin P. *Political Manhood: Redbloods, Mollycoddles, and the Politics of Progressive Era Reform*. New York: Columbia University Press, 2008.

Murray, David. "The Anti-Rent Episode in the State of New York." *Annual Report of the American Historical Association* 1 (1896): 137–73.

Murray, David, ed. *Delaware County, New York: History of the Century, 1797–1897. Centennial Celebration*. Delhi, NY: William Clark, 1898.

Nash, Gary B., and Jean R. Soderlund. *Freedom by Degrees: Emancipation in Pennsylvania and its Aftermath*. New York: Oxford University Press, 1991.

National Governors Association. "Alfred Emmanuel Smith." Accessed July 12, 2011. http://www.nga.org.

National Governors Association. "Charles Seymour Whitman." Accessed July 12, 2011. http://www.nga.org.

National Governors Association. "Martin Henry Glynn." Accessed July 12, 2011. http://www.nga.org.

National Governors Association. "Nathan Lewis Miller." Accessed July 12, 2011. http://www.nga.org.

National Governors Association. "William Sulzer." Accessed July 12, 2011. http://www.nga.org.

Nelson, Eric. *The Royalist Revolution: Monarchy and the American Founding*. Cambridge, MA: Harvard University Press, 2014.

Nelson, Paul David. *William Tryon and the Course of Empire: A Life in British Imperial Service*. Chapel Hill: University of North Carolina Press, 1990.

Nelson, William E. "Legal Turmoil in a Factious Colony: New York, 1664–1776." *Hofstra Law Review* 38, no. 1 (2009): 69–162.

Newman, Charles L. *Sourcebook on Probation and Parole*, 3rd ed. Springfield, IL: Charles C. Thomas, 1968.

New York State Education Department. *Preliminary Guide to Mental Health Documentary Sources in New York State*. State Archives and Records Administration, 2000.

Nourse, Victoria. "Rethinking Crime Legislation: History and Harshness." *Tulsa Law Review* 39, no. 4 (2004): 925–39.

Nunez, Richard I. "New York State Constitutional Reform—Past Political Battles in Constitutional Language." *William and Mary Law Review* 10, no. 2 (1968): 366–77.

Nunn, Remmel. "Using Digital Newspapers to Explore American History and Culture." *Redex* 1, no. 1 (Spring 2006). http://www.newsbank.com.

O'Brien, Geoffrey. *Fall of the House of Walworth: A Tale of Madness and Murder in Gilded Age America*. New York: Henry Holt, 2010.

Odem, Mary E. *Delinquent Daughters: Protecting and Policing Adolescent Female Sexuality in the United States, 1885–1920*. Chapel Hill: University of North Carolina Press, 1995.

Olds, Irving Sands. *Judge Elbert H. Gary (1846–1927), His Life and Influence upon American Industry*. New York: Newcomen Society, 1947.

Pagden, Anthony. "Law, Colonization, Legitimation, and the European Background." In *Cambridge History of Law in America*, vol. 1, *Early America (1580–1815)*, edited by Michael Grossberg and Christopher Tomlins, 1–31. New York: Cambridge University Press, 2008.

Palk, Deirdre. *Gender Crime and Judicial Discretion, 1780–1830*. Suffolk, UK: Boydell and Brewer, 2006.

Paul, Julius. *"Three Generations of Imbeciles Are Enough": State Eugenic Sterilization Laws in American Thought and Practice*. Washington, DC: Walter Reed Army Institute of Research, 1965.

Peck, William F. *History of Rochester and Monroe County, New York, from the Earliest Historic Times to the Beginning of 1907*. New York: Pioneer Publishing, 1908.

Petersilia, Joan. *When Prisoners Come Home: Parole and Prisoner Reentry*. New York: Oxford University Press, 2003.

Peterson, Merrill D. ed., *Democracy, Liberty, and Property: The State Constitutional Conventions of the 1820s*. Indianapolis: Liberty Fund, 2012 [1966].

Pfeifer, Michael J. "Introduction." In *Lynching Beyond Dixie: American Mob Violence Outside the South*, edited by Michael J. Pfeifer, 1–12. Urbana: University of Illinois Press, 2013.

Pillsbury, Samuel H. "Understanding Penal Reform: The Dynamic of Change." *Journal of Criminal Law and Criminology* 80, no. 3 (Fall 1989): 726–80.

Pisciotta, Alexander W. *Benevolent Repression: Social Control and the American Reformatory-Prison Movement.* New York: New York University Press, 1994.

Pivar, David J. *Purity and Hygiene: Women, Prostitution and the "American Plan," 1900–1930.* Westport, CT: Greenwood Press, 2002.

Platt, Anthony M. *The Child Savers: The Invention of Delinquency.* Introduction by Miroslava Chávez-García. New Brunswick, NJ: Rutgers University Press, 2009.

Platt, Anthony M. "The Triumph of Benevolence: The Origins of the Juvenile Justice System in the United States." In *Youth Justice Critical Readings*, edited by John Muncie, Gordon Hughes, and Eugene McLaughlin, 177–96. London: Sage Publications, 2002 [1969].

Platt, Warren C. "The Volunteers of America: The Origins and Development of its Ideology." *Journal of Religious History* 16, no. 1 (June 1990): 35–50.

Pleck, Elizabeth Hafkin. *Domestic Tyranny: The Making of American Social Policy Against Family Violence from Colonial Times to the Present.* Oxford: Oxford University Press, 1987.

Pleck, Elizabeth. "Wifebeating in Nineteenth-Century America." *Victimology* 4, no. 1 (1979): 60–74.

Porter, Theodore M. *The Rise of Statistical Thinking, 1820–1900.* Princeton, NJ: Princeton University Press, 1996.

Potter, Claire Bond. *War on Crime: Bandits, G-men, and the Politics of Mass Culture.* New Brunswick, NJ: Rutgers University Press, 1998.

Preyer, Kathryn. "Penal Measures in the American Colonies: An Overview." *American Journal of Legal History* 26, no. 4 (1982): 326–53.

Pringle, Henry F. *Alfred E. Smith: A Critical Study.* New York: Macy-Masius, 1927.

Quigley, David. *Second Founding: New York City, Reconstruction and the Making of American Democracy.* New York: Hill and Wang, 2004.

Rabin, Dana Y. "Searching for the Self in Eighteenth-Century English Criminal Trials, 1730–1800." *Eighteenth-Century Life* 27, no. 1 (Winter 2003): 85–105.

Rafter, Nicole Hahn. *Creating Born Criminals.* Urbana: University of Illinois Press, 1997.

Rafter, Nicole Hahn. *The Criminal Brain: Understanding Biological Theories of Crime.* New York: New York University Press, 2008.

Rafter, Nicole Hahn. *Partial Justice: Women, Prisons, and Social Control,* 2nd ed. New Brunswick, NJ: Transaction Books, 2004 [1985].

Rafter, Nicole Hahn, ed. *White Trash: The Eugenic Family Studies, 1877–1919.* Boston: Northeastern University Press, 1988.

Ramsey, Carolyn B. "The Discretionary Power of 'Public' Prosecutors in Historical Perspective." *American Criminal Law Review* 39, no. 4 (2002): 1309–93.

Ramsey, Carolyn B. "Intimate Homicide: Gender and Crime Control, 1880–1920." University of Colorado Law School Legal Studies Research Paper Series, Working Paper no. 06–11 (2007): 101–91.

Rawley, James A. *Edwin D. Morgan: Merchant in Politics*. New York: Columbia University Press, 1955.

Ray, Gerda W. "From Cossack to Trooper: Manliness, Police Reform, and the State." *Journal of Social History* 28, no. 3 (1995): 565–86.

"Records Relating to Criminal Trials, Appeals, and Pardons." New York State Archives. http://www.archives.nysed.gov.

Richter, Daniel K. *The Ordeal of the Longhouse: The Peoples of the Iroquois League in the Era of European Colonization*. Chapel Hill: University of North Carolina Press, 1992.

Ridolfi, Kathleen, and Seth Gordon. "Gubernatorial Clemency Powers: Justice or Mercy?" *Criminal Justice* 24, no. 3 (Fall 2009): 26–40.

Riker, John. *"Evacuation Day," 1783, Its Many Stirring Events: With Recollections of Capt. John Van Arsdale of the Veteran Corps of Artillery, by Whose Efforts on That Day the Enemy Were Circumvented, and the American Flag Successfully Raised on the Battery*. New York: Crichton and Co., 1883.

Ritchie, Robert C. *The Duke's Province: A Study of New York Politics and Society, 1664–1691*. Chapel Hill: University of North Carolina Press, 1977.

Roberts, Timothy Mason. *Distant Revolutions: 1848 and the Challenge to American Exceptionalism*. Charlottesville: University of Virginia Press, 2009.

Robertson, Stephen. *Crimes Against Children: Sexual Violence and Legal Culture in New York City, 1880–1960*. Chapel Hill: University of North Carolina Press, 2005.

Rosen, Deborah A. *American Indians and State Law: Sovereignty, Race, and Citizenship, 1790–1880*. Lincoln: University of Nebraska Press, 2007.

Ross, Richard J. "Legal Communications and Imperial Governance: British North America and Spanish America Compared." In *Cambridge History of Law in America*, vol. 1, *Early America (1580–1815)*, edited by Michael Grossberg and Christopher Tomlins, 104–43. New York: Cambridge University Press, 2008.

Ross, William G. *A Muted Fury: Populists, Progressives, and Labor Unions Confront the Courts, 1890–1937*. Princeton, NJ: Princeton University Press, 1994.

Rothman, David J. *Conscience and Convenience: The Asylum and Its Alternatives in Progressive America*. Revised edition. New York: Aldine de Gruyter, 2002.

Rothman, David J. *The Discovery of the Asylum: Social Order and Disorder in the New Republic, Revised Edition*. New Brunswick, NJ: Transaction, 2002 [1971].

Rothman, David J. "Perfecting the Prison: United States, 1789–1865." In *The Oxford History of the Prison: The Practice of Punishment in Western Society*, edited by Norval Morris and David J. Rothman, 111–29. New York: Oxford University Press, 1995.

Rothman, Meah Dell. "The Pardoning Power: Historical Perspective and Case Study of New York and Connecticut." *Columbia Journal of Law and Social Problems* 12 (Winter 1976): 149–220.

Rotundo, E. Anthony. *American Manhood: Transformations in Masculinity from the Revolution to the Modern Era*. New York: Basic Books, 1993.

Ruckman, P.S. Jr., "The Study of Mercy: What Political Scientists Know (and Don't Know) About the Pardon Power." *University of St. Thomas Law Journal* 9, no. 3 (2012): 783–837.

Salkin, Barry L. "The Pardoning Power in Antebellum Pennsylvania." *Pennsylvania Magazine of Biography and History* 100, no. 4 (October 1976): 507–20.

"Sam A. Lewisohn in Memoriam." *The Prison World* (March–April 1951). In *Sam A. Lewisohn*, 30–32. Stamford, CT: Overbrook Press, 1951.

Sampson, Robert. *John L. O'Sullivan and His Times*. Kent, OH: Kent State University Press, 2003.

Sarat, Austin. *Gruesome Spectacles: Botched Executions and America's Death Penalty*. Stanford, CA: Stanford University Press, 2014.

Sarat, Austin, ed. *Law, Violence, and the Possibility of Justice*. Princeton, NJ: Princeton University Press, 2001.

Sarat, Austin, ed. *Merciful Judgments and Contemporary Society: Legal Problems, Legal Possibilities*. New York: Cambridge University Press, 2012.

Sarat, Austin, and Nasser Hussain. "On Lawful Lawlessness: George Ryan, Executive Clemency, and the Rhetoric of Sparing Life." *Stanford Law Review* 56, no. 5 (2004): 1307–44.

Savell, Isabelle K. *The Executive Mansion in Albany: An Informal History, 1856–1960*. Albany: New York State Office of General Services, 1982.

Scheuerman, William E. "American Kingship? Monarchical Origins of Modern Presidentialism." *Polity* 37, no. 1 (January 2005): 24–53.

Scheuerman, William E. *Between the Norm and the Exception: The Frankfurt School and the Rule of Law*. Cambridge, MA: MIT Press, 1994.

Schlossman, Steven L. *Transforming Juvenile Justice: Reform Ideals and Institutional Realities, 1825–1920*. De Kalb: Northern Illinois University Press, 2004.

Schmitt, Carl. *Political Theology: Four Chapters on the Concept of Sovereignty*. Edited by George Schwab. Chicago: University of Chicago Press, 1985 [1922].

Schneider, David M., and Harry Elmer Barnes. "The Rise of Humane Institutions." In *History of the State of New York in Ten Volumes*, edited by Alexander C. Flick, 273–98. Port Washington, NY: Ira J. Friedman, 1962.

Schneider, Eric C. *In the Web of Class: Delinquents and Reformers in Boston, 1810s–1930s*. New York: New York University Press, 1992.

Segrave, Kerry. *Shoplifting: A Social History*. Jefferson, NC: McFarland, 2001.

Segrave, Kerry. *Women and Capital Punishment in America, 1840–1899: Death Sentences and Executions in the United States and Canada*. Jefferson, NC: McFarland, 2008.

Sellin, J. Thorsten. *Slavery and the Penal System*. New York: Elsevier, 1976.

Severance, Frank H. *Publications of the Buffalo Historical Society*. Vol. 22. Buffalo, NY: Peter Paul Book Company, 1918.

Seward, Frederick W. *Seward at Washington as Secretary of State: A Memoire of His Life with Sketches from his Letters, 1861–1872*. New York: Derby and Miller, 1891.

Shapiro, Ian, ed. *The Federalist Papers: Alexander Hamilton, James Madison, and John Jay*. New Haven, CT: Yale University Press, 2009.

Shaw, Ronald E. *Erie Water West: A History of the Erie Canal, 1792–1854*. Lexington: University Press of Kentucky, 2013.

Silverberg, Helene, ed. *Gender and American Social Science: The Formative Years.* Princeton, NJ: Princeton University Press, 1998.

Simon, Jonathan. *Poor Discipline: Parole and the Social Control of the Underclass, 1890–1990.* Chicago: University of Chicago Press, 1993.

Smith-Rosenberg, Carroll, and Charles Rosenberg. "The Female Animal: Medical and Biological Views of Woman and Her Role in Nineteenth-Century America." *Journal of American History* 60, no. 2 (September 1973): 332–56.

Spaulding, E. Wilder. *His Excellency George Clinton: Critic of the Constitution.* New York: Macmillan, 1938.

Spencer, Ivor Debenham. *The Victor and the Spoils: A Life of William L. Marcy.* Providence, RI: Brown University Press, 1959.

Spillane, Joseph. "Did Drug Prohibition Work? Reflections on the End of the First Cocaine Experience in the United States, 1910–45," *Journal of Drug Issues* 28, no. 2 (Spring 1998): 517–38.

Spillane, Joseph F. *Coxsackie: The Life and Death of Prison Reform.* Baltimore, MD: Johns Hopkins University Press, 2014.

State of New York. *New York in the Revolution as Colony and State.* 2nd ed. Vol. 2. Albany: J. B. Lyon, 1904.

Stern, Alexandra Minna. *Eugenic Nation: Faults and Frontiers of Better Breeding in Modern America.* Berkeley: University of California Press, 2005.

Stevens, Harriet Weeks Wadhams. *Wadhams Genealogy, Preceded by a Sketch of the Wadham Family in England, With Illustrations.* New York: Frank Allaben Genealogical Company, 1913.

Stolberg, Mary M. *Fighting Organized Crime: Politics, Justice and the Legacy of Thomas E. Dewey.* Boston: Northeastern University Press, 1995.

Strange, Carolyn. "The Unwritten Law of Executive Justice: Pardoning Patricide in Reconstruction-era New York." *Law and History Review* 28, no. 4 (November 2010): 891–930.

Streib, Victor L. "Rare and Inconsistent: The Death Penalty for Women." *Fordham Urban Law Journal* 33, no. 2 (2005): 101–32.

Strum, Harvey. "New York Federalists and Opposition to the War of 1812." *World Affairs* 142, no. 3 (1980): 169–87.

Summerhill, Thomas. *Harvest of Dissent: Agrarianism in Nineteenth-Century New York.* Champaign: University of Illinois Press, 2005.

Tanenhaus, David S. *Juvenile Justice in the Making.* New York: Oxford University Press, 2004.

Taylor, Alan. *The Divided Ground: Indians, Settlers, and the Northern Borderland of the American Revolution.* New York: Alfred A. Knopf, 2006.

Taylor, John M. *William Henry Seward: Lincoln's Right Hand Man.* New York: HarperCollins, 1991.

Teaford, Jon C. *The Unheralded Triumph: City Government in America, 1870–1900.* Baltimore, MD: Johns Hopkins University Press, 1984.

Theriot, Nancy M. *Mothers and Daughters in Nineteenth-Century America: The Biosocial Construction of Femininity*. Lexington: University Press of Kentucky, 1996.

Thomas, Tracy A. "Elizabeth Cady Stanton and the Notion of a Legal Class of Gender." In *Feminist Legal History: Essays on Women and Law*, edited by Tracy A. Thomas and Tracey Jean Bouisseau, 139–55. New York: New York University Press, 2011.

Thompson, James Westfall. "Anti-Loyalist Legislation during the American Revolution." *Illinois Law Review* 3 (1908–9): 147–71.

Tiedemann, Joseph S. *Reluctant Revolutionaries: New York City and the Road to Independence, 1763–1776*. Ithaca, NY: Cornell University Press, 1997.

Tighe, Janet A. "The New York Medico-legal Society: Legitimating the Union of Law and Psychiatry (1867–1918)." *International Journal of Law and Psychiatry* 9, no. 2 (1986): 231–43.

Tiro, Karim M. *The People of the Standing Stone: The Oneida Nation from the Revolution through the Era of Removal*. Amherst: University of Massachusetts Press, 2011.

Tomlins, Christopher. *Freedom Bound: Law, Labor and Civic Identity in Colonizing English America, 1580–1865*. New York: Cambridge University Press, 2010.

Travis, Jeremy. *But They All Come Back: Facing the Challenges of Prisoner Reentry*. Washington, DC: Urban Institute Press, 2005.

Umphrey, Martha Merrill. "Dialogics of Legal Meaning: Spectacular Trials, the Unwritten Law, and Narratives of Criminal Responsibility." *Law and Society Review* 32, no. 2 (1999): 393–423.

Umphrey, Martha Merrill. "The Trouble with Harry Thaw." *Radical History Review* 62 (Spring 1995): 9–23.

United States Census Bureau. *Measuring America: The Decennial Censuses from 1790 to 2000*. Washington, DC: United States Government Printing Office, 2002.

Ury, John L. "American Society for Colonizing the Free People of Color of the United States." *Phylon* 44, no. 3 (1983): 187–97.

Volk, Kyle G. *Moral Minorities and the Making of American Democracy*. New York: Oxford University Press, 2014.

Walker, Samuel. *Popular Justice: A History of American Criminal Justice*. 2nd ed. New York: Oxford, 1998.

Walkowitz, Daniel J. *Working with Class: Social Workers and the Politics of Middle-Class Identity*. Chapel Hill: University of North Carolina Press, 1999.

Ward, Geoff K. *The Black Child Savers: Racial Democracy and Juvenile Justice*. Chicago: University of Chicago Press, 2012.

Ward, Harry M. *The War for Independence and the Transformation of American Society*. Oxford: Routledge, 1999.

Washburne, George Adrian. *Imperial Control of the Administration of Justice in the Thirteen American Colonies*. New York: Columbia University Press, 1923.

Wesser, Robert F. *Charles Evans Hughes: Politics and Reform in New York, 1905–1910*. Ithaca, NY: Cornell University Press, 1967.

Westervelt, Sandra D., and John A. Humphrey, eds. *Wrongly Convicted: Perspectives on Failed Justice*. New Brunswick, NJ: Rutgers University Press, 2005 [2001].

White, Richard. *The Middle Ground: Indians, Empires, and Republics in the Great Lakes Region, 1650–1815*. New York: Cambridge University Press, 1991.

White, Shane. "The Death of James Johnson." *American Quarterly* 51, no. 4 (December 1999): 753–95.

White, Shane. *Somewhat More Independent: The End of Slavery in New York City, 1770–1810*. Athens: University of Georgia Press, 2004 [1991].

White, Stephen. "Alexander Maconochie and the Development of Parole." *Journal of Criminal Law and Criminology* 67, no. 1 (1976): 72–88.

Whitehead, John, Kimberly Dodson, and Bradley Edwards. *Corrections: Exploring Crime, Punishment, and Justice in America*. 3rd ed. New York: Routledge, 2014.

Wiebe, Robert H. *The Search for Order, 1877–1920*. Foreword by David Herbert Donald. New York: Hill and Wang, 1967.

Wilkerson, Isabel. *The Warmth of Other Suns: The Epic Story of America's Great Migration*. New York: Random House, 2010.

Witt, John Fabian. *Lincoln's Code: The Laws of War in American History*. New York: Free Press, 2012.

Wolin, Robert E. "After Release: The Parolee in Society." *St. John's Law Review* 48, no. 1 (June 1973): 1–41.

Wood, Marcus. *The Horrible Gift of Freedom: Atlantic Slavery and the Representation of Emancipation*. Athens: University of Georgia Press, 2010.

Wood, Sharon E. *The Freedom of the Streets: Work, Citizenship and Sexuality in a Gilded Age City*. Chapel Hill: University of North Carolina Press, 2005.

Young, Alfred F. *The Democratic Republicans of New York: The Origins, 1763–1797*. Chapel Hill: University of North Carolina Press, 1967.

Zilversmit, Arthur. *The First Emancipation: The Abolition of Slavery in the North*. Chicago: University of Chicago Press, 1967.

Zimmerman, Joseph F. *The Government and Politics of New York*. 2nd ed. Albany: State University of New York Press, 2008.

INDEX

abolition of slavery, 46–47, 234n39, 234nn36–37, 235n40; at constitutional debates, 78–79, 241n87
abuse accusations: in prisons, 13, 39, 80, 108, 110, 115, 169; at Elmira Reformatory, 142–43; against executive discretion, 71–74
Account of the State Prison or Penitentiary House (Eddy), 42
accountability, 66, 121, 266n88
Act Declaring the Jurisdiction of the Courts of this State, 59
Act for the Gradual Abolition of Slavery, 46–47
Act in Relation to Pardons, 99, 101
Act Respecting Convictions in Criminal Courts, and to Procure Statistical Information Concerning Convicts, 73
Act to Amend the Prison Law, in Relation to Paroles and Commutation, 193–94
administrative discretion, 146, 160, 173, 181, 191, 204–5, 214, 216; abuse of, 116; historiography, 3, 6. *See also* Board of Parole; Brockway, Zebulon
African Americans, 19, 42–43, 48–9, 51, 106–7, 181, 257n41; pardons for, 50, 165–66, 260n85; parole, understanding by, 154–55, 258nn48–52; paroles for, 175, 262n12; women, 154–55, 258n52. *See also* racism; slavery
African Free School, 91
alcohol, 120, 158, 174, 250n29; parole, understanding and, 152–53, 155, 257n42
Alger, George W., 191–92, 203–4, 212, 266nn88–89

American Association for the Promotion of Social Science, 108
American Correctional Association, 270n4
American Prison Association, 149, 175
American Society for the Collection and Diffusion of Information in Relation to the Punishment of Death, 78
amnesty. *See* pardons
Amnesty Proclamation, 112
anarchists, 187–88, 264n61
Andre, John, 28, 230n62
antebellum period, 11; capital cases in, 70–71, 73, 77. *See also* constitutional debates
Anthony, Susan B., 120
anti-rent crisis, 242n107; Boughton in, 84, 87, 242n109, 243n1; deaths in, 83–85, 242n108; Indian disguises and, 82, 83, 84, 86; media scrutiny on, 242n106, 242n108; pardon in, 84–85, 243nn110–12; Young in, 84–85, 243n110, 243n112
arbitrariness, 8, 61, 115, 143, 148
arson, 44
Articles of War, 26–28, 107
assault, 35, 118, 129, 165, 209. *See also* rape
Auburn State Prison, 1, 11, 14, 69, 184, 216, 250n20; establishment of, 44–45; overcrowding at, 199, 201; pardons at, 97, 117; paroles at, 151, 153–55, 160, 175, 186, 199; scandal at, 62; sexuality at, 159; solitary confinement at, 68–70
Augur, Amy, 31, 71, 231nn76–77

Report on the Prisons and Reformatories of the United States and Canada (Wines, E. and Dwight), 109–10, 247n74
reprieves, 19, 21, 35, 54, 56, 65, 77; Clinton, G. and, 31–33, 71; Morris and, 24–25; Platt for, 70; race and, 48–49
republicanism, 23, 63, 86; British justice compared to, 24, 65
Republicans, 36, 63, 74; Crime Commission and, 193; crime control and, 188, 190, 265nn71–72; criminal law and, 35; 1926 elections and, 194, 267n105; against Roosevelt, 200, 269n139
Revolutionary New York, 17, 23–25. *See also* Clinton, George
Revolutionary War, 17–18, 226n2; Articles of War in, 26–28; colonial governance and, 22–25, 228n26; Iroquois Confederacy and, 52; mercy in 25–30. *See also* Clinton, George
riots, 15, 199, 233n12, 269nn136–37
robbery, *209*
Robinson, Lucius, 130; pardon by, 133, 253n83
Rochester Work House, 118
Rogers, John J. "Bum," 195, 197–98, 267n107
Roosevelt, Franklin D., 15–16, 197; with Baumes, 203, 208, 270n151; Baumes Laws and, 199–200, 269n137, 269n139; commutations by, 199–200, 202, 269n139; against crime, 198–99, 268n129, 268n131; discretionary justice of, 201–2, 207, 269nn146–47; hearings with, 210; legislature and, 176; Republicans against, 200, 269n139. *See also* pardon board
Roosevelt, Theodore, 131; against Brockway, 144, 149, 254n117, 256n25
Root, Erastus, 64, 238n16
Rosen, Deborah, 58
Rothman, David J., 7–8, 44, 175, 225n34
royal prerogative. *See* mercy; monarchy

rule of law, 12, 49, 135–56, 144
Rutledge, Edward, 24
Ryan, George, 3, 5

sanity: in clemency files, *219*; of Druse, R., 136, 254n98; of Freeman, 102–3, 246n57; law and, 71, 78, 103; 123; Morgan and, 122, 251nn37–38; of Thompson, A., 70–71, 240n48; of Walworth, F., 132–33
scandals, 13, 15, 167, 191–193, 195, 260n93; at Auburn State Prison, 62; Dix and, 168–69, 261nn100–105, 261n108; at Elmira Reformatory, 142–43; Whitman and, 169–72, 261n109, 261n112
Schaack, Peter Van, 230n71
Schuyler, Philip, 26, 36
Scott, Thomas Morris, 26
secretary of state, 124
Seneca, 53–54, 56, 58–60, 243n116
sentiment, 33, 39; Christianity and, 104; of Clinton, G., 33, 36; at constitutional debates, 64–65, 67; Edwards on, 64–65; Fish on, 99; of legislature, 35; politics of, 76–77, 86, 179–80; reason and, 70–73
severity, 29–31, 85, 109, 231n75
Seward, William H., 74, 82, 100, 122; executions and, 76, 179, 241n81; pardons by, 112–13, 248nn87–88, 249n12; Sing Sing Prison and, 92, 244n20; statistical thinking of, 75–76, 241nn72–73; Wright and, 103, 246n57
sexual offenders, 157–60, 259n65, 259n70. *See also* rape; sodomy
sexuality, 35, 94,159
Seymour, Horatio, 111
Shepard, Lorenzo B., 80–82, 242n101
shoplifting, 198, 268nn123–25
Sickle, Daniel, 251n38
Simmons, George A., 80, 82
Simon, Jonathan, 5–6, 183, 233n6

ABOUT THE AUTHOR

Carolyn Strange is Senior Fellow at the Australian National University. She has published extensively in the fields of criminal justice history and the history of gender and sexuality. A specialist in modern North American history, her work, spanning the fields of history, criminology, law, and gender studies, has appeared in leading journals in the United States, Canada, Britain, and Australia.